THE SLOVAK EPICS

(Svatopluk, the Cyrillo-Methodiad, Sláv)

This book was published with a financial support from SLOLIA,
Centre for Information on Literature in Bratislava

THE SLOVAK EPICS

(Svatopluk, the Cyrillo-Methodiad, Sláv)

by Ján Hollý

Translated from the Slovak and introduced by
Charles S. Kraszewski

This book was published with a financial support from SLOLIA, Centre for Information on Literature in Bratislava

Cover image "Apotheosis of the Slavs" by Alphonse Mucha (1926)

Publishers Maxim Hodak & Max Mendor

Introduction © Charles S. Kraszewski 2025

© Glagoslav Publications 2025

www.glagoslav.com

ISBN: 978-1-80484-195-2
ISBN: 978-1-80484-196-9

Published in English by Glagoslav Publications in August 2025

A catalogue record for this book is available from the British Library.

This book is in copyright. No part of this publication may be reproduced, stored in a retrieval system or transmitted in any form or by any means without the prior permission in writing of the publisher, nor be otherwise circulated in any form of binding or cover other than that in which it is published without a similar condition, including this condition, being imposed on the subsequent purchaser.

Ján Hollý

THE SLOVAK EPICS

Translated from the Slovak
and introduced by Charles S. Kraszewski

GLAGOSLAV PUBLICATIONS

Contents

Introduction: New Beginnings: the Epics of Ján Hollý
and the Creation of Modern Slovak Literature. 7

The Slovak Epics

Svatopluk 72

The Cyrillo-Methodiad 238

Sláv 311

Bibliography 396

About the Author 399

About the Translator 400

New Beginnings: the Epics of Ján Hollý and the Creation of Modern Slovak Literature

Charles S. Kraszewski

The modern period of Slovak literature begins with the poet Ján Hollý (1785–1854). Štefan Krčmerý calls him 'the first great poet of the Slovak language',[1] by which he means of *Bernolákovčina* — the state of the language as newly codified by Anton Bernolák (1762–1813) on the basis of the western dialects of Slovak. This fact deserves some emphasis. For whereas the roots of the Slovak language reach much farther back in history than the nineteenth century,[2] it was necessary, at the time, for political reasons to distinguish Slovak from its near-twin Czech. And thus, while Hollý is considered a classical author in spirit, creating in neoclassical tropes at a time when, as Stanislav Šmatlák points out, Polish and Russian literature, in the persons of Adam Mickiewicz and Aleksandr Pushkin, had already passed on through Romanticism toward Realism, and in Bohemia Karel Hynek Mácha had astounded the Czech readership with something totally new in his Byronic epyllion *Máj*[3] — the fact that Hollý is a moving force behind the national revival movement in Slovakia sets him firmly in the ideological camp we associate with Romanticism. Indeed, this was the period when the 'Czechoslovak' poet Jan Kollár was creating his magnum opus

---

[1] Quoted by Milan Pišút, 'Klasicizmus (roky dvadsiate a tridsiate)', *Dejiny slovenskej literatúry*, ed. M. Pišút (Bratislava: Vydavateľstvo Osveta, 1962), pp. 187–215; p. 206.

[2] There is some justice in beginning an overview of Slovak writing as early as the ninth century — as do the editors of the two-volume anthology *Z klenotnice staršieho slovenského písomníctva* (Bratislava: Tatran, 1984) — with works in Old Church Slavonic composed by and about Saints Cyril and Methodius, the apostles of the Western Slavs, who began their mission in areas that were to become Slovakia.

[3] Stanislav Šmatlák, 'Ján Hollý — Klasik slovenskej poézie', in *Pamätnica z osláv dvojstého výročia narodenia Jána Hollého*, ed. Juraj Chovan (Martin: Matica slovenská, 1985), 123–133, p. 123.

Slávy dcera [The Daughter of Sláva], and the Magyar poets Károly Kisfaludy and Mihály Vörösmarty were engaged with legends from ancient Hungarian days; it was at this time that Hollý himself was initiating a current in literature that would continue throughout the Romantic period proper, from J.M. Hurban and Ľudovít Štúr through Samo Chalupka.[4]

THE HEROIC POEMS AND SLOVAKIA'S BATTLE FOR AUTONOMY

To fully understand the grandeur of Ján Hollý's epics, or 'heroic poems' [*víťazské básne*] we have to consider the fact that at the time they were written (1833–1839) the Slovak language was just being established as a modern literary idiom, distinct from its near twin-sister, Czech. As a matter of fact, Czech itself was also undergoing a revival. Despite the antiquity of both languages, and the Slavic group in general, in the lands of the Dual Monarchy centuries of linguistic centralisation — the imposition of German as an official language in the Czech lands, and of Magyar ('Hungarian') in Hungary — had a deleterious effect on the autochthonous languages of the regions. People who wished to advance, either in the civil service, law, the army, or any of the professions requiring an education beyond the most basic level had to study, and later work, in these two dominant languages. This resulted in the deracination of the intellectual crème de la crème in Bohemia and Slovakia, as Czech and Slovak were shunted aside from the main highways of intellectual and artistic discourse, confined to the cottage, the farm, and the servants' quarters.

---

[4] Pišút, pp. 206–207. The fact that Hollý wrote in Bernolák's idiom is seen by certain scholars as something that was already anachronistic during the poet's lifetime, for modern literary Slovak was to develop according to the usage established by the younger poet and scholar Ľudovít Štúr, based on the central dialects of Slovakia. 'When he wrote his work Bernolák's movement was in decay', stresses J. Hanák, and Paul Selver concurs: 'It was unfortunate for him that he selected Bernolák's artificial and clumsy dialect as his medium of expression'. However, it is a bit much to suggest, like Selver, that Bernolák's literary dialect 'was intelligible to a restricted circle of readers', or, like Hanák, that for this reason 'his poems remained in the main alien to the people'. Given Hollý's popularity, during his lifetime and later, throughout Slovakia, such statements are patently wrong. What is more, Štúr and his followers looked to Hollý as a revered oracle, and made at least two pilgrimages to his rectory. For Hanák and Selver, see: J. Hanák, 'Slovaks and Czechs in the Early 19th Century', *The Slavonic and East European Review*, Apr., 1932, Vol. 10, No. 30 (Apr., 1932), pp. 588-601, p. 592; Paul Selver, 'The Literature of the Slovaks', *The Slavonic and East European Review*, Apr., 1934, Vol. 12, No. 36 (Apr., 1934), pp. 691-703, p. 692. A very good source for Hollý's influence on Štúr and the young protestants of Bratislava is Lenka Rišková, 'Z korešpondencie Jána Hollého. Niečo o vzťahu Jána Hollého k protestantským autorom', *Slovenská literatúra*, 62, 2015, nr. 6: 495–511.

With the uprise of Romantic interest in 'folk' culture, spurred by the philosophical writings of J.G. Herder, among others, and fuelled by the general rebellion against multinational empires throughout Europe on behalf of the political emancipation of their smaller constituent nations, language began to be strongly associated with ethnicity, ethnicity with nationality, and nationality with statal and governmental aspirations based on the 'folk'. In both the Czech lands and Slovakia, the late eighteenth and early nineteenth century constituted a period of 'national revival' [Slovak: *národné obrodenie*, Czech: *národní obrození*]. Literati and scholars such as Josef Jungmann (1773-1847) in Bohemia, and Anton Bernolák (1762-1813) in Slovakia were at work raising national consciousness through literature, and — especially in the case of the latter — by codifying the spoken language of the people into a rationally determined linguistic entity worthy of comparison with any other tongue in the world, in short: not a peasant jargon, but a national language, a national language based upon the language of the ethnic majority.

This was an especially important task in Slovakia. The mountainous regions of the Hungarian kingdom, bordering the Polish lands north of the Tatras, were subjected to such a fierce Magyarisation that even the ethnic Slovak nobility 'Magyarised' to get ahead. The Kossuth family is a good example of that. One of the national heroes of Hungary is Kossuth Lajos (1802-1894) who came of Magyarised Slovak stock — a background he rejected. Meanwhile, his uncle Juraj Košút (1776-1849) was a Slovak patriot who opposed Magyarisation and corresponded with Ľudovít Štúr (1815-1856), poet and linguist, one of the great architects of the modern Slovak nation. In Hungary, where the language of education and government had remained Latin up until the nineteenth century (so as to accommodate the various linguistic groups present in the kingdom: Slovaks, Croats, Romanians, Germans, and Magyars), the revolutionary Romantic movement, which sought independence for Hungary from Vienna, replaced Latin with Magyar, and sought to define Slovak as a mere dialect of Czech. Politically speaking, if this were to be acknowledged, that would define Slovak as a 'foreign' linguistic import to the country, and thereby a tongue deserving of no official standing in the land. All the more so, then, did the Slovaks — including the Lutherans, who traditionally cleaved more to the Czech language than did the Catholic Slovaks — work feverishly to establish a universally accepted and codified version of the language of the people in order to cement it as a language native to the region. Indeed, it is difficult to see how this could ever have been doubted, since Magyar arrived in the lands of modern day Slovakia and Pannonia only in the ninth century with the influx of the Magyar tribes. Magyar itself is chock-full of borrowings from the Slovak. Significantly, most of these are agricultural terms, and vocabulary relating to permanent dwellings — terminology introduced to the consciousness of the nomadic tribes from the east only after their settlement along the banks of the Tisa and Danube and their peaceful commerce with their Slovak neighbours.

So much for politics. As far as literature is concerned, the ennoblement of 'new' or rather 'newly renovated' languages happens in two ways. On the one hand, products of the folk culture are disseminated through the world by translation into more universal languages. This happened with Slovak when Goethe found the folk poems brought him by Ján Kollár (1793–1852) worthy of being translated into and disseminated in German. More significant, however, is literary movement heading the other way: the translation of the great works of world literature into the 'young' languages, with the intent of proving the latter capable of bearing the weight of the content and beauties of the original in the native vocables. In Czech this occurs with Jungmann's translation of Milton's *Paradise Lost* [*Ztracený ráj*, 1811 — more of this later], and in Slovak, with Hollý's Slovak version of Virgil's *Aeneid* [*Vergiliova Eneida*, 1828]. Just fifteen years after the death of Bernolák, one of the great classics of the Western tradition was brought over into *bernolákovčina*. The remarkable suppleness of the newly-codified and far from clumsy Slovak language is astoundingly confirmed thereby. Comparatively speaking, it is as if the *Aeneid* had been translated into Anglo-Saxon by Alfred the Great, not having to wait more than half a millennium for Gavin Douglas to come along. And then, what is arguably more impressive, Hollý further enriched his literary tradition by not one, but three original epics on the Virgilian pattern: *Svatopluk* (or *Svätopluk*, 1833), the *Cyrillo-Methodiada* (1835), and *Sláv* (1839).

Indeed, Lucia Jechová begins her article on 'Mythology and Mystics in J. Hollý's Epos Svatopluk' with the bold assertion: 'The skilful epic *Svatopluk* was a work unique in its day and age. In it, Ján Hollý showed the world that Slovak literature is something independent and vital'.[5] It is true that Hollý's epics are intended as even more emphatic proof of the expressive capabilities of Slovak — and a point of reference for Slovaks, threatened with pressure from official Magyarisation. They were to underscore the antiquity, bravery, heroism, and significance of the nation's protoplasts.

The chronology of the epics proceeds backwards, from the mediaeval period into the far distant past of the Slovaks in particular, and Slavs in general — what in his lectures on Slavic literature Adam Mickiewicz calls 'the mythical period of Slavdom'.[6] For the first epic, centring on the eponymous hero who led a

....

[5] Lucia Jechová, 'Mytológia a mystika v epose J.Hollého – Svatopluk' *XLinguae.eu A Trimestrial European Scientific Language Review* 4/2011:40–44, p. 40.

[6] Adam Mickiewicz, *Literatura słowiańska. Kurs pierwszy* [Slavic Literature. Course I (1840–1841)] (Warszawa: Czytelnik, 1997), p. 26. This edition: Volume VIII of Mick-

successful struggle of the Slavs in the Great Moravian Empire against German hegemony, is set in the closing decade of the ninth century. The action of the *Cyrillo-Methodiad*, which takes as its theme — so unusual for epic poetry — the Christianisation of the Slavs inhabiting the Moravian state, develops a few decades earlier, as it begins in 862 with the request sent by Svatopluk and Rastislav to the Emperor Michael III in Constantinople, for the Apostles of the Slavs Cyril (Konštantín, Constantine) and Methodius to travel to the Slovaks on a mission of evangelisation. Finally, *Sláv* ventures even farther back in time. Its six cantos are a detailed development of Svatopluk's recounting of the migration of the Slavic people from their original homeland in the Indian subcontinent to Central Europe, which he gives at a banquet in the presence of the Bavarian king Karolman. According to the chronology presented in Canto VI of *Svatopluk*, this took place at least five hundred years before Svatopluk's imprisonment among the Bavarians, and so — somewhere around 300 AD at the latest.

SVATOPLUK

The first of Hollý's epics is also his most classical in construction. Like most of the European epics following Virgil, it is divided into twelve books. It centres on a heroic war of great significance for the nation, and unfolds on a dual plane of action: that of men, and that of supernatural — in this case, the Christian Heaven and the triune God.

The story developed by Hollý is fairly straightforward and simple to relate. The eponymous hero of the work, Svatopluk, has been imprisoned by the Germans to whom he had originally fled for protection from his vengeful uncle Rastislav. Shut in a dark dungeon, the innocent Slovak ruler is not abandoned by God, Who commands the Bavarian king Karolman to release him, lest he suffer the same fate. Karolman, moved by the visitation of God's angel in dream, summons a diet of the German elders in order to discuss the matter with them — although he has already determined upon heeding God's command. After some debate, the vote goes Karolman's way. Svatopluk is released, outfitted with arms, and provided with an army to move against Slavimír, who had reluctantly ascended the throne at Svatopluk's disappearance. Svatopluk's release is conditioned upon his agreement to remain in a feudal relationship to Karolman once he regains his sceptre, to support him in war, and to pay an annual tribute. Svatopluk agrees to the terms, although it is debatable whether

----

iewicz's *Dzieła* [Works]. Mickiewicz delivered his course of lectures at the Collège de France, during his Parisian exile.

or not he intended to keep the troth he pledged to Karolman (who betroths his daughter to him to make the alliance all the more stronger). For although he does return to his homeland at the head of a foreign force and even leads a clever cavalry charge against his own Slovak people that sweeps them from the field, at a lull in the fighting he heads to the Slovak fortress of Devín on his own to plead his case before the Slovak diet. Initially rebuffed as a traitor, following his arguments of alliance under duress, some of the Slovak elders make a counter offer: What if Svatopluk should abandon the Germans and reascend his throne? Would that not be a better solution, to fight at the head of his own people and, in repulsing the Germans, win a kingdom independent of feudal obligations, rather than to hold to Karolman's terms and 'enslave' the Slovaks to the Bavarians? Having been accused of treason for abandoning them, and Rastislav, to the Germans, and now tempted to break his word to Karolman, Svatopluk is, understandably, at a moral crossroads. However, national sentiment wins out in this man who had, just hours before, brought fire and sword against his own people. He accepts the offer and Slavimír, rather relieved, transfers authority to him. The offer he sends to Britwald, the commander of the German forces, to retreat homeward in peace, is, of course, spurned and the war continues, this time with Svatopluk leading his own people. In masterful lines that testify to Hollý's solid classical grounding in Virgil and Homer, the Slovak war of independence (in which the neighbouring Slavs, the Czechs and the Poles, also take part) batters on to the final victory, and the Great Moravian Empire is established on a firm, independent footing.

SVATOPLUK AND THE EPIC TRADITION

The classical epic genre in the West (and not only), is characterised by the following traits:

Exalted theme. For a small nation such as Slovakia, submerged for centuries in a multinational empire dominated by a foreign élite, and threatened by progressive cultural annihilation, there can be no greater or more exalted theme than the establishment of a national identity and cultural integrity. We have already mentioned the significance of Hollý's epics for the development of Slovak as a literary medium, which, it would not entirely be an exaggeration to suggest, is on a level with Dante's significance for Italian. But the content of *Svatopluk* is also important, as through it Hollý emphasises not only the heroism of the Slovaks, but the antiquity of their state as the foundational basis of the tenth-century Great Moravian Empire, the first and only independent Slavic state in the early middle ages, until the consolidation of the Polish kingdom to the north.

Formal poetic language. All epics are 'high style'. The great formal triumph of Ján Hollý, as far as poetics is concerned, was his establishment of the Slovak line, which basically consists of fifteen syllables, and the powerful poetic narrative he builds around its supple core, sustained over the twelve books of *Svatopluk* (as well as the twelve others that constitute the *Cyrillo-Methodiad* and *Sláv*). His translation of Virgil's *Aeneid* provided, of course, a solid foundation for his verse-line. For a poet whose career falls between the Enlightenment and Romanticism proper, it is noteworthy that he eschewed couplets for a stately blank verse much more in line with his Italo-Grecian models.

Generous narrative length. Modelling himself on Virgil — as so many did before and after him — Hollý contains his account within twelve books. Taking five hundred lines as the average length of *Svatopluk's* cantos, this gives us more or less six thousand lines of verse. That is a little over half the length of *Paradise Lost*, which exceeds ten thousand, and closer to, but still less than the *Lusiads* of Camões, which come in at 8,816. Still, it is more than enough space for Hollý to produce an engaging and well developed account of the German-Slovak war, with many of the trappings found in the *Aeneid* (as we will describe below).

Extended metaphors. Again like Virgil, whose metaphors tend to be among the lengthiest in the ancient epics, Hollý delights in vivid comparisons. Most of them are taken from nature, and more than a few refer to the specific nature of his Slovak homeland. The introduction of Slovak toponymy both validates the 'reality' in which his fictions play out, and draws the Slovak reader close to the stories, referring as it does to places he knows, and lives among.

Beginning 'in medias res'. *Svatopluk* begins with the hero in gaol. As he makes his plaint to God, and during Karolman's address to the diet he calls in order to discuss his plan of liberating Svatopluk, the backstory is filled in, per usual epic narrative style, by recollection.

Invocation to the muse. It is to a particularly Slavonic muse that Hollý appeals, calling upon 'Umka', who resides on Bílá Hora, and has watched the sometimes dramatic history of the Slovaks unfold from that height. But whether or not we are to suspend our disbelief and take the Slavic muse as a figure separate from the poet himself is debatable. The word *Umka* seems to be a coinage of Hollý's own.[7] Based on the Slavic root *um*, meaning 'reason' or 'mind', it

---

[7] In *Slávy dcera*, Kollár also refers to *umky* in a way that suggests a Slavic version of the Graces. It is possible, and even probable, that he borrowed the word from Hollý.

is conceivable that Hollý is personifying his own inspired poetic abilities of narration, which 'dwell' in contemplation upon the historical heights of his nation.[8] For it is also true that, like Milton, at least once Hollý invokes the Holy Spirit, asking Him to enlighten 'Umka'.

War, duel, quest. Just as the *Aeneid* is divided into two halves, the 'Odyssean' half recounting the travels of the Trojans (Books I–VI) followed by the 'Iliadic' half dealing with the war between the Trojans and Latins (Books VII–XII), so is *Svatopluk* divided into two portions, though unevenly. Cantos I–VII of Hollý's work recount the preparations for war, from Svatopluk's deliverance from prison, through a tournament arranged to decide who will command the German hosts in Karolman's name, a banquet at which Svatopluk gives a lengthy account of the Slavic nation's generation in India and wanderings to Central Europe, and a catalogue of the troops who set out on Svatopluk's behalf. Cantos VIII–XII describe the fierce war per se, including Svatopluk's switching of sides and the eventual victory of the Slovaks. The war will conclude with Svatopluk's dispatching of Britwald in a duel, although Hollý will not 'humanise' his hero by tarnishing his scutcheon with raving and cruelty, as Virgil so curiously does in the case of Aeneas, who takes vengeance upon the defeated Turnus kneeling before him.

Dual plane of Action. In the earlier cantos of the work, Hollý introduces the vengeful demon Černobog, and the rest of the legions of Hell, who bitterly hate Svatopluk for his role in establishing the Christian religion in Slovakia/Moravia and depriving them of the latreia they had enjoyed from the pagan Slavs. This idea of the reality of the pagan gods as demons, fallen angels who deceived the pre-Christian peoples into worshipping them as deities, is derived from Milton, who thus explains the Greek oracles in a manner somewhat curious for a Protestant. For he does not deny the 'existence' of the pagan gods, he just unmasks them, showing forth their true, infernal nature. The emergence of Černobog from Hell is lifted nearly *in toto* from Milton, as is Černobog's address to his fellow toppled deities, which is similar to the pandemonium scenes from *Paradise Lost*. Thus, though not to the same extent as the more classically conceived battles waged by the pagan deities in *Sláv*, Hollý preserves the epic conviction of the vital interest of supernature in the doings of men here on Earth. Dream sequences, in which inspiration is brought to sleeping mortals (from God Himself, in the case of Karolman in Canto I) are also a part of this dual plane of action. However, insofar as the Lord God Himself takes an interest in the men here on Earth,

---

[8] According to Karol Rosenbaum, Umka 'frequents the summits of his native region, and thus is something of a good genius of the Slovaks'. See Karol Rosenbaum, 'Poznámky' to Ján Hollý, *Výber ź básní* (Turčiansky Sv. Martin: Matica slovenská, 1947), p. 184.

sending forth His angel to make His will known unto them, in this we see more of a characteristic of the mediaeval chanson de geste, such as *The Song of Roland* and *The Song of My Cid*, than the pagan epics. This makes sense given that *Svatopluk* is a Christian epic, set in the mediaeval period.

Epic hero. Svatopluk is indeed an epic hero. He embarks upon a traditionally-conceived monomyth as described by the late great Joseph Campbell, departing from the Slovaks out of fear of treachery at Rastislav's hands, 'crossing the threshold of adventure' during his Bavarian imprisonment, and then returning to his people in the manner of Odysseus returning to the Ithacans, bringing to the Slovaks the 'elixir' of a restoration of independence and order following the successful war against the Bavarians.

The underworld journey. Of all the characteristics of the epic, perhaps the only one lacking from *Svatopluk* is the hero's descent into the underworld. That is, unless we consider the opening scenes of the work, in which we meet the Slovak king fettered in his dark dungeon. Yet that would be a stretch, as the underworld journey is supposed to be one of discovery. In Book VI of the *Aeneid*, the greatest of all of those west of Yudhishthtira's journey through Hell in the *Mahabharata*, Aeneas comes to know the future history of the city his descendants are to found, and what the special mission of Rome will be. Likewise, Gilgamesh would never have completely understood that the fate of all men is death had he not crossed the mythical waters to visit Utnapishtim, the Sumerian Noah. Hollý's Svatopluk does not undergo so nearly dramatic an enlightenment in his dungeon. Aware of the injustice of his sentence, he appeals to God for aid. The closest he comes to an acquisition of new wisdom is his realisation of the fata morgana of royal rule, which often leads, as it does in his case, to sorrow. Yet the nature of this intimation as life-changing wisdom is undercut as the story continues, for Svatopluk is to triumph as a king, after recovering his sceptre from his placeholder Slavimír at the diet, and then affirming it in war. But in this lack of an underworld journey Hollý doesn't completely depart from his epic patterns. In Milton's poem, for example, Adam, like Svatopluk, is depicted as a human being around whom supernatural powers group, and in whom they take an interest, and (apart from the revelation of the war in Heaven imparted by Raphael) he undergoes no journey of discovery either.

In short, then, it can be clearly seen that Hollý is a fine classical apprentice in his construction of the great Slovak epic. Significantly he is also mature enough of a poet not to work slavishly, but to select from the epic vineyard those clusters that best suit his purpose, in vinting new Slovak wine to be poured into the old wineskins of the Virgilian epic.

SVATOPLUK AND VIRGIL'S AENEID

Speaking of Hollý's translation of the *Aeneid*, Jaroslav Vlček writes: 'once again one marvels at the faithful rendering of the sense of the original, the polished diction and the richness of poetic expression of the Slovak translator, who was labouring without predecessors or previous patterns on which to model his work'.[9] There may not have been any Slovak or Czech[10] models to draw on for his *Aeneid*, but the Latin work was certainly a model for his original Slovak epics. Indeed, as a translator, recreating the original in a new poetic setting, Hollý knew the Latin original better than many a passive receptor or critic of the work. In order to see to what extent Hollý places *Svatopluk* in the Virgilian epic tradition, let us consider the following chart that breaks down the contents of the *Aeneid*, listing alongside the Slovak narrative equivalents:

Book	Aeneid	Svatopluk	Canto
I	Aeneas at Sea, Venus' plea	Svatopluk Imprisoned, St Cyril's plea	I, XI
II	Narrative of fall of Troy	The Indian Pedigree of the Slavs	VI
III	Odyssean search of Hesperides	(Migration of the Slavs)	VI
IV	Dido and Aeneas	(Ojda and Miloslav, Palislav)	XI
V	Funeral Games of Anchises	The Tournament of Heroes	II
VI	Journey to Underworld	Černobog's Escape; Pandemonium	III
VII	The War Stirred by Juno and her fury	Černobog and his demons stir the Slovaks	IV
VIII	Aeneas and Evander; Shield of Aeneas	Svatopluk and Karolman, Shield of Svatopluk	VII
IX	Little Troy; Nisus and Euryalus	Siege of Devín, Zemižížen and Slavboj	VIII, XI
X	Battle on the Shore; Aeneas' Rage	Battle on the Shore; Svatopluk's Escape	VIII, IX

---

[9] Jaroslav Vlček, *Dejiny literatúry slovenskej* [The History of Slovak Literature] (Turčiansky sv. Martin: Nákladom vlastným, 1890), p. 46.

[10] The first translation into Czech verse was done later, by Karel Alois Vinařický, like Hollý a Catholic priest, in 1851.

| XI | Latin Senate; Amazons | Slavimír's Diet, Dobroslava, Prekrasa | V, IV, XII |
| XII | Aeneas and Turnus | Svatopluk and Britwald | XII |

To speak of these briefly, Svatopluk's imprisonment, with which his epic opens, is similar to the pickle in which Aeneas and his men find themselves, storm-tossed by an angry Neptune, at Juno's urging. But whereas the Trojan hero's divine mother hastens before Jove at this first sign of danger facing her son, a similar scene is not to be found in *Svatopluk* until ten cantos later. When the battle for Slovak independence is well underway, St Cyril (formerly known as Konštantín, apostle to the Slavs), 'pleads the cause of those he had converted' before the Almighty. Just as Venus knew that it was not merely the elements that were battering the Trojans, but the inimical gods, so Cyril is concerned here, not with the earthly plane of battling men, but with the demonic legions of Černobog, who threaten, as he sees it, to plunge the Christian Slovaks back into the glooms of paganism. The Lord responds in soothing tones that both assure Cyril of the Slovak triumph, and also foretell a bright future for the Slovaks similar to Jove's promise of Roman empire without end:

> This I grant heroic Svatopluk: taking the field,
> He shall fell the German war-chief himself in battle,
> And cast the foreign yoke from off his people's shoulders.
> The borders of his kingdom shall extend far and wide;
> The kindred Slavic nations shall support his sceptre,
> Though like all earthly things subject to vicissitude,
> They shall endure the varied shocks of change, and sad falls.
>   XI:146-152

There may be a flirtation with Pan-Slavism in these lines, which would not be strange for a Slovak poet of the national revival period. But given that the centre of this empire is Slovakia (something which even the most patriotically minded Slovak Pan-Slavists would never dream of suggesting), it is obvious that Hollý is here having God enunciate a more humble glory: the foundation of the Great Moravian empire, which indeed for a while did stretch 'far and wide', from the Lusatian Serbs in East-Central Germany to well within modern day Romania, and from Little Poland and Silesia in the northwest, past the Tatras, through Pannonia to swathes of modern day Serbia and Croatia.

In Book II of the *Aeneid*, when Aeneas recounts the fall of Troy, he is narrating current events, rather than history — after all, he was involved in the conflagration; it was the destruction of his city, despite his best efforts, that led to his roundabout journey to Carthage. The same is true of his story of the 'Odyssean' adventures undergone along the way. Canto VI of *Svatopluk* contains a much more ancient story. Karolman, who has Slavs within his own realm, is interested in learning from the Slovak king where his people come from. Svatopluk embarks upon a long tale of the Slavs' journey from their original homeland — India — to Central Europe, centuries before, chased there by flood and famine. They have their own harrowing passages on the way to their own 'Hesperides', including a fierce war against the cannibalistic 'Doghead' tribe — more than enough of an equivalent for the bestial Cyclops or the fanciful half-human Harpies.

This idea of the Slavs' kinship with the Hindus and other tribes of the Indian subcontinent was popular amongst other Slavic Romantics, such as Adam Mickiewicz and Ján Kollár. As fanciful as it may sound, there is some linguistic kinship to build upon; the Slavic tongues, like ancient Sanskrit and modern Hindi, belong to the *satem* branch of the Indo-European family of languages (English, like German, is of the western, *centum* group), and the ancient cognates between them are often surprising. Slovak *piect'* [to bake] is a cognate of the Sanskrit *paçati*, and the same ancient word is at the root of the Slovak verb *budit' sa* — 'to awaken' — and the noun 'Buddha' — 'the awakened one'. I do not know to what degree Hollý, the meticulously trained Latinist, was aware of Indo-European comparative linguistics, but in the catalogue of troops in *Sláv* III, Mount Matra is said to have been named in honour of the Indian homeland. Is it merely a homophonic guess, or did Hollý know that *mātarah* means 'divine mother' in Sanskrit?

To whatever extent any of the theories of Slavic migration from India might be true, the desire of Hollý to pin the Slavs onto the Ancient Indian past is reasonable enough. How better to underscore the antiquity of the Slavic nation than by claiming it to be an offshoot of the ancient culture that gave us the *Vedas*, the *Mahabharata* and the *Ramayana* — especially given the paucity of mention of the Slavs in the writings of the Western historians of ancient Greece and Rome?

The Indian descent of the Slavs possesses an additional interesting aspect. That the Slavs themselves are immigrants to the territories they now occupy is a strong corrective to any racist understanding of nationhood. They do not despise the Chudes, or the Avars, or the Germans, because they are racially different; they battle against them because they are rapacious, murderous, and unjust. This is further emphasised by the generous offer extended to Dízabo in *Sláv*, and at the end of the epic even to Bondor, for them to settle amidst the Slavs, giving over rapaciousness, and working the land with them. It's all about peaceful usage and coexistence — that's what the Slavs are after, who, as Svatopluk says, only occupy the lands abandoned by others, so as to bring what's fallow into fecund use.

And thus, in Canto VI, the Slavs continue on their trek to their own 'Hesperides', of which, like the Trojans, they know to have been fated to them. This destiny is first mentioned by the god (Brahma) himself, through his prophet, before they leave famine-stricken India, and is confirmed at their stop in Armenia by the king, who recalls an old prophecy of a 'kindred folk' who were to pass through Armenia for Europe.

The Armenian episode is an interesting one for several reasons associated with the *Aeneid*. First of all, it recalls the 'seeds of empire' strategy employed by Virgil in his epic, in which (as here) some of the old and infirm are left behind at their various stops along the Mediterranean, thus underscoring the Roman Empire as a widespread area held together not only by law or governmental authority, but linked by bonds of blood. In the case of Hollý's epic, this emphasis placed on the kinship of the Armenians and the Slavs, true enough as far as Indo-European linguistics are concerned, is part of his syncretising Pan-Slavic tendencies (as delicate as they are in comparison with other Slovak writers, such as Štúr and Kollár). While not Slavs themselves, the Armenians are Christians, and the conquest of Armenia by the Russian Tsar draws them into the Orthodox Russian Empire and out of the clutches of the Muslim Ottomans. It is safe to say that if a Pole like Mickiewicz were writing *Svatopluk*, he might rather have appealed to the kinship of the Armenians (of whom, traditionally, there had always been a large community in Poland), above all as a people enslaved like his own to that same Russian Tsar.

Also, as some of the Slavs start to get used to Armenia and slowly — just like the lotus-eaters — begin to forget the destiny and responsibility fated to them in Europe, word must be sent down from on high to get them started on their road again — just as Jove sends down Mercury to the 'uxorius' Aeneas in Carthage.

The fact that the Armenian king 'would have liked it' had the Slavs remained 'to form one kingdom' with him in the Caucasus is, of course, an echo of Dido's welcome given to the Trojans even before Aeneas is revealed to her eyes. The same is true of the generous outfitting of the Slavs as he finally sends them on their way. We should not, however, expect Hollý to cover every episode in the *Aeneid* — Virgil himself does not do so with his Latin reinterpretation of Homer's epics — only a much worse poet would have slavishly imitated his original inspiration. However, a lamenting woman can be found in Canto XI. The one woman who stands out in this epic, as does Dido in the *Aeneid*, is Ojda, bewailing the loss of her last remaining son in the battles against the invading Germans. Her vituperation of Miloslav's squire Palislav for emerging from battle unscathed, while his master's body lies in the dust, is Hollý's equivalent to Dido's 'Hyrcanian tiger' rant, and, like Dido, Ojda will die too, embracing her son's body — with God dispatching a merciful angel to snip her golden thread.

The funeral games in celebration of the life of Aeneas' father Anchises, which take place in Book V of Virgil's epic, provide a respite of sorts between the harrowing destruction of Troy and the war for survival of the Trojan people, which is about to commence upon their landing in Italy. It is full of good humour, the sort of thing where 'prizes for participation' are given out (witness the footrace in which Nisus and Euryalus take part) — although tragedy is never far away. The 'lusus Troiae' are broken off abruptly when some old women, under the malign influence of Juno, fire some of the ships so as to impede further wandering. Hollý's equivalent, the 'tournament of heroes' that takes place in Canto II, serves a more serious purpose: the determination of who is to lead the armies in Karolman's stead during the invasion of Slovakia.

Just as during Aeneas' absence on his meandering mission to the Arcadians, when the camp of the Trojans becomes the scene of a second, miniature, siege of Troy, the Slovaks, routed by Svatopluk's unexpected cavalry charge, are bottled up in Devín. The curious fact here is that while Aeneas is merely absent from his men, Svatopluk is actually fighting against his own country. It would be a bit of an understatement to say that Svatopluk's actions here are morally ambiguous. This seminal hero of Slovak independence — a traitor? It is as if the Americans were to begin celebrating Benedict Arnold Day, or the British give Lord Haw Haw an OBE in recognition of his services to the Crown.

Svatopluk's history begins in the shadows of betrayal. He accepts the armour given him by Karolman, and the army that will escort him to his homeland, and the hand of the king's daughter, who weeps at his departure into the unsure environment of war. Whether or not Svatopluk knew all the time what he was about to do, Hollý, at the very least, heavily foreshadows the treason:

> 'This armour, which I have had forged for you, expressly,
> Take now unto your mighty limbs, and visit the troops.
> Go now, engage in the cruel fray with steadfastness,
> And batter the resistant to their knees, to the dust,
> To occupy your throne usurped, and wield the golden
> Sceptre of your nation. Never break your plighted troth'.
>   Thus said he, knowing not that he armed his own ruin.
>   (VII:8–14)

'Never break your plighted troth' — ominous words indeed, as this is exactly what Svatopluk will do. When he switches sides, he will be going against an implicit vow, repaying good with evil. The situation is made even more equivocal when we consider the design on the shield. It is no depiction of Slovak history — past or future, as in the case of Aeneas' prophetic buckler — it recounts a much graver act of perfidious ingratitude: the fall of the angels (VII:27–34).

This matter of Svatopluk's treachery is problematic to say the least — unless we consider Zemižížen's expression of shock at Svatopluk's original 'troth breaking' with the Slovaks — which we know did *not* happen. For in such a case Karolman's words might be applied to Svatopluk's first oath — to defend the Slovaks — and this oath we know that he did not break, certainly not of his own free will. Granted, this is a bit of convoluted reasoning, but in order to square the circle of a foundational national hero who seems not to keep his word, it makes sense. The oath to one's country is the main thing. Any deception practised on others, especially on the enemies of one's country, is excusable, if never entirely laudatory.

It is just such reasoning that Všeslav, once Svatopluk's archery instructor, presents to the Slovak diet in Book IX:

> Was it so totally evil, what Svatopluk did,
> Abdicating his own freedom, so sweet to all men,
> Subjecting himself to a Bavarian liege lord?
> Such was the price of escaping long imprisonment
> In dungeon dark, and regaining his royal sceptre.
> That's what we call extenuating circumstances.
> Can there be any here who can state with certainty,
> That had the same hard fate been visited upon him,
> He would not do the same, but return to his prison,
> Abdicating rather his possessions and his life,
> Than to re-emerge to the sweet light of day and regain
> His honours lost? Even at the cost of serving one
> Already set above him?

And he carries the day. Along this train of reasoning, Svatopluk's troth-breaking against Karolman is actually a fulfilment of Karolman's injunction: in taking the opportunity to turn on the Germans, he is acting in accord with his first and most important 'troth', being true to the Slovaks. As for that shield with its design of the war in heaven, it is perhaps not insignificant that it was carved by Rukoslav — a Slav himself — as if a reminder to his fellow countryman where his loyalty ought to lie.

Broadly speaking, as far as the composition of *Svatopluk* is concerned, the remainder of Virgilian analogies refer to the Battle itself (and Aeneas' rage), the Trojan Senate scene, the duel of Aeneas and Turnus, the night sortie of Nisus and Euryalus, and the Amazons. Not only does Hollý eschew a mere slavish copying of these themes, he constructs them in such a way that the Slovaks are seen to surpass the Trojans in virtue.

As for the Amazons, for whatever reason, the idea of women warriors whose martial prowess doesn't detract, but actually augments their pulchritude, has been a key element of European culture since its earliest days. This rather odd component of the European psyche stretches from Achilles and Penthesilea in the *Iliad* all the way through Clorinda and Tancred in Tasso's *Gerusalemme liberata.* In both of these cases, eroticism is mixed with violence in that the male knights overcome their fiercely-battling rivals, only to melt in regret and passion when the dying maidens' casques are removed and their beauty revealed. The psychological roots of macabre, voyeuristic dramas such as this are beyond my experience and powers of explanation. In Virgil's *Aeneid*, Camilla is a Volscian warrior princess fighting for the Latins; we also find there Turnus' supernatural sister Juturna, who desperately, though vainly, tries to save her brother's life. Hollý's Prekrasa,[11] Ludomír's wife, is more lucky, or more skilled. Sharp-eyed (and how!) she follows her beloved husband's warring from her perch on the battlements of Devín, her crossbow always at the ready, it would seem. For once, when she finds him in grave mortal peril, she loads her weapon, fires it, and shatters the elbow of the foe who raised it to bring down a sword upon Ludomír's head. It's a shot worthy a modern sniper, but the point here is not so much Prekrasa's skill as the great philosophical divide that lies between the pagan world of Greece and Rome and the Christian dispensation. Juturna is eventually unable to save her brother because Turnus is fated to die. There is no such destiny, for good or ill, in the Christian religion, where free will is preeminent; Ludomír is no more fated to die than Žarkoslav, who sought to bring him down — it was Prekrasa's presence of mind and steady hand that delivered her husband. Her dart, unlike that fired by the precocious Ascanius at the braggart Romulus was not borne to its target by any god.

As far as the battle scenes, which make up the largest portion of the epic, are concerned, Hollý's descriptions of the slaughter in an age when hand to hand melees were the norm does not go far afield from the usual epic fare. If there is any special characteristic of the fight scenes in *Svatopluk*, it may be the attention the poet pays to anatomy. Hollý's imagination is a sharp one, and in

---

[11] Predictably, in true Amazon fashion, the archer is not only skilled, but comely as well. The name Hollý invents for her means 'sublime beauty'.

his descriptions he is exact, technicolour-exact. Consider Warnefríd's death in Canto VIII:

> The bolt caught him between his nape and shoulders, its tip
> Slicing his tongue and smashing his lower row of teeth,
> To emerge from his mouth like some grotesque appendage.

It is often suggested that Homer must have been a military surgeon, judging from the detailed exactitude with which he describes battlefield wounds. By the same token, one might wonder if our poet had not been a soldier himself, given how good Hollý is at describing scenes of maiming, which underscore the horror of war in close combat. (He never was, which is but additional confirmation of his exceptional powers of imagination).[12]

For example, in his description of Ľuboslav's raging amongst the Germans in X:135–142 we have a marvellous example of the furious chaos of close combat, the frenzied fog of war. The blows and thrusts fall on whatever body-part happens to be in the vicinity of the whirling sword-arm. Ľuboslav is not shown here as a deft fencer, planning his thrusts, but rather as a wildly milling propellor that minces whatever blunders into its path:

> [...] First Wolhart he fells,
> Slashing his right thigh, then beauteous Malching the left;
> He hacks through Firt's brow, helmet and all, and separates
> Arfríd's arm at the elbow, hand still gripping his sword.
> He ran Trost through the eye, and marred Hildebrand's visage
> Once comely with a cruel slash; he severed Máro's
> Head, which, still helmeted, flew away from his body,
> Eyes blinking in astonishment, to roll far away.

No epic worth its salt can do without a showdown between two black brothers: Achilles and Hector, Aeneas and Turnus, Arjuna and Karna — and here, Svatopluk and Britwald. In comparison to these more famous showdowns, Hollý's comes up a little short. There is no moving, and so believable, hesitation as in the case of Hector, when he sees death approaching in the guise of the 'dog star' Achilles, and ponders flight, tempted by his parents from the battlements. There is no even more jarring despair like Karna's, when he learns that the promises of the gods are not always kept, as his 'invincible'

---

[12] As Milan Pišút puts it: '[the images of warring] are as plastic as one finds in the *Iliad*. In this respect, Hollý could have no better inspiration, as he himself had no soldierly experience'. p. 207.

dart of Indra flies wide at the very wrong moment and the earth itself begins to swallow his chariot-wheel, leaving him helpless; there is no moral quandary as that faced by Arjuna when his half-brother, struggling at the wheel, begs for his life and Krishna urges him: 'Kill!' Nor is there the questionable slaughter of Turnus, kneeling before Aeneas, defeated, begging, but not in any vile fashion, for his life. This is one of the more memorable scenes from Virgil's *Aeneid*. The noble protoplast of the Romans is about to spare his defeated rival's life when his eyes land on the belt of his pupil Pallas, which Turnus stripped from his body after defeating him on the battlefield, and rage gets the upper hand of reason — he slays the helpless man one would have reckoned on him sparing. Whatever the reason for this may be — perhaps Virgil wished to humanise his nearly perfect, other-centred hero in this way, as an almost negative encouragement to us mere mortals (even heroes make grave mistakes!). It is certainly a much more complex and satisfying scene than what Holý presents us with. For here, the courageous Britwald merely has his men step aside and he approaches Svatopluk with a proposition to end the fray there and then:

> 'Tell your men to set aside their swords in present truce.
> Let us, you and I, enter the gallant lists alone.
> Should you emerge the victor, you shall reign in your land
> Over a people free of Bavarian lordship;
> Just spare these other soldiers, send them home to their hearths.
> But should I overcome you, and strip you of your arms,
> Your land and people shall revert to Bavaria'.

Svatopluk's speech is not recorded by the poet. Mention is only made of his rejection of the paroling of the Bavarians — again, for what reason, we may only speculate, although there is certainly nothing nefarious behind the refusal — before the slugfest begins. All Holý gives us is another vicious, sumptuously described, battle, until Britwald's soul is 'released from the flesh, and the holy light / Soon vanished from his eyes, ceding place to endless night'.

As we have just mentioned, Holý is unsurpassed in his battlefield descriptions, even by his classical masters. The battle in Italy, however, provides Virgil with the first opportunity of making his otherwise perfect hero stumble. In Book X of the *Aeneid*, when news reaches Aeneas of the death of Pallas, Evander's son, the Trojan begins to rage in a very un-Roman way: slaughtering men who are kneeling before him having cast their weapons aside, chasing down priests in their vestments, and — worst of all — reserving eight boys to be sacrificed over the funeral pyre of his deceased friend. Why? Is Virgil seeking to 'humanise' this son of Venus, as we suggest above, making him a more believable hero by giving him some rather garish flaws? Perhaps he is underscoring the fact that Aeneas is not a Roman *yet*. Unlike the Carthaginians, from whom Aeneas and his men had just parted, the Romans held human sacrifice in the greatest horror. As earlier Virgil made use of such realia as the speech from the rostrum and the *lusus Troiae* as evidence of how far back some familiar Roman traditions reach, was he now foregrounding this reprehensible behaviour to show the Roman receptor how far his nation had come since its earliest days?

It may be suggested that Svatopluk's escape to Devín after the initial rout of the Slovaks, and his decision to switch sides, is just such a conscious scuffing-up of the pristine hero by the poet, providing him with the flaw of infidelity (such as that may be). To some extent, this may be true. On the other hand, the Slovak comes out on top, morally speaking. However we are to understand Aeneas' actions, he is morally reprehensible. It is not the 'fog of war' that is leading him astray, for he indeed does lead the boys out to their gruesome death on the next day of truce; he is not acting under the duress of fresh emotion. Svatopluk may be acting vilely towards the Bavarians — how many died on his behalf? And now he just switches sides? — but his actions may also be excused, or at least understood, on the basis of the higher fealty he owes to his own people.[13] And even though Britwald bitterly thinks that Svatopluk always had this treachery in mind, his hesitation at the Slovak diet, as brief as it may be, suggests the opposite: that he was aware of the equivocality of his position, and took his decision only after reflection.

Speaking of the parliamentary scenes in both epics, there is no invidious Drances seeking to belittle his better, Turnus, before the Latin elders. Everyone gathered at the diet in Devín, at the beginning of the invasion in Canto V, and during the heated interview with Svatopluk in IX, is noble, devoted, and there with only one thing in mind — the rescue of the motherland. No Slovak taints himself with villainy — excepting Svatopluk himself, whom we have already excused twice — the only Drances character in the epic is German: the 'choleric Wilbert' who rises in the Bavarian diet in Canto I to oppose leniency for Svatopluk. Indeed, although he strives 'to cloak his hatred in terms of gallantry and praise, / His hard eyes and unkind demeanour [give] him away'. This is that same Wilbert who will come across Svatopluk on the battlefield and mock him, launching into an extended and somewhat ribald brag of how he will wed his Bavarian spear as a bridegroom to the 'maiden' Svatopluk. But, like Ascanius facing down the rant of Romulus taunting the 'twice defeated

---

[13] Numbers of whom he also slew, during his brilliant cavalry charge, while still fighting on the Bavarian side. We do not mean to muddy the waters here, but it's worth pointing out.

Phrygians' by running the gloater through with the 'answer' of his arrow, thus Svatopluk wastes no breath on divorcing Wilbert from the light of day with his own weapon, crowing only briefly over the felled man before moving on to other deeds.

Whether one should wish to see this as a fault or not, Hollý constantly paints his Slovaks in brighter colours than his Latin models are tinted with. To bring our chief comparison chart to an end, let us consider the night sortie of Zemižížen and Slavboj in Canto XI. Night sorties are commonplace in classical epics. The two most famous are those of Ulysses and Diomedes in *The Iliad*, and of Nisus and Euryalus in *The Aeneid*. These are missions of espionage. The Greeks are penetrating the Trojan lines, where they wring information from the unfortunate Dolon; Virgil's Trojans volunteer for the dangerous mission of breaking through the Latin lines and bringing word of their besieged camp to Aeneas, who is away seeking allies for the coming war. The same is true of Zemižížen and Slavboj, who volunteer to sneak into the Bavarian camp to learn Britwald's intentions. Will he be content to head home with the remnants of his troops? Or does he intend to continue the war on the morrow?

The morality of such endeavours is none too straightforward, especially when violence occurs during the nightly truce, when both sides are supposed to withdraw to camp to refresh themselves for the coming day. Let us remember that Odysseus slaughters poor Dolon *after* he promises not to, in exchange for his information, and Nisus and Euryalus don't merely cut through the lines on their way to their absent leader, they linger there, revelling in the slaughter of their sleeping enemies. Is all fair in love and war? Or is this simply not cricket, at all? There is an interesting moral progression in the epic sequences from Homer through Virgil to Hollý. Homer makes no moral pronouncement whatsoever on Odysseus' actions. Is this cruel betrayal of trust merely one more example of the 'many wiles' of the king of Ithaca, who always comes out on top? Returning to camp after the sortie, Ulysses merely wades into the sea and washes the gore from his skin, after which he goes off to his tent for a late supper and a refreshing nap. Virgil is more censorious of Nisus and Euryalus. He notes with distaste their psychosexual (?) arousal as they stab the sleeping men — quite unnecessarily — and then has them pay the ultimate price for their gory distraction. Euryalus is betrayed to a Rutulian patrol by the moon flashing off the helmet he looted during his frenzy, and Nisus, even though he had gotten through the lines by now, returned to sacrifice his life out of sorrow for his friend, captured and slain, choosing (in a very un-Roman way) private grief and the chance for revenge over the good of his nation, by returning to certain death rather than pressing on with the mission. Although he doesn't explicitly state it, Virgil is disgusted at the bloody capers of the two Trojans, and the story of the night sortie is a monitory fable: what *not* to do — how greed and personal feelings should never overcome duty.

It is only the Christian Hollý who sees the matter in its proper moral context.[14] Sending off Zemižížen and Slavboj to the sleeping German camp, Svatopluk admonishes them:

'Off with you, then, godspeed, to discover everything we need
To know. Then hurry back safely with the news you glean.
But see you take the life of no defenceless sleeper:
There is no crime so silent as raises no alarm'.

This is not mere prudence — v.g. 'stay under the radar' — it is hortatory advice: 'stain yourself not with crime'. *Svatopluk* is a Christian epic, and both hero and poet speak as Christians. This is not only historically significant, it also plays a key role in the story itself. The Slovaks are Christians no less than the Germans. There is no religious justification for the Bavarian onslaught; it cannot be explained as a justifiable use of force with the aim of spreading the Christian faith among pagans (although Paweł Włodkowic put paid to that sort of reasoning at the Council of Constance), nor can the rationale be the altruistic setting of Svatopluk upon the Slovak throne, which is his inheritance. Since he is being helped to that throne under conditions of vassalage, this is a German war of conquest, pure and simple, and Svatopluk's switch of sides, consequently, is heroic. To return to Zemižížen and Slavboj, not only is their mission a success (they penetrate the camp, and bring back the news desired by Svatopluk) they also do some — justifiable — pillaging of their own. Before they part to encircle the camp from different sides, they come across a stable of horses, in which they recognise two steeds that had been stolen from them earlier by the Germans. The horses recognise their masters as well, and Zemižížen and Slavboj return, whole, not only with information, but also 'made whole' once more, retrieving their equine friends, balancing accounts.

We bring this section of our essay to an end with a comment applicable to all three epics. Just as Shakespeare's histories always tend to the restitution of order, so each of these three narratives ends with a liberation. Svatopluk liberates his people from Karolman's overlordship; after their labours to liberate the Slovaks from paganism and deficient Christian doctrine, Cyril and Methodius receive a blessing from Pope Adrian which frees them from the overlordship of the Bavarian Church. Finally Sláv once and for all delivers the Slovaks from the depredations of the Chudes.

....

14   Yes, you read that right. I state it unabashedly: this is the *only proper* moral context.

We should also point out that Hollý has a tendency to use 'Slovak' 'Tatran' and 'Slav' interchangeably in his epics — interestingly enough, in the same way in which his contemporary Jernej Kopitar (1790–1844) treats 'Slav' and 'Slovene'.[15] What are being described here are not wars of territorial acquisition or the self-determination of one small West Slavic people, but rather a 'gathering together' of all the Slavs — the first Pan-Slavic appeal in history. It is significant that a Polish contingent mentioned among the catalogue of Slavic troops in *Svatopluk* is led by a man called 'Swojski' — which name means 'one of our own'. Finally, when Černobog appears to Slavimír in his deceptive, yet all the same prophetic, dream, the first thing he frightens him with is not his own personal danger, but the ravaging of his country. Slavimír is first and foremost worried about his people — the Slavs.

THE *CYRILLO-METHODIAD* AND *SLÁV*

Just two years after the appearance of *Svatopluk*, Hollý brought out his second epic, the *Cyrillo-Methodiad* (1835), followed by the third, *Sláv*, four years later. Except for Milton (of whom we will have occasion to speak), and Dante (if we consider the three portions of *La Divina Commedia* to be separate poems in their own right) Hollý is the first poet since the mythical Homer to compose more than one epic.

In this period of national rebirth, Hollý is basically creating a mythology for his nation. As *Svatopluk* would have the Slovak reader look with pride upon the Great Moravian Empire, the *Cyrillo-Methodiad* reminds him of the great apostles to the Slavs, who spent much time in the territory that was to become Slovakia, and finally, *Sláv* takes up the purported descent of the Slavic peoples from ancient India, providing them with the ancient civilisational past that their neighbours in the nineteenth century would deny them.

If an epic centring on preaching and conversion seems counter-intuitive, Hollý endows the mission of the brothers Konštantín and Methodius with all the glory of a cosmic battle. And why not? Is not salvation, the war waged against sin and the devil, a goal that surpasses all the hegemonic strivings of any Napoléon or Aleksandr I? 'For our wrestling is not against flesh and blood' says the Apostle Paul, 'but against principalities and powers, against the rulers of the world of this darkness, against the spirits of wickedness in the high places'.[16] The triumph of the Thessalonian brothers over paganism, and later the

---

[15] Giuseppe Dell'Agata, 'S. Toscano, Ján Hollý (1785-1849) cantore di Cirillo e Metodio, *Studi Slavistici*, xvii, 2020, 2: 271-272, p. 271.

[16] Ephesians, 6:12.

lukewarm Christianity of Bavaria, is a triumph with greater significance than any victory over an earthly oppressor, as it leads to an eternal liberation. In *Paradise Regained*, Milton sets the question before the reader with even greater force, locating the victory of Christ over Satan not at the dramatic moment of His salvific death on the Cross, but in His obedience to God the Father, His victory over Satan's temptations in the desert, which as the English poet sees it already redeems humanity as the New Adam makes up for the sins of disobedience committed by the Old.

Both the *Cyrillo-Methodiad* and *Sláv* are much shorter than *Svatopluk*. Whereas Hollý's first work follows the conventional twelve-book Virgilian template, the two later epics are more or less the size of *chansons de geste* — each of them six cantos apiece. Six and six — the reader of Virgil is reminded of the thematic halving of the *Aeneid* into 'Odyssean' and 'Iliadic' portions — can it be that the *Cyrillo-Methodiad* and *Sláv* are to be considered two halves of one epic?

It might be a bit too much to suggest that, as the topics of both, and the time-frames presented in them, are too widely ranging. What is true, however, is what we have already mentioned: that all three of Hollý's epics share the same general thematic thrust: towards liberation. In *Svatopluk*, the liberation of the Slovaks from Bavarian overlordship is celebrated. In the *Cyrillo-Methodiad*, the Slovak people are both liberated from the darkness of paganism by the two apostles, and, with the establishment of the Slavonic Rite and Slavic administration of the Church in Moravia, Slovakia, and Pannonia, from the careless cure of the German priests from Salzburg, who disdained even to learn Slavonic in order to preach effectively, and whose establishment in Slovakia is proved to have been little more than a German ploy for political expansion. As for *Sláv*, Hollý reprises an element mentioned in Svatopluk's account of the Slavic migration to Central Europe from India: their defeat of the horrible 'Psohlavci' [Dogheads], a barbaric nation of cannibalistic horsemen from the southeastern steppes of Europe, here identified with the Chudes. The successful defence of the Slovak homeland from these invaders is not just a liberation from the threat of enslavement — it is that, too — but more, it is a paean to the pastoral civilisation of the Slovaks. Agriculture is shown here to be a civilisational advancement — a liberation — from hunting, gathering, and rapine. It is not too much of a stretch to see in the Chudes a thinly-veiled allusion to the Magyars.[17] If that is the case, the epic

---

[17] In his *Slavic Antiquities* (1836), Pavol Josef Šafárik mentions just such a theory, linking the Magyars with the Chudes (though he offers this as only one possibility). *Slovanské starožitnosti*. Vol I: 'Starožitnosti slovanské okresu prvního' (Praha: Bedřich Tempský, 1862), p. 51. Rosenbaum suggests that 'among the Russians, the original meaning of the word *Chude* means foreigners in general, while in the ethnic sense it means the whole great Ural-altaic tribe, to which the Magyars also belong'. p. 192.

is both as forward-looking as it is historical. For after settling in Pannonia, the Magyars not only accepted Christianity, but also the ways of the Slovaks — most of the words dealing with agriculture and fixed abodes in the Hungarian language derive from Slavic terms.

The plots of the two shorter epics are simple, yet engaging. In the *Cyrillo-Methodiad*, Rastislav, already a Christian, and Svatopluk his nephew, send to Emperor Michael in Constantinople for Slavic-speaking priests to travel to their country and instruct their subjects in the true Faith. For:

> [...] how unlearned we remain! How unfamiliar
> With the Way of that Truth, which is Life! How can a man,
> Whose mind is still wrapped in the gloom of error, take sure
> Steps from the darkness, without any light to guide him?
> That eye is no better than blind, which sees no daylight!
> And who is to blame for this our sad, purblind state?
> Who but the Germans? Who've sent such men to convert us
> As know our language not, or mangle it in speaking?
> What's more, these men are not scholars; they've no wish to whet
> The blade of their tongues to address us with precision.
> They'd rather make Germans of us!

Thus, the theme of the threat of Germanisation, never far from Hollý's purview or that of the majority of western Slavs of the Romantic period, makes its appearance in Canto I. Michael gladly sends to them the brothers Konštantín (Cyril) and Methodius, who had already succeeded in converting the kindred Volgars. The Slovak people themselves, though nominally converted by the Bavarians sent from the archiepiscopal see of Salzburg,[18] still hold to pagan practices, and indeed, there are quite a few pagans still among them who refuse to convert, such as Oslav, high priest of Belbog, who sees Christianity as a German invention. Oslav, a Moravian, is distrustful because, as he sees it, the conversion of neighbouring Czech princes resulted in nothing but an extension of the hostile sway of Ludvík, the Bavarian prince:

> Twice did he fall upon them so, yes, three times, when they
> Uprose to struggle free of the tight German halter.
> Is this what you would bring us, too — just such misfortune,
> Imposing this your foreign faith upon us, and driving

---

[18] In Canto I of the *Cyrillo-Methodiad*, Rastislav informs the brothers that the Christianisation of the Slavs there began under the reign of the Marcomanni — thus, as early as the fourth century — when the baptised king and queen established a church in Nitra.

Us from our homes to knock about foreign parts, begging?
Would you like the Moravians to die for your faith,
Bringing the Germans here too, to make us into slaves?

And so the struggle of Cyril and Methodius as presented by Hollý is a three-fold battle. First, they must overcome the distrust of the peace-loving Slavic people, chary of German hegemony; second, they must implant true Christianity among them, not only baptising them, but preaching to them in the Slavic language (which indeed convinces even some of the most reluctant pagans, once the truth of Christianity is finally revealed to them); third, they must overturn the pagan 'gods' themselves by hacking apart their idols, destroying their fanes.

The introduction of the Slavic gods to these epics, as nefarious beings in *Svatopluk* and the *Cyrillo-Methodiad*, and benign ones in *Sláv*, allows Hollý to provide the reader with a more pronounced dual plane of action, the heavenly in addition to the earthly, crucial to the classical epic. Poetically speaking, it allows Hollý to showcase his familiarity with his other great model, John Milton, as some of the scenes he depicts are lifted in pious appropriation directly from *Paradise Lost*.

While we actually know little about Slavic religion prior to the advent of Christianity, the mission of Cyril and Methodius is historically documented. This is especially apparent in the closing, triumphant, cantos of the work descriptive of their trial before the Pope. The introduction of Slavonic ('Old Church Slavonic') to the liturgy of the Mass was a controversial step, and the brothers were indeed summoned to Rome to explain this elevation of a vulgar tongue to the liturgical status of Latin and Greek. As Hollý sees it, this summons came not of the Holy Father's theological misgivings, but rather from the invidious Bavarian clergy, who saw the mission as a threat to their influence — and enrichment. And so the theme of German rapacity — even in things of God! — mentioned at the outset of the epic, returns in force at the end, although the brothers, and the Slavs, eventually win the day.[19]

....

[19] The triumph was short-lived. Although use of the Slavonic liturgy in the Roman Catholic Mass was authorised alongside Latin and Greek, it soon fell into disuse in the West with the reimposition of Latin uniformity at the decline and fall of the Great Moravian Empire. However, that the Slavic identity remained strong among Latin-rite Catholics is emphasised by the famous saying of Aleksander Cardinal Rudnay (1760–1831), a contemporary of Hollý's, Cardinal Primate of the Hungarian Kingdom: 'Slavus sum; et si in cathedra Petri forem, Slavus ero!' [I am a Slav, and even should I find myself on Peter's throne, I will be a Slav!]. Of course, a Slavic bishop was elevated to the papal see in 1978, with the election of Karol Wojtyła — Archbishop of Kraków and native of Wadowice, both of which locations once found themselves within the Great Moravian Empire. See Stanley B. Kimball, 'The Austro-Slav Revival: A Study of Nineteenth-

As for *Sláv*, Hollý's last epic is a development of an episode from the Slavs' ancient trek from India to their new homeland. As Svatopluk tells the story, after departing friendly Armenia, the migrants were set upon by a wicked, savage nation known as the Psohlavci [Dogheads], one (it seems) of a number of violent tribes inhabiting the regions bordering the Black Sea. Svatopluk describes the initial battle between the Slavs and these brigands (described as half-human creatures, rather than men), and then notes that initial Slavic settlements along the Dnieper were under constant threat of invasion.

In *Sláv*, which begins with the great nation already settled in Slovakia, these wild men are identified with the Chudes. This is rather incongruous, as the historical Chudes (or Chuds) were a Finnic people, living far to the northeast of the Tatra regions. This may have been politically-motivated sleight of hand. For the real threat of national deracination faced by the Slovaks of Hollý's day was not from the Germans to the west, but from the Magyars, who had come to assume a dominant role in the multinational state of Hungary. During the nineteenth century, when nationality came to be associated with language, the 'national revival' of the Magyars led to the imposition of the Magyar tongue upon nearly all educational, legislative, and legal activity in the state, shunting aside the Latin tongue, which had for centuries been an official lingua franca shared by the Slovaks, Croats, Romanians, Germans, and Magyars inhabiting the kingdom. The raw 'Chude' invaders, then, who fall upon Slovakia twice in the epic, and are routed (to their astonishment) by these farmers 'unskilled in arms', are perhaps to be understood as the horsed invaders from the south-east, the Magyars themselves — who cannot be so named by Hollý, as such would certainly have threatened the book with suppression.

On the one hand, then, the *Cyrillo-Methodiad* and *Sláv* are monitory epics on the same theme: the threat to the Slovaks of being submerged by stronger, expansive, foreign elements. In the first, the poet warns against the threat from the west (Germans), and in the second, against that from the east (Magyars). As far as the latter is concerned, in Canto I of *Sláv* the gathering of 'all [Chudes] capable of war / For murder and pillage in the land of the Tatrans' is described thus:

Soon time matured unto that fateful hour when the horde
Should mass, as ordered, on the limitless rusty sands
Of that desert oceanic, stretching endlessly
On all hands, pitiless and barren.

....
Century Literary Foundations', *Transactions of the American Philosophical Society*, 1973, Vol. 63, No. 4 (1973), pp. 1-83, p. 52*n*.

It is hard to read lines like this without seeing the men and horses massing on the famous Hungarian plain, the *puszta* — which Magyar word is, after all, a borrowing from the Slavic adjective *pustá* in its feminine form, meaning 'empty'.

Can it be that Hollý progressed in this manner with one eye on the censor? Did he plan, for example, to have the more benign epics on the Great Moravian Empire's victory over the Bavarians, and Cyril and Methodius' struggles against the Salzburg clergy, in print and widely known before turning to the delicate subject of Magyarisation? So that, as it were, his position as a known and accepted epic poet would be strong enough to permit *Sláv*, so critical of the Magyars (if our reading is correct) to slip through into print?[20]

In any event, the chronology of the epics, if we follow the dates of publication, is unusual, for it proceeds backwards in time. First, we have the historical struggles of the Great Moravian Empire, in connection with Bavarian (East Frankish) expansion in Central Europe. Then comes the description of the mission of Cyril and Methodius to the Slovaks — a relatively contemporary, yet still earlier event, and finally, Hollý leads the reader into the mists of antiquity: the first solidification of a pre-Slovak state, while the Slavs were still entirely pagan. It is as if the poet wished to slowly initiate his Slovak reading public into the history of the nation, starting with the familiar and moving backwards towards the unknown.

In essence, Hollý is creating a mythology for his nation — nothing new in the context of the Czechs and Slovaks during the period of 'national revival'. However, the way in which he does so is interesting, and praiseworthy. The desire to cement the antiquity of nations just (re)emerging from a suffocating overlay of a foreign, imposed culture allegedly led Czech poet Václav Hanka (1791–1861), in collaboration with his friend Josef Linda (1789/92–1834) to forge poetic documents purporting to contain verse in an older form of Czech dating in some cases from the eighth century. Named for the location of their purported discovery, these are the *Rukopis královédvorský* (Dvůr Králové manuscript, 1817) and *Rukopis zelenohorský* (Zelená Hora manuscript, 1818). Whether or not the overwhelming suspicion of counterfeiting be true (and even today there are

---

[20] Of course, truth is never black and white. In his article 'Slovenská literatúra v literárnohistorických prácach napísaných po maďarsky' [Slovak Literature in Works of Literary History Written in Magyar], *Slovenská literatúra*, vol. 68, 2021, nr 4, pp. 408-431, Ivan Halász gives a fine overview of the many studies and translations of Slovak literature amongst the Magyar population of the Kingdom of Hungary. Still, despite sympathies and a seemingly benign attitude to Slovak cultural autonomy, the ruling majority both feared and battled against 'Pan-Slav' tendencies, whether real or merely apparent.

some who defend the authenticity of the manuscripts),²¹ the probability of the fraud cannot help but detract from the poetic value of the works themselves. As contemporary Czech poet Rio Preisner once said, 'it would have been better had Hanka published the poems under his own name'²² — as did our poet, for example. Ironically, the fact that Hollý makes no mystery about himself being the author of these epics lends them an 'ancient' authenticity which the *Rukopisy* are completely lacking. In the case of *Svatopluk* and *Sláv*, we are ready to suspend our disbelief and assent 'Yes, it might well have been like that', playing along with the poet as he begs, and wins, the inspiration of 'Umka' that gives him a glimpse into the doings of ancient Slavdom, whereas with Hanka, as soon as the supposed authenticity of the *Rukopisy* are called into question, we reject them out of hand as 'counterfeits' not worthy our consideration. They are worthy of a better fate, but any allegation of fraud, even a *pia fraus*, tends to negate the work in question entirely. As to Hollý's 'inspired authenticity', the manner in which his soul vibrates in harmony with the misty traditions of his people, if we are to credit the testimony of the Russian Slavicist Izmail Ivanovich Sreznevsky (1812–1880), who visited Hollý at his home, there might well be something in that: 'He speaks of times long past as if he had it all right before his eyes. He feels it all so viscerally; he sobs when he recalls something great, or beautiful, or evil'.²³

The catalogues of names — some authentic, most of Hollý's own invention — seemingly evoked from the misty past, which we find in the descriptions of battle in *Svatopluk* and *Sláv* and in the descriptions of the completely faded pagan past in the *Cyrillo-Methodiad* somehow create the sense, not of a modern poet creating modern works in his own personal style, but rather of a historian passing on the ancient sagas of his people in a bardic succession, as it were. The uniformity of the descriptions creates an aura of textual contemporaneity, and not necessarily that of the nineteenth century — and thus is more akin to translation than to falsification. Hollý is above-board with his reader, and it redounds to his credit.

THE CLASHING OF THE PLANES: THE *CYRILLO-METHODIAD* AS EPIC

'Going therefore, teach ye all nations', commands the Lord at the conclusion of Matthew's gospel, 'baptising them in the name of the Father, and of the

---

[21] In his lectures, Mickiewicz too lends credence to the surprising 'discovery'.

[22] In conversation with the author.

[23] In May of 1842. The Pan-Slav in Hollý emerged when Sreznevsky introduced himself, crying 'Rus? Rus? Ó Bože môj!' [A Russian? A Russian? O my God!] Sreznevsky's account of the meeting, which he published in *Slovenské pohľady* (1894, p. 116) is cited by Rosenbaum, p. 181.

Son, and of the Holy Ghost'.[24] It is a peaceful, triumphant scene, as befits the resumption of man's friendship with God at Christ's resurrection. But before we cue the soft music of Alfred Newman, it is worth remembering that the progress of the Church from that hilltop in Galilee throughout the world will not fit within the soft boundaries of a Protestant Easter film starring Victor Mature and Richard Burton. St Peter was to be crucified upside-down, St Paul beaten and decapitated, St Bartholomew skinned alive, and our St Matthew, to whom we refer at the beginning of this section, was martyred at the altar — as many years later were to be St Thomas Beckett in Canterbury and St Stanisław ze Szczepanowa in Kraków. And this is only a representative example of the most famous soldiers of Christ. The catalogue of martyrdoms — witnessing to Christ unto the death — stretches from St Stephen in the years preceding Saul's conversion into St Paul, through the steadfast heroes of the Roman and Elizabethan persecutions, through Andrew Dung-Lac and Maksymilian Kolbe, Jan Zahradníček and Job Chittilappilly in our own times. As the previously quoted St Paul reminds us: 'our wrestling is not against flesh and blood but against principalities and powers, against the rulers of the world of this darkness, against the spirits of wickedness in the high places'. This is a war a thousandfold more frightful than any invasion of Phrygia or Normandy, with stakes immeasurably higher than the struggle for any throne or political system. Why should it not be worthy of traditional epic treatment?

This is worth keeping in mind, especially when one comes across the not-entirely baseless opinions of contemporary critics like Miloslav Vojtech anent the *Cyrillo-Methodiad*, who feels that Hollý's second epic 'is stuck in stereotypical rhetoricality without the [proper] use of dynamic narrative and epic breadth'.[25]

That's a questionable statement, especially when one considers the three strands of the story, Christian vs. Pagan, Orthodox Christian vs. Jobbing Priests, and finally Slav vs. German, which are wound throughout and fully developed in the space of six short books. But to restrain ourselves to the question of dynamism here: in the *Cyrillo-Methodiad*, the long battle scenes between Bavarian and Slovak, Slav and Chude, found in the other two 'heroic songs' are replaced by the shattering of idols throughout the Tatran region by the brother apostles. The catalogue of idols overthrown by Konštantín in Canto III, and Methodius in Canto IV, is like the catalogue of heroes slain in battle in *Svatopluk*. It is this more than anything else that raises the *Cyrillo-Methodiad* to the rank of epic

---

[24] Matthew 28:19.

[25] Martina Taneski, 'Epos *Cirillo-Metodiada* v peripetiách literárnohistorickej recepce', *Konštantínove listy* 11/2 (2018), pp. 143–150, p. 147.

poetry. Again, these battles, both against the false idols and their worshippers who from time to time oppose the Christian missionaries, are more crucial than any mere human wars. Their extent is just as impressive and important, underscoring just how immense a task the brothers took upon themselves. Thus, in our opinion, rather than to speak of 'a poorly-managed composition and further generic deficiencies',[26] we should rather pause in wonder at the poet's compositional daring in outfitting a missionary story in Virgilian tropes.

To return to the pagan deities, whether or not all the gods mentioned by Hollý are historically confirmable, the feeling the reader gets is of a Herculean struggle like few others. What is more, the sheer number of the gods speaks volumes to their irrationality. It is much more reasonable to accept the proof of St Anselm, that none can be God but He Who is the absolute highest, beyond which there can be no other perfection. St Augustine's argument in *The City of God* against the multiplicity of Roman deities: 'What? the goddess of childbirth can only do that? Not much of a god, is she?' — is also implied.[27]

This approach is found in other of Hollý's works as well. In Canto IV of *Svatopluk*, for example, the poet underscores the powerlessness of the pagan gods in an interesting way. Svatovít is described as having four faces — not, as in Slavic mythology, so that he might behold the world in all four directions at once, like some powerful guardian deity, but so that he might be seen himself from all four sides, as the people gather around the blind, inert idol. Further, we find another description of the weakness of the pagan gods in XII:327–356. Radislav, a pagan, fighting on the Slovak side (a defective man fighting in a good cause), prays to Svatovít for help in felling Chocil, a Slovak Christian fighting on the Bavarian side (a good man fighting in a bad cause). Radislav's spear goes wide: not only is Svatovít powerless, he has already been chased from the field with the rest of the pagan gods by St Michael, at God's command — while Chocil, who prays to the True God, casts successfully and takes down the pagan. Nowhere is the succession of times, with better dispensation replacing worse (*nota bene*: regardless of national considerations), better shown than here.

As for the descriptions of the destruction themselves, the depiction of Methodius' hacking apart of Bobák, for example: 'slicing him clean into two portions' (IV:232), is similar to those used to describe the felling of the warriors on the battlefields of *Svatopluk* and *Sláv*.

---

[26] Taneski, p. 147.

[27] In Chapter 21, he asks: 'What need had women in childbirth to invoke Lucina, when, if Felicity should be present, they would have, not only a good delivery, but good children too? What need was there to commend the children to the goddess Ops when they were being born; to the god Vaticanus in their birth-cry; to the goddess Cunina when lying cradled […]?' (Translation by Marcus Dods).

When we come to discuss *Sláv*, that epic of pagan Slovak antiquity, we will see that Hollý's approach to the pagan deities of Slavdom will be somewhat different. As for now, it is important to point out that, in *Svatopluk*, among the demons called forth from Hell by Černobog, Perún is conspicuously absent. Perhaps the poet was already mulling the theme of this god being 'the ruler of the cosmos' — God Himself, Whom the pagan Slavs worshipped under that name (as the Muslims of today call Him Allah).

And so, the traditional epic possesses two planes of action, the spiritual and the human. Sometimes they mix, and the gods themselves descend to earth to enter the fray on behalf of their favourites (we shall see something of this sort in *Sláv*) — although in both the *Iliad* and the *Aeneid* there comes a point when Zeus or Jove forbids their active participation. In the *Cyrillo-Methodiad*, the entire epic, save the question of Slavic/German ecclesiastical issues, is built around the clash of these two planes. The human plane (Konštantín, Methodius) directly battles against the spiritual plane (the pagan idols and pagan ignorance). Considering the matter from the Christian point of view, Hollý's work, in a very satisfying way, shows Christians fighting on behalf of God against forces inimical to Him, 'helping' Him (rather than repeating *de rigueur* epic depictions of quarrelling gods helping their favourites on Earth). It is a battle of spiritual enlightenment. Whereas in Book V of the *Iliad* Athena endows Diomedes with divine sight so that he might be able to distinguish between god and man engaged in the fray around him (whom he should avoid, and whom he is free to attack), the situation in the *Cyrillo-Methodiad* can be better likened to the concluding scenes of the *Bhagavad-Gita* in the *Mahabharata*. There, Krishna (Arjuna's charioteer on the human plane, the incarnate god Vishnu on the spiritual) bestows divine sight upon his friend so that he might perceive Krishna's true nature and understand the cosmic significance of the war he is so reluctant to join. Who knows but there's not a bit of the Indian in the Slav Hollý after all?

SLÁV, OR JOHN FORD'S FAVOURITE SLOVAK EPIC

Of course we have no evidence that the great Hollywood pioneer was even aware of Ján Hollý, the *národné obrodenie*, or Slovak literature in general. But it's a safe bet to assume that, if he had, he would prefer *Sláv* to the other two epics of the Slovak poet, for it best fits the template of the Western genre, which he did so much to shape. The white hats are easily distinguishable from the black, right is obviously right and wrong indubitably wrong, and virtue and civilisation triumph in the end over vice and barbarity. Matters will be decided by a showdown, and even though a child might recognise these villains when he sees them, Hollý's black hats — the Chudes — sometimes (if infrequently) rise to a nobility of character that complicates and humanises them beyond painted devils.[28]

The Slovaks are right and the Chudes are wrong. In *Sláv* we have an analogous situation to that of Charlemagne's Frankish troops and the 'pagans' in *Le Chanson de Roland*, where 'Paien unt tort e chrestiens unt dreit' [The pagans are wrong and the Christians are right, Laisse LXXIX:1015]. However, there is nothing racial about this; the Slovaks, settled, peaceful farmers who work the land, are more civilisationally advanced than the marauding Chudes, and at least twice the offer is made to them by the Slovaks — *Leave off your rapine, come, live among us and learn to live from the fruits of your labour, and we shall be friends* — at which all reason to battle will vanish (something that seems to have happened in the case of the domestication of the Magyars). For the Chudes are not evil because they are Chudes, different, 'the other', they are evil because of the evil things they do (looting, cannibalism, the lawless life they lead). Only these must be put aside, not their nationality.

The story told by the poet is a simple one. The Chudes, vicious neighbours of the Slavs inhabiting a none too well-defined latitude that seems to be located somewhere in the regions of southern Russia and Ukraine,[29] survive by raiding nearby states, pillaging them of goods and cattle and enslaving that part of the population they choose to spare from the sword. It seems that the Chudes send out expeditions in waves. While one horde goes a-looting, the others remain at home, salivating in anticipation of their share of the take. Just as the *Iliad* begins with the anger of Achilles, *Sláv* begins with Bondor, the Chudan king, infuriated at the news that an expedition led by his brother into the Tatras has not only failed to bring home booty, but has been decimated, scattered by the inhabitants of that land. This enrages Bondor all the more, as defeat at the hands of 'farmers untutored in war' seems to him a black mark on the whole nation. In his wrath, he summons all men capable of bearing arms and organises a punitive expedition.

The six books of the short epic will be made up of accounts of the battles that ensue. Here as well Hollý will distinguish himself with vivid descriptions of the fierce struggle. Sláv, the eponymous leader of the nation, who first beat back the Chudes, is called upon again to meet the renewed threat. This he does, with the help, not only of Slovaks, but kindred Slavs living nearby: Czechs, Moravians, and Poles.

....

[28] See, for example, Dízabo's beautiful and stirring metaphor of the caged eagle in Canto V.

[29] They are not Slavs, however, although some of them have names with a Slavic tang to them.

Of course, the Slavs will be victorious. Yet as Milan Pišút informs us, of all Hollý's epics, *Sláv* made the least impression on the readership of the time:

> Romantic historicism demanded at least some approximately proven historical facts. A certain disruption was also caused by Hollý's introduction to his work of a mythology more appropriate to Greece — with which a great cultural epoch of Europe is associated, whereas nothing remains of the Slavic deities, so stylised here in antique fashion, except for their names. Other nations possessed, at least in their folklore or in mediaeval literary texts, some legends and tales from pagan times. And so as an epic Sláv runs out of steam, although the poetic language of this work is just as masterful as it is in Svatopluk, and its composition even more perfect.[30]

There may be some truth in this for such readers as set historical authenticity above invention, but in our opinion this all is rather beside the point. For what sets this epic apart from others — both of Hollý's pen and those further afield — is, on the one hand, its characterisation as a cultural war: peaceful agrarianism vs. wild savagery, and on the other, the very manner in which Hollý treats the pagan gods. They are not demons in this work, but benign, angelic figures, fighting on behalf of justice, under the ultimate direction of Perún, the supreme god, whose name, as we say above, Hollý treats as the Slavic denomination of the one true God.

THE SLAVIC IDYLL

Svatopluk, who first recounts the ancient pedigree of the Slavs, speaks of them as lovers of peace (though brave), tillers of the soil, and hospitable to all guests. Their original homeland is India, which they would never have abandoned (they have no interest in wars of conquest) had Brahma not commanded them to, first by the plagues he sent down upon the subcontinent, and then through the mouth of his prophet (*Svatopluk* VI:197–206). They are also a fair-minded people. Among those who decide to leave India with the group setting out for Central Europe are such lovers of democracy who reject the Hindu caste system, and wish to live in equality with all (VI:212–213). 'In peacetime / They cared not for any permanent governor' VI:540–549, he says, implying that the Slavs enjoyed a tradition of harmonious anarchy in times of peace. They needed leaders only in time of war — hence the appellation *voivode*, which still exists in the Slavic tongues today in the meaning of a 'regional governor', but which ultimately derives from words meaning 'war-leader'.

---

[30] Pišút, p. 208.

War, however, they wage reluctantly. In all of his epics, Hollý describes the Slavs as lovers of freedom, and it is only on behalf of freedom that they will engage in defensive wars. This is the theme of all three epics. In *Svatopluk* they do the battle against the Germans who would enslave them; here, it is against the rapacious domineering of the Chudes that they will fight (as we say above, one of the purposes of the Chudes' invasions is to enslave the conquered peoples). It is also noteworthy that although there are Slavs in the army of Karolman, when he mentions the Slovenes and Carinthians who owe him allegiance, he points out to Svatopluk that it was only after long and ferocious fighting that they were at last subdued by German arms. Indeed, when Svatopluk changes sides in that epic, he will rally the Slovak troops on behalf of freeing those brothers of theirs currently 'in German slavery' (XII:89–94). Finally, even the *Cyrillo-Methodiad* can be read as an epic depicting the brothers' efforts to liberate the Slavs from, on the one hand, the slavery of paganism, and on the other — dependence on German (foreign) ecclesial administration.

Liberation from the foreign yoke is a very familiar theme in the Romantic literature of the West Slavs — Slovaks, Czechs, and Poles. While the Poles had a long history of independence stretching from the end of the first millennium until 1795, and therefore had both a strong sense of their identity and an aversion to any sort of Pan-Slavism that would posit the Russians as leaders of the 'nation', the Czechs and Slovaks were just re-shaping their national identity after long years of Germanisation and Magyarisation. Unlike the Poles, who were overly familiar with just what Russian hegemony means for peoples subjected to Petersburg/Moscow, Czechs and Slovaks frequently turned longing eyes towards Russia as a fraternal saviour, with whose aid they might cast off the 'foreign shackles' of Vienna and Budapest. And thus in *Sláv* III:106–109 Hollý voices a thinly-veiled Pan-Slavic threat, such as would not be foreign to the mouth of Ľudovít Štúr: Watch out Germans, Hungarians, and all the rest! Start treating the Slavs equitably, for you will not be able to withstand their power should they unite in arms against you!

> Destroy the evil Chudes! And may our German neighbours,
> The haughty Thracians and even the warlike Greeks see
> What brave and excellent warriors we Slovaks are!
> What terror we might sow ourselves were war our custom!

There are quite a few echoes of the *Aeneid* here as well. In one of the most easily recognisable, Živa, the Slavic Ceres, goes before almighty Perún, and pleads for the embattled Slovaks as Venus does for her son and his Trojans tossed by the raging waves:

> Of all the nations, the Slovaks are dearest to me,
> For eagerly they heed me, wholly devoting themselves
> To the soil, which rewards them ever with abundance.
> No other people is so wedded to sweet tillage!
> They know no weaponry, they are not a warlike tribe.
> Rapine and pillage are terms unknown to them, who earn
> What they enjoy from honest toil. They need no war-chief!
> Far from vice and harm, they live in peace. Fearing the gods,
> They raise our images amidst their broad, fertile fields,
> And on wooded hills they erect us splendid temples.
> They honour us with annual holidays and rites
> Of frequent feasting — for all these reasons, I've chosen
> To live amongst them particularly, protecting
> Them specially, bestowing my favour upon them.

This peaceful character of the Slavs, their devotion to agriculture, is what particularly endears them to her. In a very interesting way, she shapes her argument so as to suggest — along the lines of Ovid's description of the ages of man — that it was her intent, as the goddess of vegetation, that man should be vegetarian:

> Since the earth's fertility was entrusted to me,
> To provide all nourishment, both daily and festive,
> It was my desire to lead people to batten on
> Beechnuts and acorns, both sweet and bitter windfalls,
> Fresh leafy vegetables and crisp nutritive tubers
> And roots, rather than — as savage beasts — to feed on meat.
> I wished to incline them to a gentler husbandry!
> And thus did I teach them to yoke the plodding oxen
> And groove the sillion in even rows for planting.
> Thus I presented them with the seeds of varied plants —
> I taught them to sow and reap when the crop matures;
> To winnow the chaff and to mill the health-giving grain,
> And how to prepare the yield in succulent dishes.

Since such is her aversion to even the killing of animals for meat, all the more so does she hold the Chudes in repugnance, as slaughterers — and consumers — of men as well as beasts.

Before we continue with any discussion of Slavic meekness and Chudan savagery, it is worthwhile noting Perún's comforting prophecy to Živa, which more than smacks of Jove's promise of Roman greatness to Venus:

Your monuments despoiled will rise anew, your temples
Shall rise again from their ashes in all their beauty,
And you shall live again in honour there, enjoying
The daily sacrifice raised by your most pious Slavs.
What's more, their nation shall spread far and wide, the people
Multiplying in peace, waxing in power, until
Their holdings stretch from the Northern to the Southern Sea.
They shall occupy the lands where others dwell, including
The Chudes', which lies fallow. Such desert wastes they shall cause
To flourish with abundant culture. The Slavic folk
Shall swell into the most numerous of all nations,
A realm immense! And as they are now, so shall they be
Forever your faithful worshippers. Never the plough
Shall be far from their calloused palm, which shall never reach
For the sword, unless it be in need, when strangers attack
As now, when in defence of their land they shall be fierce:
A terror of inexorable, mighty warriors!

Hollý packs Perún's answer with so much significance, that it is difficult to say where to begin, and where to end, the citation. First of all, we need to point out the Pan-Slavic conflation of the Slovaks with the Slavic people as a whole. Whatever the truth of the matter may be — wherever the ur-Slavic homeland was located before the kindred nations spread west, north, and south throughout East-Central Europe — in Hollý's mythology that homeland (saving India) is the Tatras. Once they have defeated the Chudes, they will spread out in all directions, becoming the 'most numerous' of all nations in Europe — words to cheer the heart of any Pan-Slav, and prick the ears of the Germans, Magyars, and all the rest, as in the aforementioned monition that Hollý delivers about their might and valour.

Yet the Slavs are not a nation bent on conquest. They will spread, for sure, but only into such lands as are unoccupied, and lie fallow. In this way, the spread of the Slavs brings blessings upon Europe, causing the wilderness to bloom. It is an analogous mission to that of the Romans as predicted by Anchises in Book VI of the *Aeneid*, who are to spread the rule — not of Rome but of the law — throughout Europe. This is a theme first sounded by Svatopluk in his recounting of Slavic history before Karolman and the Germans. He goes even further (not only in emplacing the Slavs on the coast of Brittany and even on the British Isles!), but in stating that some of the lands the Slavs occupied were abandoned by quarrelsome tribes who went out to kill, and perish in turn, by the sword. Agriculture, therefore, is an advancement over martial glory, and of much more advantage to the world — and the Slovaks, 'Tatrans', or Slavs in general, are its greatest practitioners.

THE CHUDES — THE ANTI-ROMANS

In a manner that recalls the chauvinistic descriptions of the *Chanson de Roland*, where the armies ranged against Charlemagne are described as beasts,[31] Hollý conflates the Chudes in *Sláv* with the *Psohlavci*, the 'Dogheads', who rush upon the Slavs on their journey from India, as recounted by Svatopluk in his epic. Blood-thirsty cannibals, their only delight is in bloodshed and theft, as the haughty Bondor spits at Sláv just before their final duel. There is little, if any, redeeming qualities to this angry and hateful enemy of man. Bondor is an elemental character; there is no subtlety to him. He thinks only of slaking his own thirst, sating his own hunger, satisfying his own desires. He has no fellow-feeling. At the start of the work, his reaction to the news of his men's catastrophe, including that of his brother, is not sorrow or pity, but rage. Not rage at the Slovaks for depriving him of his brother and friends, but rage at his brother and camorades for their 'cowardice' and the 'shame' they've brought upon the name of the Chudes. In Canto I he is motivated by a desire to avenge the harm done to *him* by their lack of valour. In the deceptive dream sent by the Slavic gods in Canto II, when Oslad appears to him in the guise of his brother Ednek, Bondor reacts in the same wise — not with sorrow or love, but with anger and vituperation. Nor is he alone in such savagery. The Chudan champion Kondok says much the same in reference to the fallen, who now, supposedly, are suffering in Hell: 'Our comrades suffer? They should not have lost the battle!' (II:515).

In *Sláv*, Hollý employs the *Aeneid* allusions in a novel and interesting way in reference to the Chudes. Take Bondor's dream, which we have just mentioned, as one example. God, His messengers, or pagan deities often appear in classical epics and chansons de geste, delivering the will of Heaven to sleeping protagonists. The one instance that leaps to the reader's mind is the appearance of Hector's ghost to the slumbering Aeneas in Book II of Virgil's epic. Troy is aflame, all is lost; seeing that there is no hope now, Troy's greatest hero commands his living comrade to escape the conflagration, rescuing the remnant of the people and the gods of the city, to found the 'new Troy' destined to arise in the Hesperides.

---

[31] Characteristically, for the uninformed poet of the *Chanson* (unlike he of *El Cantar del mio Cid*, who was familiar with the Moors), amongst the pagan/Islamic enemies ranged against the Christian Franks are included 'Esclavoz' [Slavs] and troops from 'Hungres' [Hungary]! (Laisses CCXXXII: 3225; CCXXXIV:3254).

Characteristically, the appeal of the revenant spirit arouses compassion in the dreamer and spurs him to positive action. The message is a call to pity, and Aeneas, the first 'other-centred' hero in our tradition,[32] sets off on the arduous trek on behalf of something greater than himself: his people, his nation, the will of the gods. But here, on the contrary, Bondor responds to his 'brother's' request for mercy with disdain: *You're in Hell? Well, suffer on, you wretch, who have brought shame upon the Chudes!* He only springs into action when he himself feels threatened with the same fate. Hollý paints him as a true cannibal — selfish, concerned only with himself, deprived of all sense of fellow feeling. The epic machinery of the prophetic dream is here inverted. It matters not that the dream is a false one in the sense that it is actually the Slavic god Oslad, and not Bondor's brother Ednek, who he pretends to be; it matters not that the appeal he brings to Bondor — to perform the funeral rites for the slain Chudes and thus deliver them from their suffering — is a ruse intended to retard the Chudan march while the Slovaks prepare to meet them. The point is, Bondor believes that his brother has appeared to him, and his reaction is viscerally true to his nature: he is the anti-Aeneas.

We have an exact correlation to this 'inversion' of the *Aeneid* in Canto III. Part of Perún's stratagem in sending Oslad, the Slavic 'god of wassail' (whose name is based on a Slavic root meaning 'to sweeten') is to possess the minds of the Chudes with a desire to relax at banquet, to eat, drink, and be merry, in order to buy time for the Slovaks, who are on the march to meet their enemies in battle. This is a clear reference to the possession of poor Dido in the *Aeneid* by Venus. As we recall, in order to ensure that the Carthaginian queen receive her son and his companions graciously, Venus instructs her other son, Cupid, to infect Dido with an overwhelming desire for the Trojan hero. She changes the appearance of Cupid into that of Ascanius. Dido, dandling on her lap the boy she takes to be Aeneas' son, is suddenly pricked by the god's golden arrow, and soon is overcome with lust for Aeneas. This looks to be overly facile and mechanical. It is actually brilliant. For Dido does not fall in love with Aeneas — to give yourself to someone, you must first be in complete possession of yourself — she is drugged. Her mind is poisoned — the widow who determined to be ever faithful to her first husband Sychaeus (she wants to remain a *univira*) — struggles against the overmastering urge like a 'stricken deer trying to run away from the pain of the arrow in her

---

[32] In his notes to the *Aeneid*, R.D. Williams describes Aeneas as a 'new type of hero' and 'unheroic' (in the traditional selfish sense of the classical hero, in that 'he is spoken of as *insignem pietate virum,* and we see in him an honest and honourable endeavour to shoulder his immense social, religious, and military obligations'. See R.D. Williams, ed. *The Aeneid of Virgil* (Walton-on-Thames: Nelson, St Martin's Press, 1992). Vol. 1, p. 155.

side', before she succumbs to a passion that, in her right mind, she would have none of. The poison (for such it is) courses through her veins and keeps her a prisoner of the gods' will until the time has come for Aeneas to set out from Carthage for Italy. Virgil, who has much affection for Dido, is kind to her at the end of her story. Once Aeneas and his men are safely a-sea and beyond reach of any pursuit, once the gods have no more need of her, Virgil has the effects of the 'roofie' wear off. Dido, literally, comes back to herself. Realising how she has been used, all of her lust vanished, she rages in anger against 'that man' who abused her hospitality — and thus the stage is set for the Punic Wars. The point is, when we first meet Dido (and before she meets Aeneas), she is presented by the poet as a queen, an ideal woman in beauty, wisdom, and authority. Because of the gods' evil trick, she is transformed into a 'love'-sick teenage girl. But once the long fit passes, she becomes a queen again: her true, regal nature, which commands our respect, is once more revealed.

In *Sláv*, again, we have a similar scene, but inverted. Once Perún and the Slavic gods have achieved their purpose, and the Slovak hosts have drawn near the Chudes distracted by merrymaking, Oslad is commanded to leave their camp and return home. And then:

> As soon as he'd left the unpleasant tent of Bondor,
> And set off on the road leading home to Radostov,
> The black bile once more coursed through the veins of the raw Chudes.
> Astonished, they blinked around at the feast in disgust.
> Again 'twas blood they thirsted for, not wine; not music
> But screams and the groans of the slain would they gladly hear!
> Once more the cold lust of rampaging set them aflame.
> They grabbed their arms and nearly fell to blows then and there,
> Irate at having wasted so much time in softness!

Their true nature is once more revealed, and it is not flattering at all. Whereas, although Dido became worse through the intervention of the gods, but at the end of their meddling, her noble and praiseworthy nature is revealed again, here, the intervention of the gods made the Chudes *better* for a short space. When their minds are released from the gods' influence and their free will is restored, immediately, all gentleness, peace, and indeed humanity leaves them with the disappearance of the charm that made them better, and they regain their horrid nature, lusting for blood, not wine, and the groans of murdered victims rather than music. In such a way then, Hollý makes use of the *Aeneid* like the true poet he is: not pedantically, but creatively, brilliantly.

It would take long to fully draw out the manner in which Hollý depicts the foul villainy of the Chudes. Whereas even in the one skill of which they boast — warring — there is no beauty or intelligence, merely brute force, as they flail about with their weapons chaotically, the Slovaks are civilised warriors: they fight fiercely but in controlled fashion, with discipline, 'according to plan' (IV:149ff).

It is significant that the strategy chosen by the Chudes for this new incursion — one massed assault — had once before ended in catastrophe: for Ednek's men. They too fell upon the Slovaks in one swoop, achieving success at first, only to be slaughtered later. This inability to learn from past mistakes is but more evidence of the Chudes' barbarity. Indeed, the description of the earlier expedition's destruction — at a narrow throat of a river valley between high cliffs — is similar to the place where Sláv's men will slaughter Bondor's.

We needn't dwell overmuch on cannibalism and human sacrifice — such things need only be mentioned in order to characterise barbarity. However, there is one example of a sacrifice offered to the disgusting Chudan god Ár that is worth mentioning. Among the Chudes there is a beautiful Scythian lad named Tirák, taken prisoner during an expedition in Asia Minor, and raised, it seems, in Bondor's own household. Everyone who lays eyes upon him falls in love with him, including (believe it or not) Bondor himself. But Tirák is still a non-Chude, and hence an outlaw. Those who wander into the Chudan homeland are mercilessly killed — Tirák the exception has been living on borrowed time. And at last, in order to win the foul Ár's favour before his punitive invasion of Tatrania, Bondor determines on sacrificing him, 'the dearest I might ever offer'. Even the murderous priest in the foul grotto hesitates before raising his axe at such a beautiful head — but not Bondor!

> The cruel priest had never before hacked at such a face,
> Though more than two thousand men he had thrust from this world
> With cruel axe-blows, but then — his arms grew limp, the blade
> Thudded to the floor of the filthy grotto, harmless.
> Seeing this, Bondor was not moved to pity; the black
> Flames in his hard heart but bellowed to wilder raging.
> He unsheathed his own sword and plunged it into the breast
> Of the youth, to the very hilt.

Obviously, we have another inversion here, but not Virgilian. Bondor's sacrifice of Tirák is a perverse retelling of the Abraham and Isaac story — yet Hollý, intentionally, does not dwell upon it. The 'sacrifice' of Tirák is described tersely, although one might have expected pathos, and in so doing Holý deprives Bondor of all humanity, Abrahamic or other, and us of any possibility of weeping for and with him.

Holý constantly harps on the savagery of the Chudes. Pun intended. Their songs, such as they have, are wild ululations (what would you expect from the Dogheads?) and the instrument that their bard Kopolt uses is a primitive 'lute' of four bows bound together. Compare this to the Slovak's ability to forge real weapons on the model of those captured from the Chudes. There are armourers amongst the Slavs, but no luthiers amongst the Chudes — that gentle skill is beyond them.

Finally, insofar as *Sláv* is not just a story of warring between peoples, but models of civilisations, it is worthwhile to bring this discussion of Chudan barbarism to an end by taking a brief look at Bondor's speech to his troops in Canto I. This is also indicative of savagery and primitive culture. Bondor holds the Slovaks in contempt because of their agriculture, which he understands not as people living in harmony with nature, but warfare — hacking at the earth with ploughs and shovels — ripping 'vegetable loot' from her bosom:

> [...The Slovaks] know neither battle, nor
> How sweet it is to ride to war and return with loot,
> Expert at nothing but slave-labour, at war with dirt,
> Incessantly hacking the tired earth with horse-drawn blade,
> Stabbing it with their hoes and battering with shovels,
> Heaping as treasure whatever loot — in vegetables! —
> They tear from her womb.

More than being just the type of figurative language one would expect from a marauder, this makes the war between Chude and Slovak a struggle between primitive hunter-gatherers (to put the kindest spin on the ball) and an advanced, stable civilisation based on settled towns and peaceful farming.

THE SHIELD OF SVATOPLUK

The struggle of Slovak with Chude is also presented as a struggle between good and evil, between those beloved of God and the demonic powers ranged against them. It is a Christian epic through and through, in that the result of the tussle is never in doubt — God will prevail; during His interview with the worried Živa in *Sláv*, He, as Perún, suggests that He allowed the bloody incursion of the Chudes into Slovakia for the very purpose of bringing them down in final defeat, and such a resounding one that they will

[...] serve as an evident example
To other bandits, who the patient work of ages
And other hands would ruin in one frenzied moment,
Who find their joy in murder and rapine.

In *Svatopluk*, too, the spiritual plane of the epic emphasises the same. Černobog, the Satanic character of Hollý's elaborate Slavic mythology, appears at the very outset of Canto III rejoicing at the news of the fall of Svatopluk, whom he hates for his role in introducing Christianity to the Slovak lands and depriving him of the worship he heretofore enjoyed. Finding him nowhere in the underworld (Why should he hope to? The very fact of his reckoning that so great a Christian hero might be sent to Hell upon his demise witnesses to the demon's blindness), Černobog decides to undertake the arduous journey into the upper world again, where he and his minions will remain until they are toppled back into the pit of Hell in Canto XI by the archangel Michael, and the vent they emerged through is sealed again for all time.

Černobog's ascent mirrors that of Milton's Satan in Book II of *Paradise Lost*, including the characters of Sin and Death who stand watch at the nine gates of brass,[33] iron, and 'Adamantine Rock'. It is more than obvious that Hollý knew *Paradise Lost*, perhaps in the Czech translation of Josef Jungmann, which first saw the light of day in 1811— twenty-two years before he brought out his *Svatopluk*. The most extensive evidence of the Miltonic strain in Hollý's epics is found in the first and longest one, in Canto VII, where the shield of Svatopluk is described.

The motif of the elaborately decorated hero's shield is a characteristic of the classical epic, initiated by Homer, when the shield forged by Hephaistos for Achilles following the loss of his armour at the death of Patroclus is described. Achilles' shield, which in our day and age W.H. Auden so pessimistically (realistically?) parodies, is an image of fulness. The River Ocean is embossed around the edge, and the shield itself, as circular as the world, is decorated with scenes of human life, from agriculture and dance through a city besieged. Hollý's hero Virgil repeats the theme, and, as usual, betters his master, as the one that Vulcan bestows upon Aeneas following his return from the underworld is carved with scenes of Rome's future glory. Coming right after the commissioning scene with Anchises, who, after displaying to his son the parade of souls destined to lead the empire that is yet to be founded, imposes upon him the Roman's civilising burden, it is a marvellous poetic metaphor of Aeneas' devotion to duty. For he doesn't understand the

---

[33] In *Svatopluk*, the first of three gates is copper.

images (obviously), yet he rejoices in them, and at the end of Book VIII *attoll[it] umero famamque et fata nepotum* ['took upon his shoulder the fated deeds and fame of his descendants'].

The shield that Hollý has Karolman bestow upon Svatopluk in Canto VII describes the war of the fallen angels with the hosts of Heaven. Lifted entirely from *Paradise Lost*, it recounts the rebellion of Lucifer, who induces a third of the angels to follow him in his hopeless war against God, the devils' invention of cannonry, and the final, decisive triumph of Christ on his magnificent chariot. Hollý's retelling of the war in heaven is a masterpiece of condensation. Whereas Raphael's account of the rebellion stretches over a thousand lines — two hundred and fifty at the end of Book V and all of Book VI — Hollý's description takes up little more than one hundred and seventy.

How much Hollý owes to Milton — or to Jungmann, if indeed he knew *Paradise Lost* through the Czech intermediary — can be seen by comparing the descriptions of Christ's chariot. This is the English original:

And the third sacred Morn began to shine
Dawning through Heav'n: forth rush'd with whirl-wind sound
The Chariot of Paternal Deitie,
Flashing thick flames, Wheele within Wheele undrawn,
It self instinct with Spirit, but convoyd
By four Cherubic shapes, four Faces each
Had wondrous, as with Starrs thir bodies all
And Wings were set with Eyes, with Eyes the Wheels
Of Beril, and careering Fires between;
Over thir heads a chrystal Firmament,
Whereon a Saphir Throne, inlaid with pure
Amber, and colours of the showrie Arch.
Hee in Celestial Panoplie all armd
Of radiant Urim, work divinely wrought,
Ascended, at his right hand Victorie Sate
Eagle-wing'd, beside him hung his Bow
And Quiver with three-bolted Thunder stor'd,
And from about him fierce Effusion rowld
Of smoak and bickering flame, and sparkles dire;
Attended with ten thousand thousand Saints,
He onward came, farr off his coming shon,
And twentie thousand (I thir number heard)
Chariots of God, half on each hand were seen:

Hee on the wings of Cherub rode sublime
On the Crystallin Skie, in Saphir Thron'd.[34]

Jungmann renders this in Czech:

Počalo pak třetí svaté svitati
jitro, rozednívaje se na nebi.
Zvukem vichrovým a lítým plamenem
jede prudký nebeského otce vůz,
beze spřeže, ducha zvodem vlastního
puzený, a podlé něho podstaty
Cherubínů čtyř , a čtyry majících
divné tváři, cválají, co hvězdami
celá těla jich a křídla stkvějí se
mnohooká; mnohooká z berylu
kola jsou, a mezi nimi míhaví
plamenové. Křišťálová obloha
nad hlavami jich a safírový trůn, plný ambry,
plný barev duhových, stane na voze,
kde on, v své nebeské zbroji,
ze třpytících Urim, díla božského,
vstoupiv posadil se jest; s ním po pravé
ruce sedne orlokřídlé vítězství,
po levé pak jemu visí luk a toul
plný hromů trojzubých, a valí se
vůkol něho kouře mrak, a výlevy
líté plápolu a blesku žhoucího.
Obor svatých, deset tisíc tisíců
silný, vyšel s ním, a v dáli stkvěl se jda;
dvadcet tisíc vozů Páně (slyšel jsem
počet jich) s ním jelo, na dvě zdělených
strany. Tak se vznáší, jeda na křídlech
Cherubových v výši po křišťálové
obloze a sedě na safírovém
trůnu, stkvoucím široko a daleko.[35]

---

[34] John Milton, *Paradise Lost* VI:748–772 from *Poetical Works edited after the Original Texts*, ed. H.C. Beeching (London: Humphrey Milford / Oxford University Press), 1913.
[35] John Milton, *Ztracený ráj*, trans. Josef Jungmann, from Josef Jungmann, *Sebrané spisy veršem i prosou* Vol. III (Praha: I.L. Koreb), 1873.

[Then the third morning began to dawn, / brightening in the sky. / With the sound of winds and liquid flame / rolls the swift chariot of the heavenly Father, / without harness, set in motion by the impulse of its own spirit, / though next to it came four Cherubim, having four / wondrous faces, galloping, with stars / their entire bodies and wings flashing, multi-eyed; many-eyed with beryls / are the wheels, among them dart / flames. A crystal firmament / above their heads and a sapphire throne, full of amber, / full of rainbow colours is set upon the chariot, / where He, in His heavenly armour, / flashing with Urim, the work of divine hands, / mounting, placed Himself; with Him to the right / hand sits eagle-winged victory, / on His left hangs a bow and quiver / full of trident thunders, around Him roll / billows of darkness, and outpourings / of liquid flame and glowing flashes. A line of saints, ten thousand thousands / strong, came with Him, brilliant in the distance; / twenty thousand chariots of the Lord (I heard / their number) rolled with Him, divided in two / flanks. And thus He soars, flying on wings / of Cherubs aloft through the crystal / firmament and sitting on the sapphire / throne, flashing wide and afar].

Hollý's description of the image on Svatopluk's shield runs thus, followed by a literal translation:

> Nádherný vídať je tu vóz , nad míru podivný,
> Najremeselnejšou vykovávan ze zlata prácou:
> Bez všetkých žrebcov, bez všetkých oprát a štverní,
> Bez biča bez všeho aj štvoronožných správcu ťahúnov:
> Len kola plápolavé a horáce bahry, čo vlastnou
> Obracajú sa mocou, a letá svou od seba vládou,
> Najprudším ho točá na spósob víchora hurtom.
> Tam štvoro hvezdovaných vókol Cherubínov a toľko
> Uhľadať postav, prepodivné tvári majúcích:
> Každá šesť jasných rozkládá prez tela krídel;
> Každá nad to plná aj zókolvókol i znútra
> Stríhnúcích je očí, i bedlí vždy a nikdy nezasne.
> Na prostred voza trón najďáľ diamantami žárný:
> Kdež večný Boha Syn, lavicou svou berlu držácí,
> Pod duhovými sedí vysoký oblakmi; a pred ním
> Čerňý strach cválá a ukrutná tiskne sa hróza.
> Napravo okridlané mu letí víťazstvo; morácí
> Od lava lúk, a plný žeravých strel a hromby nebeskej
> Pozvesený má túl; vókol neho mračna kaďácé,

Prudké blýskání a perúcé žúrily ohne.
Vystrojených též s ním dvoranov šli tisíce tisícov,
A dvoma na skvúcích sa vozoch brali radma. Tu verné
Hneď po pravém i ľavém pripojá sa mu zástupy krídle.[36]

[A splendid chariot was to be seen here, beyond passing wondrous, / a work fashioned with greatest craft, all of gold: / without any stallions, without any harness or reins, / no whips to control four-legged beasts of propulsion / only fiery flaming wheels, which of their own / power spin, flying of their own will, / as swift as the rush of the mightiest wind./ Four starry cherubim surrounded the vehicle, / [and] just as many figures of awesome countenance: / Each one spreading about his body six bright wings / Covered with eyes unsleeping, keeping watch on all hands. / In the midst of the chariot was a throne set with diamonds: / Where the eternal Son of God, gripping His sceptre in His left hand sat, beneath towering, rainbow-coloured clouds. / Before Him black terror galloped and cruel horror pressed on. / Eagle-winged victory flew to His right; / from His left shoulder hung a death-dealing / bow and full of blazing arrows and the thunderbolts of Heaven / hung His quiver, round Him billows of incense rising / thick with lightning and roaring fires. / Thousands of thousands of courtiers all in armour went with Him; / Two legions on shining chariots. Here the loyal / hosts to His left and right flanks were attached.]

Once more it is not slavish repetition, but creative homage to the English epic poet, better than whom no one ever imagined the battle of the angels that preceded the history of mankind. What is important here is not how much Hollý borrowed from Milton (or Jungmann) and how he did so, but rather *why*. Whatever we may think about Svatopluk's treason towards Karolman (and, as we have said before, what is a promise worth, when extracted under duress?) the armour that Svatopluk now bears in battle proclaims his nature and allegiance: Svaotopluk is fighting on the side of God.

AND GOD IS ON HIS

As we have already noted in reference to Svatopluk, it is God, the one God, the God of Hollý and Milton, who determines that Svatopluk must be freed and restored to his throne in Canto I, and sends his archangel Michael down

---

[36] Jan Hollý, *Svatopluk*, from *Jána Hollého Spisy Básnické. So životopisom a zprávou o pomníku i spisoch jeho*. Sporiadal a vidal Josef Viktorin (Pešt: Sklad kníhkupectva Lauffera & Stolf, 1863).

to Slovakia in Canto XI to thrust — once more — the demonic forces of Černobog into the pit of Hell. This is a very interesting poetic passage. In Milton's great epic, the battle of the good angels against the rebels is, already at the telling to our first parents, 'ancient history'. It is a relation of something that happened long ago, predating even Adam and Eve. In Canto XI of *Svatopluk*, insofar as we suspend our disbelief and enter into the present action of the epic, we witness the victory of St Michael and the hosts angelic over God's enemies as it unfolds before our very own eyes, in real time. In this way, Hollý is emphasising the continuing interpenetration of eternity and time, God's continued presence and intervention in the world, here and now. It is just the same sort of strategy that the great Caravaggio employs on his canvases such as *The Calling of St Matthew*, or *The Supper at Emmaus*, in which he dresses up Levi, his fellow tax-collectors, and the two sorrowing disciples, in contemporary, seventeenth century garb, in order to stress to the onlooker that these are not merely mythological tales — they are images of God's activity in the world which did not cease in the first century ad but continues to this day. In a literary sense, to the north of Slovakia, this is the foundational idea of Polish Monumental Drama, first established by Adam Mickiewicz in *Forefathers' Eve* some ten years before *Svatopluk* was written, in which the spirits of the departed have just as much a right to interact on the stage as do those still encased in the flesh.

Just before the Lord sends Michael down to rout Černobog and his foul legions, St Cyril, one of the two great apostles to the Slavs, comes before the Lord to beg His mercy for the Slovaks as they struggle against the Germans (who were once, we remember, something of his enemies too). The scene with St Cyril is similar to that of Živa before Perún (and Venus before Jove), and the Lord delivers a very similar answer to his saint's petition:

> [...] They shall have their victory.
> This I grant heroic Svatopluk: taking the field,
> He shall fell the German war-chief himself in battle,
> And cast the foreign yoke from off his people's shoulders.
> The borders of his kingdom shall extend far and wide;
> The kindred Slavic nations shall support his sceptre,
> Though like all earthly things subject to vicissitude,
> They shall endure the varied shocks of change, and sad falls.

God was on Svatopluk's side at the start of his epic, and He remains with him to its victorious climax. For those of us still having a problem with the question of Svatopluk's breaking his troth to Karolman (to which we shall still return), there is nothing for us to do now except, just like Dante in those moments when God seems to be acting not according to human logic, shrug and remember that 'His thoughts are not our thoughts', His reason, though unfathomable, is always right.

Hollý often makes use of such thematic rhymes, or repetitions, to emphasise a point. In Canto IV (15ff) of his epic, for example, when Sláv addresses his men before the battle, he uses nearly the same words as Perún delivered to Živa earlier, cited above— that the catastrophe of the Chudes would be an example to all nations who wish to thrive by rapine, stealing the goods of others. He was not privy to that conversation, of course, so how is it that he expresses the same sentiments? Obviously, he is on the same page as the god; his spirit shares in that of Perún — (like Aeneas) he is entirely bent to the will of the god, he is 'inspired' of the god naturally, unconsciously even.

Toward the end of his epic (VI:511 ff), Hollý once more shows Sláv as something of a prophet — or at least a leader uncannily in tune with God. In his last speech to the dying Bondor, Sláv declares that the Chudan king had been warned many times by the flashing anger of the gods, and that he would indeed have been carried off in punishment of his crimes, had Sláv not killed him first. Sláv, therefore, is not only a 'prophet', but also an instrument of God's will, a scourge in the hands of justice.

The gods — in *Sláv* benign and propitious, not demonic — are so on the Slavic side, that in Canto IV:94ff Stribog is at home alone amongst the deities ruling the winds, for he had sent off all of his 'subalterns' to dry the Pripet marshes toward the day when the Slavs would expand and occupy them and bring them under cultivation. It's not far from this to a description of the Slavs as something of God's chosen people. Perún, the supreme God, is not drying the marshes so 'men' can cultivate them, he is readying them for the *Slavs*.

Stribog is enlisted to help the Slavs by Perún who, whether the ancient Slavs considered him supreme heavenly Father or not, was a wielder of the thunderbolt like the Germanic Thor — and thus Sláv's words referred to above concerning the 'warnings' sent to Bondor as the 'flashing' anger of God are eloquent. Stribog sends adverse winds upon the Chudan archers, which time and again turn their missiles around in mid-flight to hurl them back upon them — a metaphor of sin slaying the sinner.

As for the Chudan god, he is certainly as demonic as Černobog is ever depicted in *Svatopluk* or the *Cyrillo-Methodiad*. Actually, he is much worse, given that he is not satisfied merely with animal sacrifice and misplaced latreia usurped from God, but demands — and receives — human sacrifice in his foul grotto.[37] Yet he can do nothing for his men. At least twice in the epic, Chudes

---

[37] The foulness of Ár, and the benignity of the Slavic gods, is underscored in *Sláv*

call upon him and chide him for his failing to aid them. But even when he wishes to help his worshippers, his efforts turn out to the advantage of their enemies. For example, at one point in the vicious final struggle, the Chudes are trapped on a narrow tongue of land between two cliffs, surrounded by marsh and wetland. When Ár snaps the tendons of the Slovak bows on the heights above them, he is doing nothing but unwittingly furthering the slaughter, as the Slovaks re-string them immediately with fresh tendons, and the arrows they now shoot speed all the more swiftly. He, like Goethe's Mephistopheles, is 'part of that power, which would do evil, but ends up doing good'.

IF GOD IS FOR US, WHO IS HE AGAINST?

The short answer to that, in *Sláv*, is the Chudes, and in the *Cyrillo-Methodiad*, paganism. It is a more interesting question in *Svatopluk*, for the answer there must be — the Germans — which makes sense as far as the politics of the *národné obrodenie* are concerned, but is problematic insofar as the Germans/Bavarians are Christians just as much as the Slovaks are. Indeed, it was through the Bavarians that the Good News first came amongst the Slavs of the Tatra region.

Still, as Jesus says in the Gospel, 'Not every one that saith to me, Lord, Lord, shall enter into the kingdom of heaven [...] And then will I profess unto them, I never knew you: depart from me, you that work iniquity'.[38] It's not enough just to be a Christian.

In the *Cyrillo-Methodiad*, when Methodius begins his description of the apocalyptic painting he'd worked up to convert the king of the Volgars, he describes the lot of heretics and schismatics (II:278–285) — and those who are led astray by the doctrine of crooked preachers. It's not so much Hollý the Catholic priest castigating Protestants here (that sort of overt condemnation doesn't seem much in the character of the friend of Kollár, Štúr, and the other Slovak Protestants),[39] rather, it returns to the theme of why the Slovaks need

....

when Hollý describes the Chudan god's lonely, gore-splattered grove, where 'No gentle Veles there toots love-songs upon his pan-pipe; / No Vila's gentle foot taps the earth in wheeling dance-steps; / No Rusalka adorns her hair with such reeking weeds'. It is so noxious that 'Even werewolves, who terrorise men, avoid the place, / Shuddering to enter the terrifying thicket'.

[38] Matthew 7: 21, 23.

[39] Lenka Rišková reminds us that 'Hollý's orientation to persons from Protestant circles cannot be characterised as hostile, certainly not hostility based on confessional differences'. What annoyed him was anyone who belittled Bernolák's codification of the Slovak — especially such as preferred Czech as a literary language, or the melding of Slovak into a 'Czechoslovak' idiom. One of these was his friend, the Protestant pastor Ján Kollár, who once, in an anonymous preface to a collection of Slovak folk songs

Cyril and Methodius in the first place. Rastislav is above all motivated by his desire that the baptised Slovaks be taught the pure Faith, and not be led astray by the 'unlettered', lazy, and rapacious German clergy:

> And who is to blame for this our sad, purblind state?
> Who but the Germans? Who've sent such men to convert us
> As know our language not, or mangle it in speaking?
> [...] They'd rather make Germans of us!
> (I:47–49, 52)

In *Svatopluk*, Karolman is presented as just such an imperfect Christian. Indeed, he has a 'direct line' to God, in that an angel visits him and instructs him concerning what he is to do: free Svatopluk. This he does, out of holy fear, but... conditionally. The conditions he places upon Svatopluk for his liberation (marriage to his daughter, and a rather onerous fealty to his crown) were no part of the message brought him by the angel — which was monitory, more than anything: do unto Svatopluk as you would have others do unto you. Perhaps his fate might befall you one day. In exceeding the commandments of God, is Karolman not sinning thereby?

Take that betrothal of Svatopluk and Karolman's daughter for one example. In I:520 Karolman 'bestows' his daughter on Svatopluk and 'calls him mine'. That seems like an advancement, doesn't it? And yet, he gives the Slovak king the hand of the girl (or the hand of Svatopluk to his girl) without even asking him if he desires it! He 'calls him mine' indeed. The woman — who disappears from the epic as soon as she is mentioned[40] — is just one more way for Karolman to remain in possession of Svatopluk, or keep him in his control, even as he frees him, ostensibly, to the light of day. Again, this is not part of the

---

stated that Bernolák 'had few followers and even fewer who praised him amongst the more knowledgeable'. In a letter to Jura Palkovič (to whom he dedicated both *Svatopluk* and the *Cyrillo-Methodiad*), he wrote: 'Truly those Lutherans are having a bold go at us with their tongues!' [*Veru sa smele vozá hubú po nás ti luteráni*] — though he had no idea who the author of the words was. Rišková states: 'it is clear that in the cases where Holly speaks of Lutherans, he has in mind those who adhere to "biblictina" [Czech as a literary language, known as 'bible-speak' as deriving from the Czech translations of scripture used in Slovak Protestant circles], as far as Czech as the literary language of the Slovaks is concerned, and not the faithful of the Lutheran Church', p. 498.

[40] Perhaps because of his priestly vocation, Hollý is unable, or unwilling, to rise to the level of painting great erotic passion — as does Virgil in his creation of the Dido and Aeneas myth. Still, writing in the 1890s, the poet Tichomír Milkin is perhaps a bit too harsh in his appraisal of *Svatopluk* because of its 'wooden' approach to women. See Pišút, p. 208.

angelic command; Karolman is to free Svatopluk, not retain him. And thus the metaphor of the eagle in the gilded cage, spoken by Dízabo in the one passage from *Sláv* where a Chude is shown as valorous, is exemplified before the fact. By 'hooping him unto himself' with such bonds, and setting terms of tribute and fealty as conditions of his release from prison, Karolman is not only exceeding God's command, he is going against it. A dog held on a long lead is still a dog controlled by his master. This spitting of fiats left and right by Karolman — which also might be taken as impiety, as he is acting like God Himself — sets Svatopluk's 'breaking of his troth' to him in a new light. Karolman is brought low by the man he trusted, as he well deserves. How far did he trust him anyway, since he trussed him up in all those 'if's and 'as long as'es?

This, however, is the way of the Germans, Hollý suggests. If Karolman does obey God's command to a certain extent, as his hands are tied in the matter, it is nonetheless instructive to consider how he reveals his intentions to the German princes called together in moot in comparison with another parliamentary scene: the Diet of the Slovaks when news of the German invasion reaches their ears (V:99–104). When the Bavarians' intention to invade his land becomes patent, Slavimír calls his nation to moot and asks their opinion: shall we fight, or not? He may be expecting the answer he wants, but at least we have the sense of him reaching for counsel. Karolman, on the other hand — though bound by God's command that cannot be overlooked — announces to his diet what he plans on doing, and just seeks their rubber stamp. Although Slavimír is under the influence of a dream, and although he has already tested it by sending Ľudomír spying, and frames the question in a manner that reads: 'fight or be slaves', we get the sense that this is a real deliberation. Karolman's diet, on the other hand, is merely an audience for his announcement. We witness deliberation in both parliaments, but there is a stronger sense of real consultation in that taking place in Devín — which is very much in line with the Slavs' mythical democratic anarchy in times of peace, as presented us by Hollý in his idyllic descriptions of the Slavic past.

Karolman falls into impotence with the decimation of his army at the hands of Svatopluk and the Slavs. The sway that he might have had over Svatopluk's nation had he done what God required of him and simply released the Slovak king — loyalty based on gratitude, the loyalty of free allies — is taken away from him when he seeks to enforce loyalty upon him through imposed conditions that have nothing to do with God's will, and are even, conceivably, against it. As a Christian king, Karolman should know that his will is not the ultimate instance, his law not supreme. The Christian monarch is a custodian of eternal law, not its legislator. 'He who does the will of God proves worthy of His grace!' so says the angel to Karolman in that dream (I:194). Karolman listens, but exceeds the command, selfishly, releasing Svatopluk only on condition that he should rule Slovakia as a German fief. That's not what the angel told him: he was simply to 'do what he had long wished / to do' — release the Slovak king. Svatopluk's 'treachery' is thus no treachery at all. Promises extracted under duress are not to be honoured.

At the diet in Devín, when the looming invasion is laid before the Slovak leaders and their advice solicited, Zemižížen [41] gives vent to his disappointment in Svatopluk with the words: 'Were you not once the greatest advocate of freedom?' (V:135) Zemižížen's shock is well founded, as is his reading of Svatopluk's character. Indeed he was, and is, the greatest advocate of Slovak freedom, as he shall shortly prove again…

There also remains the matter of Svatopluk's treachery towards his uncle Rastislav, in which the Germans are involved as well. In the shifting sands of the history presented by Hollý in his three epics, it's hard to find many characters who always remain steadily good, or steadily bad. The exceptions to that rule, of course, are the mythical characters Sláv and Bondor. As for the historical characters mentioned in the three works, our assessment of them changes, quite realistically, accordingly as their acts and behaviour change. In the *Cyrillo-Methodiad*, Rastislav is heroic, on account of his role in the evangelising mission of Konštantín and Methodius. In *Svatopluk*, his character has a tyrannical tinge to it, as he sought to capture and kill his nephew by deceit.

Whether or not he had a reason to — it is suggested that Rastislav wanted to kill his nephew in the first place because of an alliance Svatopluk had made with the Germans — it would take us far afield to determine who is right and who is wrong in this family quarrel. The point that bears consideration is that introduced by Britwald at Karolman's moot. He tells us that when Rastislav fell into Svatopluk's power, the latter handed him over to the Germans, not for murderous purposes, but *for arbitration* in the matter of Rastislav's intended treachery towards him: 'At last, after cruel slaughter, / Svatopluk took Rastislav, and set him at our bench (I:464–465)'. That proved to be a mistake — not only did this lead to Rastislav's imprisonment and maiming, but to his own capture, as the Germans saw an opportunity of snatching two birds where one was on offer, and took it. Once more, Hollý emphasises what he sees as the leading characteristic of the German nation: rapaciousness, imperiousness, a willingness to exceed the bounds of right and wrong in order to satisfy their own desires, to work things to their own advantage. And it is out of their own mouths that they stand condemned, as Britwald continues in his speech (I:436–439):

---

[41] Zemižížen (whose name, ironically, means 'Land-thirst') plays a key role in both *Svatopluk* and the *Cyrillo-Methodiad*. He is a historical character. See Rosenbaum, p. 186.

> We all know quite well that when Svatopluk entrusted
> Himself, and all he had — his very realm — to our care
> We paid him back by bringing sword and fire, destruction
> Through all the marches of his monarchy.

Following the line, just or not, established by Romantic historiography in the Slavic nineteenth century, Hollý depicts the Germans as the ancient enemies of the Slavs. This is hinted at in his references to the founders of Devín, the mythical Dobroslava and her Slavic Amazons. In Canto IV Dobroslava is described thus:

> As long as the sweet light of life bathed her countenance,
> Dobroslava, with her regiments of Amazons,
> Defended her city and realm from all armed assault —
> Without any man to rule her as husband or king,
> Though there was no lack of princes, native and foreign,
> Who begged the maiden's mother for her hand in marriage.
> (IV: 13–18)

The virgin queen who leads her people against invading foes, fiercely determined to give her hand to no one, native or foreign, is a legend that savours strongly of a foundational myth of the Wiślanie — Slavs just a tad to the north of Slovakia around Kraków — whose maiden queen Wanda chose suicide in the River Wisła over marriage to a German prince. And that these invaders mentioned above were Germans is made clear by the images kept at Devín, examined by Černobog as he waits for Slavimír to fall asleep so that he might invade his dreaming mind:

> [...] most of all he marvelled at the maiden
> Of many gifts, ever-unvanquished Dobroslava,
> Who led her troops in fierce battle against the Germans,
> Panting with blazing fury, in the swelter of war,
> Tall in the saddle, shoulder to shoulder with lovely
> And many-wiled Ludomíra protecting her back,
> Along with thousands of their comrades in arms — women,
> Skilled at war, battling down the Bavarian troops.
> (IV:76–83)

This is a main thesis of Hollý's epics, especially *Svatopluk* and the *Cyrillo-Methodiad*. Characteristically, he uses repetition to reinforce it in the reader's mind.

When Černobog insinuates himself into Slavimír's mind in dream,[42] the reader 'sees' Slavimír's nightmare of German destruction along with him. Then, shortly thereafter, he hears Slavimír repeat it — twice: To Ľudomír upon waking, and again to the assembled moot. It is as if the poet wished to keep German treachery and threat, didactically, always before the eyes of the modern-day Slovaks.

That saying, we must still point out that, in his mythology, Hollý still respects historical truths. The Germans may be rapacious and ever seeking to expand at the Slavs' expense, they may be double-dealing, but the fact that the Bavarians were the first to introduce Christianity to the Slavic lands, even before Konštantín and Methodius, is respected and noted. It is no Nordic deity, but the Christian God who sends his angel to Karolman in dream; in the banquet hall of the Bavarians (Canto VI), besides the obligatory portraits of his forefathers, paintings of Christ's miraculous multiplication of the loaves and fishes are also found. In the *Cyrillo-Methodiad*, even if the Bavarian hierarchy will be shown to be inimical to the Slavic rite, their Christianity is not brought into question. In this, Hollý proceeds like the poet of the *Cantar del mio Cid*, who deals with the Muslims justly, as people, not demonising them does as the poet of the *Chanson de Roland*, and who points out that the main enemies of the Cid are Christians, not Muslims. They, like the Germans here, are not his enemies because they are Christians, but despite that fact. 'Ye shall know them by their fruits, and according to their works they shall be judged'. It is also similar to Dante's approach to the popes in Hell. He does not put the popes in Hell because they are popes, but because they have sinned despite the high spiritual office to which they were called.

THE SLAVS: PAGAN OR CHRISTIAN, EVER TRUE

In speaking of mythology, we must address the manner in which Hollý treats the question of Slavic paganism. For the reader who presses backwards through

---

[42] Significantly, despite Černobog's evil nature, this is not a *lying* dream, but the truth. Wishing to stir up war between the Slovaks and Germans for his own nefarious purposes, he gladly makes use of truth in order to further his advantage. It is the same situation as that of the Nazis upon discovering the mass graves at Katyń. Their decision to reveal the Soviet crimes had nothing to do with devotion to truth or any fellow-feeling for the murdered Poles, or the Polish nation. They wanted to drive a wedge between the Allies, and the magnificent thing — from their point of view — was that their propaganda did not have to lie or spin anything here to work their advantage: they just told the truth — the Soviets murdered fifteen thousand Polish officers in cold blood and buried them in mass graves. It does not excuse *Nazi* crimes against the Polish nation, and the only reason they revealed this to the world is because it was to their advantage (had the Soviets remained the allies of the Nazis, as they were at the start of the conflict, the Nazis would conceivably have helped them cover it all up). But it was nevertheless the truth.

the *Cyrillo-Methodiad* into *Sláv* is sure to be puzzled at the manner in which the villainous deities of the missionary period are depicted as the benign guardians of the nation before the Slavs' introduction to Christianity. The whole history of Slavic paganism is puzzling as it is. Whether it be that the Slavs readily accepted Christianity or that it was forcibly imposed upon them, very little save a few legends and names enshrined in folklore, as well as inscriptions and cultic statuettes catalogued by Josef Růžička in his popularising, but for all that encyclopaedic, *Slovanská mythologie pro lid Českoslovanský*. [Slavic Mythology. For the Czechoslovak People],[43] remain as material evidence of pre-Christian Slavic belief. Certainly the pagan Slavs developed no advanced religious civilisation such as that of the ancient Greeks, and despite the pious sighing of Pan-Slavic pilgrims such as Ľudovít Štúr, who — somewhat ironically for a Lutheran pastor — shed tears while visiting the 'obelisks and pyramids of far-distant Slavic antiquity'[44] on Mount Prašica, no temples of the sort we see in Athens, Siracusa, or even Stonehenge remain in the Slavic lands. That said, the most magnificent find, the four-faced stone statue of Svatovít discovered in the eastern Polish Zbrucz River in 1848 confirms both the existence of a cult of the all-seeing god and the toppling of idols carried out by missionaries, such as we witness in the *Cyrillo-Methodiad*. The sixth century Byzantine historian Procopius, writing about the Slavs in his history of the Gothic War, speaks of 'one god, demiurge of the lightning bolt [whom] they regard as the one lord of all',[45] which sounds quite like Hollý's Perún, who in *Sláv* takes on the attributes of the Triune God from *Svatopluk* — a supreme deity, to whom the lesser gods such as Stribog and Svatovít and Oslad are as the angels of the Christian tradition. Curiously enough, the continued existence of the name Perún in the

....

[43] Josef Růžička. *Slovanská mythologie. Pro lid Českoslovanský* (Praha: Alois Wiesner, 1924).

[44] Ľudovit Štúr, *Slavdom. A Selection of his Writings in Prose and Verse*, translated and introduced by Charles S. Kraszewski (London: Glagoslav, 2021), p. 201. Ján Kollár, also an evangelical pastor, compares his trip around the 'ancient Slavic' lands of east Germany to a trip to the Holy Land (*Slávy dcera*, II:18). The one distinction he draws is: the infidels who have control of the Holy Sites in Palestine have preserved them, whereas the German Christians have 'shattered and trod beneath their feet' the Slavic 'temples, groves, mounds, and altars'.

[45] Quoted by Henryk Łowmiański, *Religia Słowian i jej upadek* (Warszawa: PWN, 1979), p. 82: θεὸν μὲν γὰρ ἕνα, τὸν τῆς στραπῆς δημιουργὸν ἁπάντων κύριον μόνον αὐτόν νομίζουσιν εἶναι. He goes on to comment that many researchers (in whose company Hollý would feel at home) saw this as evidence of proto-monotheism amongst the Slavs, while the staunch positivist Brückner feels rather that Procopius was merely Slavicising Zeus. p. 83.

Polish word for thunderbolt — *piorun* — offers some parenthetical proof of the existence of this Slavic Thor.

Now, how much of ancient Slavic belief is Hollý's invention is an open question. That he was informed about a great deal of it can be determined on the basis of Svatovít and his prophetic horse. None other than the great scholar of Slavic mythology Aleksander Brückner reports myths handed down by priests from the German areas (especially the Island of Rügen) once inhabited by Slavs, speaking of 'Świętowit, who frolicked about at night on his own horse'.[46] So, our poet must have had some access to sources upon which to draw. More important to us is not how much authentic information the poet possesses and passes down to us concerning the Slavic pantheon, but how he makes use of it, and why.[47]

First of all, Hollý creates his mythology, or more precisely, presents it to the reader, as a counterweight to inimical historians (especially German ones) who would assert their cultural superiority over their Eastern neighbours by comparing the richness of Germanic religious folklore, from the Icelandic sagas to the Nibelungs, to the paucity of pagan prehistory among the Slavs. Perhaps this is why Hollý so emphasises nineteenth century theories of the Slavic descent from India in order to go them all — Germans, Latins, and Greeks — one better, by inserting his people into arguably the most ancient, developed, and still vibrant, religious tradition in the Eurasian sphere: Hinduism. He is not the only one to do this: in the ancient Slavic pantheon Mickiewicz finds 'traces of Hindu gods', giving as an example of this 'Trigław', whom he takes as the 'equivalent of the Hindu trinity Trimurti'.[48] Hollý's countryman Ján Kollár composed

---

[46] Aleksander Brückner, *Mitologia Słowiańska i Polska* (Warszawa: PWN, 1985), p. 49.

[47] The matter of sources arises already during the composition of *Svatopluk*. Peter Podolan informs us of a letter that Hollý wrote to Jura Palkovič (his friend and mentor, to whom he dedicated the epic), in which he confesses: 'Potrebné bi mňe nade všecko, čoho sa já pre nedostatek kňih úplňe dočítať ňemóžem, bolo nasledujíce: 1. Čí bol sin Svatopluk? Jedni píšú, že otca mal Mojmíra, druhí, že Radislava a tretí, že Boleslava. 2. Kďe bíval Karolman? v kterém mesťe roku 871' [Above all the following information is necessary to me, which for lack of books here I am unable to ascertain: 1. Who was Svatopluk's father? Some write that it was Mojmír, others Radislav, and still others Boleslav. 2. Where was Karolman? In what city was he found in the year 871?]. Peter Podolan, 'Veľká Morava a veľkomoravská tradícia u generácie Kollára a Šafárika', *Český časopis historický* 117/2019, nr. 1:59–91, p. 64.

[48] Adam Mickiewicz, 'Lecture VII (19 January 1841), *Literatura Słowiańska* in *Dzieła*, Vol. VIII (Warsaw: Czytelnik, 1997), p. 79. It is also true (see his lectures from 3 and 14 March 1843), that the Polish bard derived not just Slavic culture, but all of European culture, Latin and Greek included, from Indian Mythology. In the earlier lecture, where he asserts that 'of all languages, Sanskrit is the richest', he makes the bold statement that

an entire work treating the Slavic and Hindu cultures comparatively.[49] Josef Dobrovský himself, the founder of Slavic philology (1753–1829) ascribed to the theory of the Slavs arising in India, basing his theories:

> on the similarity between European, especially Slavic, languages, and Indian languages. [...] Dobrovský drew on the work of the Czech Jesuit Karel Přikryl (1718–1785), who had been sent to India in 1748. Přikryl wrote a grammar of the Konkani language entitled *Principia lingua brahmanicae*. Dobrovský came across the book around 1791 and noticed the structural similarities between Slavic languages and Konkani, and developed an interest in India and Sanskrit [...] Later also the Polish scholar Walenty Skorochód Majewski (1764–1835) discovered similarities between Indian and Slavic languages in his book *O Słowianach i ich pobratymcach* [The Slavs and their Brethren] (1816). Consequently many Slavic scholars began to see India as the Slavic homeland.[50]

In *Svatopluk*, it is Brahma, 'the highest of all gods' who indicates to the Slavs that a portion of them must leave the Indian sub-continent. If this sounds like an attempt on Hollý's part not only to set the Slavs in antiquity, but also to make of them something of a chosen people, it gets even better once they leave India.

For Hollý even resorts to the Hebrew Bible in order to emphasise the antiquity of the Slavs. On their journey to Europe from India, as described by Svatopluk, we read of the Slavs passing by Nineveh, Babylon, and 'where Noah of legend / Sensed his ark scrape to ground after the destructive flood' (VI:243–244). Granted, it is the early-mediaeval Christian Svatopluk who is employing this nomenclature. It's kind of like a modern archaeologist saying 'Traces of the earliest Hopi culture have been recently been found in a shallow depression near the off-ramp of I-10 in central Phoenix'. Neither Phoenix nor

---

'the Indians took nothing from European antiquity, but rather gave the Greeks and the Egyptians their priests and wisemen. History tells us that renowned Greek philosophers visited the regions along the Ganges'.

[49] Jan Kollár, *Sláva Bohyně a původ jména Slavů čili Slavjanů v listech k velectěnému příteli Panu P.J. Šafaříkovi, s přídavky srovnalost indického a slavského života, řeči a bajesloví ukazujícími* [The Goddess Slava and the Etymology of the Names of the Slavs or Slavjans in Letters to His Most Worthy Friend Mr P.J. Šafařík, with Additional Comparison of Indian and Slavic Life, Language, and Folklore, Pest: Trattner-Károlyi, 1839]. The goddess 'Sláva' that Kollár invokes in his great sonnet cycle *Slávy dcera* [The Daughter of Sláva] is identified in this work with the ancient Indian goddess Sváhā. See Róbert Gáfrik, 'The Image of India in 19th-Century Slovak Literature', *Porównania* 2 (21), 2017: 163–170, p. 166.

[50] Gáfrik, p. 165.

the I-10 were around when the ancient Hopi left their crockery in that ditch, but the modern reference allows contemporary people to visualise the space with immediacy. Still, in making use of Old Testament coordinates and figures, Hollý emphasises the antiquity of the Slavic nation — they passed by there — and, what is more important, sets them in the current of Old Testament history, the general current of Christendom's history, even before their conversion.

Another such biblical reference is provided in Canto III of *Sláv* (377ff). When the Slovaks set out for battle, the god Svatovít marches at their head in a 'pillar of cloud'. Readers of scripture will immediately recall Jahwe leading the Jews (Exodus 13). None of the soldiers see him, we are told, but they see the cloudy mass, and hear the clatter of armour coming from within.

We have already spoken of Hollý's treatment of Slavic 'monotheistic' polytheism. In his exhaustive study of Slavic paganism, which sets their beliefs in the context of religious sentiment in general, Łowmiański seems to confirm Hollý's understanding of his forebears' religiosity. The Slavs, he suggests, had a 'cult of the heavens' rather than a pantheon. They were 'fixed in the sphere of polydoxy — a form of *prototheism* being a phenomenon characteristic of Indo-European religions like that of the Slavs, which had not developed polytheism'.[51] Parom (Perún) is the supreme god of all, but has nothing to do, directly, with the lesser regions below the atmosphere he rules with thunder and lightning. The lesser gods govern the elements below in his stead — or so 'human reason', as yet unenlightened by the Christian revelation, held. The Slavs were monotheistic, in that they believed in a supreme God; they were polytheists of a quasi-Stoic[52] sort, unable to conceive of a God omnipotent, able to rule everything, everywhere, without the agency of lesser deities as assistants.

To return to the shifting character of the Slavic gods in Hollý's descriptions, the same gods who are benign spirits in *Sláv*, who constitute stages in the religious development of a people always under the care of the One True God, in the *Cyrillo-Methodiad* and *Svatopluk* are shown as demons. The best single example of this is the 'water-man' — a lesser Slavic sprite, the male equivalent

---

[51] Łowmiański, p. 37. His subsequent footnote refers the reader to Schrader-Nehring's *Religion*. Polydoxy, as Łowmiański defines it, is a 'belief system of pre-Classical or pre-literate peoples developed from four basic characteristics: magic, belief in the souls of the departed, a cult of nature, as well as a secondary form — demonology'. p. 9.

[52] 'Quasi' Stoic, because the Stoics, it seems, believed in one god, invoked under different names in accord with the divine context of the human phenomena referred to. Thus, this god is addressed as 'Minerva' when divine wisdom is being referred to, 'Mars' when his anger or military attributes are invoked, 'Venus' to describe divine love, and so forth. In the pantheon developed by Hollý from whatever scanty evidence of Slavic paganism remained, there is one supreme god, and a host of minor gods, subject to him, to whom their particular milieux and responsibilities are entrusted.

of the Rusalka. He aids the good Slavs to demolish the bad Chudes in *Sláv* by drowning those pressed near the shores of his domain, trapping in a reed net those who seek to swim across the flooded lakebed. In the *Cyrillo-Methodiad* he is a ghoulish character who drowns the inhabitants of the regions where his watery lair is located. In his epic of the conversion of the Great Moravian Empire, Hollý presents us with a lesson about pagan worship. Now, in the new, Christian dispensation, latreia paid to the pagan gods is demon worship, and those who call them close do so at their own great peril. For they no longer serve the people who worship them, but prey upon them.

There is a time and place for everything, and the intent is all. What is a virtue in Konštantín and Methodius, i.e. the hacking apart of the pagan idols with hatchets — which in their epic takes the place of the battles in *Svatopluk* and *Sláv* — is a heinous crime in the Chude raider Borkol, who takes the hatchet to two idols of Perún. However, Konštantín and Methodius are replacing the diabolical, or at least defective, pagan religion with the true dispensation of Christ, whereas Borkol is destroying objects of piety for personal gain — thirsting for the golden chaplets the idols wear. Konštantín and Methodius are other-centred, serving God; Borkol is thinking only of his own advantage, serving himself. And, of course, as Catholicism in its Old Church Slavonic form was to be a characteristic trait of the converted Slovaks, so was worship of the Slavic god Perún a national signifier in these pre-Christian days. So Borkol is also attacking the Slovak nation here, sinning 'nationally' — a grievous offence during the national rebirth of the nineteenth century. In the *Cyrillo-Methodiad* the binary opposition is: Christianity = good, paganism = bad, in *Sláv* we have Perún = good, Ár = bad.

Another curious example of 'that was then, but this is now' occurs in *Cyrillo-Methodiad* IV, where the widow Ľuboslava decides, in her despair, to commit sati on her husband's funeral pyre. Whether such things happened in ancient Slavdom or not, or whether it is just one more Indian interpolation of Hollý's, is beside the point. What is important is that Methodius steps between her and the flames, explaining the futility of the act, 'at which her faithful friends blocked the path at once, / Forbidding her to cast herself onto her husband's pyre'. Even though the majority of the pagans gathered at the funeral 'received the pious words / Of Methodius unwillingly, shaking their heads', he is invited by the dead Milko's father, the village chief, to preach at a more convenient time — at which he, Ľuboslava, and others convert. Just as in the case of the Slavs departing India in *Svatopluk*, amongst whom went a large number of souls who had no more use for the caste system, the keynote here is evolution, development. What was acceptable, even pious, in the misty age of the old gods' rule is no longer so now, in the new age — here, of the Christian dispensation; there, with the establishment of a new homeland.

Hollý does not entirely refrain from mockery, as he addresses the absurdities of paganism. For example, the destruction of the temple of Svatovít on Mount Sitno contains the description of the priest Vitoslav being forbidden to breathe inside the sacred precinct 'so as not to infect the deity with mortality'. Passing by the question: if a deity can be 'infected' with mortality, can he be a god at all? a comic scene ensues:

> [...] So, constantly he'd hasten out,
> Again and again to the threshold, blue in the face,
> To exhale and draw a fresh breath before going back!
> (III:268–270)

Sorcerers and pagan bards are frequently the butts of Hollý's bitter irony; both Chudan soothsayers and Bavarian skalds are often depicted as being incapable of predicting their own fate, as in the case of Sigmar (*Svatopluk*, X:289–290): 'Wise old Sigmar the oracle, who outriddled / The future to his folk — but foresaw not his own doom' — a fact that calls their whole métier into question.

In short then, as Hollý tells the story across his three epics of Slovak antiquity, the pagan Slavs, both in India and in the Tatras, are shown to be pious folk. Even if 'seeing through a glass darkly', and worshipping polytheistic images in their nation's infancy, still in their ignorance they worshipped the One True God (called Brahma in *Svatopluk*, and identified with Perún in *Sláv*), and it is He and no one else Who sent them on their way after saving them from flood and drought in India. Cyril and Methodius' mission then, is not so much one of conversion, as it is of enlightenment — a re-calibration of religious focus, a clarification. In a sense, we might risk saying that the Slavs are a more obedient chosen people, who accept the new dispensation revealed to them, growing out of their previous traditions, as it were, not inimical to them.

Thus it is remarkable, yet logical, for an agricultural people who 'do not need a war-chief', who are untutored in war, to be so unafraid at the onslaught of a people like the Chudes, whose only delight is pillage and murder. Sláv, and his people as well, are calm throughout the entire ordeal — certainly because of their piety, and their assurance of God's favour.

As far as the mission of the two brothers is concerned, if the victorious march of Cyril and Methodius does not seem dramatic to our eyes, it is because those eyes of ours have been trained by Hollywood to fear the power of evil as a real threat. Hollywood does not believe 'if God be for us, who is against us?' Money is made by devils that can't be exorcised, ghosts that can't be lain, zombies that can't be killed, evil murderers who come back to haunt and slash for sequel upon prequel upon sequel — in short, evil that is not an absence of good, but a powerful entity. The Christian truth that all these false gods and 'dark powers' are powerless before the might of the one, good God, and that wooden idols are defenceless against a simple axe blow doesn't make for a good plot (or a good take at the box office). What phrase is more memorable from *Jaws* than 'don't go into the water'? The wizards of poster and trailer want us to 'fear the water' only because they want to make *Jaws II*, and for that, they need an audience of primitive animists, tremulously picking their nervous way through a world filled with danger on every hand, danger that must be respected, propitiated. Here, to continue the metaphor, Methodius marches right into the surf — and the shark — naturally! because he's a shark, not an overwhelming evil force! — swims right past in search of the natural breakfast God provides all His creatures. Shark attacks are rare; sharks do not lurk in the shallows waiting for the opportunity to pounce on people for the mere joy of working evil. And no wooden idol of god or demon can harm a human, unless it totters the wrong way and falls on him. But those sort of stories don't film well.

Methodius' description of the manner in which he converted Boriš is similar to Dante's Johannine infixes in the *Divine Comedy*. In setting forth the deadly seriousness of opting for Christianity over paganism, Hollý not only gives the reader a template for the actions of the brothers that are about to commence in Slovakia, he also justifies the matter of the story as worthy of epic treatment. 'You agree that the struggle for Heaven is important, Reader, do you not? That we should strive to win Heaven and avoid Hell? What, then, can be a greater war than this, and what can be more heroic than the struggle of the saints against the demons, on behalf of men's souls?' (Hence the reaction of those Slovaks who listen to his account: Methodius wishes to 'satisfy the pious, / and jolt the hearts of the sluggish to penitence'. II:5–6).

MY NATION (SMALL OR GREAT) NO MATTER WHAT

National epics have a mythological significance, important to the intellectual cohesion of the nation, the spirit of which they seek to express. In the great *Cantar del mio Cid* (c. 1140) the historical protagonist Ruy Díaz is shown to be an unstoppable warrior routing the Moors like a force of destiny, yet one who becomes so even-handed and gentle a lord to his conquered peoples, that the Muslim inhabitants of Jalén, for example, who had earlier resisted his troops, 'weep' at the departure of their new governor, as he sets out upon new conquests.

Similarly, in Luis Vaz de Camões' (1572) *Os Lusíadas*, the conquest of India by the Portuguese is sanctioned by the Rivers Ganges and Indus themselves, who visit King Manuel in dream, urging him to impose the 'new dispensation' of Christian faith and European culture on their heretofore unvanquished people as civilisational advancement.

It's easy to smirk at these passages as facile justifications of might, the self-congratulatory re-writing of history by victors. But, despite Camões' frequent suggestions that history is superior to poetry, that one cannot have heroic poetry without actual heroic deeds to inspire the poet, such carping, popular in our rudderless postmodern age, misses the point of these writings entirely. They are *not* history; the historical Ruy Díaz, upon whom the poetic Cid is based, may not have been really as noble and flawless as his anonymous poet describes him to be. However, he played a significant role in early modern Spanish history, and that story becomes part of the national myth wherewith generations of Spaniards understood the significance and nobility of their nation. Ruy Díaz is unstoppable, because the *reconquista* was inevitable, sanctioned by God, irreversible; if not for the *reconquista*, Spain would be much different today; the *siglo d'oro* might never have come about, and the breathtaking century, during which Spain (and Portugal) divided the globe between themselves might never have occurred. Both the Old World and the New would have developed along entirely different paths.

Of course, post-modern Atlantic thinkers, who like nothing more than to foul their own nest by harping on the 'black legend' of colonialism, would perhaps be thrilled by that prospect. But what they call paternalism in the description of the grateful Muslims of Jálen is a mythopoetic expression of the Spaniards' desire to see themselves as a fair-minded people, whose relations with their Arabic neighbours is no straightforward story of black-and-white hostility. This same self-expression of Spanish fair-mindedness can be seen in the structure of the story told in the *Cantar* itself, where the chief villains — the Ordoñez clan, the Infantes of Carrión, Berenger, the Duke of Barcelona — are all Christians, and one of the key heroes, Albengabon, is a Muslim, who is virtuous because he is virtuous, not because he 'sees the light' and becomes a Christian himself — something he never does.

Likewise, in Camões' epic, the (so-unpopular these days) Eurocentricism of the author, which sounds absurd in the mouths of the sacred rivers of India, is the expression of something that seemed obvious at the time. European culture, of which the Portuguese saw themselves as the torchbearer, and Christianity, which they were determined to spread, were understood by them as incontrovertibly of a higher order than the oriental mores of the Indian subcontinent, and the polytheism of the Hindu world, which Europe had grown out of some fourteen hundred years previously. The question posed by Jared Diamond in his fascinating study *Guns, Germs, and Steel*, i.e. 'why weren't Native Americans, Africans, and Aboriginal Australians the ones who decimated, subjugated, or exterminated Europeans and Asians?',[53] would never have occurred to Camões, and if it were posed to him, he would certainly squint his one eye at the questioner, wondering if he were off his rocker.

Just as the Romans, to whom we owe our civilisation, weren't always angelic, but the mission given Aeneas by Anchises in the underworld is a succinct summation of important civilisational ideals:

> Roman, remember by your strength to rule Earth's peoples
> —for your arts are to be these: To pacify, to impose the rule of law,
> To spare the conquered, battle down the proud[54]

so are the words of the Indus and Ganges, as a confession by eternal beings who see more clearly than the frail human creatures who inhabit their banks, a pithy expression of the civilisational altruism of the Portuguese, spreading their sway across the world not merely out of self-interest. It is a moot statement that the Iberian colonisers did not always act in ways of which we would, or should, approve. Good old Bartolomé de Las Casas provides a proper example of Spanish self-reflection on the potential evils of the *encomieda* system at the very time it was in force. But ideals are important; without them, the few (or many?) who would wish to live by a more elevated code, would have little wherewith to direct their virtue.

The word 'myth' often has an undeservedly pejorative meaning in modern languages, used as it is interchangeably with 'fanciful story' or outright 'lie'. This, beyond their distaste of Spain, is perhaps what has recently motivated the separatist government of Catalonia to vote to remove 'imperialist' artworks from the Palau de la Generalitat in Barcelona. As reported in the *Times* of London, some murals depicting key events from Spanish history, including Columbus' reception by the Catholic Monarchs in Barcelona following his first voyage to America, and the Battle of Lepanto, are to be effaced because:

> They exalt militaristic values, a class order opposed to parliamentarianism — the perennial and sacred monarchy and the state based on Catholicism as a social order — and the fight against Islam, as well as belligerent and imperial patriotism.[55]

---

[53] Jared Diamond, *Guns, Germs and Steel. The Fates of Human Societies* (New York: W.W. Norton, 1999), p. 15.

[54] Virgil, *Aeneid*, VI:1152–1154 (Robert Fitzgerald's translation).

[55] Isambard Wilkinson, 'Catalonia waves goodbye to "imperialist" Spanish art', *Times* 2 May 2023, p. 29.

What some might see as a noble attempt at 'righting historical wrongs' or 'debunking imperialist myths' is nothing more than a stab at the creation of a new μῦθος — a new cultural self-expression. It is the replacement of one myth with another. Which is not to say that the new myth is any more true than the old myth. For example, Spain *is* identified with its Catholic heritage, no less, and perhaps even more, than is Slovakia, and modern Spanish history *is* concomitant with the 'fight against Islam', however unpopular Catholicism and 'religious intolerance' may be in twenty-first century Barcelona. We all construct myths, some more engaging and infectious than others, and Ján Hollý is no exception. Without him, and Anton Bernolák, and Ľudovít Štúr, and so many other lights of the Slovak *národné obrodenie*, the self-awareness of the Slovaks would be much different today — if indeed they were still to exist as Slovaks, not having vanished into the more dynamic masses of Magyars, Czechs, or Austrians. Even if some of us do not appreciate the myths of our fathers, we should respect and preserve them as they are — so as to understand how those who created them saw themselves, where they came from, and where they were headed: to us.

THIS TRANSLATION

seeks to approximate the feel of the original Slovak poetry for the English reader. As with Hollý's originals, it is unrhymed — where rhymes do occur at the end of lines in the English translation, this is purely coincidental. My original, ingrained instinct was to render the stories in blank verse. However, it soon became apparent that the English classical line cannot bear the weight of all the information that Hollý packs into his much longer verse-line, which stretches to an average length of fifteen or sixteen syllables. In order to distinguish the poet's introductions to each canto from the cantos themselves I have employed blank verse in *Sláv* and the *Cyrillo-Methodiad.* In *Svatopluk*, the introductions are in prose, as they are in the original.

Like Czech (and Latin for that matter), Slovak metre is based on tone: a variation of long and short syllables. In his discussion of the epics, Karol Rosenbaum gives a good explanation of what constitutes long and short syllables in Slovak poetry,[56] which is probably only of interest to those who can read the Slovak text. Although it is not for me to say whether the English translation 'rolls on like a great river' as Rosenbaum speaks of the prosody of the original,[57] it is my hope that the English line, lengthened to thirteen syllables and eschewing sudden breaks at the end of the line, will approximate the incanta-

---

[56] Rosenbaum, p. 181.
[57] Rosenbaum, p. 180.

tory rhythm of the Slovak original when read aloud by a performer sensitive to the spoken word.

Traditionally, Slovak commentators on Hollý's epics seem to sense an obligation to explain — if not indeed apologise for — the poet's manners of linguistic expression. Just like the above-cited Hanák and Selver in the thirties, so Jechová today states that 'as in the nineteenth century, so today, especially for the contemporary receptor, this epic is relatively difficult to read'.[58] To her credit, she places the blame for this on the poet's intentionally archaicised language. The fairest dealer in this matter is Ján Horecký, who, in an interesting note that calls for a closer philological treatment of Hollý's language, admits that in his poetry

> we find words of older coinage, created by word-forming procedures that are unused today, or seen as unproductive. At the same time, however, one cannot deny the poet's clear motivation, and, consequently, the significant semantic impact of such words.[59]

(Horecký also gives vent to his exasperation with those who constantly shake their heads at Hollý's *bernolákovčina*: 'and after all, we're speaking here of the poet who stands at the very beginnings of Štúr's codification of Slovak').[60]

Context, indeed, is everything, and Jechová herself explains that the anachronisms are due to Hollý's 'writing according to an ancient pattern, to which the author draws us near thereby, creating a work that affects the reader with more authenticity'.[61] In modern English translation, to imitate archaism comes off as parody, and there can be no greater treason to an original work than that. Therefore, except for a very few instances where archaic language actually supports or strengthens the poet's original expression, we eschew the practice completely.

Córdoba — Ortigia
7 May 2023 — 29 August 2025

---

[58] Jechová, p. 40.

[59] Ján Horecký, 'Ján Hollý — básnik a zakladateľ', *Kultúra slova*, XIII/9 (1979):289–293, p. 290.

[60] Horecký, p. 292.

[61] Jechová, p. 40.

SVATOPLUK
A Heroic Poem in Twelve Cantos

CANTO I

Svatopluk, King of the Slovaks, in prison, where he was confined by the Germans on account of their fear of him, appeals to God for his liberation. God hears his prayer and sends His messenger to Karolman, ordering him to release Svatopluk from prison. He vows to do so. However, first he assembles all the elders at a diet and lays before them the command he received of God. He wishes to grant Svatopluk the lands of Rastislav, under certain conditions. Radbod approves the plan. Wilbert, however, protests that if they were to do this, they would be preparing their own ruin. Britwald, on the other hand, advises that both Rastislav's lands, and the hand of Karolman's daughter in marriage, be given to Svatopluk. All present, including Karolman, are pleased with this advice. Svatopluk is brought before the diet. Karolman presents the elders' intentions to him. Svatopluk acquiesces, accepting the proposed conditions as well. The diet is dissolved.

    I sing the bitter war that Svatopluk with Karolman
    Waged, and how victorious, himself and his whole nation
    From German yoke did liberate to independence,
    Father of the great kingdom of the manly Slovaks.
      Sweet Umka, if ever Thou didst deign inspire my songs,
    Come to my aid now! For Thou knowest well the martial
    Spirit, having thy residence on Bílá Hora
    Or Kobyla or Devín, where Thou once gazed thy fill
    On frightful armies massed! Come, shed thy light upon me,
    Waft gentle inspiration, dispel the darknesses
    That I may sing of those heroes who, up until now,
    Have had no worthy bard to tell their mighty battles,
    And of Svatopluk, who from sad and gloomy dungeon
    Was raised to royal dignity, set upon a throne.
      O Thou, who hast the fullest skill and kenning of deeds

Famous and ancient of our forefathers, O Delight
Surpassing all delight, great Glory of our nation!
Look now upon me with clement eye, and if only
Thou hast a moment free from toiling with the mighty
Bards of the great Lord God, and the clamorous appeals
Of the more humble rhymers begging inspiration,
Incline a patient ear unto this labour of mine
And as Thou hast gathered beneath thy aegis other
Songs that Thou hast reckoned worthy of thy support,
May it be welcomed too among the Slovak nation
Kindly and gladly, as something of thy fashioning.
   The seventh month had passed, and now the eighth moon arose,
Unseen by Svatopluk in his dark prison pining,
Into which the German, savage, caused him to be hurled
In the despairing hope that this would shatter his faith.
So there he sat, yearning for his freedom, bewailing
His hard fate. There, as his sorrows swelled, his pains increased,
He unburdened his sad heart, lifting up this complaint:
  'Ah me! Miserable wretch, sorely persecuted,
Is my age to dissolve thus in torrents of distress?
Once more this head is pummelled by blows of misery!
No sooner had I emerged whole from one catastrophe,
Evading the cruel talons of fierce Rastislav,
Who would have swept me from the world, than I land in worse!
O, wretches who scramble after a royal sceptre!
And you who envy the ermine, believing it soft —
Learn this from me: learn what wisdom comes of my sorrow.
Look upon my suffering, learn from my example.
The higher you climb, the more violently shivers
The pine-tree in the gusts that batter it from all sides.
Such are the thrones of kings! The fires of heaven play but
On the sublimest masts that pierce the dark thunderheads!
How I would rather be somewhere in the far meadows
Of the high Tatras, a simple shepherd! A calm life,
A gay life, delightful, free of all burden and care.
How sweetly flows one's age there, amidst the simple joys
From which hap tore me, thrusting me on a throne. This throne
Of rotten straw, this realm pitch-black of pain, pining,
To gnaw upon my own heart's gristle in vain remorse!
And for this too I have to thank my royal sceptre,

That through no fault of mine I languish in this prison,
Where darkness, deep and endless, sears these two eyes of mine,
Where no sun rises, nor does the pale moon ever glow.
Nevermore shall I see the scattered flames of heaven
Nor their reflections on the fields: blooms and sparkling dew.
Neither breeze-flutings, nor streams' thunder pierce these deaf walls,
Nor music sweet, nor the trillings and songs of the birds
At break of dawn or when the soft gloom of dusk gathers
Before the night spreads its deep blue wings over the land;
It's all the same to me — I know not when the dawn breaks
Nor when the resplendent day marries the languid evening —
Here darkness broods unending with wings blacker than night.
Behold the joys of kingship, the recompense of rule!
Why am I here imprisoned? For what reason, Germans?
What is my crime? What evil have I done unto you?
Unwise was I, for entering into your friendship
When in my wretched need I sought protection here
While you cruelly ravaged our outposts with fire and steel!
Because through me Rastislav fell into your clutches
When he sought my life, laying covert traps before me,
Envenomed, abandoning that king to league with you?
Fresh is the memory of your defeat at his hands;
And even now he'd be thrashing your Bavarians
Had he not fallen into the snares he plaited for me,
And been dragged here before you, under guard, bound in them.
And lo! Now he has met with the same misfortune as I!
He, sad in his prison, I pining in prison too.
O my countrymen, and you my cousin Slavimír —
Are there no spears among you now, have you no armour
That you rush not to free me from this horrid gaol?
Have you too been charmed by regal glory, Slavimír?
But what are my vain pleas and complaints worth, anyway,
Since my raw-throated anguish will never reach your ears?
Perhaps you think I've died here, crushed by an evil fate?
O, if only I were to die in these darknesses,
At least my wretched suffering would come to an end!
Ah, fool! What are you thinking, trusting in human might?
Hope turns delusion when it's placed in human hands.
Should you not rather turn from them and entrust yourself
To the mercy of the Most High Ruler of Heaven?

If He deign not to help you in your need, no one can.
He who places his hope in Him is never undone.
And so, O mighty Ruler in the sky, behold me,
O Thou, who comfortest the saddened and sendest aid
To prop up the needy, who leadest forth from darkness
Of dungeon blind into the pristine light of freedom,
Look down upon Thy servant who with mind and whole heart
Trusteth in Thee; look down upon me now, abandoned
By all, and buried deep beneath endless suffering —
And lead me forth, if I be worthy, from this prison.
O, deign to stretch forth Thy mighty arm, and lead me home!
So that I might bring to a successful end the task
I began: uprooting from the garden of my land
The rank weeds of paganism, which yet do flourish
In scattered parts, to lead all my people unto Thee,
To spread the one true faith, and gather all to worship
Pure, so that Thou, heavenly Father, alone shouldst reign,
Receiving praise and glory meet from a worshipful nation
Who serve Thee always, and everywhere, with ardent hearts'.
   Thus groaned Svatopluk, complaining of his wretched lot,
Just like a nightingale captived within the stiff bars
Of a narrow cage for some thoughtless person's pleasure,
Who thinks, to hear him trilling, that it's from joy he sings,
The while the eyes of the poor creature well with hot tears,
Beholding him who deprived him of his liberty,
And while he crouches on his collar-beam, he sorrows,
Trilling his melodious dirge until, exhausted,
He's emptied quite the contents of his brimming heart,
And all the house echoes with his dying, sad laments.
   Now the Lord omnipotent, in the heights of Heaven,
Seated upon His golden throne flashing with diamonds,
Gazing upon the bright constellations as they roll,
And down upon the earth and all its people, at once
Beholding all things that are, were, and are yet to be,
Heard Svatopluk's lament, and had mercy upon him.
He called before his throne one from his splendid legions
Selected (one from the ranks who serve as messengers
And comfort men in sorrow with words from on high).
Clad in refulgent armour and tunic bright with stars,
His face he covered in his pied plumes as he drew near

God's throne — from piety, and also because the Face
Divine so radiates with light, out-shining the sun.
The angel came with alacrity and, bending low,
Attentively awaited the command of the Lord,
Which rang thus in his ears as the Omnipotent spoke:
   'Take thee off, youngster, to the city of Karolman,
And this command impart to him: "You must put an end
To the cruel captivity of guiltless Svatopluk.
The King must be led out into the bright light of day
And sent back to his realm, the land of the Slovaks".
Let Karolman consider the fickle ways of Fortune —
What's befallen Svatopluk might well befall him too.
Go now, and bring my command to him without delay.'
   Thus spoke the Lord. The angel then withdrew in a haste
His mission to accomplish. All the hosts of Heaven
Parted before him as he sped on, clearing his path;
Sooner than thought he's at that golden gate, which of all
Portals the greatest is, and the nearest placed to earth.
Its massive leaves opened before him without a sound
Revealing to his eyes the fixed fires of Charles' Wain,
As he sailed on amidst the numberless galaxies,
Comets and flashing stars throughout the sky unnumbered;
Far off he saw the sun, the pitted horns of the moon,
Beyond it: the earth, from this perspective no larger
Than a disk of stone that six brawny lads might bear off —
Thus she appears on the measureless fields of Heaven.
There sped the angel, cutting the air with mighty strokes,
Then he banked and descended, resting his limbs from rowing,
Hovering motionless, with pinions hardly beating,
Like some errant eagle, fledged on the Wallachian heights,
Poised in the blue above the highest summit, weighing
With sharp eye where to stoop, when, on the banks of Danube
Or Dvina he catches sight of a swan, snowy-white,
And down he plunges in speedy rush meteoric,
In well-aimed free-fall, no longer twitching a feather,
As if he had no wings, until he sinks his talons
Into her flesh, unfurling them then to strike aloft.
Thus did he plummet anew through the earth's blue atmosphere.
It was now past midnight when the angel alighted.
All men were submerged in sleep after the day's labour;

All beasts in their dens, all birds nested, in deep silence
The universe, no echo resounding through the fields;
No whispering breeze set the forest leaves a-rustle;
Only now and again came a streamlet's soft chuckle
Soothing sweetly the dreams of the slumbering mortals.
'Twas then that God's messenger arrived at the city
Of Karolman, splendid with spires soaring to the clouds.
He entered its gates, and hastened to the king's chamber,
Where he found Karolman wrapped in the deepest slumber,
And, approaching the richly spread bolster, the angel
Bent low, and such words sifted into his sleeping ear:
   'Think not, O Karolman, that your reason be muddled,
Nor that this be an empty dream that deceives your mind.
I hasten to your side, sent by God Omnipotent,
To bring you His command: Do now what you long have wished
To do: No longer hold captive guiltless Svatopluk,
But free him from his prison to the bright light of day,
And send him home now, to his realm, the Slovak kingdom.
Consider well the fickle spinning of Fortune's wheel:
What's befallen Svatopluk might well befall you, too.
Do now what the supreme Ruler of Heaven commands!
He who does the will of God proves worthy of His grace!'
   Then did God's orator step away from the embers
That with his breath he'd blown into a raging firestorm
And, his gigantic wings unfurling, set off skyward
To soar back, eagerly, to his home-hearth in Heaven,
Vanishing through the thin air and brightly burning stars,
Leaving nothing behind save a sweet fragrance that fell
About the palace, repanding through all the chambers.
Then came a thunderclap that made the earth to tremble.
   And slumber fell from the eyes of Karolman. Numb, cold
With sudden terror, his mighty limbs were shivering,
His heart was pounding madly, and the hair on his head
Bristling. Just the same as when a traveller, surprised
By the onset of a sudden storm, roaring and black,
Seeks shelter — anywhere — beneath a bridge or large cliff,
And lightning strikes an elm before him, blinding his eyes,
Shattering the tree down to its deepest roots, it falls
With a crash; so did the stunned king leap up out of bed.
Flinging off his bedclothes and clasping his hands, he cried:

'Was this a dream merely, deceiving my mind seduced,
Or was I truly visited by God's messenger?
For dreams can brew illusions impregnating the mind
With terror, but — Why should I be terrified at this?
A splendid young man of a radiant countenance,
His wings spread above me, dewy-moist, and rainbow-hued;
His voice in my ears like the roaring of cataracts!
Whence is this bright aura that sets the black night aglow?
Whence comes this perfume, if not wafting from high heaven?
Is it Thy will then, O Lord, Father Omnipotent,
Who rulest both Heaven and Earth with Thy might divine,
That Svatopluk the King should be led from his dungeon?
This I shall do, Lord, and that without further delay —
Sending him home with a large escort and many gifts;
With an army returning him to his fatherland,
That thus he might shake the sceptre from Slavimír's hand
Should he but grip it tighter, refusing to give back
Royal authority into the hands of the king.
But Thou, who art Goodness immense and everlasting,
Thou, who hast heard so many prayers rising unto Thee,
Hear too my voice that approacheth Thee in earnest suit:
If without just cause King Svatopluk was imprisoned,
If he unjustly suffered insult at these my hands,
Be merciful unto me and forgive me my sin
And that of those near me who led me with slant advice;
However deserving, deflect Thine anger from us
And let Thy castigation slip from Thy memory.
And thou, ambassador divine, soaring now homewards,
I give thee thanks for the commands thou hast delivered.
Be thou gracious unto me, plead my case before God'.
   Thus spoke Karolman. But now his mind was in a tumult:
How might he fulfil the Lord's command just delivered?
Should he release the King without the others' knowledge?
Or assemble the elders and reveal God's command?
The latter seemed the best way of taking it in hand,
And so he'd call a diet and set all before them.
Thus calming his racing heart he abandoned his bed
And, donning his royal robes, with ardent soul he flew
To the cathedral, where he poured forth his prayers to God.
The hour was conducive, for the church was empty now,

And there he knelt in fervent and groaning petition,
Remaining thus, until the dawn poured forth its splendour.
   As soon as the lips of morning overtopped the hills,
The ruddy-cheeked daystar smiling down upon the earth,
Karolman called the peers to gather in a diet —
All those who had excelled in martial skill or wisdom,
Whose names were therefore graced heroic for their merits.
A great many such worthies were gathered at the court.
There was a spacious hall there, as long as it was broad,
So long, the sharpest eye could barely make out its end:
The Rathaus, in the midst of the palaces royal.
'Twas there they went, as soon as the summons was given.
Just as the bees, who spend the day circling broad meadows,
Flitting from flower to flower and, when they alight,
Sipping with their tiny mouths the sweet and fragrant juice,
Fill their sacks with golden booty, until the evening
Flows in on dark shades, beglooming the fields, and they return
To the hive from all directions, from the misty bounds
Of the north, from the darkling east whence the night slips near,
From the south and from the western rim where the sun sets,
To spill their liquid treasures into the honeycombs,
Thus did the Germans bustle along the roads, crowding
Highway and path as they made their way to the Diet,
Until the Rathaus was crammed and the latecomers spilled
Out the doors and into the capacious courtyard. All
Were then assembled, taking their appointed places.
Then the babble of voices, like a swelling ocean,
Was stilled by the king rising in his golden mantle,
And, raising aloft his sceptre, he began his speech:
   'Noble Bavarians! Carinthians, Styrians —
It shall not be kept from you, the reason why we're here.
'Tis no petty matter, even amidst the troubles
With which we are beset, that prompts me to summon you
To gather in Diet from the early morning hours.
Have you any idea what has befallen me?
Hear what I have to say, and set it firmly in mind.
Exhausted with my day's work, slumber overcame me.
The horses of the night had not yet half run their course
When a messenger of the Lord appeared before me,
His countenance radiating a brilliant light,

His splendid, pied wings fanning a delicious fragrance.
Stunned into wakefulness, the blood ran cold in my limbs
As he drew near me, and directed at me such words:
   "'Think not, O Karolman, that your reason be muddled,
Nor that this be an empty dream that deceives your mind.
I hasten to your side, sent by God Omnipotent,
To bring you His command: Do now what you long have wished
To do: No longer hold captive guiltless Svatopluk,
But free him from his prison to the bright light of day,
And send him home now, to his realm, the Slovak kingdom.
Consider well the fickle spinning of Fortune's wheel:
What's befallen Svatopluk might well befall you, too.
Do now what the supreme Ruler of Heaven commands!
He who does the will of God proves worthy of His grace!'"
   When he had finished speaking, he spread wide those broad wings,
And swept up into Heaven. I vowed to do God's will,
Fulfilling the Lord's command without any delay.
And this in addition: to send King Svatopluk home
With gifts and a large armed force, back to his fatherland.
And so, the manner in which I intend to do this
I would reveal to you now. Rastislav, no petty
Ruler of the Slovaks once, now deprived of his sight,
His sway and his country, has no son to inherit
His throne and power by right of primogeniture.
But Svatopluk his nephew is closest him in blood.
So let us add the lands of Rastislav to his realm.
The wretched Rastislav himself intended just that,
Wishing to place his sceptre in that successor's hand.
The elders there were in support of his intention.
Of this then I intend to enfeoff him; after all,
He'll still be our retainer, and send yearly tribute
Of horses one hundred, oxen double that number,
And like talents of silver; bound too in time of war
To come to our aid with auxiliary legions.
So let us now gather an army from all regions,
A force to accompany him to his fatherland.
With these he shall shake the sceptre from Slavimír's hand
Should he be unwilling to acknowledge Svatopluk
King, and deliver the nation into his power.
This I intend to do, for our own good, I reckon.

Consider this well then, and reveal to me your thoughts'.
   He finished speaking. And then, thunderstruck at his words,
Each man remained mute, submerged in the deepest silence,
Until Radbod, one of the most exalted, arose:
Of clan illustrious, in war and council foremost,
Of splendid posture and most pleasing countenance,
Who enjoyed the respect of all of his countrymen.
For his entire concern was love of his land and people.
On this account, all eyes were ever turned toward him.
His bearing, proper and true, won him the hearts of all.
Such was the man who suddenly broke the strange silence:
   'O, wretched we! Who have so raged in our conniving,
In our crooked judgement of the Slovak king's treason,
Casting him into a dungeon, and he innocent!
The outrage we have done! So now, my splendid lord,
Almighty God, ruler of all, has made you aware
Of His command through His angelic emissary,
Has poured His grace upon you, shown you His high regard:
Boldly then, let us fulfil His will without delay.
For even should we be unwilling and resist Him,
What the Omnipotent wills shall come to fruition.
A futile gambit it is, to kick against the goad,
And for such sinful disobedience to His will
Harsh punishment would fall upon us, a discipline
Inexorable. Heed we then the King's good advice,
And with our own arms, aid Svatopluk to his sceptre.
Let us bestow upon him Rastislav's wasted land,
In this way to allay the bitterness of prison,
Righting a wrong, soothing the just anger in his heart
Before it sours to hatred. In this way, dependence
Upon our empire, thaneship, will not seem a burden'.
   So spoke Radbod. At this, choleric Wilbert arose,
Who in his swelling heart nursed hatred toward the Slovak
King; he was the one who, more than all the others, urged
Svatopluk's imprisonment. And when he rose to speak
It sounded like the roaring of mighty, massed waters.
   'Most excellent King! Fulfil the command of the Lord
From start to finish; after all, it is in your hands
To do whatever you wish, whatever you deem right.
But do not toss Rastislav's realm to the prisoner!

For such a generous gift will bear quite other fruit.
Indeed, it will bring great destruction upon us all.
Recall how deftly Slavimír destroys our armies!
Now Nitra, now Fraštak, now Bratislava he takes,
Seizing the castles Pezinok and Devín quickly;
Why should I go on, listing the towns that he's taken?
If he, less trained in arms, should take measure of us now,
— And these are merely Slavimír's deeds with his army! —
What shall a real hero do, one accomplished in arms?
Svatopluk, when to his realm is added Rastislav's,
King Svatopluk, when his power is doubly increased?
I knew him when he was young — already so able,
So wise beyond his tender years — the court was in awe
Of his sharp intellect, and the valour of his heart;
Immense the power of his limbs, his thew unflagging;
Ever, it seemed, in armour clad, skilled in manly sports,
Be that to ply the bow upon the archery range:
His fleetly whizzing arrows always split the bullseye;
And how he swung the sword — how he flung the javelin!
All of his sudden deeds — as if thought out beforehand!
His greatest delight was to race through the dark forest
On a steed he'd broken himself, shooting at the game.
All of his thoughts, like his bearing, were martial, warlike.
'Twas war he sought; he found no delight in anything
Else; he'd only give ear to songs of ancient battlers,
Terrible wars and the expeditions of heroes.
Ah, then would you see him come to life — then his heart thumped!
Already then I thought to myself, should he ever
Grow into manhood, and grip the sceptre with his hand,
He'd cast off vassalage with a light shrug and set to fight,
Tearing power from our hands to become his own lord.
And this is what he shall desire now, and accomplish,
Should he become even stronger, with Rastislav's realm
Added to his own; doubly strong. And so I beg you,
Ye fathers gathered together in this moot: think!
Consider well my words: Are we to provoke his might?
Enabling, in our despite, an enemy's power?'

   Thus he brought his clever speech to an end. Though he strove
To cloak his hatred in terms of gallantry and praise,
His hard eyes and unkind demeanour gave him away.

When he had done, enormous Britwald rose to his feet,
His face glowing brilliantly with sharp wit and good sense —
Like the azure sky free of any taint of grey mist.
There were none present who even approached brave Britwald
In flinging spear or slicing through the enemy ranks
With sword, or with speech to set afire the hearts of men.
There was no greater advocate of truth and justice,
Always ready, when asked, to give his folk good advice,
Equal to all, and to those most in need, generous.
With such words then, he arose and revealed his reckoning:
  'As I see it — for my part, I think I see it well —
We should subject our wills to our monarch's clear judgement.
Let us aid Svatopluk to his sceptre lost, with arms
Of our mighty forces, and let us bestow the realm —
The whole of that, which belonged to his uncle — on him.
The very law demands it; he is closest in blood
To Rastislav, who intended to make him his heir.
Nor was there any opposition from the elders,
Who gave to that great king's will unanimous consent.
And this too holds valid — that any new regions won
By warring, subjected realm and fiefdom overcome,
These too belong to him; they are his accomplishments.
For tell me — how did this unmastered ruler win them
If not with arm victorious and clever warring?
We all know quite well that when Svatopluk entrusted
Himself, and all he had — his very realm — to our care
We paid him back by bringing sword and fire, destruction
Through all the marches of his monarchy, and what then?
Rastislav, at the unexpected news: his nephew
Coming to these our lands and forming an alliance,
His mind enflamed with bitter wrath, indeed overcome
With floods of ferocity that swept him quite away,
Determined to murder Svatopluk: first, by deceit.
He gave a banquet, hoping there to seize Svatopluk,
But some of his retainers rescued him from peril.
Because before the lackeys who were to murder him
Entered the keep, one of the guests, whose name was Výslav,
Who was well aware of what was about to happen,
Nodded his head slightly, winked an eye at Svatopluk,
Who caught on at once to what the good man meant to say,

Rose, and called for falcons, as if he would go hawking,
Escaping the impending doom, avoiding the trap.
Before Rastislav caught wind of his treason lain bare,
Distraught, Svatopluk fled with his fleet army, in pained
Mind skittish of pursuit, eyes wide, ears pricked for new traps,
Like a stag spooked by raging wolf, feeling on his nape
The hot breath, bounding in terror, speeding to cover
Until at last he reaches his own grove. And once there
He called his councillors together, each man ready
For battle, urging his fellows to battle, fervent
They set to war. The clash of armour pounded by swords!
The streams of blood that flowed! On this side soldiers perished
And on that side too. At last, after cruel slaughter,
Svatopluk took Rastislav, and set him at our bench.
And thus he, who until recently had pummelled us,
And surely thereafter would have bested us in war,
Was placed into our hands, his mighty power broken.
For that alone would it not be a proper reward,
The land he conquered with his sword, a realm far-stretching?
Or do you think he's earned imprisonment, four dark walls?
Is this the sort of justice we uphold, this, our truth?
And if we fear that when his kingdom waxes in might,
When the realm we bestow on him should one day sprout horns
And buck the yoke of fiefdom, to bolt at liberty
(And do you think he'd do that, if once he does submit?)
Gripping the sword to hack himself away from our grasp —
Are we so lacking in capable arms and manliness?
We've all of Germany at our beck and call for aid
To tame his pride if he should prove stubborn, think you not?
But I've another means to keep him tethered to us,
To bind him to our rule — O my Lord magnificent!
He is a bachelor, and you, my Lord, have a daughter:
A splendid girl of marriageable age, in virtue
As beautiful as in her countenance and carriage —
How many mothers throughout Europe have sought her hand
For their sons princely! Offer her to him, and bind him
With charms of love as son-in-law to your throne; a firm friend
To us he shall remain, nor shall he ever betray
A faith so sanctified. How many kings and heroes
Unmoved by threat of arms or violence, by one word

Of their sweet helpmeet, one soft touch, were set to labour?'
   Thus Britwald argued. Suddenly, a murmur swept through
The moot, as when a stormcloud from high mountains spills down
Into the valley, and the whistling winds precede it,
Striking the forest, to resound the more: moans and booms
Echoing off each trunk and leaf-thick branch it sweeps through,
While thunderclaps crash as the storm now rages — just so
A rush of words passed through the lords assembled at court,
For all were pleased at what had been suggested. Britwald
Was duly praised by all — except for Wilbert, who glared
With angry eye on all, swelling with rabid venom —
His breast appeared about to burst with gall. His gorge rose
Thrice with opposing speech; and thrice he stifled his words
Of opposition, biting back his tongue, deception
Seeming the better path to overturn the counsel
That irked him. For the king saw that his thanes were agreed,
Thinking as one man. So he spoke again in such terms:
 'I see that you are pleased with my intentions, against
Which I see no hands raised in opposition, and therefore,
Go now, my noble Gottfried, and lead forth from prison
The king of the Slovaks, and bring him here. We meanwhile
Shall send messengers throughout the reaches of our realm
To call our men to arms, for that cruel war shall break out
We do not doubt. But you also advise my daughter
Be wed to him, so that he remain true to our throne;
Faithful ally in war and peace. For my part, I too
Agree this will be good; you but outpaced my own will
Before I might have suggested it myself. Her now
Upon him I bestow, and call him mine from now on.
Now let his happiness be our study, repaying
His pains and sadness with rejoicing; both with deep bowls
And tournaments — to which summon all. Who triumphs
In these lists shall be set as my lieutenant over
All of my armies, in my place'. Thus spoke Karolman.
   Then Svatopluk was led inside the chamber, his face
Pale, but proud; uncertain as to this change in fortune;
But as he knew himself innocent, his fierce eyes blazed.
All that were present rose from their places before him,
The king himself arose, and went to greet him, cheerful.
He took him by the hand and led him to the dais,

And words most affable directed to him, saying:
  'Gallant King of the Slovaks, hold it not against us
That, misled by ill counsel, we covered you with shame.
You know yourself how prudent every ruler must be,
How providential in his actions, mistrusting all,
Whatever seems to tend to his realm's disadvantage.
You know as well how easily he may be deceived.
Know now: just such a misfortune has befallen me.
But what's already happened cannot now be undone;
Yet hear what we've determined just now in parliament.
Released from gaol, we send you back to your fatherland,
To which we also add the lands held by Rastislav,
But in exchange you must subject yourself to our rule.
Each year one hundred horses, and two hundred oxen,
Silver talents two hundred — you must pay in tribute,
And hold yourself ever in readiness to make war
Against our enemies should hostilities erupt.
Know too that I have a splendid daughter, my delight,
Beautiful of face and form, lovelier in virtues,
Of marriageable age. Many royal mothers
From all over Europe have sought her hand for their sons.
To you I shall betroth her, and I do it gladly,
That we may be bound in love and friendship forever.
What is more, we have commanded that a stout army
Should be drawn up quickly and set at your disposal,
With which to batter Slavimír, and retake your realm,
Should he refuse to render unto you your birthright,
To recognise you as king, and voluntarily
To acknowledge your sceptre, relinquishing his sway'.
   He finished. Then, shaken by these words of Karolman,
King Svatopluk found himself tossed here and there in thought.
As when the pleasant sun shines down, but burly clouds borne
On the winds cast down their dark shadows on the hilltops,
Light and shadow are interweft on the earth below,
And those who stood in the sunlight are now enveloped
In gloom, while those once in darkness are now bathed in light,
Thus Svatopluk was overwashed with joy — and caution.
Glad he was at the thought of returning to his home;
Glad at the thought of the sceptre, the army — the land
Of Rastislav too, annexed to his inheritance,

But at the price of subjugation to a foreign prince?
Obliged to such a yearly tribute? His blood ran cold!
But since it could not be otherwise, he determined
To agree to the terms — even such terms; after all,
Time and fortune rule even government and monarch;
Nothing's immutable on this changing globe. And so:
   'Great King', he said, 'and you elders assembled in moot,
Although I've lost my taste for the glories of kingship,
Which led but to imprisonment and cruel torments
— Both hard to bear — because you now intend to lead me
Back to my fatherland at the head of an army,
Bestowing the whole realm on me — and a splendid wife —
I agree, once more, to take command of an armed host
To bring Slavimír to heel should he not relinquish
The sceptre of his own will, nor my authority
Acknowledge, as hereby do I, my subjugation,
To you, my liege lord, accepting all your conditions.
Nor do I wish any longer to hold you to blame
For my months in that dark dungeon — as you were deceived
Yourselves in adjudging me that harsh portion'. He spoke,
And Karolman dismissed the parliament, the elders
Out-filing in meet order of their ranks; meanwhile, he
Led off to his own chamber encircled round about
By royal councillors, Svatopluk the Slovak king,

CANTO II

As soon as the news of the war spreads abroad, the entire land immediately finds itself in tumult, with all men readying themselves for battle. Meanwhile, Karolman, Svatopluk, and the leading men set out to the fields appointed for the tournaments that were to be held for Svatopluk's delight; each of the victors is presented with an oak-leaf chaplet. Britwald is victorious in clubs, Svenčar is first in piercing the target with the spear. Bojmír is first among archers for speed; for aim it is Vratislav, and in hurling the shot it is Merisáv.

    As soon as from the palace tower the war-banner
Flapped in the wind, as soon as messengers were sent out
To all corners of the land with bronze trumpets blaring
The news, the realm entire was gripped with martial ardour.
The farmer abandoned his ploughshare in mid-furrow
Or dropped the seed-bag and raced off the fresh-tilled sillion;
All the works of hands and days, without hesitation
Broke off as spears were unsocketed, dull blades whetted,
Rust scraped off arrowheads, vambraces touched with the damp
Wiped clean of mould, and armour neglected flashed like new.
Some plait defensive shields from stiff wickets of osier,
Stretching a well-tanned ox hide over the frame, sewing
It all tight; others form pauldron and breastplate, faithful
Defence against arrows light. Thick chain-mail is woven
To cover the joints and limbs, ply over threaded ply.
Axemen rough-cut the ash-forests for spear shafts, and yew
Is carved into longbow, while bowstrings are spun from hair
Or sinew and tested: Shall it snap at the first draw?
Or bear wingèd death on the tip of the dart, afar?
Many a ploughshare, coulter, scythe, and spade are melted,
Along with whatever other iron comes to hand,
To prepare new arms for the clash with the enemy:
From every chimney 'round about the thick smoke rises.
Some of the men will go as infantry, while others
Upon the frisking backs of colts would ride to war,
Cruel war; so each his steed outfits in armour too:
Chanfron and harness, snaffle, crinet, petrel, crupper,
But first he plaits the mane in ribbons gay, and his palm

Caresses the trembling flanks, giving the horse courage.
The saddle is measured, the rider swings upon it,
And spurs the steed into a gallop, toward the lists.
   Then neared with quick strides the day on which the tournament
Was to be held. As the sun broke over the hilltops,
Karolman set off for the jousting grounds, and with him
Rode King Svatopluk in the company of those lords
First in the German Empire. It was a broad expanse
Where the men were to compete, surrounded on three sides
By black woods; in the centre, thickly spread with white sands
Made firm by the constant pounding of the chargers' hooves.
It was there that whole legions of onlookers gathered,
From all corners of the realm, above all: worthy youths.
Some came only to watch, others to meet in combat,
Eager to have their names bruited far and wide by Fame.
Nearby was a bare hillock, from which the view was clear
To all sides. Here the greatest number of spectators
Gathered; this too the king ascended, and all gave way
To their monarch, who set his throne beneath a grand oak
As old as time itself, from the leaves of which were weft
The chaplets of the victors in the lists. Here he sat,
Setting Svatopluk to his left, the throne of honour,
While the rest of the council spread out upon the sward,
Surrounding the kings on their left hand and on their right.
Like two oaks themselves, the pride of the forests, which lift
Their heads above the lesser growth, and spread wide their boughs,
In the shade of which shelter the striplings and the shrubs,
So seemed the two kings amongst the crowds assembled there.
And then, when all had taken their allotted places,
The clarions sounded, their calls echoing afar
In brassy blasts, and everyone gave ear, for the king
Then arose to establish the order of contests,
His voice resounding loud and clear throughout the valley:
   'First will be the jousting, and after that, the gold ring
Suspended from a hair, to be threaded by a lance,
And that at a full gallop. Thirdly, swift javelins
Shall strike at the Avar helmet; sharp-eyed archers
Shall draw their strings taut, measuring the bull's eye target;
Lastly, shot-putters, hammer-throwers shall prove their skill.
Fame shall broadcast the victors' names afar, and oak-leaves

Grace the triumphant brows. Now let the lancers approach
And set themselves to the fierce battle on the tilt-field'.
   Thus spoke the king, his words stirring the heroic hearts.
The knights then mounted, armour on their chests, and lances
Firm at the left forearm. Visors slid down from shining
Helmets topped with ostrich plumes and bobbing horse-hair crests.
They raised their armoured heads on high to heaven and swept
Their mighty lances aloft, in their right hands, now;
They reared on eager mounts as high as oaks cloud-piercing
On the heights of Suchánka or Zobor braving all
Thunderheads and lightning bolts with their crowns, leafy, proud,
Their eager stallions pawing up the sand, ready to charge.
   A trumpet blaring loud gave the signal for the joust.
The first to canter out upon the sand, Jesutbor,
A stout warrior, lifted his voice and called out his slogan:
   'Let him who trusts in his strength and has a valiant heart
Swing up into his saddle and meet me at lance-point.
But he won't sit there long! I'll knock him flat on the sand!'
   He finished his boast. Then, burly Agilmund, aroused,
Advanced to hurl such an answer back into his teeth:
   'If indeed you trust to the skill you vaunt, just the same
I boast of my own craft, which budges not before yours.
We'll soon see if that big mouth of yours will be stopped up
With sand. This lance has cast down better men than you, sir'.
   He spoke, and both knights turned their swift chargers to the track,
One to the right, one to the left, champing at their bits,
Each to the farthest limit to gather momentum
At which they wheeled their steeds around, then spurred them onwards,
Hooves drumming at the sand, lances tensed, level, their plumes
Bobbing above their helmets. So fast did they race on,
No freshet in the spring plunging down a mountainside
Swollen with melting snow roars on with more force, no cloud
Disburdens with more violence thunderclap; arrows
Speed on with no more raw velocity than they, rushing,
The drumming of the hooves drowning out all other sound.
The dust and sand kicked up in dark clouds obscures the sun.
The crowd then roared, their cries reverberating from hill
And wood encircling the tourney-pitch. Charging near
They met, and with an awesome splintering the lances
Boomed against breastplates. As when a lightning bolt crashes,

Splintering a granite cliff, sending rubble tumbling
Down the rock-face onto the valley floor, Jesutbor
Fell, rocked from the saddle of his prancing steed, his back
Slamming the pitch concave. The whole earth seemed to tremble
Beneath the blow. His shield rolled far off, wobbling at last
Still like a saucer. Bloated with pride then, Agilmund
Cried out with laughter, 'Lie there on your back, who vaunted
Vainly your might; how do your words savour, mixed with sand?'
He spoke, and then he cantered off to where the victors
Were to be honoured; his mates rushed close and lifted him
Upon their shoulders. They bore him to a spring, and there
He rested on soft grass. Once more the trumpet sounded,
Summoning new competitors to the jousting.
First Mutimír the spearman emerged onto the field
And bellowed a loud challenge to one and all — to fight!
Without a moment's hesitation came Gromislav;
They met, and parted, again each to the farthest extreme,
The nostrils of their stallions snuffling the tense, charged air.
Turning their steeds, they pricked their sides with the iron spur,
Each aiming his wroth lancetip at the metal helmet
Of his opponent. Before slick Mutimír parried
The shaft rushing upon him, swift it came crashing on,
Striking his crown and slicing away crest and feather,
But when his lance struck the smooth copper, of a sudden
It shattered into a thousand splinters; sparks showered
From the battered helm of Gromislav. Then, beholding
Spearhead and shaft asunder, he slid from his scabbard
His sword, and with it hurled himself upon Gromislav,
Who, stunned and reeling as if he had been thunderstruck,
Hardly could move, his head buzzing, slumped in the saddle.
His lance fell from his hand, and darkness weighed his lids shut.
Tottering thus, his horse carried him on, and his friends
Caught him as he began to slide from the alarmed steed;
They bore him, swooning, to a cool, shaded retreat
While Mutimír galloped in triumph, a champion.
   Once more the trumpet sounded, urging knights to the lists.
Valiant Britwald trotted forth into the arena.
In his right hand he bore a spear of knotty oak-wood,
And a shield in his left; fierce is his coat of arms:
A hydra-dragon, belching fire from its black gullets.

He called out boldly, challenging one and all to fight.
Radbod then raised to the clouds his awesome staff, with which
He'd menaced many a roaring bear's poll in the hunt,
And thrashed out of their coverts — and out of their hides, too —
The foaming forest boars. No less fierce a battle loomed,
To which he stood, with his proud heart unflustered. Intent
Upon the broil at hand, the two champions parted, turned,
And like two bellowing bulls, with angry horns lowered,
Rushed at each other, hooves thundering the sand. They met,
And Radbod's left arm was cruelly battered by the bolt
Of the iron-tipped lance, his wooden shield was shattered,
And hung from the dead limb unable to heft it more.
Britwald turned and approached, ominous, intending
To strike anew, but Radbod's horse, sensing limp harness,
The bit loose in his foaming mouth, spurred by lance falling
Upon his flank, set off at a gallop, arrow-quick,
To where the other chargers wait, bearing his master dulled
By the blow, his whinnies answered by his stablemates.
  But when the trumpets blared again with metal voices,
Great-soulled Britwald retreated not from the tourney pitch;
He called aloud again, challenging all to the lists.
Swiftly-horsed Hartung pranced onto the arena sand,
To and fro feinting, his steed skipping forwards and back,
Slitting the sandy pitch with hooves swifter than the wind.
They charged, but just before their ash-lances could strike home,
Hartung the witty — ever adroit and resourceful —
Avoided impact by slipping somewhat to the right:
Thumped by a clever blow of Hartung's staff, Britwald's lance
Flew from his hand deceived to plough a trench in the sand
A fathom deep; the shaft trembled, having missed its mark.
But Britwald was not to be daunted by such foul chance;
Swelling with venom, he unsheathed cruel sword from scabbard
And with one swipe he shattered Hartung's spear; thereupon
Feinting himself, his next blow crashed down upon his helm.
The light hooves of his steed availed Hartung nothing now,
For he fell battered from the saddle onto the sand
With crash and clatter of his armour jangling to earth.
His mournful comrades then dragged him off into the shade.
  Once more the trumpets blared, calling forth men to the lists.
But bold-hearted Britwald, reflecting on his success,

Confident in his arm, did not abandon the field
Though twice the call sounded. It was hard for him to bear
That doughty Mutimír and Agilmund the mighty
Were seated — so lofty! — on the thrones of their triumphs.
And so he gripped the errant lance buried in the sand
And pulled it free, with booming voice baiting all to the fight.
The first man who rose to the challenge was Agilmund.
Parting, the knights withdrew each to his end of the track.
Then, wheeling their mounts around, there was no need of spur:
The fiery steeds flew to the clash like angry storm-winds.
When the distance between them narrowed to certain blows
And sharp lance-heads were trained implacably on breast-plates,
Unfortunate Agilmund's shaft shattered, while Britwald,
Skilled lancer, rammed his copper between groin and navel,
Piercing the armour. Unsaddled by the momentum,
Fending a swift mace-blow with his buckler, Britwald seized
The stallion's reins and delivered a resounding blow
That opened a cut near the base of the horse's ear.
Stunned with the sudden pain, the steed reared on its hind legs
And shivered, casting its master down from the saddle.
His comrades rushed up to draw him aside to safety.
   Again the raucous voice of the trump sent forth the call.
At once, many-skilled Mutimír, although having seen
So many mighty heroes overthrown at the hands
Of Britwald triumphant, set firm his unflinching heart
To the fray anew. Taking in hand the thick fir lance
Of Gromislav, as the shattered fragments of his own
Lay bright, scattered on the sand, he trotted to his place
Before Britwald began his boast. Like a grand oak tree
Powerful, vigorous, towering over the grove
Of lesser growth, was Mutimír, ominous, patient,
As when he led his men against the cruel Kozárs
Or smote the restless legions of the raw Polovtsy,
Dotting whole steppes with the grave mounds of his enemies.
Yes, thus menacing Mutimír loomed above the pitch.
And then they rushed to combat, copper-tipped lances poised
For the collision. They seemed like two high crags speeding
Together across a plain that shrinks from them in fright;
Opposing cliffs tumbled by earthquake or lightning-bolt,
Boulders clashing in wrath; all nature in an uproar

Of groaning and roaring of the elements at war.
Thus did they leap at one another: the tight impact
Was a horror of violence. Both lances splintered
Into a thousand pieces when Britwald the robust
Collided with Mutimír. Their chargers, head to head
Impacted and recoiled, sent squatting upon the blackened sand.
The men leaped to their feet, and, balanced on the firm ground,
Unsheathed their fang-like swords, and set to the fierce battle.
Thickly the blows fell as they hacked at their opponent,
Sword against sword clanged, blows battered upon their armour,
The horrid clamour echoed from the surrounding woods.
The feathers that bobbed so proudly from their crowns were slashed
And whirled about them in the dust their struggle kicked up.
Like twin tornados opposing at Chválenské Brody,
From each side, neither giving way, thus their cruel war:
From this side Britwald, from that Mutimír, limbs milling,
Neither giving way, yet neither advancing. Like sea
Ramping at heaven, and wind battering down the waves
Which burl and leap anew, so did they surge without pause
Or quarter (unasked!) neither man wishing to give way
Though bathed in sweat, battered, deafened by the clanging blows
Which fell again, again, upon the pair exhausted,
But thrashing still. On both sides all their comrades arose
And with their cheers encouraged their champions, raising
A raucous clamour that battered the clouds; six times now
They'd tangled angrily, pounding with swords, mace;
Six times the sparks flew from the whining metal; clashing,
The swords bit, caught in chinks, and were torn away again,
Until Mutimír swelled his mighty thew and lashed forth
A horrid blow upon Britwald's head, splitting his helm.
And yet before his exhausted arm could pull it back,
The heavy sword, Britwald, enraged at the thunderous blow,
Spun and swung, landing a gigantic blow of his own
On Mutimír, whose sword flew from his mailed grip, landing
With a great thud upon the sand. Britwald's upon him
Inexorably, once, twice battering his bevord
Until the pummelled visor flew apart; Mutimír,
Battered, tottered, fell with sparks exploding in his eyes.
His mind a fog, unbalanced, his head sank to the side,
His limbs relaxed, though once more they sought to lift him up —

Deflated now, he lay stretched on the arena floor,
The echoes of his mighty crash just then dying off.
His comrades ran up to drag his bulk off to the side
Where they revived him with fresh, cold water poured in streams
That steamed when splashed upon the heated chain-mail gorget.
The horn resounded, calling an end to the jousting,
While Britwald's proud friends surrounded him, cheering, leading
Him to the king's throne, who placed the fair oaken chaplet
Upon his brows, with words of praise, declaring him now
His champion, the warrior-chief to lead his troops.

   The horns again with raucous voice called forth the young bloods
To new contests, echoing from the woods their summons
Brassy. The king arose from his throne and took voice thus:
'Who now shall test his fortune, and with his lance, the ring
Suspended from the elm-tree pierce, and strip, at full gallop?'

   The most dexterous of the youths then gathered, mounted
On bonny-draped chargers proudly stepping, spangled
With ornaments, their eager muzzles lifting on high
Haughtily, this way and that, catching the bright sun's rays
To reflect in dazzles. The foresightful Regenbald
Produced his dice, and setting the young men in a row,
Had each toss them in turn. It fell to Wilbert
To try his luck the first; following him came Kučbor,
And in his train were Erchenbert and Humboldt the strong,
And last of all: Svenčar. Tall in the saddle, Wilbert,
Upon his steed immense, pricked the charger's flanks with heels
Iron-shod, and set off at a gallop, measuring
The tiny target with his thick fir lance, unblinking
His steady eye and peaceful, trained on the glinting ring
Suspended from its filament. And yet he raced past,
Unable to centre the lance-point in the circle,
Glancing its right side, sending the loop wildly spinning.
Or was it set in motion by the lance's slip-stream?
Defeated and disappointed, without the trophy
Upon his lance, he trotted back to his first station.

   At once the sod was drummed again, as fair-cheeked Kučbor
Sped at the target — 'twas so like the ring he just now
Sought to exchange with Ratimír's beautiful daughter,
Through matchmakers pleading his case until the news came
Of cruel war looming — and the games to precede it;

At which he called off all his wedding plans, postponing
The blessed day for happier and more peaceful times,
And set off to contend at the spectacle of arms.
It was he that streaked then towards the ring with his lance,
Reflecting all the while on his beloved, and praying
That he might win a chaplet he'd then send her, binding
Her heart to him in greater love. He yearned for the prize,
And conjured Fortune to befriend him now, fervently
Whispering: 'Now, O Fortune, now, if ever you have
Deigned support me with your grace, O now, bring me good luck!'
Straight on he sped, and true, urging the stallion to flight
As swift as any arrow loosed from a Cossack's bow.
But Fortune, though she favoured him before, otherwise,
This time, when most he needed her, she failed him, merely
Nudging the spear-point towards the thick knot at the crown
Of the golden hoop. And so he turned aside, blaming
His hands recusant, and Fortune for letting him down.

   Then Erchenbert's turn came round, and he spurred on his horse,
Who flew so fast, his hooves hardly seemed to touch the ground.
His mane flared in the wind, whistling from the impetus.
But Erchenbert pierced not the ring hanging from the tree:
The impact of the lance sent it jangling and spinning.

   Then Humbold quickly leapt astride his thoroughbred mount
And set him prancing here and there, gracefully dancing,
As if to notes plucked sweetly on lute or sprightly bowed,
Traipsing now here, now there, just as the tune commands him,
The while the onlookers, delighted, applauded, cheered.
Not otherwise did Humbold, upon his proud-legged steed,
Carouse and prance along the pitch, forward and backward,
Until at last he reigned in the steed's exuberance.
Pressed now to a gallop, like a loud mountain freshet
Thus he raced, lowering his lance toward the target.
But as he neared the goal, a hawk, by chance alighted
Upon the elm-bough from which the ring was suspended,
Gazing in wonder at the people there assembled,
Gave out a screech of surprise, spreading its wings to fly.
The sudden movement spooked the horse, who snuffled and reared,
Pounding the sand with jamming hooves, his mane thrown forward.
Humbold, irate at the bad luck, cursing mightily,
Flung at the bird for depriving him of victory.

With a less springy tread, he returned to his station.
   Then it was Svenčar's turn, on his sleek, sable stallion;
Pale white is his mane, however, and white is his tail,
With a white apple-like patch adorning his forehead.
The horse was gifted him by the Volgar Radislav,
From the stables of Styria; Svenčar himself trained
The horse to rear and mill at the clouds with his forehooves,
To prance in complicated arabesques on the turf,
And more than that: to overleap ravine and hollow,
And to break off at once the most violent gallop.
There was no need to urge him on to a swift career:
One needed but to loosen halter and reins a bit:
At once the winged-hooved steed would bolt off with a leap
To fly faster than a stone launched by mightiest sling-man.
Just such a charger the canny Svenčar now mounted,
Aiming his lance at the small hoop. And this time Fate
Was kind: he pierced the target and carried off the ring,
Bearing it to his liege. He showered him with praise
And wound about his shining brow the oaken chaplet.
   The trumpets sounded to summon the men to new games.
The king arose from his elevated throne and spoke:
'Whoever now would like to present his skilful aim
Before us here assembled, let such a one approach
And fill the Avar warrior's mouth with an ashen spear'.
Walter first advanced to the target range thus prepared,
And a painted image of an Avar warrior,
Hair and complexion true to the cruel reality,
Affixed to a post as if it were a severed head.
Sunken eyes, and a mouth spread open in a horrid grin
— About the size of a pine-cone was the opening —
To this the young hopefuls approached bearing javelins.
To Madalbod fell the lot to fling the first missile
Swiftly at the target — it sliced off the left ear.
Dipold followed him, first pumping the missile thricely
Behind his back before he let it fly with all his might
At the target; it buried itself in the right cheek.
Jarohnev stepped up the third, nevertheless in vain:
Although at other times he was favoured by Fortune,
Bringing down many a wild beast with his piercing shafts,
Now, as he ran to gather momentum for the throw,

Planting firm his foot to release the javelin,
He tripped on an unlucky root, and his bolt flew high,
Sparing the head by a broad measure as it whizzed on.
Ludolf then took his turn, and with much better fortune,
Struck the horrifying effigy straight in the forehead.
At last came two proud brothers, Dobroslav and Bojmír,
In face and figure unvaried one from the other,
They bore the same weapons and wore a like livery
So that even their close friends could not tell them apart;
Even their parents sometimes were unsure which was which.
From early youth they'd trained in archery, their delight
To let fly dart and spear. Now, Dobroslav to Bojmír:
  'My dear brother, I have always heeded your advice,
And you mine. Listen to me now and don't refuse me —
Let others aim at the mouth; you and I — for the eyes:
I'll measure at the left, and you take aim at the right'.
  Bojmír was pleased with his brother Dobroslav's advice;
The two then rushed off to their places and launched their spears.
Alike the shafts flew, screaming through the air like eagles;
Alike their predatory beaks bit into the eyes.
But now Otto stepped to the line, the seventh to go.
Speedily from his mark he raced and released with skill.
True sped his spear-shaft to pierce the horrid target's mouth.
He ran before the king and begged the oaken chaplet,
At which the brothers objected! Dobroslav first spoke:
  'If Otto is to reap such laurels of victory,
Even greater adulation is due the brothers
Daňkovič, who flung their two missiles at the same time,
And hit their marks as one, plunging through the two sockets!'
  The king replied: 'Indeed you are both worthy of praise,
As much as he: so I will have you all hurl again.
And he whose missile pierces the mouth of the target
(Such the rules, such ancient custom) shall be the victor'.
Each then extracted his spearhead from the riddled mark.
The brothers permitted Otto to be first to throw.
He raced up, hurled: the spear thudded between the eyebrows
Black-painted. Because the spearhead had blunted somewhat
From the first impact, the shaft now sagged limply, but held,
Blocking clear access to the scowling mouth. He went off,
Otto, with anger, irate that the oaken chaplet

Which he'd already won, should now be taken from him,
And from the circle of champions he must step down.
At this Dobroslav whispered to his sibling Bojmír:
'Brother, so that your path to the target should be clear,
Let me throw first, and with my missile I will dislodge
Otto's spear hanging loose'. No sooner did he finish
Than up he raced and hurled — and his missile hit its mark,
Splitting the hanging shaft and knocking it to the turf.
His brother then let fly, and he pierced the Avar's mouth.

  At once the trumpets sounded, calling men to new feats;
The king, wreathing the brows of Bojmír with the chaplet,
Called out: 'Who now would show their deftness with archery
Step forth and take the measure of the distant bull's-eye'.
At once the men approached, extracting their swift arrows
From their quivers and affixing them to their bowstrings.
Scattered near the very limit of the arena
Stood birches, lifting their heavy crowns to the heavens,
And one of these had, just beneath its bifurcation,
A small round hole, gouged into the papery white bark
By some woodpecker's beak, hammering in search of food.
At this, the archers in turn were to shoot their arrows.
First Alfríd pulled his reluctant bow's taut sinew
(A feat of strength itself!) and shot the dart at the mark.
It whistled through the air, and struck the tree on the right.
The skilful Grajsa next took aim — with no better luck.
He split the breadth in two — alas, beneath the target.
Then, third approached Vratislav, a renowned marksman,
Whose greatest pleasure and recreation was to tie
Two pigeons together by their feet and release them,
To measure them with eagle-eye and frame tensed like stone,
And cut them free with speedy dart, harming neither bird.
'Twas such an eye that scanned the target then, and almost
Without his fellows noting when, sent his dart whizzing
Straight to the hole — its impact set the dry punk flying.
Others followed him in turn, with uneven results —
Their missiles struck the tree, some closer to the target,
But none within the narrow bounds, none piercing the mark.
And yet it cheered the leader that their aim was so good.
And as the blacksmiths hasten to the forge, when pressing
Need urges weapons fashioned or ploughshares need repair:

These shovelling coal, and those expanding the bellows
To puff the flames hot; another the molten horseshoe
Plucks from the fire with pincers to place it on the anvil
And hammers strike, and star-like sparks fly off on all sides
From the still-soft metal, while the smithy rings like bells
Clamouring wildly, just so the young archers hurried,
Swishing their bolts at the target in constant showers
Until the birch tree bristled like a porcupine's back.
At last the trumpet signalled the end of the contest
And bade the archers set aside their bows. The king praised
Vratislav the victor, binding his brow with chaplet,
While lauding as well all the young marksmen for their skill.
One final time he called forth men to vie for glory:
'Let those of brawny shoulder now approach to display
Their skill at putting far afield the shot, the dense stone'.
So many men arose and made their way together
Into the ring, each eager to display his prowess.
But when they saw the immense stone brought forth by Bogdán,
Who bore it on his back, the ardour of many cooled;
Only Budimír and Dragšo remained undaunted,
The one a Slovene, the other a Carinthian
From the town of Želenec. Merisáv too joined them,
A Croatian of gigantic frame. Only these three
Feared not the boulder's challenge, and set to the contest.
Budimír first approached the stone — 'twas no light labour!
With one swift motion he hefted it above his head.
Spinning with lightness four times upon his own axis,
Swiftly releasing the stone into the clouds, grunting
Loudly, he fell to the turf under the momentum
And ploughed a ditch in the clean sand. The stone flew afar.
Then Bogdán approached the boulder at a sprightly pace,
And with strong arms, his veins bulging, he lifted it up,
Spun for momentum, and with strength incredible
Hurled the rock, which came to rest a bit beyond the first.
Third stepped forth Dragšo, no flimsy battler in war he,
But jealous as he was for victory in this broil,
Fortune smiled upon him not. For as he lifted high
The boulder with swift jerk, he swung it too far backwards,
And back he stumbled straining, until the weight won out
And fell behind him. He barely kept from tumbling down

Himself. Then, there stepped forth Merisáv, brave, many-skilled,
Like to the oak-trees of his fatherland strong, immense,
A master of his art, proud of his ability,
Up till now never bested in such games by any.
For on the River Sáva's banks, at its widest point,
From childhood on he'd often hurl stones across the flood,
Heavier, ever heavier were the stones he'd throw —
This is what won him the monicker of Merisáv,
Though he had been christened Slavomil by his parents —
Because he would *measure* the *Sáva* with his boulders.
Now, once he had killed a man resting in the pleasant shade
Of an alder on the far bank — fell, misguided throw! —
And as the man was known, and his kin armed for revenge,
Merisáv left his fatherland for Slovenia,
Where he lived a new life in banishment, near Ljubljana.
He lifted up the stone with one hand. It seemed light to him,
For he was used to flinging boulders greater by far.
And so he flung this stone using his right hand only
— No need of its sister's aid! — and on it whistled, clean
Past all the markers, falling to earth with such a crash
It shook all that was standing near, like to an earthquake.
All of the Germans trembled astonished, pale, speechless.
He loped then before the king who showered him with praise
And graced his victorious brows with oaken chaplet.
The trumpets blared a retreat: the games were at an end.

CANTO III

Furious at Svatopluk for commanding his idol to be tossed into the flames, and hearing, in Hell, news of his vanishing, Černobog decides to ascend to earth. Overcoming the gates of Hell, he passes through the darkness of eternal night by way of a bridge until, at last, he emerges once more into the light of day. At once he sets off for the land of the Slovaks. Disguising himself as Bytsa, once his priest, he begins to harangue the people, tempting them to raise another idol to him to worship as a god. But he is rebuffed everywhere with laughter, since the people have been taught the true Faith by the brothers Constantine and Methodius. And so he hastens off to Pannonia to take revenge upon Methodius, for by that time Constantine had already passed on to his reward. It is then that he learns that war is brewing. Setting aside his plans for vengeance, he takes himself to Karolman. And there at the tournament he catches sight of Svatopluk, and, learning that Karolman wishes to help him to regain his throne — under the condition of him holding his kingdom in fief from him — he hastens off to Slavimír on Devín with this news.

    Such was the entertainment grand with which the Germans
Feted Svatopluk the king. But that evil spirit,
Whose name was Černobog, nourished a cruel hatred
Towards him; indeed, he was swollen with bitter bile
Ever since the day when Svatopluk caused his idol
To be toppled and cremated, its ashes scattered
To the four winds so that no trace of it should remain.
From that time on he never ceased to scheme against him,
For no longer did the stench of goat flesh sacrificed
In holocausts by the Slovaks reach his nose in fumes
Of greasy smoke; rather, pummelled by the acrid swells
Of the infernal lake stinging him with their sulphur
He was whelmed in endless pain. But then Pikulík, sprite
And toady, brought him news that made his black heart rejoice:
King Svatopluk, his greatest enemy, had fallen;
And more: some over-haughty men in the Slovak council
Set Slavimír, however reluctant, in his place,
Threatening him with death and universal disgrace
Should he refuse the sceptre they thrust into his hands.
Swollen with infernal delight at this news, he rose
And spoke within his foul soul such evil words as these:

'At last time presents me with the opportunity
To win a full recompense for my loss, and regain
My former glory! All in vain then, did Svatopluk
Topple my idol and reduce it to mere ash!
For he now leaves the world, while I return thereto.
You'll set no obstacle before me now, Svatopluk!
I'll have free rein to wheedle the people back to me,
To serve me once more, bowing before me as a god!
So fickle is the human heart, easily deceived!
But first let's see whether the great Slovak king is here,
In Hell, amidst the horrors infernal, the searing flames.
How I would laugh at that! What a delight it would be
To gaze upon his torture and bank higher his flames!'
  Thus he, at once setting out to scour the foul pit
For any trace of him — but of course, without success.
And so he set off for the world, crossing the black plains,
The gore-befouled cliffs and offal-spewing volcanos
That ring the world of pain, past lakes and streams of hot pitch
Seething with fire and reeking with the stench of sulphur;
Thus he passed on to the far soot-slimy walls of Hell,
Which thrice ring the sewer of Tartarus. Ominous,
They arch inward to foil all attempts at scaling them;
Between each ring a boiling river flows,
Swelling with angry billows and dashing caustic foam.
Here stood three gates, so broad, that fully armed regiments
Could pass through them abreast when setting off to battle.
One gate is of poured copper, the second of iron,
And the third is chiselled of the hardest adamant.
Each (it is said) has locking-bolts as thick as millwheels
That seal it impenetrably to the wall, and more:
Two monsters hideous and evil blocked all access —
Abominations, no human pen can conceive them.
One had human form, the other half-female, hellish
Spawn both of them. One to each side they stood sentry there:
The dam, aborted fully grown from Lucifer's brain
While still on high, is of bright beguiling countenance,
But beneath her torso writhe scaly, viper-like tails
(Thick, each ends in a sting oozing with mortal venom,
Of reptiles and repulsive drakes in size surpassing
The dragons, which the ancient sorcerers used to ride

In days of old toward the seething ends of the earth,
Beyond the eastern sun, on whirlwinds splitting the skies
And tearing up whole forests by the roots). Her belly
Was — O filthy womb! — a cavern crowded with vicious
Dogs, baring their rabid fangs, snarling, barking, howling,
Stifled somewhat only when bestial hunger gripped them,
When they fell to a cruel banquet on their dam's guts,
Tearing at her intestines. Colder horror never
Harried that sea-hag, the abominable Scylla,
Whose pack disgusting never so fearfully gambolled!
And furthermore, beneath her breasts there coiled a huge snake
In a reel, secreting in her womb its foul poison,
And in the pauses of the howling of the glutted dogs
It flicked its forked tongue and hissed, whistling like three times
Six shepherds, or discordant winds battling in a cave,
Filling the bogs 'round about with terrible moaning.
When he'd aroused the dogs to their clamour once again
He'd sink his greedy fangs into her heart, to feast there.
In her right hand this filthy, repulsive, and cruel hag
Held an arrow, in her left a bow, mortal weapons;
Her name is Sin. Across from her there stood a monster
Crueller yet, the daughter of the former horror —
Might such a whelp be any more comely than the dam?
Her frame is skeletal, bones loosely bound together
By sinews, a mangy hide hardly covers her ribs;
Instead of eyes she has hollow black sockets. The scythe
She grips in her hand she never twitches in vain, blighting
All its shadow crosses to destruction. Lipless chaps
Reveal sharp teeth, snapping in constant hunger to fill
Her throat voracious, suffering ever with famine.
So gluttonous, that she would gladly swallow alive
Everything found in the earth and the sea and the sky,
And still her vile hunger never would be satisfied.
So vicious she is, and yet puffed up like royalty:
A crown she wears, and a rattling dry champion's laurels,
For she would never be bested by any hero —
Able to undo great warriors with a finger-flick,
Her name is Death. Such were the ghouls set to guard the gates,
Opening them to none, jealously clutching their keys —
And yet they spread them wide before their father Satan,

After he promised them release from the dark prison
And access to the upper, forbidden world of light
Where, in the pure air befouled not with the stench of Hell
They would live continually enjoying pillage.
First it was sharp-toothed Death who snatched her keys and turned them
Thrice in the locks, where they grated with evil clamour,
'Twas then that the gates, both of metal and chiselled rock,
Fell open with a deafening rumble resounding
So, that all Hell cringed in terror at the commotion.
But although the ghouls might open the gates infernal,
They could not close them, and since that time both day and night
The gates of Hell have been spread open wide, a black gullet
That belches forth smoke sulphurous, sable, through which flit
Evil shades of all types, dragging there and hurling in
The souls of those condemned to eternal punishment.
Through these, therefore, passed cruel Černobog, setting off
Across the same footbridge that Satan once had hung there
Spanning the black abyss, by the monsters Sin and Death,
When they set forth to attack our very first Parents,
Deserting the sentry posts at which they had been set.
   Broad it is, huge and firmly fixed with great iron fetters,
Stretching over the chasm from the gates of sorrow
To this, the world of men. This the evil spirit ascends,
Blinded at first by the blackness, his hearing deafened
By the chaotic cacophony mysterious —
It sounded like avalanches rumbling down the heights
Of the White Carpathians, smashing ancient oakwoods,
Beauteous forests, whose crowns had stretched to the skies,
High Mlíč or nearby Kolostina levelling; thus
The horrid clamour roared on, an eternal chaos
That swirls and eddies forever through the black vortex.
Here in eternal wrangling the elements battle:
Earth wars with air, turbid water with molten fire,
Heat with blistering cold, wetness with aridity;
Smooth with rough, light with the ponderous, as eternal
Enemies they fight, locked in an unending grapple.
As he stumbled along this black road, the evil thing
Met up with many demons bearing off sheaves of damned souls
To Hell's granaries, but he recognised no one
On account of the deep darknesses; only screaming

And imprecations met his ears from the hopeless lost.
For nine whole days the creature traversed the black desert,
At a quick pace, battling the vacuum with oar-like wings —
So far the road from the depths of Hell to us here;
Then less and less his ears were assaulted by the howling,
And the horizon cracked dimly gleaming to his sight;
Faintly, the plains below began to appear, flurries
Of wings parting before him in terror sounded, light
Tinged a cloud far-off, and toward it he sloped his course —
Before him spread our world then, and again he banked off,
Skimming near the earth — making for the Slovaks' country,
Speeding in his flight all the way to Bílá Hora
To alight at last on a cliff at Havranica —
Just there, where in days long past his idol used to stand,
Which clever Drevoslav Modranský carved from smooth log,
Chiselling with care a figure with a human face,
But down beneath its torso, the hoofed legs of a horse,
With a horse's tail too dangling from its hindquarters;
From the forehead sprouted long horns twisting upward;
A fat black tongue lolled obscenely between its wide lips.
Its eyes: open wide in a vacant stare of horror;
Its gnarled fingers ended in razor-sharp talons,
The blackness of the limbs bruited the name: Černobog.
Although horrid, to him that idol had been something
Beloved, as over the years it had given him
Much cattle, though the place there was quite deserted now;
All had been swept away but blackened splinters and stumps
About which ravens wheeled, cawing above their dire nests —
All shattered, though in past years many had worshipped him,
Sacrificing black goats, and cocks of varied plumage,
Raising their mournful dirges to appease his anger.
He gnashed his teeth at the memory, howling loudly
Until the very trees and hillocks trembled 'round him,
His wailing bellows echoing from the plains below:
  'O happy demesne, as long as my idol stood here!
How I would hasten here, from the farthest recesses
To the solemn sacrifices, the fattened goat-thighs!
O, the aroma that then filled these nostrils of mine!
There were times when the thick billows of smoke made me sneeze!
But now Svatopluk the cruel has stolen that from me,

By smashing my image and chasing me off to Hell.
So great the evil done to me, wretch, unbearable!
But now I'll serve his turn! Now I'll pay him back, and how!
If only I might clutch him in these talons of mine…!
So now I go to tempt his people to raise anew
An image in this high place, that they might worship me
Once more! The dice are thrown: let's see how it will turn out'.
   He finished, and descended from high Bílá Hora,
First changing his form to that of the aged Byksa,
From whom the settlement of Byksád derives its name —
He had once been a priest of Černobog, but now, dead,
Long ago having abandoned the sweet light of day
His ashes moulder in the gloomy grey tumulus.
Swarthy of face, he dressed in the black hide of a bear.
But his hair was white, as was his beard and whiskers.
Thus identical to him in face and in carriage
Černobog, full of wiles, made the rounds of each village,
Tempting the people with words such as these: 'O wretches!
How joyful and peaceful was the life you used to lead!
How bursting your goat-pens, how foison your fields of grain.
Drowning in wealth you were, as long as you paid homage
To my god Černobog! He turned away all evil,
He held terrors at bay, there was nothing you need fear.
But since that time, fools! when you abandoned his service
To worship a novel God, a foreign deity,
All your delight has vanished, all your ancient joy fled!
How much anxiety, how much misery is yours!
Cruel war is rushing near — hear you not the clatter
Of armour and weapons? The heavens thunder, the winds
Of war are whistling loud, clouds obscure the golden sun.
All of you shall suffer, and think you this not vengeance
For unfaithfulness? More death, more punishments await
You all — just such as met with your old king Svatopluk,
Reaping the death he'd sown by his own foul deeds, justly
Brought low by the punishing hand of great Černobog.
You know he died, suddenly abandoning the world;
And Mach and Zrost, who raised their hands in foul blasphemy
Against the image, hewing it to shameful splinters
With hatchets, also met with a righteous penalty:
Once, when they came together, bragging about their deed,

Černobog descended in a black cloud. In revenge
For their sacrilege, he skewered each on a harpoon
And dragged them off in each hand to deep Hell. Go and see:
The hole that opened wide to engulf them is still there.
Now, here's what I advise: cast away that foreign God
Unknown to your forefathers, and return to their faith,
The ancient faith, and raise anew here the old image —
Renew the sacrifices, renew the old worship!
Under Černobog's throne all this misery will cease;
Peace shall return, and your flocks and harvests shall increase;
You'll dance once more, and while away your lives rejoicing'.
  Thus the black evil disguised sawed away at his lies,
Striving to tempt the people and draw them to his side.
But all in vain, his efforts: he was greeted with jeers.
He reaped only mockery and shameful rejection.
Wherever he went, the folk rebuffed him with such words:
 'You shameless seducer! You boldfaced liar, you!
How dare you come so brazenly before us with such
Plain, horrid untruths, seeking to lead us to — that stump?!
Promising us the benediction of shattered wood?
What sort of help can he bring others, who's unable
To help himself? Tell us why that mighty god of yours
Allowed the hatchet blows to rain down, and permitted
His idol to be dragged off to the flames? He, a god?
How can you shatter God with axes and burn Him up?
There is another God, the living God — Konštantin
And Methodius, brothers, taught us to worship Him;
He is the Lord of Heaven and of Earth; He rules Hell;
All that there is came about once at His mere command:
The sky, this world, the sun arising on the first day,
The moon and all the stars that spangle the sky at night;
He makes the trees to blossom, and fills the skies with birds;
'Twas He created man. He rules and provides for all.
He disperses the clouds, and still He wields the lightning;
The storm submits to His governance. Now you, lost soul,
You weaver of deceit, if you do not wish to bow
Before the Almighty Lord of all along with us,
Follow that abomination of yours straight to Hell,
Quick as you can, be off with you, fly! Before our dogs
Rush up and tear your foul hide into tatters! For know:

Both Mach and Zrost, about whom you would spread such foul lies,
Are alive and healthy, and might take it into mind
To turn their hatchet staves to your backside! O, you'll see —
Both are above ground, neither has abandoned the light!'
   When the malignant abomination heard these words,
His heart swelled full to bursting with a bestial venom,
But he tamped down his black bile, and with shameful meekness
Asked — Where he might find those brothers? — those two apostles?
Humbly he asked, but all the while conniving vengeance.
At which he learned that three harvests had been gathered in
Since Konštantin left for Rome, which city he in turn
Abandoned for Heaven, but Methodius remained,
Residing now at the court of the pious Kocel,
Preaching the Gospel to the Pannonian people,
Instructing them in the worship of the one true God.
So he set off for there, but suddenly halted, stunned,
Catching sight of men arming for war — as he foretold
By chance — set for the invasion of Slovakia!
Cunning now took the place of ire; he set aside plans
Of revenge for later, and sped toward Velehrad,
Which Kocel's pious father Pribina himself built,
Encircling the whole with bastions and walls of rubble
(Which at the time in their tongue the Germans called Mosburg)
And from thence in speedy flight to Karolman's dwelling
There to take cognisance of the reasons for the war.
And while he was on his way he came across countless
Legions of people arriving at the tournament
To behold the games being held at the arena.
How dumbfounded he was, how he quaked in bald terror
To behold on the dais, next to King Karolman,
The King of the Slovaks enthroned in great honour there!
Then, waking from his stupor, he growled with bitter bile:
  'What a strange thing is this! Resurrected from the dead
King Svatopluk, the horrid — here in Bavaria?
What circumstances find him here, amongst the Germans?'
   Thus wondered he, and so, unmarked, he mixed in among
The crowds there, disguised as an old man in pilgrim's garb,
With bundle slung across his shoulder, and staff in hand,
As if he were some pious soul bent against the sun
Making a penitential pilgrimage, as it were,

On the long road to Záhrušica or to Šaštín,
Out of breath, panting, robes grey with the dust of the road,
But lightening his way with hymns from a raucous throat.
Thus he arrived at the tournament grounds, where, pausing,
His eyes feigning great wonder, he asked those standing near
'Tell me, my sweet sons, why have so many gathered here?
What does it mean, this great congress of so many folk?
What festival is this? And in whose honour given?'
   At this, the prudent Unwert, sitting nearest to him
On the springy carpet of soft meadow grass, answered:
'Grandfather, you alone in all the world know nothing
Of what is being prepared throughout our whole country?
The hammering of the skilled blacksmiths in their smithies
Day and night blazing, forging arms, has not met your ears?
On your way, have you not met with the crowds of men,
Of men at arms hastening here to swell the legions
And march off beneath the colours of King Karolman
Against the Slovak chief? Thunderheads are gathering
Towards the greatest tempest of war this world has seen!
His aim? To set Svatopluk upon the Slovak throne.
Then he shall hold the Slovak land in fief, and pay us
Yearly tribute. What you gaze at now's a tournament
In his honour, that he might rejoice with us, forget
The heavy wrong done to him, put far out of his mind
The pains of dank imprisonment suffered unjustly.
But come now — sit you down closer and behold the games —
You're sure to see nothing of the like ever again'.
   Thus said Unwert the wise. As soon as the deceitful
Spawn of Hell, clad in the lying robes of a pilgrim,
Heard what he said, he danced in the black depths of his soul.
Knowing his next step, feigning still, he answered with lies:
   'Where I live, in the deserted summits, no man's voice
Let alone clangour of blacksmiths's smithy meets my ears;
But long ago, when these limbs yet swelled with strength, this head
Was not yet white with the snowfalls of old age, I too
Had been a warrior, and many a Slovak thane
Had smarted from my blows. Mighty-limbed Kraslav himself
Might bear witness to the truth of what I say, how we
Pummelled in stout battle the troops of doughty Mojmír,
Swinging hammers such as none of you might heave today.

How many of our men were lain low, how many graves
Of our heroes bewept, until this right hand smote him
And swept him off to Hell! The buckler at my bosom
Deflected many a lance-thrust too in tournaments;
These locks that now pale with grey have also been enwreathed
With chaplets of victory envied by my rivals.
But now war and martial games no longer delight me;
It's quiet I seek, the solitude of still forests;
Let worthy Svatopluk win the throne of the Slovaks,
Or any other for that matter, it's all the same
To me, as long as he serves the good of our homeland.
No, you stay and enjoy the games; I've already had
My fill of such sport. It behoves me not my senses
To glut with such delights, being on my yearly tramp
Of pilgrimage in honour of God's Holy Mother'.
   Thus the sly goblin, who at once disappeared from sight,
With haste heading for Devín, with news for Slavimír.

CANTO IV

At night, Černobog comes to Slavimír at Devín, where, taking on the appearance of Rastislav, he appears to him in dream, revealing unto him that the Bavarians, along with the army of Svatopluk, who has subjected himself to the Germans, are on the march, aiming at depriving him of his crown. He sets before Slavimír's mind vivid images of the destruction with which these armies will ravage the countryside — how they set Svatopluk upon the throne, and how they cast Slavimír into prison after first blinding him. Upon awakening, Slavimír sends Ľudomír off on a secret mission to determine what the Bavarians intend. Retreating then to Hell, Černobog leads back into the light such comrades of his whom the pagan Slovaks had been wont to worship as gods. He addresses the assembled, instructing them, that as soon as the people are summoned to war, they should possess them with fury and direct the greatest number of them at Svatopluk himself, with him to grapple. They then scatter about the country to await the call to war.

    The sun by now had vanished from the fields, though not yet
Sinking beneath the smooth level surface of the sea;
It still stroked with its rays the summits of the mountains
Though in the valleys grey mists tumbled from the shoulders
Of Night as she spread her black wings, when on a high cliff,
Steep and exalted, foul Černobog beheld Devín.
The ancient legend speaks of Dobroslava, robust
And brave the maiden, who with *devy* no less stalwart
Raised on high above Moravia, where the Danube
Falls upon her bosom, this impregnable redoubt.
Sturdy it is, and beautiful, like they who built it,
And from them — *devy* — maidens — Devín derives its name.
As long as the sweet light of life bathed her countenance,
Dobroslava, with her regiments of Amazons,
Defended her city and realm from all armed assault —
Without any man to rule her as husband or king,
Though there was no lack of princes, native and foreign,
Who begged the maiden's mother for her hand in marriage.
Thither this plague of Hell now hastened on speedy wing.
Just as a hungry hawk hovering on the thermals
Speeds down to pierce the harmless dove or tuneful linnet,
Grasping her in his talons before she is aware

Of the attack — the piercing pain, the jolt of inter-
-rupted flight comes simultaneously with the rush
Of whooshing raptor's wings at the nape — the startled prey
Has barely time to peep in terror — futile protest
Of innocence when a predator is petitioned!
Mercy and pity are foreign to the carnivore;
He is not turned away from violence by sweet song,
And once having gripped his prey, he will not let it fall!
Thus did malicious Černobog rapidly descend
As soon as he'd sighted Devín from his soaring gyre,
At which he alit on the peak of the highest tower.
None of the people noticed him there, but the guard-dogs,
Fur bristling, lifted snouts in his direction and howled,
Raising together a panicked warning of danger.
There he paused, musing how to raise in Slavimír's soul
Cruel frenzy toward Svatopluk, blazing hatred.
The queen of night, the moon, by then had barely travelled
Half her path, dispersing the shadows with her golden sheen;
The exhausted people were deep asleep, the birds
And drowsy beasts were all submerged in deep, calm silence;
Only the nightingale trilled beneath the castle walls.
Decided and ready, his plans full-formed in his mind,
Certain that Slavimír was sunk deep in slumber too,
He suddenly swooped down to earth like a fallen star.
Smouldering, extinguishing each torch as he passes,
He threaded the deepest recesses of the keep.
Everyone there was asleep — except for Slavimír:
Watching, and coaxing pleasant melodies from his lyre,
Songs such as Jesse's son David, bard inspired of God,
Himself sang, and handed down to the chosen people.
So Černobog waited, impatient, till Slavimír
Should be overcome by sleep too, in the atrium
Glaring upon the famous images there gathered —
Unable to draw near the pious lord Slavimír
And listen to the hateful psalms that battered his ears.
With scowling mouth he gaped (for he could see well at night,
Better than in the clear light of day): Sláv, first of all,
Who gave a name to his people, who call themselves Slavs.
Next, the clever Morav, and the other forefathers
Who left their homes with their families (reluctantly)

To settle the Tatra regions (then empty mountains);
The greatest of these were Váh and Hron the courageous,
From whom the Rivers Váh and swift Hron have their names.
Morav himself settled on the banks of a river
Full of fish, which still today is called the Morava;
Father of Slovaks, known from his name 'Moravians'.
There too he beheld the fearsome Sám, gigantic-limbed,
Whose very countenance seems death, his eyes bright with sparks;
There Samomír, and tall as a cypress Samoslav;
And many other heroes of the motherland's wars
Beautifully imaged, in glorious succession.
Further on he beholds Mojmír, hateful to him, sword
Unsheathed in his right hand, and in his left — golden pledge —
The Cross. But most of all he marvelled at the maiden
Of many gifts, ever unvanquished Dobroslava,
Who led her troops in fierce battle against the Germans,
Panting with blazing fury, in the swelter of war,
Tall in the saddle, shoulder to shoulder with lovely
And many-wiled Ludomíra protecting her back,
Along with thousands of their comrades in arms — women,
Skilled at war, battling down the Bavarian troops.
But as he gazed further upon the heroic deeds,
The battling doughty victors, the stallions flashing
With gold, the ostrich feathers bobbing on the helmets,
The metal-tipped lances, the many-coloured hauberks,
He seemed to hear Slavimír's breathing grow more even,
At which he turned away from the lovely images
And made his way to the draped bedroom forbidden him,
First changing his appearance to that of Rastislav,
Whom the Germans deprived of both Kingdom and eyesight,
Tormenting him imprisoned in cold and bare dungeon.
And so the demon usurped both the visage and voice
Of Rastislav the king — blinded eyes moist with weeping,
Sightless, his mighty frame deprived of light's captaincy;
Thus he approached Slavimír sunk in first deep slumber
And with deceptive fatherly concern, tears streaming
From mutilated eye-sockets, he addressed him thus:
   'O sacred prince of Father reigning beyond the stars!
O mighty war-chief of the mighty Slovak nation!
Are you asleep, unaware of the catastrophe

That menaces you? You know not that when unfaithful
King Svatopluk vanished, ruined, when against your will
You were forced to take the throne to unyoke your nation
From Bavarian harness unto sweet liberty,
Believing that all was in order now, all secure,
You were merely fooling yourself! My clever nephew
Lives yet, indeed, lives to the ruin of the nation!
It wasn't enough for him, traitor, to betray me
Into the hands of the wrathful Germans who judged me
Worthy of the most shameful death — merciful Ludwig
Took pity, commuting one sharp pain into thousands,
Bursting the jellies of my two eyes with white-hot rods
And hurling me into an endless imprisonment.
Nor was this enough: he took upon himself
More shame, more evil, selling his own nation, that's right —
Involving his own people in his mischief, bending
A knee abased before the Germans, promising them
Servitude and vile, usurious, yearly tribute
Unbearable — and all so that he himself might reign,
But in subjection to a cunning German woman —
To roll in the sty each night with a Bavarian wife!
Arms have been forged, a numberless host is assembled,
All aimed at toppling you, and upon the vacant throne
To set him king, so he might raise a blunted sceptre.
And still you do not call for arms to shatter this foe?
Was it for this mere mouthful of sweet freedom — so brief! —
You freed your people from the yoke of foreign serfdom?
To see them fettered anew in baser slavery?'
   This, as if through the lips of Rastislav, the foul sprite
Thundered at Slavimír, whose cozened mind beheld him,
And what he bellowed, he heard. In blind terror, he thrashed
Upon his bed from side to side, just like a fish jerked
From its swift native stream, gasping on the riverbank,
Or as the fieldfare surprised by deceitful birdlime
Struggles in panic to free herself; alas, the more
She kneads the foul putty with her feet, the more it grips them;
The more that she beats her now useless wings, thrusts upward
Her aching shoulders, the more she gums them, becoming
The unwitting lackey of her gaoler — Slavimír
Thus struggled with slumber thrice, pushing from the bedclothes

On weak elbow; thrice striving to pry open eyelids
As heavy as lead, and muster the powers of speech
With lips reluctant, tongue numbed and sluggish — so gripped he
By the overwhelming nightmare that tormented him.
With ever more vivid images of disaster
The evil spirit strove to chafe Slavimír to rage,
The sharpest of these being (and it might well suffice
Alone) how an immense force of Bavarians spill
Into the country of the Slovaks from all sides — wild
The thunder of horses' hooves and tramping feet, stallions
Neighing — the dust they kick up obscuring the sunlight.
He saw cities engulfed in flame, villages afire;
His nostrils seemed to scent the acrid odour of smoke.
Surrounded on all hands he seemed by an inferno.
He saw, he heard — bitterness pummelled him from all sides:
Pillaging everywhere — gold, silver, all costly things;
Horses, sheep and goats, milch-cows and whole herds of oxen
Were whipped away bellowing, the herdsmen barely escaping
The emptied pastures, panic everywhere, all the air was charged
With terror. He beheld anguished mothers looking on
While armoured murderers struck down the husbands and sons
Who dared attempt to protect their goods; with hair unbound
They raced here and there, lifting their eyes to the heavens;
They wrung their hands or raked fingers over tear-stained cheeks.
He heard their fearful sobbing, the frightful whimpering
That reaches the very stars in accusation, beats
In echoes from the deaf crossroads and squares of Heaven.
Mingled with these, his name — anathematised for weakness,
For failing to protect his country from the Germans —
Then he beheld the victorious Bavarians
Ascend the slopes of Devín and enter the stronghold
Unopposed, having slaughtered the pickets who crossed them
With swords unsheathed, to enter his chamber and haul him
Roughly from his bed, to fetter his arms and his legs
In rough chains. And then he beheld haughty Svatopluk
In royal robes ascend the throne, taking the sceptre
— Gift of the Germans. Before him he is roughly dragged
To the jangle of fetters that spark at the friction!
He shall be cast into a dungeon, deprived of light.
The last thing he saw: glowing pokers approaching him

To spit the organs of sight, leaving behind sockets
Sizzling, smoking — (here the evil sprite wafted a breeze
From the hearth embers to his nose — he smelt the rank stench
Of the bright jelly fouled; in his sleep he jerked away
As if he couldn't bear the searing pain. Thus he thrashed,
Like some lion roused from his cool rest by a spark
Blown on the breeze from an aspen-grove where a shepherd
Was smoking beehives to becalm the bitter drones
At honey-gathering; the ember falls by blind chance
Upon his nape; awakened from his slumber, he rears
And shakes his mane, and shudders in angry arousal.
Just so Slavimír leapt from out his bedclothes, roaring —
So great was the clamour that his bodyguards rushed in.
As sleep fell from his eyes still sighted — no glowing rods
Menacing their lights — he looked around for Svatopluk
And saw neither him, nor his Bavarian allies.
He shook his arms and legs and found they were unfettered,
No cruel, heavy, jangling chains hampered his movement.
His eyes then swept the chamber for wretched Rastislav,
But nor did they find the unfortunate, blinded king.
And though at first he foundered in the foul morass of dream,
Flailing in panic with his limbs at the unreal threat,
He was suddenly bathed with relief: An empty dream,
A horrid nightmare it was, but nothing more than that.
Just as when a black storm has raged long with violence,
Quaking the earth and shaking great cliffs, winds lashing,
Lightning stabbing, suddenly the tempest passes on,
The thunder ceases growling, the rock-faces are still,
The earth is soft again, and the thirsty soil drinks in
The cool rain falling from the gentle clouds, nourishing
The grainfields, and smiling beasts pad through copses refreshed —
So now Slavimír, calmed, summoned his aide Ludomír,
A trusted friend, his cleverest advisor, always
Ready with sound advice in every situation.
Friends they had been since childhood, and comrades-in-arms too.
Such words he spoke to him upon his having entered:
    'Good Ludomír, my ever-worthy friend, and my peer!
The leaves of my heart have never been closed before you,
And now I need to let you know what I've just been through.
Rastislav, our former ruler, deprived of his sight,

Appeared before me in a dream — just now, I saw him,
And heard a menacing prediction from his own lips —
He sang that Svatopluk lives yet, and is conniving
To sell his own nation once more into slavery
To the Bavarians, promising them fealty,
Harsh tribute and shameful servitude of the Slovaks,
If only to obtain our sceptre and a woman
Of their nation. Legions already stand under arms
Preparing to invade us, and set him on our throne.
I shall be taken then, my two eyes pierced, my limbs chained.
His spirit urged me now to call for arms and beat back
The cruel invader at the gates. Indeed, I beheld
Our borders forced, our cities aflame, and pillaging
Of all sorts; Bavarians storming Devín, slaying
All men faithful to me, overwhelmed by their attack.
I saw haughty Svatopluk enthroned, glaring at me;
I saw the glowing white-hot rods nearing my two eyes
And felt the shackles pinned to both my wrists and ankles
Before they hurled me into a deep dungeon. Such things
I saw. My faithful friend, I place no trust in visions;
Dreams are mendacious things, and empty. Yet all the same,
For our security, and clearer intelligence,
Take you off to Bavaria now, and with sharp eye,
Unseen yourself, study the lay of the land — find out
If they seek peace, or are preparing war against us
Slovaks. Take care not to reveal the slant of your trip,
So as neither to offend them, nor cause us disgrace,
Lest cunning get the upper hand of truth, and foil us.
Then make your way back to us as quickly as you can.'

   Thus Slavimír. At once his friend went off, eagerly,
Making his swift way into Bavaria. Meanwhile,
Dawn arose from her golden bed in the east, and spread
Wide the rosy gates of the fresh morning. Presently,
The evil spirit, having worked Slavimír's terror,
Scurried off to summon forth from deepest Tartarus
His comrades, who in ancient pagan times had also
Been gladdened by the sacrifices of the Slovaks,
But since then had been sunk in sulphurous lakes and bogs.

   There is a place in the region of Bílá Hora,
Set against the rising sun, to which it bows, sloping

From Havrana, not far from Skala, known as Šaštin —
All meadows now, but back then, covered in thick birch woods.
And here a pit yawns, as deep as the gullet of Hell,
Into which thunder great waters with a frightful din.
This gorge was used by demons to ascend to the light
To terrorise people and harm them as they might,
Until the pious Horislav, the hermit, bound them
Deep in the pit with prayer, from which time forth there never
Arose from thence anything save malignant vapours
And puffs of steam rank with sulphurous stench. It is there
That Černobog descended and with iron bellow
As loud as he could manage summoned forth his cronies.
So loud he shouted, that the earth around him trembled,
The dire sound echoed from the mountains, the animals
Raced to their dens and coverts trembling. Then the clamour
At last reached the ears of his infernal brotherhood.
As soon as the name of Černobog beat their eardrums
They took heart and rose again through the abysmal air.
The first to emerge was Radogosť, who not long ago
Received latreia on Radhosť — which still bears his name.
There, on a sacred meadow, where his foul idol stood,
Many an ox was slaughtered, many a sheep was slain,
Many a sweet jug of mead swilled at the banqueting,
The air reverberating with the sound of singing,
Droning instruments and feet beating the turf in time —
Such orgiastic rites and ceremonies (they thought)
Would guarantee them victory in battle, and fame.
Following him came Chásoň, purported deity
Of sun and light, once worshiped on the heights of Zobor,
But now discarded, sunk in gloom and darkness fretting.
Svatovít rushed forth, a monster of gigantic limbs,
Four-faced, so that he might be gazed upon from all four sides.
His idol stood in a large temple on Velehrad —
A god prophetic, gripping in hand a full wine-cup,
And yet he was unable to foretell his own fall.
Trigláv came in his train, and Stríbog, lord of the winds:
The former frequented Kriván, where glitters the lake
Called Morské Oko, the latter worshipped in Buchlov.
Behind them stumbled Rarach (said to chase off horrors).
And then the greatest lover of the pan-pipe, worshipped

By shepherds and farmers, Veles, courted by sundry,
Then Zmok, Pikulík and finally, tiny Škrátek,
Said to protect the home-hearth, while those watched over wealth.
More demons followed them, once feared by ancient Slovaks,
Whom they induced to honour — as gods! — logs and kindling
With praise due only to the eternal, living God.
Now, when they had gathered in a narrow cliffside chink,
Černobog rose before them, his eyes flashing with ire,
And in their midst addressed such spirited words to them:
  'O brethren! Residents once of starry palaces,
Now fellow-sufferers in the deepest pit of woe!
Remember how we, by our own might, once re-emerged
From the darknesses into this upper world of light,
To usurp unto ourselves the worship due to gods —
Slight recompense for the honour once stolen from us!
O, how we were regaled with sacrifices of fat
Bulls, sheep, milk-fed goats and the flesh of black-plumed roosters,
Reduced to greasy ash in unceasing holocausts!
How many libations of foaming wine and sweet mead
Were poured into our thirsty gullets by the thousands,
Our ears caressed by music frolicsome, ribald song!
Then, there was nothing but delight, nothing but dancing;
So much so, that we no longer regretted our loss,
The great deprival of our starry homes and demesnes
Heavenly; but now, cast down into the glooms of Hell,
We're made to suffer the torment of hunger and thirst —
And the worst pains that any cruel mind might devise.
Nothing remains us now but hot vengeance — but it too
Burns him who wields it, unless he slakes its scalding heat
With results. Now, who is to be blamed for our exile?
Rastislav, Mojmír, and Svatopluk, who's living still.
And who was first amongst our envious enemies
To urge on, and give occasion for our overthrow,
And set the bolt-wielding Lord of Heaven in our place?
Was it not the Bavarians who seduced them thus?
It is they who are the first cause of our misfortune,
Our ruin. Are we not then obliged to take revenge,
And drown the ever-burning embers that scald our hearts?
There's nothing sweeter to the heart than to take revenge —
Have we no right to cast again for honours divine?

Hope hasn't quite abandoned us, not yet! Now's the time,
Now the moment has come, as it seems Bavaria
Is gathering legions numberless from every land
And Svatopluk, so firmed, is aiming to seize the throne
With violence, to wrench away the Slovak sceptre,
Unless Slavimír himself, or the other Slovaks,
Acknowledge him their king of their own unfettered will.
But he has bent a servile knee before the Germans,
Swearing to them the base enslavement of his people,
And usurious tribute, well-nigh unbearable.
So now, disperse yourselves throughout the land entire,
And when you hear the trumpets blare, calling men to war,
Enrage the people, ignite a cruel flame in their hearts;
Make Svatopluk disgusting to them, smear him traitor,
Have them all hate him, egg them on to war against him.
Should he fall, the Germans would suffer a mortal blow;
And, by some chance, should Slavimír meet with ruin too,
Light work 'twill be to tempt the victorious remnant
Of the Slovak folk to our side, to cast off the yoke
Of foreign dependence, to abjure their foreign God,
And reestablish the ancient rituals in praise
Of us. Now, to the task: tickle their pride-bloated souls,
Fill them with volatility and the rage of beasts.
When you've well-banked their fires, congregate at Plaveč.
There, in the empty cavern, await my further words'.
   Thus spoke the black one. With tongues lolling, long they listened
To his haranguing. Nary a one made a grimace,
Snorted, or shook their polls. As a sign of their pleasure
At what he planned, what he revealed to them with his speech,
Thrice did they nod their horned heads, thrice they lashed their tails,
Thrice did they pound the shuddering earth with their cloven hooves,
And just as many times they twisted their lips in grins,
And with a horrid bellow, proclaimed aloud his praise.
And then, like to a murder of ravens taking flight
Around the Slovak land, they dispersed, seduced by dreams
Of coming glory, to await the blare of trumpets
And the slogan of their leader, calling them to war.

CANTO V

Upon Ľudomír's return, Slavimír assembles the leaders of the land to parliament and reveals to them what Rastislav uncovered to him in his dream. Ľudomír confirms it, reporting on what he saw during his mission among the Bavarians: that is, that they have given over to Svatopluk command of an army, as he has sworn subjection to them, so that with these troops he might force the Slovaks to acknowledge him as their king in the event that they refused to do so of their own free will. Slavimír then asks the assembled men if it is war, or subjection, that they prefer. Zemižžen advises armed resistance, upon which all the assembled opt for war too, as does Slavimír. Heralds are then sent out throughout the land announcing to the people that they are to prepare for war, and gather at Devín. Černobog and his minions as well set about inflaming the people to reach for the sword. A ferment of anger ensues. The first to set off for war is Zemižžen, followed by Milín, Slavboj, Ľuboslav and the rest of the leaders with their men.

   As lion cubs await with yearning their dam's return,
Their stomachs pinched with hunger and their throats parched with thirst,
While the lioness stalks afar through thick savannahs,
Or on her daring hunt prowls through the nearer thickets
To drag near some fallen carcass of the timid cow,
Or grapple with the buffalo, who when cornered
Lowers his horns in rage, so Slavimír awaited
In fraught expectation the return of Ľudomír,
And in anticipation of the news he would bring
Back from Bavaria, he sent forth all his heralds
To summon to a moot all the great ones of the land.
In haste these assembled, and set down to counsel, while
Slavimír directed such words at those there gathered:
   'My worthy friends, we have deluded ourselves with hope,
Lulling our hearts into a false sense of security
That, freed from the yoke of Bavarian subjection
We should behold this land bloom in peace perpetual.
For a tempest of war even now is hurtling near,
The stormclouds of which will soon rain down upon our heads
The shackles and gyves of slavery. Not long ago
Our wretched king, Rastislav, appeared to me in dream
Revealing to my eyes a horrible, looming threat.

"'O sacred prince of Father reigning beyond the stars",
He said, "O mighty war-chief of the Slovak nation!
Are you asleep, unaware of the catastrophe
That menaces you? You know not that when unfaithful
King Svatopluk vanished, ruined, when against your will
You were forced to take the throne to unyoke your nation
From Bavarian harness unto sweet liberty,
Believing that all was in order now, all secure,
You were merely fooling yourself! My clever nephew
Lives yet, indeed, lives to the ruin of the nation!
It wasn't enough for him, traitor, to betray me
Into the hands of the wrathful Germans who judged me
Worthy of the most shameful death — merciful Ludwig
Took pity, commuting one sharp pain into thousands,
Bursting the jellies of my two eyes with white-hot rods
And hurling me into an endless imprisonment.
Nor was this enough: he took upon himself
More shame, more evil, selling his own nation, that's right —
Involving his own people in his mischief, bending
A knee abased before the Germans, promising them
Servitude and vile, usurious, yearly tribute
Unbearable — and all so that he himself might reign,
But in subjection to a cunning German woman —
To roll in the sty each night with a Bavarian wife.
Arms have been forged, a numberless host is assembled,
All aimed at toppling you, and upon the vacant throne
To set him king, so he might raise a blunted sceptre.
And still you do not call for arms to shatter this foe?
Was it for this mere mouthful of sweet freedom — so brief! —
You freed your people from the yoke of foreign serfdom?
To see them fettered anew in baser slavery?"
    'These words sad Rastislav spoke to me, and then vanished.
Then in my dream I saw Bavarian hordes spilling
Into our beloved Slovak homeland from all sides;
Our cities engulfed in flame, our villages afire,
Pillaging everywhere, looting everything; I saw
Bavarians ascend the slopes of Devín, and slay
The brave pickets who resisted them with swords unsheathed.
Then I beheld haughty Svatopluk in royal robes
Ascend the throne, taking our sceptre into his hands

— Gift of the Germans; — the last thing I saw were white hot
Pokers of iron thrusting near my eyes to blind them,
Before I was to be cast into prison, in chains.
Such visions came to me in dream — filling me with dread.
And that these were not vain imaginings, mere vapours
Of a troubled mind asleep, tell us now, Ľudomír,
What you saw in Bavaria just now, what you heard
About these threats?' He finished, and then Ľudomír spoke:
  'Valiant Slavimír! Sweet leader in time of need!
You sent me into the land of the restless Germans
There to discover, secretly, what they were planning
In our regard, if anything. Know then: No sooner
Had I entered in than the sound of blacksmiths smiting
Metal to weaponry met my ears, anvils ringing
In the fiery, angry forge. As I moved further on
I saw the fresh-cooled darts and swords glittering, bristling,
Amidst the legions of men in a country set on war.
Their cities are transformed to muster-camps awaiting
Recruits, whom here and there I beheld hastening in:
Young men, eager for the fray. There I also learned
That Svatopluk had bent the knee before the Germans
Cruel, swearing them subjection and shameful slavery,
And furthermore, binding us to annual tribute:
A century of horses, yearly, and of oxen
Two times that, and likewise two hundred silver talents,
And troops auxiliary in time of war — to bolster
Germanic arms; for that reason only he was freed
From his dark imprisonment, unpinned from his fetters,
Though he be chained now to a Bavarian princess;
This was the price he paid to take command of the troops —
With them, Slavimír, you, and all the rest of us as well
To dislodge from our places and lord over us,
Taking by violence what we might be loth to grant
Of our free will. And that yearly tribute I spoke of?
It will be stripped from us. There you have what I have seen
With my own eyes in Germany, and heard with these ears'.
  He'd barely finished speaking when Slavimír once more
Addressed them: 'So you see the reason for my summons,
Calling you here to moot! You well know what wretched fate
Befalls the slave: the shame, the grovelling. So tell me:

Which do you choose? Resistance, or bitter enslavement?
Here stands the Bavarian yoke: will you bend your necks?'
   The floor was now open to the elders who would speak,
But they were all so stunned at what they heard that no one
Piped up. They sat there motionless and dumbstruck, all.
As when a strong wind pushes dark clouds across the sky,
Bruising the sun's gay face with livid, broody darkness,
And in the gloom of early thickened night all is hushed:
Overwhelmed in dread of the tarry blackness, the beasts
Cringe before the coming storm, so silent grew the lords.
For none of them expected such despairing tidings;
None doubted up till now but Svatopluk had perished,
Smote in the cruel conflict. And here: he's still alive?
Then prudent Zemižížen stood up and took the floor,
A man known to be wise, and always ready to give
Sound advice, no matter how dire the situation.
Wisdom shone from his placid eyes and calm face, therefore
He was a trusted man, universally esteemed.
He was the first to break the silence, speaking these words:
   'Renowned lord, and all you elders gathered here in moot!
Has Almighty God placed our dear nation in our care
Just so that we should harness it to a foreign yoke,
Exchanging freedom's songs for the groans of bondage?
Who was it granted the Germans such a privilege
To oppress the poor, and lash them into subjection?
O Svatopluk, damned Svatopluk! What were you thinking?
How you have disappointed us in our hopes of you,
Who saw in you a manly and unflustered leader,
A doughty heart, such as should defend our motherland,
Never permitting her to be cast into fetters
Foreign! And now, wretch, you have sold her, and us as well
— So long toiling in her cause — to purchase... slavery?
Whatever could have tempted you to such villainy?
Were you not once the greatest advocate of freedom?
Far better had it been had you fallen in battle
Than lived on to commit so immense a treachery!
To drag us into misery, and cover your own name
With filth! Was it for this we warred under Rastislav
As now under our beloved war-chief Slavimír,
And spilled so much dear blood, in order to wrest freedom

Into our hands, only now — by our own free will — to
Let it fall from our grasp? What shall our descendants say
— Those future generations groaning in subjection —
Of us, for so base an act? Do you imagine us
Quaking now? Hearts a-flutter at mere rumours of war?
Do you think we shall toss away our weapons, meekly,
And approach the Germans with sloping necks, furrowing
The earth toward them on grovelling knees? Mewling, vile
Cattle, not men, shambling into the waiting harness
Without whip or prod to sting their hides? Subjection? No!
To arms, I say! Let us take in hand our weapons now
And rush to battle, to meet the haughty enemy
With the cries of men determined from massed throats booming!
Let us defend our golden freedom, rescue our land
From ruin! And should chance deprive us of victory,
Let us die proudly, rejoicing, that we die as men,
Free men, and not as slaves to the Germans, shivering!
We shall serve no German, nor bear his yoke on our necks!'
   He'd barely finished speaking when all began to cry
'To arms! To arms! And off to battle, fiercely!' No voice
Was silent, nor dissenting, and the roar of their cries
Echoed like thunder from mountain crag, vale and hillock.
Then Slavimír arose, and addressed them in such wise:
   'This arm I too raise in favour of going to war.
Better to die a heroic death! Come, let's tempt fate.
Better to be hacked apart or bled dry, drop by drop,
Fighting for liberty, than to groan beneath a yoke!'
   Thus said he, then he sent forth his swift-footed heralds
To cry unto the people to arm themselves for war
And hasten all to Devín, where shortly they did come.
   When Černobog — black abomination — had fired up
His mates, he set off in search of a steed, and found one, white
Of coat, on rough Vetrlín — the kind that Svatovít
Received at times in offering, upon which he'd ride
Clad in fierce armour, through the night, as they say, to strike
Terror into the hearts of those who wronged his faithful,
Wreaking his vengeance upon them (so the story goes).
And now, as he saw the banners flash upon the heights
Of Devín, upon which he'd kept his eyes trained, watchful,
And the swift-footed heralds set out with their tidings,

Moving the land to war, he too leapt astride his steed,
A horn in his left hand, and in his right a sabre
Gory with blood; on his helmet blood-red feathers bobbed:
Threatening, ominous, as if War herself brooded
Above his shoulders. In such wise he galloped away,
First taking the road along the River Morava.
Then, once in the fields, where no eye could note his progress,
He clipped time by flying through the air like a swift hawk.
But drawing near castle, village, or populous town,
Whenever he came across men preparing for war,
He hastened near, blaring loudly on his oliphant,
Shaking aloft his bloody sword and calling to them:
   'To arms! To arms, sweet comrades — thus our leader summons:
For Svatopluk the traitor has basely sold us out
To the Germans. Even now they are marching deeper
Into our dear motherland, burning our villages,
Pillaging our goods, and forging fetters for our necks!
And so to arms! To arms all, in defence of our land!'
   Thus does he shriek, thus does Černobog fill the ears of all.
Both near and far they hear his cries and trumpet echo,
Insidiously injecting reptilian venom
Of cruel anger and bestial ferocity
Into their hearts, poisoning them with hatred for vile
Svatopluk the traitor — urging sharp blades upon them.
Swiftly through Moravian Hana he sped his way
To the Odra, and from thence to the hillocks of Váh,
Thence to the Danube meadows he galloped, nimble
His steed — to the Hron re-bruiting the slogans of war.
From here he made his way to the Tisa, abundant
In fish, following its valley to its bubbling source;
And there he meandered criss-cross, trotting here and there,
Twice toward the rising sun and twice to where it sets;
Twice toward the freezing north and twice to the warm south —
He traversed the whole land — that gargoyle! — every region.
But as he made to set off on the road a third time,
Once more to fly through the land from border to border,
His steed balked, fainting from the constant gallop, ready
To fall, exhausted with bearing the weight on his back,
Singed with the demon's beating wings, no longer able
To race over the earth and, bounding, to clear hurdles,

Nor to skim through the light breezes. The charger stumbled,
And broke down, knelt, and rolled onto his heaving flank
Spreading his long mane upon the cool sand of the path.
Černobog cursed, and spit black bile from his evil gob.
   No less the black battalions of the hornéd goblins
Set to their task, invading the nearby villages,
All settlements, in both day and nighttime, ceaselessly,
Like shaggy cauldrons of bats when the evening falls,
Spinning and weaving with ease here and there,
Chattering folk to a frenzy, spreading truth and lie
To urge the herds on to action, pricking and spurring,
Filling their breasts with cruel ire, loathsome ferocity,
A feverish, angry rabies, hate for Svatopluk,
Rousing them to take arms against their vile countryman
The traitor, and his cohorts the pillaging Germans.
   Thus did the sable legions of evil churn the land
To a ferment, stinging the men with their demons' barbs,
Whipping them on to the dire battle. Arrows were fletched,
Spears forged and swords ground sharp, pikes turned, helmets riveted,
Bucklers were hammered, lances bound tight with copper sheathes,
Bows were planed smooth, maces, clubs tempered over the flames,
Steeds led from stables, prancing eagerly for the charge.
   Sweet Umka, muse! Who hath witnessed this old world's events,
Sing now, and say how many war-chiefs were set aflame,
From what far-flung regions did they hasten to the stour,
Leading their mighty hosts, panting eagerly for war
Through the fields obscured by the dust clouds of their tramping;
Eager for war, to defend freedom, to slay their foes.
   First of all set out, with his army, Zemižížen,
Who first advised resistance to treacherous Svatopluk,
First to take arms to chase the cruel German from his land.
Steadfastly the Belohorci accompanied him,
Brave lads from fair Bystrica, Lamač and Dúbravka,
From Zóhor and Stupava rebuilt, Lozorno, Mást,
Where once gigantic battlements soared into the sky,
But now nothing remains except sad hovels scattered
Amidst ruins and cold cinders. From Jablonový
Leváre, Sološnica, Láb, and from Závod too,
And from all three Bory set among rich fields of hemp.
From Veľký Bor, where lies the broad-spreading pasturage,

Where once, as ancient lore has it, rolled huge inland seas
Which, drying up, left behind great deposits of sand.
Immense forests took root there then, spreading far and wide.
Armed with stout weapons fashioned from the timber lopped there,
The men rush at the head of all forces to Devín
Whenever it is threatened by Bavarian arms.
Then those from the banks of great Danube, lesser Dudváh,
The cool Gidra, the briskly flowing Trnávka waters,
The swift-racing Blava never known to freeze over;
Those who herd cattle at the feet of the high mountains
And those who turn the rolling earth with spade untiring
Beneath the grapes that yield the fiery wine in Modra,
Jur, Častá, lofty Pezinok and bonny Udolíe
In which Otto, battered by the Romans, found refuge
And, falling in love with it, lived there, left it his name.
Following him came a giant — scion of Strojmír,
Who once planted the broad plains at the foot of Zobor
With wicker, and taught the people how to water it —
Milín comes, bearing a hefty javelin of stout oak
Tipped with a vicious barb that can pierce any armour.
With him came young men, all splendid, select warriors
Sent by ancient Nitra and the foothills of Zobor,
Admirable Močenok, Frašták rich in vineyards,
Čachtice, Brezová, Turá, and those who sip the rill
Of Horečka; from the healing spas at Píšťany;
They come from Nové Mesto, which gazes at the Váh,
From all the magnificent meadows spreading about
There. From the banks of the Chvojnica meandering
The mounds under Javor, delightful Myjova stream,
From the hot springs of Bojnice, craft-rich Privizda,
Especially old Topolčaný's fields of saffron.
The brawny Paderák comes from the banks of Nitra,
From cloudy Žitva's moors that stretch as far as eye can see,
Who furrows the black grainfields with deep-plunging ploughshare;
And those who live where Danube with its mouth voracious
Sucks at the Váh to bear it away to its delta —
Two thousand infantry, and three squadrons of horsemen
With lances armed, bows slung across their backs — these came too.
   Mighty Slavboj, immense of stature, swept on as well,
Bearing a sword forged by Smílo, the likes of which few

Are to be seen, if any; this in bloody battle
Swinging with one swipe he'd cut his enemies in twain.
With him came picked troops offered by that city founded
By Roman Terence in the beautiful Váh valley —
Over which tower keep impregnable and fortress
Firm on the clifftop; from magnificent Dubnica,
Townsmen from the boroughs of Žilina, from Rajec,
From Púchov, Kysuce, and Povážská Bystrica,
From Ilava, Beluša, Pruské, Varin, Čadca,
And the Beckov vineyards, where the sour grape is pressed.
Men came too from the regions watered by the swiftest
Surge of the Váh, ploughmen of the black earth it pounds through,
Collapsing their tillage when flooding it swells in might,
Each of them bold, and of a figure like their leader.
   Suddenly, Ľuboslav appeared, a bolder battler
Than he is nowhere to be found throughout the Slovak lands;
Everything about him is beautiful: his stature,
His countenance, and his attire — all gorgeous; lovely
The sparkles that flash from his gold-encrusted armour;
Lovely the accoutrements of the troops given him
To lead by that famous and proud city of Velehrad,
Whose battlements unshakeable soar unto the stars,
Seat golden and delightful of Slovak kings of old;
Its senior Prerov, between Priboň and Ičína
Lying, sent men too, as did Kyjov and Ostrov bright
With blooming meads, Polešovice and still unwalled
Brod, and farthest Bzince of flamboyant garths renowned,
The beauty of which cedes nothing to Veselí
Nor Strážnice. There came marching as well those who slake
Their thirst with the rushing flow of the Odra or Bečva
Twice-coursing, meandering around windy Radhošť.
   Further, riveted in heavy armour and mounted
Astride a Czech stallion with white mane and milky tail,
Pure white indeed down to its knees, prancing, leading
His men came fulgent Jaromír, lifting high aloft
His threatening lance, as did his soldiers behind him,
In valiant imitation of their valiant war-chief,
The greatest number chosen men from Brno and splendid
Záhrušice and Lednice washed by the Dyje;
From Boskovice, from Letovice and Slavkov

Rich in fisheries; proud Hodonín offered her sons
Too, from low-lying Bredslava and her neighbourhood
Settled by Podlžáci, broad and wide. There came whole hosts
From Ilava and Znojmo and the Dyje floodplain;
Neighbours of the evil Germans, these too seized their arms
And rushed off all together to engage in battle
Dire. As in the autumn the leaves tumble from the trees
When the bellowing wind blasts the boughs, or thick hailstones
Batter them, pelting and rebounding, spilt from burly
Grey clouds roiling in the heavens, thus came these rushing.
   Nor did that man of many talents, Hodislav, wish
To tarry at home-hearth. Although advanced in his years,
He'd left behind him the care and effort of battling,
Hanging up his weapons, devoting himself to peace,
Rejoicing in nothing but his acres of black earth,
Which he tilled with a thousand ploughshares, and his forests,
The shade that the copses provide in summer's swelter,
The dewy meadows through which his streamlets purl, often
Wandering to their banks to rest a while, he came too.
In his age, he was gladdened by shepherd's songs, the trills
Of carefree birds, the intricate plucking of the harp
Of which he was a master, rehearsing the legends
Of the great wars waged by great heroes, their mighty deeds —
A bard now, in command of caesura and metre crisp,
But since disaster loomed, menacing his fatherland,
He marched forth, tossing aside the lyre in anger
(The sympathetic strings growling as it fell); his arms
He took down from their dusty pegs, and set off to fight.
Then, able Milibor, leading the Olomouc hosts
From Unčov, Tremsko, Prostějov, from Třebová
And Slavetín. But when Milibor saw Hodislav,
He set his legions at the old warrior's command,
Who received the marshal's staff in hand once more in joy,
To lead the doughty regiments of the stout Hanáks.
   Borislav, that fearsome champion, he rushed on too,
Who'd spit the dragon that had terrorised his region,
Growing and growing, the foul beast, spewing venom, clouds
Of fatal vapour, usurer of death, of gaping
Maw that could swallow a man entire — who had ravished
The land, slaughtering far and wide, until Borislav

The brave, who could not bear such evil, rose against him.
With unflustered heart he set upon him, while the beast
Was sunning himself outside his gore-filthy cavern;
He rammed his mighty spear into that scabrous gullet
And thick his winged darts flew, the bow's tendon humming
As steadily he sent screaming arrows from quiver
Into the quivering flesh of the drake. He drew near,
And before the dragon quite comprehended the threat,
Punctured his evil eyes. Bellowing with violence,
And hissing horridly, he wrung the lance from the grip
Of the knight and shattered it against the ground. Three times
On scaly wing he strained to soar above the earth, and
Three times he fell like thunder. Writhing in his anger
To this side and that he rolled, uprooting trees, smashing
Rockface, flailing blindly with barb, clawing the void,
Missing the man with each swipe, though rocks flew heavenward.
Defeated, he dragged his bulk into the sad cavern
And there expired with one last, immense bellow of pain.
For some time yet the exhalation foul of that cave
Poisoned the air nearby to sicken each animal
Who happened near, until the people sealed it with stone.
  So great a champion as he hastened off to the fray,
His shield emblazoned with the image of the dragon
He slew, carved by clever Myslota of Vavrečka,
A seven-ply shield of hide skinned from mighty aurochs,
Taut leather, and just as many sheets of sturdy brass.
He led regiments numberless of young warriors
From Babia Hora and Kriváň of booming waters,
From Volovec and the high Tatras that scrape the clouds,
Others from the Fatras whose chaplets are weft of stars.
From the pure waters they came too: from the Orava
— Swift river — from the mighty wellsprings of Dunajec
And the lower Poprad too. Men who hold Tvrdošín,
Veľka Ves, Kutin, Trstená — so named from *trsť*— reed —
Námestovo, Hyby, Ľupča, Boca low lying
In valley deep where no blithe sparrow ever twitters;
Bela and Ľubovňa too, lovely Podolínec
And Smolník, in whose waters iron ring turns to brass
Growing beautiful, transfigured its face once severe.
Varied their glittering arms: some bore swords and lances,

Others Wallachian staves and pikes hardened over flames.
Varied their costume and cut, too: these from their far-off
Paternal hearth-stones wore brilliant caftans of white fur;
Still others there shone in black. Some were wrapped in wolf-skin,
Head upon head, cheek covering cheek, to spook the steeds
Of the enemy. Many came on foot, grudgingly:
As long as the stream could carry them, they rode the Váh
Steering their rafts along its brawny current, so as
More swiftly to arrive at the Devín battlements.
The great waters thundered with their oars, their pikes bristled
Like iron forests; bold they were, men like the mountains
That bore them, trooping along the banks of the river.
  Two brothers also came, alike in power and fame,
The sons of Jarek no less skilled and brave as any:
Šťahlav and Krup the fearsome, who founded Krupina
And had the people name it after him; all the sons
Reared in Krupina's ambit obeyed their lord's command;
From Ľubietová they came, nary a fluttering heart
Amongst them; from Brezno, famed market of cheese and meats,
From splendid Bystrica, from Zvolen strapping reapers
Came on, whose scythes in peacetime mow down the golden wheat,
Who understand how to turn iron into coppers;
From Detva, birthplace of sturdy lads, Jelšova,
Plešivec too, and Štítník, land of armourers,
Where weapons and shields — *štíty* — are forged for warriors.
From Turany and Mošovce, Sučany, Pravno,
And all the villages of Turčány, surrounded
On all sides by high mountain summits — a sublime ring.
  Bor and his dexterous son Vlastoň sped on their way.
All that their accoutrements shimmering with gold — shields and casques,
Their armour-plated bosoms, the hand-grips of their swords,
The cumbersome bows they carried also glowed with gold.
Their city, rich in gold, outfits their capable troops,
Kamnica, threaded with veins of the dearest metals,
Bounded on this side and that with the steepest looming
Hills, in which valley lie the shafts of Nova Baňa.
And Bela and Pukanec, excelling in ores rich,
And farthest on, Štiavnica, scattered on soaring knolls.
To these Tisovec threw in companies of stout lads;
Tekov sent a great number, who shun the swollen streams —

Easy-going ploughmen, who till the river's left bank.
The quarries of Hliník grew silent of a sudden:
She entrusted her sons to the war-chief in this time
Of danger, as did Sitna, from her lofty aerie,
Whose sons wage constant war against wolf and mountain bear,
Pricking their ribs with stout javelins; onward they coursed
As the Ispel, joined by the swift Hron and Rímova
Shallow nourish the victorious Danube, monarch
Of waterways, so all these joined forces for the fray.

   Nor would you, O Blizkon, shirk the chance to do battle,
Though fated to fall into a horrid trap, from which
There is no escape for anyone caught in its toils;
There would be wounds enough for you, and still you hastened
To avenge your son's bloody death upon the Germans,
As to the swift battle you led the Novohrad troops.
Your forces were supported by Halič, herdsmen
Of Lučenec and magnificent Divín, nearby
Sand, and those who can barely be seen from the cloudy
Summits of Matra, watered by the Zaďva's currents.

   And those from amidst the deep eddies of the Tisa
Teeming with fish, that river that gnaws at populous
Hernad, these came in awesome hosts as well.
Rozhoň led them, under the command of Bugartúr
The great; all of them cavalry, with shining bucklers.
Light were the bows they bore, and quivered arrows, roaming
With lance in hand; above their helms bobbed heron feathers.
And then ranks of infantry, stout lads of immense might.
The clubs they bore: no slight logs of elm! Fire-honed, clad
In six-ply metal, as their torsos with thick bear hides.

   Besides these there also came that mighty Czech Zbislav,
— Who hearing the rumours of war came to aid his kin
Bearing a hammer immense, such as none of those there
Could lift aloft, though it was a trifle in his hands,
And whenever he did, whether close at hand to smash,
Or to fling away to smite at a distance, each blow
Brought death. Five hundred men came with him, all volunteers,
All armed alike, but of course with much lighter weaponry.

   Also, from the wandering Wisła came our neighbours,
The Poles, seething for the fight, as did the Silesians
From the Odra. Amongst these three hundred Masurians

With shields, and pikes taller than they as they rode in;
Two hundred archers among them, whose darts never err,
Swojski led these, at the head of those bold Nosistrach;
Both equal in stature and in honourable, bold heart.
  So many were the skilled chiefs who led on their brave troops,
Their hearts brimming with dire venom borne toward the Germans.
The air reverberated with song, dark clouds thundered
The echoes, the earth trembled beneath their trampling feet,
The dust they kicked up, dark, obscured the sky, lifted up
In ominous whorls that thickened the gloomy heavens.

CANTO VI

Following the conclusion of the games, the Germans return to the city, to a festive banquet prepared by Karolman. Makward, the harpist, sings of the genesis of the Bavarian nation. Then Karolman asks Svatopluk to render an account of the first beginnings and adventures of his people. He relates that India is the land that first gave birth to the Slavs; she is their natural mother. The reason for the Slavs' abandonment of such a rich country was a gigantic flood from the sea, which overwhelmed many nearby kingdoms, and a subsequent, even more horrible drought. Fearing famine and pestilence, the people gathered before their high priest. As together they lifted their prayers to God, a voice was heard in the heavens saying that the drought would not cease until a portion of them had left for Europe, where they were to multiply. They fulfilled this command of God's; young people were chosen for the journey, to whom large hosts attached themselves voluntarily. And so they wandered through the outer regions of Persia, Chaldea, and Assyria, until they arrived at Armenia, where the king received them graciously and showed them where they were to go so as to bring their journey to a successful completion. He provided each man with the necessary arms. Leaving behind the weaker folk who were unable to proceed any further, they passed through the Caucasus range, after which they did battle with the Psohlavci. Passing over the Volga, they reached Europe. They settled on the banks of the Borysthenes, but when they were set upon by savage nations from the Black Sea region, they abandoned the land and took themselves all the way to the Tatras. There, between the Tisa and Danube, they established their residence. They adopted the name Slávi from Sláv, who vanquished the Chudes. Multiplying greatly, they proceeded to settle other uninhabited realms, at first, indeed, beyond the Danube, later, on the banks of the Wisła, all the way to the Bay of the Wends, and later to the Volga, to Serbia, and so on, until they stretched from the Lába past the Don, from the Adriatic Sea to the Baltic, occupying an immense space. Hating war, they lived in and cultivated peace.

> The Germans, after bringing the tourney to an end,
> The feigned battles on the arena sands, all returned
> To the large city, to a banquet of victory,
> A joyful feast, which the wealthy Karolman prepared.
> A giant banquet hall was located in the midst
> Of the royal complex; broad it was and very long,
> Beautifully adorned, walls thickly hung with portraits —
> Images of the King's ancestors in ordered rows.
> The floor as well was graced with the painter's clever art:

How God's eternal Son did nourish the multitudes
(Five thousand men, not counting the women and children)
With but five loaves of bread and two fish, satisfying
All, relieving the burden of three full days' hunger
Borne by the famished crowds who had brought no victuals;
And two times six baskets of leftovers were gathered
Which the people, sated, could no longer manage.
Into such a feasting hall, then, came the guests, to boards
Stretching deep, end to end, and at these they took their seats.
The tables gleamed with silver plate and goblets of gold
Adorned with figures and manifold intaglio.
Three hundred servers, clad in magnificent garments,
Spun about the hall quickly, softly, now here, now there,
Some of whom carried trays laden with delectables,
While others raised the emptied cups to fill them anew.
   When the first hunger had been sated, men's limbs refreshed,
They began to discuss the spectacle, the tournament,
Now praising the victors, now the nimble, eager steeds.
The vanquished, too, are spoken of, compassionately.
But most of the table-talk touched on the coming war:
The campaign was on everybody's lips. Then the king
Raised aloft a heavy goblet encrusted with pearls
And garlanded with flowers around its golden rim,
Brimming with Sirmium wine. He toasted Svatopluk:
   'Your health, dear King! Enjoy this happy feast to the full.
May your heart's least desire be fulfilled. For you are
Not to consider yourself my guest, but my son-in-law.
In such wise I greet you, no mere friend, but family!'
Ending, he passed the chalice into Svatopluk's hands,
Who received it with a bow, and then thanked Karolman
Gratefully, after which he toasted the king in turn:
'Your health, your Majesty, and yours, honoured councillors!
Your health I drink, war-chief, and yours, victors in the games,
And all you other soldiers, soon my comrades in arms!
May you defeat our foe, help me to my promised throne,
And cover yourselves with undying martial glory!'
   He finished, and then passed the goblet to bold Britwald;
Britwald tasted, then passed it on, neighbour to neighbour
It went, till it circled round the immense crowd of guests
Rejoicing. Thrice ten times it was drained and filled anew,

Until a pleasant jangling of strings was heard, and song,
For silver-tongued Makward was raking his skilled fingers
Over his harpstrings, chanting the Celts, how from the east
They wandered to the farthest shores of the western sea,
Changing their tribal name, henceforth to be known as Gauls,
Of whom a great number, led by their chief Segowés,
Took up new residence in the Black Forest. Bójmi
Their appellation, from which the name Bohemia.
Here they soundly defeated the Cimbri, to a man
Pounding them, removing a threat of nigh destruction.
He sang on, strumming his harp, of how they left that land,
Heading south, led by their chief Agilofing, across
The fish-teeming Danube, where they settled new dwellings,
Permanent now, the nucleus of Bavarian sway.
Makward had barely finished his song, graceful to all
— The faint strings longing for new metrical caresses —
When many-skilled Karolman addressed King Svatopluk:
 'Your Majesty, having now heard our folk's adventures,
We would be grateful indeed if you narrated yours.
For many things are said of the Slavs, yet we know not
Anything solid concerning your people's wellsprings.
Five hundred years have passed, if my memory errors not,
Since our Carinthians and Styrians abandoned
— Against their will — their ancient cradle to wander far
To more commodious regions. Two centuries ago
Tasil, warlike beyond all measure, led an army
Against them, subjecting them, after fierce resistance,
To Bavarian authority. They call themselves
Slovenes, while the neighbouring Germans call them Wendisch,
Although we know not the generation of the term.
And yet they are quite similar to the Indians
In their speech and customs and in the gods they worshipped.
Yet speak you rather: Whence comes your great people, the Slavs?'
  He finished, and all there present were pleased at his words,
Earnestly adding their voices to the king's request.
And so Svatopluk rose to his feet, to address them:
 'It is a great burden you place upon these shoulders,
Requiring of me a song of times passed long ago,
Days that are shrouded in the mists of antiquity.
But because every man gladly sings his own people,

And seeing as you would fain listen to the story
Of my nation's beginnings, its source, I shall relate
What I have heard from others, and chiefly from Ctislav,
The high priest of Parom and lover of our nation,
Who lived three times fifty summers and winters, and knew
The deeds of our people from the most hoary ages,
And these he handed down to me when I was a boy.
India is our natural mother, our first home;
India our origin, that happy, fecund land,
Rich beyond telling in beauty and crops, indeed first
In the world, a paragon quite unsurpassable —
A delightful paradise on earth is India,
A cornucopia brimming with every good thing:
Whatever the heart desires is found in abundance
There — twice-yearly harvests, in some regions, even three
They reap without sowing; rice thickly fills the paddies,
And so much gold and silver and precious gems are there
— As many as are the grains of sand lining these streams.
Yet no one deems it treasure, for what are such things worth
When one lives in abundance, and has all that one needs?
The people there are good-hearted, wise, lovers of peace,
Capable and clever folk, well skilled in all the arts.
Why then would one ever wish to abandon such a place?
What event might urge one to seek out a new homeland?
A fearsome catastrophe such as never before
Had been seen by man fell upon our happy homeland,
For suddenly, in bestial might the ocean rose up
And swamped our land far and wide, flooding the bright lowlands.
With new and angry whirlpools splitting the earth, it sucked
Down into its depths all we had raised there. Our cities,
The streets of which men once proudly trod, had now become
Silent submarine corridors thrid by massy whales;
Our palaces the lairs of all sorts of sea monsters,
Nor did the occupying waters ever recede.
Only the people escaped the deluge — with scarcely
Anything, having heeded the warnings of our bards
Inspired of God about the looming catastrophe
Shortly before it fell. They hastened from the seashore
Farther inland, and thus avoided death by drowning.
Then, not three months had passed since the multitudes pressed in

When a fierce drought commenced beneath a merciless sun:
No rain would fall, nor any dew moisten the parched earth.
The grass upon the thirsting meadows curled to a crisp,
The blossom fled the bough, the soil cracked unnourished.
Even the Indus shrank, the Ganges shrivelled by half,
No longer slaking the banks on either riverside.
The Beas ran short, the swift current of the Satluj
Shrank to a trickle, across which a short man might wade.
Mud caked and split, the earth crumbled away frightfully.
Harvest-time came round, but no one whetted sharp his scythe;
No field of grain rang with happy reapers' melodies.
Then the terrified people, fearing hunger — and worse:
Pestilence, which is ever the offspring of famine,
Brought no first fruits to harvest festival, no fat sheaves
Were carted to altar in thanksgiving sacrifice,
And yet they came as wont, before the aged Vyzov,
The priest most senior at the time, and remarkable
For piety and life devout, and for prophecy,
For to him Brahma spoke, the highest of all the gods,
Words he'd convey unto the people, who now begged him:
    "Most renowned father! Who have always interceded
With God on our behalf, beseeching His mercy for us
When He is angry; who always have reconciled us
When we had gone astray, speak to us now and tell us
(For He so often reveals to you His holy will),
How have we offended Him, that He sends upon us,
His servants, such punishment, such immense destruction?
What can we do to incline His mercy unto us?
How may we win His benison, beseeching an end
To these dire straits, which threaten our annihilation?"
    Then did the high priest make response to their entreaties:
"My children, night and day I spend beseeching Brahma
On your behalf, pouring forth my ardent prayers at the throne
Of Heaven's king, and yet He heeds not my petitions
However frequent, nor does He deign reveal to me
His will as in the past. Indeed, great must be our fault
In His eyes, to cause such anger. Come then, my children,
And as we are now gathered in such great multitudes,
Let us fall prostrate before Him and beg His mercy".
    He finished, at which the people knelt in contrition

While he, with arms upraised to Heaven, began to pray:
"O Lord supreme! Creator of all that lives on earth!
Sustainer and nourisher of all that moves and breathes,
All souls that tread the meadows, or pierce the swelling wave,
Or with sharp quills skim through the windy regions above,
Look down upon us wretches, and deign incline Thine ear
To this our fervent plea: bring an end to this famine
And through Thy bounty strengthen once more our withered limbs!
Reveal the cause of Thy displeasure towards Thy people.
How may we end Thine ire and once more win Thy favour?"
He'd barely finished praying when a great wind blew up,
A bolt split the clear sky and thundered in the distance,
Making the earth to tremble. The wooded hills bowed low
And then a great voice was heard calling down from the sky:
"O nation excellent and multitudinous!
You must now leave your homeland and set out wandering
To glorify your name in other parts of the world.
For this famine has fallen upon you, this sore trial
To urge you outward, on the road from your motherland,
Or otherwise you'd never leave so blessed a realm.
Go then, and direct your steps to the far northern climes,
For this sun shall not cease to pour down its scorching rays,
Nor will the dew refresh the soil, nor will new shoots grow,
Until a portion of your people leave this country
To set off on a journey to the bounds of Europe.
You'll find rich farmlands there, fallow soil unfailing;
Fat harvests await you in that land of abundance.
Go, and love peace there, keeping yourself from evil war
That slaughters men and makes entire realms to vanish.
There multiply in peace into a sturdy nation,
Earn your living from the ploughshare, and not from pillage,
Gift-giving, treat well the stranger that comes unto you,
And there in time you shall spread wide your nation's tendrils,
Taking root in great numbers in lands now left vacant
By earlier folk — the greater portion of Europe
Yours, from the southern sea to where the arctic waves beat
The shingle; from Sláva, Glory, your name shall be Slavs."
   Thus sounded the voice. Stunned, they gathered their thoughts, slowly
Coming round to an ardent desire to fulfil
God's command without further hesitation. Young folk

Were soon selected, and leaders among them chosen,
To set off on that quest in search of a new homeland.
To these a large contingent joined themselves willingly,
Such as were not pleased with a strict division by caste
But looked forward to a freer form of government.
Sám was appointed them, pious and wise, as chieftain,
To be a judge unto them when matters should arise
Ponderous; whom they were to heed as their own father.
Their sacks were filled with gold and many precious treasures,
As much as they could carry, to help them on their way,
To purchase food — for well they knew what strangers value.
   Now, when the day of the planned departure had arrived,
After the ceremonies and sacrificial rites
Had been accomplished, at the time of parting many tears
Were shed, and many the lament was groaned (for who leaves
Home happily, against his free will, when forced by want?)
Yet still they set off on that unknown road. And as soon
As the last foot passed over their motherland's frontier,
A heavy rain began to pour from the clouds, torrents
Reviving the dead earth, and all that grows thereupon.
The hosts, meanwhile, had passed over the Persian border,
And all were treated well; they journeyed on without fear.
Soon they had reached the Chaldean plain's wide steppes.
They wondered at the great battlements of Babylon,
Their skyscraping towers and gates all forged of metal,
Copper-chased. From the top of the highest ziggurat,
The brow of which defied the stars, an angelic voice
Rang out in song. Thence they passed into Assyria,
Without pausing, where they beheld no smaller cities,
The largest of which Nin, son of Baal, had erected,
That proud king, who named it after himself: Nineveh,
Where vines and gardens spilled down from its crenellations.
The level path ceased as they approached Armenia,
And neared the soaring summits, where Noah of legend
Sensed his ark scrape to ground after the destructive flood.
Nearby, King Armén gazed out upon the multitudes,
And recognising them as kin, greeted them with joy.
With arms outspread, he inquired as to their journey's aim:
Whence do they come, whither go? Why such great pilgrim hosts?
   To this their wise chief responded in words such as these:

"O best of kings! Not of our free will do we wander,
Leaving our motherland dear, but commanded of God.
(Indeed, who would of his own free will abandon home?)
He bids us find a new homeland in distant Europe,
And that we aim at, gropingly, knowing not the way.
But since the northern regions are well known unto you,
Advise us in your wisdom, where is it we shall find
The fat earth destined unto us, yearning for the plough,
Ready for tillage, and burgeoning nigh with produce?
That land we wish to occupy in peace, its bosom
To be our home forever, where we shall age secure".
   Thus spoke the chieftain. Armén the king, astonished, mused,
Revolving an ancient prophecy that came to mind,
And then he broke the silence, speaking such words to them:
"When things come to such a pass as this, it is best
To beg inspiration of God, how to serve one's folk,
As you have done, to the glory of yours. The prophet
Gerzen once proclaimed — some three hundred years ago —
That from the same regions that saw our generation
Another nation of kindred seed would come some day,
Following in our traces in quest of sweet Europe.
These, one day, were to grow into a mighty people,
Outnumbering all nations bordering on their land,
To found a generous and widespread kingdom, the sway
Of which would extend even unto our own realm's bounds.
But come now, friends, into our gardens, to our hearthsides,
For you are tired with your journey. Come, refresh your limbs.
Then you shall learn of me where you are next to travel,
To find the new homeland which has been foretold you".
Thus Armén. Then, leading a portion to the city,
While settling the rest in fine quarters in the country,
He had his folk provide their guests with all they needed.
Five months they spent there. When the fifth moon was on the wane
— The while the happy feasting went on incessantly,
Until our people near forgot God's great command
And all things else, grumbling about further travelling,
Giving rein to their own will, — once, while Sám was asleep,
God Himself appeared to him at midnight, in a dream,
With mighty threatenings should they refuse to move on.
He leapt up from his bed and swept his hands to the stars,

Beseeching the Lord of Heaven in ardent appeal.
He went before his people then, and bade them prepare
To leave, after which he went to see the king and said:
  "O most benevolent Sire! The time has come for us
To bid farewell to you and set off on our journey.
For God himself this night appeared to me in a dream
To prod us on our way, threatening dire consequences,
Should we tarry here longer. The gifts you have bestowed
Upon us are immense, far exceeding our powers
Ever to repay, though our hearts brim with gratitude!
But now I beg you, fulfil the promise made us,
And tell us whither we should now direct our footsteps,
What road we are to take, and where we are to settle".
  King Armén then arose, and responded with such words:
"Indeed I would have been happy to see you remain
Here with us in one realm, making with us one people,
But as I would not go against the commands of God,
I say — heed without hesitation His will revealed!
I will not hold you back. Set out now upon the path
Given you; in a few words I shall unfold to you
As much as I know, as much as I've heard from others.
So listen closely: the road that stretches before you
Is not an easy one: through the Caucasus summits,
Along steep ranges teetering deep chasms it leads,
To conquer which will require much courage and firmness
So dangerous it is. There is but one mountain pass,
One valley long that allows a respite from climbing.
But when you've passed through it, turn not unto the right hand,
For that region, as far as the boisterous Chvalenská
Plain, is inhabited by the savage Psohlavci —
A monstrous, evil nation, hideous. Psohlavci
They are called, for their heads are like to dogs",
Their snouts are long and fanged, their ears are pointed and keen,
Their fingers end, not in nails, but in sharp, tearing claws.
Their bodies, otherwise, are like to a proper man's
Except for this: they are covered in a shaggy coat
And have no need of any clothing. They eat horse-flesh,
And men, too: at their banquets quaffing blood with delight!
They have their own language of barks and hideous howls:
One's flesh crawls, and blood runs cold in one's veins to hear it.

Speed on your way without a moment's hesitation
And cross the Don, the great ravine carved by which river
Divides Europe from her sister Asia. Then strike left,
Avoiding the whirlpools. Settle not by the Black Sea,
For savage and unwelcoming are the peoples there,
Who plunder their neighbours and subsist on brigandage.
Take the straight mountain route, rather, and head to the north,
Where empty fields, untouched as yet by any ploughshare
Await the husbandry of patient agrarians.
The climate there is cooler, true, the winters severe,
But the summers can be sweltering, and anyway,
Man can adapt to anything: raw cold, blazing heat.
It's better to have peace in a cold climate that war
In a temperate zone. There you shall live securely,
Free from the threat of banditry. There settle your folk,
And work the fecund black earth, multiply and prosper".
  He said such words, and this good counsel given, each youth
He armed with weaponry: long pike, sharp sword, full quiver
And bow; to each man a round shield and copper helmet;
And more: he gave them horses — wing-footed stallions, mares
Caparisoned with saddles of Armenian workmanship.
Many silver pieces too, and food for the journey
He gave them, while Sám received the greatest hoard of gold
And precious gems, which sparkled brightly with living fire.
Then all made ready to set out, except for the weak,
And old folk bent under their years, who remained behind.
The hosts then departed, limbs refreshed, and rejoicing
That from their loins was to arise a mighty nation,
Lords of broad lands, exceeding other tribes in numbers.
Many a foot pressed into the Caucasian mountains
Fearsome, descending again through the narrow ravines,
The vault of heaven high above them, on both hands sheer
Walls of rock — as when the son of Abraham the sea
Split with his rod to make a dry passage for the Jews,
And the ocean grew tame at his command, and Jacob's
Nation passed through it dry shod, as if an avenue
Promenading. But soon, worn out with the arduous
Climbs and descents, wearied, they sought for a place to rest,
Where food might be prepared, skewered meats roasted on coals.
No sooner set they to this task than a vicious howl

Met their ears, and screams and whimperings. They grabbed their arms
And set out racing to that place, swords at the ready.
The first one there was Sám, mounted on his swift charger,
Filling the ranks with heart, urging them to be manly.
It was a pack of hideous Psohlavci, weaponed
And viciously falling upon the shocked outliers.
Wretched those men surprised — before they could grab their arms
And form up in line defensive to beat back the swarm
That tore infants free of their mothers' frenzied embrace,
Lovely, nubile maidens and lads helpless, overwhelmed —
All these they tore apart, quartering them savagely
With claws like sickles, lapping their blood with long and rough
Tongues, crunching torn limbs in their hideous maws, gorging
Their unholy guts. But when they saw the armed legions
Bearing down upon them like an avalanche unchained,
They left their gory repast and, with a howl, attacked,
Tensing the tendons of their bows, winging swift arrows
At Sám's men, who, no less adept at fighting, whirled out
Squadrons of darts themselves from their defensive phalanx,
Shields linked, Armenian bows hurling death at the Dogheads
So thickly that the sky above the field was darkened,
The rafts of missiles blocking out the sweet light of day,
Until the two lines moved close for a fierce grapple, wildly,
At spear's point and closer, hacking thickly with their swords —
A cruel, bestial battle it was, horrid slaughter.
Soon a great number of men rushed at the Psohlavci
Hordes. They cut down the strongest to quiver in the dust,
And yet in their rabid bloodlust most kept raving on
To the cruel fray; none would give up, none turn tail and run.
Their king (if such a title may be bestowed on beasts)
Kept urging them on with fierce yaps, great howls, in a rut
For the filthy feast he lewdly smelt in the offing.
Then Sám, the many-wiled leader of the men, hit on
This strategy: He had his picked archers fix their darts
With flaming pitch and send them whizzing at the Doghead
Leader; they wrapped their arrows in tarred rags and, kindling
Them, sent them in a searing blizzard at the monster
As soon as the order rang out. Their aim unfailing,
The wind bore the missiles straight into his foetid maw.
Such a piquant morsel that wicked gullet never

Swallowed! His nostrils snorting smoke, his eyes exploded,
Jellies bursting to darkness, blind, his fur caught fire, soon
His poll unholy raged aflame. Still the storm of darts
Rained down, and all the Psohlavci in range were burning,
And even those unpierced caught fire from the others,
Fur setting fur alight, skin crackling — an inferno!
Writhing in horror, for on all hands the flames burst forth,
As in the open steppe, when lightning bolts strike thickly,
An overwhelming storm of fire searing juniper
To ash, the tarry smoke and whirlwinds of winking sparks
Swirled to the clouds, everywhere the stench of burning flesh
Burdened the gloomy air. Soon the Psohlavci ran off,
Trailing cruel embers, unable to bear this onslaught,
Coarse though they were to pain, with howls and panicked barking,
They turned their backs and loped with haste back to the thick brush,
The hosts of Sám in close pursuit, who would cut them down
In vengeful wrath, but their chief would not permit it,
To task he recalled them — the road that lay before them.
   Then began the sombre collection of the gnawed limbs
Of their companions. Once they'd been laid in the dark peace
Of the tomb, and the rites funereal accomplished,
Having refreshed their strength at a feast sad with keening,
They set out again, leaving the dire vale behind them.
Many other obstacles had to be surmounted.
But then, after the longest passage of time, the grand
Broadly-spreading river Don was reached, and its ravine,
Which urged them on the more. They crossed the booming river
And entered long yearned-for Europe with great rejoicing,
Greeting the land hospitable, falling to their knees,
Kissing the earth in sacrifice of prayer beseeching
Her kind protection, peace. But barely had they begun
Their rites of thanksgiving than their able leader Sám
Urged them on farther, mindful of King Armén's warnings.
Then, skirting round those treacherous whirlpools, they struck north.
Soon, near the banks of a large river, which at the time
Still bore no appellation, unsettled by nations,
Far from the black plain, they meant to dig their foundations.
But when their dwellings were raised upon the riverbank,
They named it Boristen, for in its wrathful flooding
It battered walls — *boril steny*. Still, plots allotted,

And laws decreed, inscribed on birchbark, they set to work:
Soon were the fields tilled, soon the fecund soil brought forth crops
In abundance — that black earth, a cornucopia!
Their flocks and herds fattened and multiplied on the rich grass
And all so prospered — who could wish for a better land?
Until the savage Meotaks and Cimmerians
— Uncultured rabble — and other Black Sea mobs
Began their depredations: looting and pillaging
All of a sudden, again and again creeping close
Stealthily, driving off herds of cattle, sheep, and goats,
And even people too, as slaves, to serve those bandits.
Whatever they couldn't carry off with themselves, all
Structures and gleanings preserved, they burnt to ash, destroyed.
Then did our people, in council, determine to leave
That land, in search of a more secure place to settle;
Better to wander anew, than to toil as vile slaves!
And so they left that place, heading towards the sunset,
Until, after a long trek, they came to the Tatras,
Those summits high that scrape the clouds, and here they settled
Between the Tisa and the swelling Danube — for good.
And since that time our people have lived in these regions
Of ours, their yearnings for peace fulfilled three times over;
No one disturbed them there, no one destroyed their peace,
Nor rustled their herds, nor rifled the goods they amassed.
There, gaily have we lived, leading a life free of war
And banditry, enjoying the generous harvests
Of a foison land in harmony with her husbands —
Until some three hundred years later, a tribe of Chudes
Crept near and rustled seven herd of stallions, and more:
Three times that many oxen, and six times flocks of sheep.
These they unpenned, and began to drive back to their land,
A task as greedy as immense, and impossible:
For at this time there was one man, courageous and great
In both wisdom and chattel — the wealthiest by far.
His name? No one knows that given him by his parents,
Although he earned another; well, he gathered his able clan
And set off in pursuit of the thieves. Chasing them down,
He toppled their savage chief with one hurl of his spear.
The rest he scattered, although the greater part he took
Captive, and these he drove back, along with the rescued

Beasts. Of course, the Chudes, learning of the catastrophe
Their brothers met with, gathered all their troops together
To take revenge upon the victors. That famous man
Expected no less, for which reason he appointed
Pickets to keep watch over our borders, day and night,
Bidding the people be on guard at home, weapons
At arm's reach, ready to rush upon the enemy
At a moment's notice. And thus it came to war, yes,
The Chudes again were routed by his might and prudence —
All of their spearmen were slaughtered, none of them returned
Alive to their homeland. During that fearsome battle
He cut down a hundred (he fought as well as led),
He slew one hundred of their stoutest men, their monarch
Himself, with his right arm hurling to the nether shades.
For this he won eternal fame, defending with valour
The land of his birth, that victor bold, saving it from ruin,
Securing its peace and prosperity thereafter,
And more: ruling it with just, measured hand, dispensing
Justice to all. As all he did was righteous, his fame
Became his name — Sláv — from *sláva*, glory, Glorious One,
Sláv — this the name bestowed upon him by our ancients
In thanks and honour; this the name that spread far and wide
As his descendants waxed into a great multitude,
After him naming their ancestors Slavs, the Slavic
Tribe, and rightly too, for in virtue and might and sway
They were, almost to a man, identical to him:
Thus 'Sláv' became a cherished term of honour, gladly
Adopted by all tribes who trace their generation
To him, to them, who were renowned for glorious deeds:
Sláv, a title commemorative — and a duty.
Thereafter the people multiplied in great numbers
And wave after wave moved on to settle vacant land
Like swarms of bees when the springtime sun wheels to Taurus
To tempt them from their overbrimming hives. The Danube
First they crossed, where after the circling of many years
They stretched from the Black Sea to the salty Adriatic.
And there they linked up with their brethren the Venedi
From whom they'd last parted when leaving Armenia —
Whence later they migrated to Paphlagonia
And the land of the Medes, and from there on to Adria.

But as there was no end to long frays in those regions,
Constantly harried as they were by the warlike Celts
Striving to seize them and harness them to slavery,
They retraced their steps to their brothers in the Tatras.
Over that range they spread to settle the Wisła's banks
And follow that winding river to the Wendish Bay
So named for them, while others to the mighty Volga
And sweet River Srb — taking thence the name Serbians —
And farther to Silín and the inhospitable
Metic marshes to reach anew the black riverbanks
Of Boristen. No prince ruled over them at this time,
No chiefs or kings (except in times of necessity
Urgent — as when wars broke out, demanding leaders
Picked for the duration of the conflict; in peacetime
They cared not for any permanent governor). Oh!
Had such been their intention, their desire, as other
Nations, to carve a crooked fame for themselves with arms,
Blindly hacking onward; if such had been their desire
It would have been an easy thing for them to fetter
All Europe at the feet of one Slavic tyranny!
But we've always been the fiercest foes of war itself.
Never have we mixed into our neighbours' broils; killing
And cruelty have never been to our liking, nor
Looting and pillaging, nor the shameful trade in men.
The ancient Slavs preferred to live in peace, possessing
All goods in common, thinking all men brothers, equal,
Sharing both wealth and dearth in even portions: now joy,
Now burdens borne in common. Our fathers were our kings,
Their realms marked by tilled furrow, their subjects: sons, daughters;
For these they laws established, and those obeyed with love.
Thus through their preference for peace, their hatred of war,
They were spared, through long ages of migration, the harsh
And horrid falls of fortune, pogroms and destruction
That nations fond of brigandage endure. Ever true
They were to their sweet fields and homes, once they were settled.
But each time that the nation waxed full of multitudes,
They sent out settlers to new vacant lands — an excess
Of population, never draining their motherlands —
To regions depopulated by those who set out
To slaughter others, leaving behind a shameful void,

Or when such met with annihilation, through their greed
Slaughtered by others. Thus on they surged, renewing earth
Laid waste by those who scorched it and moved on. To the west
They pressed, crossing the mighty Odra, to the very
Banks of the Elbe, spreading over the River Saale,
While others for the second time moved south, the Danube
Crossing anew to regain territories once held
And found now permanent new settlements covering
The plains between the Black Sea and the Adriatic.
Theirs was Pannonia, theirs the land that stretched to these
Your borders; they even pressed into proud Italy.
Then did the circuit of their lands — gigantic ambit! —
Stretch from the pulse of Elbe far past Silín, from Baltic
To Adriatic Sea; it was not strange to find them
Settled upon the Belgic seashore. To Brittany,
And even England did our people come. That they till
The fat soil on the Rhine, this you know well, close neighbours
That you be: but because those were but smallish outposts
In varied lands, this mighty nation, fragmentary
In colonies, lived on without any king or lord,
And only later, when such tribes had waxed in numbers
Did they elect, from among the boldest and wisest,
A ruler, yet whose authority was circumscribed
To regions he could traverse mounted. To such a king
The common people subjected themselves happily.
Remaining faithful to their way of life, as of old,
When once they settled a land permanently, they stayed,
Busied with tilling the soil, animal husbandry,
Tending orchards, grafting trees... and music. Ah, they sang
While they laboured, their gay voices always filled the air —
Rejoicing, or soothing their bruised hearts when deep sorrow
Afflicted them, with song. But they raised great cities, too,
Invented arts and necessary crafts, unstinting
Their hands in varied trades, vending the bumper produce
Of their lands, importing goods, transporting through their lands
The rich resources of the eastern climes north, and west
To where the sun sets. In hospitality as well
They excelled all other nations. No sooner stranger
Appeared in their fields than they welcomed him, quite all there
Gathering, wishing to learn whatever he could teach.

Whoever afield saw the stranger first took him home,
Hosting him, having him sit to a copious board,
Refreshing him with food and with drink, outfitting him
For his further road with provisions, sweet honeycomb,
And going along with him on the road till he reached
The next settlement. And this our generosity,
The fact that we were mild and quiet, industrious,
Led by no princes cruel thirsting for blood and slaughter,
Induced other vicious nations to invade our lands.
For thus the Chudes, and the Alani from the highlands
Of the Caucasian range, the nomadic Goths, the wild
Hordes of the Huns and rabid Avars marauded us,
And with their overwhelming numbers and violence
Made our realms to vanish. Yet those savages received
A just reward for their brutality: *they've* vanished,
Leaving nothing behind but infamy, a vile name,
While we're still alive, and always shall live, with *sláva*
— Undying fame — despite the looming threats and pressure
Of neighbouring folk who still sometimes press upon us'.
   Thus Svatopluk narrated to the gay revellers
The origins of his people, and their history
As far as it was known to him. Meanwhile, the dark night
Spread slowly over field and battlement, enticing
All men to refresh their limbs with sleep. Soon all were still.

CANTO VII

Karolman presents Svatopluk with the armour that had been swiftly forged for him. Svatopluk examines it in wonder, especially the cleverly crafted shield, on which the battle waged by the Prince of the Angels, Archangel Michael, the leader of the faithful hosts of Heaven, against Satan and his forces, had been beautifully carved. In the first and second battles they fight alone, and the true hosts repel the rebels, but in the third, the Son of God Himself, mounted upon a splendid chariot, batters down the revolting crew with thunderbolts and pitches them into Hell. Taking his armour, Svatopluk hastens to where the army is gathered and inspects them. The first he sees are the Austrians led by Agilmund, then the Bavarians with their leader Hartung, the Tyroleans under Dipold. Further, the Styrians, led by Humbold and Gromislav, the Carinthians under their leader Svenčar, the Krajuce with Jesutbor leading them and the Pannonians led by Radbod, accompanied by Mutimír, Chocil, Salak, Erchenbert and Ludolf, and among them too, the commander in chief of the entire army, Britwald. Svatopluk addresses them, encouraging and inciting them.

    The two horns of the golden crescent moon met to shed
A brighter glow upon the earth, at which the joyous
Banqueting wound to a close, replaced by war-councils.
The regiments prepared for the coming war, the king,
Karolman, summoned Svatopluk his guest, who now yearned
To set off for his homeland as soon as possible.
Then, when he stood before him, the king addressed him thus:
   'This armour, which I have had forged for you, expressly,
Take now unto your mighty limbs, and visit the troops.
Go now, engage in the cruel fray with steadfastness,
And batter the resistant to their knees, to the dust,
To occupy your throne usurped, and wield the golden
Sceptre of your nation. Never break your plighted troth'.
   Thus said he, knowing not that he armed his own ruin.
King Svatopluk, on his part, was gladdened at the thought,
And with great wonder examined the given armour —
Turning the helmet this way and that with its bobbing
Tufts, hefting the sword in its golden sheath with black stones
Fresh-flashing — fatal blade, someday, to many thousands,
Among them, his host's own Bavarian regiments.
There was a long pike too, immense, and triple-weft mail

With gold inwoven, such as no dart might penetrate,
And a seven-ply shield of the leather of oxen,
Rough war-beasts, covered with just as many metal plates,
Flashing with ominous sheen, as if blazing lightning.
A cruel war was carved thereon, a battle fearsome.
He saw the hetman heavenly, Archangel Michael,
Chief of the hosts angelic ever faithful to God,
Messiah's champion, leading his fearless army
Against Satan the rebel, who had once been glorious,
First of all angels, who had once of the Almighty
Received the greatest honours, resplendent like the sun
Above all others shining, until in jealous bile
— Resenting Him! The Son of God! — he swelled with venom,
Spiteful at the King of King's anointing. He would not
Submit, and, first deceiving a full third of the hosts
Of Heaven with underhanded, wrathful dissembling,
He sought — the fool! — to storm and overcome the ramparts
Of the eternal City of God, and topple Him
From His almighty throne! Which he sought to occupy —
Seizing the universal sceptre to brashly rule
In base apotheosis, alone amongst the stars.
There was described all the densely-packed legions at war,
Grappling together in tangled scrums, whole phalanxes
Of foot-soldiers here, there — cavalry on flaming steeds.
Some brace their legs on flashing chariots, tensing bows
Strung with darts forged in celestial armouries, while
High above on wings shining like rainbows swoop squadrons
In combat mid-air, now here, now there, some strafing
The enemy below. And neither of these armies wavers,
Neither condones retreat. The scorching arrows streak past.
The clouds above swag blood-red. Immortal brawn swipes, hacks,
Arms flail in constant hewing, thick sparks swirl up from shield
And helm in blizzards or flare like angry pennons flapped
By the dark wind, or as when hot thunderbolts flash forth
From stormclouds' murky wombs to set whole forests aflame.
Michael, nimble and mighty, wielding the sword of God,
Sharp and gigantic, of adamant forged and gold, hot
As the summer sun, this he brings crashing down upon
The helmet of Satan, lopping its overbold tufts
With the impetus of doom. The holy blade severs

The metal casque, and as the lightning splits some windy
Ural summit, so Michael's blade shears the demon's brain,
Splattering what was once ichor, now black, noxious gore
Such as pulses through the rank conduits of immortal
Spirits now fallen, befouling the once-burnished shield.
Satan, toppled headlong, writhing in pain, tosses it
Away. It rolls, as gigantic as the moon at full.
His pike, three hundred fathoms long, to which the tallest
Fir that grows in the mountains of Orava
Would be as a stake that props grape vines, comes crashing down
And sweeps away a thousand infantry in falling.
Then gallant Gabriel opposes the lieutenant
Of Satan, roaring Belzebub, and with his axe cleaves open
His side. With a stout lance of pine Raphael skewers
Belial's throat, muting his foul larynx with the blow.
Uriel cuts off Dagon's legs from underneath him,
Zephon meets Asmodeus, and with one mighty blow
Shatters to smithereens the left nave of his rib-cage.
Nimble Abdiel lays the fallen angel Molorch low,
While mighty Uziel, with his sharp, double-edged broadsword,
Rushes at God's enemies, mowing down regiments.
Moloch falls, as does Fegor and Alastor the sprite.
Dramelech the cruel and Alfit (who beat the tocsin)
Are battered down with Babuel, who blared foul slogans
On Hell's bugle, urging forth the legions of the damned
— Deceptive encouragement! — he falls, with Amiden
And Nizrok, no less the liar, while those who soared high
On wing, blazing, battling in the air, are pierced by dart
And sharp missile, and now plummet headlong in terror
Upon their own infantry, crushing them like millstones,
Breaking their own necks upon impact. The larger part
Of Lucifer's generals by now have been lain flat;
The blue fields of heaven are thickly strewn with lances,
Shattered swords, and shrapnel, scrapped armour and battered casques;
Fire-breathing steeds stumble, chariots teeter like drunks
On split axles and wobbling wheels, crashing into heaps.
Chaos reigns among the ranks of the fallen angels.
No thought is given now to counter-attack, no arm
Can be raised in defence, no leg but blunders backwards
As the rebels, routed, flee. But on another field

The war renewed is carven, as blind hatred again
Spurs the proud fools onward to renewed self-massacre,
No sooner than the wounds they received close up and scar.
For spiritual bodies are like air, which allows
For penetrations that sunder not permanently,
Let the blade be ever so sharp, thrust ever so fearsome.
Aethereal matter heals itself, leaving behind
Nothing but the mark of shame, which is never effaced.
Although the evil hordes recovered from the smiting
They brought upon themselves by pride, they would never lose
The horror of their sin, which burns deep inside them,
The eternal worm of their disgrace, never at rest,
Never giving them peace. Still, they renewed the battle
As soon as their flesh was whole, scarred fast, their second wind
Caught, but having proved their might unequal to the hosts
Of Heaven, seeing that nothing could be expected
That road but new stripes, new pain, they resorted to guile.
Under the truce of night they forged new machinery
Of war unseen before: whole ranks of hollow pillars
As long as mill-sluices, their gullets packed with sulphur
And leaden shrapnel, their mouths trained at their enemies.
A twist of twine mysterious was set at the breech.
When this was touched by the vital spark, of a sudden
A flash and a roaring unheard before filled the air
With smoke and flame, as all along the axis guns belched
Their bad contents, discharging chaos upon the hosts
Angelic, who, unprepared for such a novel shock,
Were bowled over in their thousands. Not long, however,
Were the evil ranks of fallen sprites to exult;
Short-lived their jollity, for, before they could reload
Their clumsy artillery, God's army recovered
And rushed upon the imps milling round the batteries.
As arms and stout lances are no match for cannon,
The mountains of Heaven they uprooted, might and main,
To hurl upon them in an avalanche titanic,
Overwhelming the cannons, knocking askew the aim
Of those unburied by the first great Alpine salvo,
Which thundered upon gun and gunner alike. The sprites
Out-burrowed their way from under suffocating piles
Displaced upon them with difficulty, to renew

The battle once more with equal arms, that is to say,
They fell to pitching cliffs themselves. Hill upon mountain
Flew, jostling in the space above the darkling battlefield.
Confusion filled the once-ordered sky, fall upon fall
Of ruins cluttered with chaos the meads of Heaven.
  But this was not the end, this not the final battle.
There was another segment of the shield, richly carved,
Showing one more encounter: this the final thrashing
Of Satan's forces. Here Svatopluk beheld a strange
And wonderful war-chariot, fashioned all of gold,
Drawn by no horses whipped on to the gallop, no reins
Or harness to control the power of the beasts —
The lambent wheels of which spun under their own power,
Speeding the chariot onward with the rush of storm-winds.
Four starry cherubim surrounded the vehicle,
Just so many figures of awesome countenance,
Each one spreading round his body three pairs of bright wings
Covered with eyes unsleeping, keeping watch on all hands.
In the midst of the chariot glowed a burnished throne
Sparkling with diamonds, upon which sat the Son of God,
Gripping His sceptre in His left hand, above Him clouds
Piled, rainbow-hued. Before Him black terror galloped
And horror, pressing on His enemies. Nike soared
Winged to his right; from His left shoulder hung a bow — Death
To those against whom it was tensed; with quiver chock-full
Of blazing arrows and the thunderbolts of Heaven.
Sublime He sat, round him billows of incense rising,
Threaded by showers of glittering lightning brilliant.
He led on hosts of angelic thanes in their thousands,
Two legions on flashing chariots on both His flanks,
Who then put up their swords into their sheaths, and set
Down pikes, all intent upon the Victor's mighty deeds:
For He rushed alone, all unaided, upon His foes,
His face obscured in mists of anger, wrathful His brows
Arched, wielding the thunderbolt in His divine right hand
As He scattered the rebels, raining blow upon blow.
Nothing saw they but moiling clouds and flashing lightning;
Nothing heard they but roaring; nothing felt they but torment.
The foul hosts fell away; those who breasted the assault
And those who hung back. The flanks on both sides were scattered.

Stunned at the overwhelming onslaught, their dark weapons
Fell from their hands, as the chariot divine sped on
Crushing the demons proud, while all the heavens shuddered
And echoed with the storm that splintered the sky in twain,
As bright painted shields and golden helmets were crushed flat
Beneath His wheels, along with the brawn aethereal
They covered. Three hundred thunderclaps sounded at once,
Followed by one loud roaring — and the floor of Heaven
Gave way into a chasm abysmal, sucking down
The damned revolters. Some even scrambled and ran
(Such was the will of God) to plunge themselves, therein
Seeking sanctuary anywhere away from Him —
They hurled themselves down, jamming the hole in writhing throngs
Until the centre caved, and whorls of black angels fell
Head downward, spinning, into the throat of Gehenna,
Where darkness everlasting reigns, and fires never quenched.
   Such was the shield fashioned by the clever Rukoslav
Which Svatopluk received; this and the weapons, with joy
He accepted, parting from the Bavarian king.
It was a tearful farewell that he shared with his bride,
Adelajda, who raced up to him, tears in her eyes,
Adjuring him with many fond entreaties to keep
Himself away from all the shocks of battle, fell chance
That might put him in harm's way, and to return to her
Safe and sound as soon as his victory was assured.
And then he mounted his steed, its coat as white as snow,
Swifter of foot than any mountain gust, spurring him
To flight towards the army on the march. Hardly had
The sun sunk beneath Ocean's waves a third time, shooting
Bright rays of fiery light into the darkling heavens
Than the clatter of many hooves and men's tramping feet
Reached his ears, with the distant neighing of eager steeds,
And his eyes beheld the spangling glory of countless
Spearpoints a-glitter in the sun's last rays, along with
Helmets with feathers bobbing, flashing shields. He pulled up
And paused, drinking in the spectacle, before spurring
His charger on. Before long he'd reached the rearmost troops
Who had just halted at a place appointed to rest
That evening, after the long day's constant marching.
   The first troops he inspected were from the eastern lands

Bordering Slovakia: Austrians — known as
Rakúsaks from the castle Rakús. Their commander
Was Agilmund. Beside him were clever Hengeswald
And cruel Manhart, smouldering with fiery vengeance
Toward the Slovaks, who once, when Rastislav was king,
Tore from him with victorious hand his pillaged estates.
   Further on he beheld the capable regiments
Of the Bavarians, outfitted in pike and sword,
Warlike beyond all measure, their breastplates and helmets
Polished, flashing in the dying light of the sunset.
Their leader was Hartung the Brave, of limbs and torso
Large, who never left a battle unvictorious.
Next to him were his comrades: Erchenpald, and Otto,
And Ernest. Besides these Waninch and Unhat the Small.
   Next to these he spotted Tyrolean mountaineer hosts
Led by that slaughterer of wild animals, Dipold,
Whose only recreation and joy in life was war.
When he was not hurling a javelin in battle
He'd train his weapons on the denizens of the woods,
Stalking the powerful bear and the foam-flecked wild boars.
With him came Alfrid, and Luprecht, tinder to anger.
   The next regiments to these, outfitted with the best arms,
Speaking in two tongues and clad in two distinct colours:
The capable nations of Styria met his eyes.
These were led by Humbold and Gromislav the steady:
The former chief to Germans from the upper reaches
Of their homeland, the latter, Slovenes of the lowlands.
Kraič, Pačemíl and Grajsa the spearman second
Gromislav, while Irmengard, Walter, and great Sigurd,
Who in the cavern of Retelstein slew the dragon,
Rounded out the staff of Humbold, no less mighty, he.
   The regiments of the Carinthian youths came next,
Their vigour unspent, though they bore such heavy armour;
Ready to leap into battle at moment's notice.
Skilful Svenčar wheeled among them on his eager steed,
While the sun flashed off his bright helmet here, glittering
Shield there, his horse's mane and helmet-tuft bobbed and waved —
Despite the fact that his right arm hung numb, still unhealed
The wound received at jousting — still he came, war-eager,
With him, his comrades Budimír and sharp-eyed Oblag.

Next to these stood the regiments from nearby Kranjska,
Led by Jesutbor, prudent, yet virile, youthful yet;
At his side rode Zaglav, his nephew, for his own son
Had fallen in battle; and Merisáv, swift Dragšo.

Lastly, Svatopluk's gaze fell upon the Pannonians
In their many thousands, varied in livery and arms;
First of all here were drawn up the Slovak regiments,
Divided in three, and each with as many war-chiefs,
At the head of all, with his men, was Radbod the brave,
In fearsome armour, and helmet tuft fiercely bobbing,
But that which filled the onlooker with more dread — his spear
Gripped in his mighty right hand, enough to discourage
All knights who beheld Radbod's stallion wheel towards him.
Stout Dobroslav trotted up close to him on his mount,
And Bojmír, his brother, of tightly-weft brawn, wielding
Each a lance — excellent picadors both, no less skilled
In archery, whose darts could bring down the swiftest bird.

Mutimír rode up, great warrior, with his comrades,
Swift-footed Mutimír, whom none might surpass, even
Fleet-footed chargers he'd outpace, and few were the feet
That still could stumble off after engaging his might
On the reddened sand of tourney-pitch. With him hastened
Ratimír, and Kučbor, renowned lord of many herds.

Next appeared Chocil with his three Slovak regiments,
That warrior valiant, leading brave souls to battle,
Who once with his pious father and lord Pribina
Was banished past the Danube by Mojmír grown mighty,
Who moved against their fatherland. There, for the faithful,
Velehrad had been established, so named on account
Of its many churches raised to the glory of God.
With him his son, the duteous and fair Vratislav
Went, still young, but not far behind his elders in wit
And clever ideas; stronger-limbed than his father.
Bogdán and the impetuous Jarohnev led the rest.

The sad remnants of the neglected Avars were there
As well — who in ages more fortunate were busied
With nothing but the savage labour of slaughtering
Other nations, spilling innocent blood, pillaging
The lands they invaded, until their banditry led
Them to their own destruction — bitter loot! A portion

Meagre were spared the sword. Those humble legions were led
By Salak, puffed-up in vain pride as the successor
To Khans of the most ancient bloodlines. The sword he bore
Once made the world entire tremble when it was wielded
By his forebears. From his massive shoulders hung a bow.
   And then, sharp-eyed Svatopluk scanned the widely-spread trunk
Of the armies — Germans, led by Gerold dutiful,
Thane of Karl — who'd once migrated to Pannonia
From the Bavarian marches, heeding king's command.
Above their legions heroic Engiškalk was placed
And Vilém — but they were still to lead them in battle
Victorious, for, wounded by skilful hurl of spear,
One had his ribs crushed, the other his thighs, defending
Their city from attack — wounds throbbing still. However
Their troops yearned for those two past commanders, they were not
Deprived of skilful warriors to lead them; brothers
Twain, breathing fire both for the coming fray now led them
To battle: wise Erchenbert and Ludolf, a brawler
Beyond all measure, the one a peerless archer,
The other unmatched with javelin. Erchenbert's son
Wato was with them, and Ludolf's Madalbot as well,
Both virgins to war's tussling, keen for experience.
Ratfréd attends them with valiant Ulrich, and Wilbert,
Broiling in anger towards the King of the Slovaks.
He took up arms against his better will in the cause,
But his pride could not bear the shame had he stayed at home.
   There amongst them all stood Britwald, gigantic of frame,
Commander-in-chief of the forces assembled there.
Taller than all by a head, his broad chest protected
By triple-weft chain-mail of gold. In his strong right hand
He bore a sharp lance, resting in the crook of his arm
To the left: metal-tipped, such as only he could hurl,
Such a log of spruce it was! Wearing a golden casque
With black plumage, through which when the rushing wind whistled
Such a terror it sent abroad, moaning, like an oak
For a thousand years growing on the Morava's banks,
Its vital juices thrusting it towards the heavens,
When the hurricane falls upon it and here and there
Its cloud-scraping summit nods, its trunk rumbles and creaks.
   When mighty King Svatopluk had pondered long the troops,

He ascended a hillock that rose there in their midst
And from this high rostrum, he addressed them in such words:
  'O worthy hosts of warriors, eager for the fight!
The long-awaited time has come for all here to prove
Their manliness and stout heart, battling in my just cause!
I know that you shall now reward my pains twice over,
Deprived as I was of throne and honour by ill chance.
Now, if you have any fellow-feeling for me,
Or if it's the thirst for glory that motivates you,
Or concern for your fatherland that weighs on your heart
And would now display your fealty to your monarch,
Grip now your hefty weapons, and fight with might and main!
Hack with your swords, let fly your arrows, fling javelins,
And batter down the throngs rebellious, into the dust!
Return me my spurned honour, return me my sceptre
And in this great trial of ordeal prove my innocence!
Thus shall you win great names for yourselves as well, glory
For your king; you shall be the flower of your nation.
Worn-out today with marching, rest your limbs and refresh
Your strength with food and wine. Tomorrow when the dawn splits
The horizon, we set off to war!' Thus he finished,
And from those thousands of hearts, enkindled with zealous flames
They cried out, ready for the fray, roaring 'Victory!'
Glorifying the shades of their fathers — 'Victory!'

CANTO VIII

Seeing that the Bavarians were now nearing Devín, Černobog incites his comrades to place an obstacle in their way. They gather the clouds and send torrents of rain crashing down upon them. The Morava swells and floods its banks. The Germans gather in council, seeking a remedy for the situation. Should they attempt a crossing of the river in flood? or wait for its waters to recede? Svatopluk urges an immediate crossing. They heed his words: they construct as many rafts as are necessary, and set out upon them across the river, under fire from the Slovaks, who shoot their arrows upon them, breasting the rafts in a long rank. A fierce battle ensues, and so many fall on both sides that the waters run black with gore. Slavimír cheers his men on. The Germans begin to retreat in a crushing press backwards, which when Britwald notices, he sharply whips them back toward the battlefield. On his part, Svatopluk, who had up till now remained on the far side with the cavalry, leads one half of the troops through a nearby wood, unnoticed by the Slovaks, and fords the river there. He and his men draw stealthily near their foes, after which they suddenly rush upon them from the flank. In a panic, the enemy retreats to Devín.

  Černobog, noting great numbers of Bavarians
Nearing proud Devín, and that the Slovaks advanced not
Against their open ranks, but formed a defensive line
Along the river, there to await the enemy,
Heavily armed to match the invaders, hastened
To rouse his lackeys, whom he addressed in angry words:
 'Look there! And see how Svatopluk and the cruel hosts
Of Germany enter Moravia, unopposed!
Soon they shall penetrate the river-gully and ford
The narrows to reach the farther bank in one stout push!
Can it be that our powers have so paled, grown flaccid,
That we're incapable of foiling this? Come, gather
The thunderheads and make them pour down rain in cascades
Upon those legions! Flood the banks of the Morava
To push them farther back! Quickly! Make haste! Herd the black
Clouds close, Prick them into a roaring storm! Draw curtains
Of rain impenetrable before the German troops!'
 Thus the black spirit. His brethren heeded his commands —
They threw themselves into their task: from the four corners
They assembled burly clouds and chafed them to anger.

Chief in these labours was Stribog, ruler of the winds.
Stifling all the others he prodded on the South wind.
The clouds thickened so, the light of day was extinguished.
The sun's face, veiled with sooty blackness, turned crimson.
The clouds burst, unable to contain their waters more,
And rain crashed in torrents like mighty rivers coursing.
Earth thundered beneath the pounding and no long time passed
Before the river valley swelled with foaming billows.
Wider and wider spread the Morava, overspilling
Its banks to turn field and meadow into morasses.
Embankment and dyke disappeared, sunk in the new sea.
The Slovaks were made to withdraw their defensive line
To find surer footing on the dry land that remained.
   No sooner had the cruel storm boomed its last salvo
Than the brave Bavarians reached the swollen river.
To their left a path led along the banks to a wood
That stretched into the distance towards the northern chill.
Pinewoods they were, for the most part, on hilly ground
Where the waters reached not; here and there a solitary
Oak raised its crown, or that fragile timber, the rowan;
Blackberries too were sprinkled about in sparse thickets
And catkins near the riverbank; alders in bogs, too,
Stretching their high brows toward the starry firmament.
'Twas there that Svatopluk led the rain-battered Germans.
Soon bonfires raged, fed by pine-logs crackling and spitting
And sending aloft dense clouds of smoke, black, resinous.
The men stopped shivering as their soaked clothing dried out,
Chafing their shuddering limbs around the great campfires.
As soon as the steaming warmth spread through their clammy bones,
The leaders of all the regiments convoked a moot.
They'd seen how the Morava, swollen, overspilled its banks —
Engulfing all the features of the land like a sea!
They'd seen their foes ready to receive them, their weapons
Flashing in what meagre light there was, forbidding them
Access at all points along the farther bank, eager
For war. But first the river had to be overcome,
Its flood increasing wildly, eating away the banks
With groanings terrible to the ears as it washed past.
Leaning on spears at the ready, without hesitation,
They took counsel: What were they to do? Set forth upon

The deep waters on rafts? An arduous labour, that!
Or wait until the floodwaters recede, and assume
Their wonted current, sliding a calmer riverbed?
Some urged the former, others were pleased with the latter,
And like a boat caught in a whirlpool, spun now this way
Now that, the prey of winds contending, teased near a shore
It never shall reach, so swirled the chieftains' discussion,
Bewildering the fraught minds of the Bavarians,
Until Svatopluk, unable to bear any more
Such hesitation, decided the matter firmly:
   'Why wait any longer? Are we such idle villains
As to let pass our best opportunity like this?
The other river-bank is made of steeper bluffs than ours —
These floodwaters are a godsend! They elevate us
To the same level as our foes! When the flood recedes
It shall reveal steep cliffs to be surmounted before
We grapple with our foe. These brave lads of ours will tire
With clambering the slippery steep bank, while those there,
Rested, will meet however few should survive the climb
And the punishing fire, holding the higher ground.
So let us dither no more — but set axes in motion,
Felling the trees for logs to construct as many rafts
As we need for the crossing. Then, with the help of God,
We'll punt our way across the swollen stream, and meet them
On even terms. Should their army wait on the dry ridge
As now, when we get close, not much shall separate us
From them — we'll pull up in the shallows and wade on in
Unfatigued. If they come closer, entering the flood
Themselves to meet us — all the better! The bed drops off
Quicker than they expect. We, on our rafts, they — below us
Amid the swirling currents… Hard it is to fight so!'
   He finished, and all the chiefs assented to a man.
At once commands were given for the men to hew down
The wood with sharp axes, and carpenters to prepare
The rafts. Eagerly, even knights set about their tasks:
Hands used to wielding swords seize saw-handles — lumberjacks
With quartered crests and squires! They felled pine trees with dispatch,
And oak-trees too, whose toppling crowns had once soared so high;
Rowan trees shivered and fell, and trembling alders as well,
Till the air was filled with a different thundering:

The cracks and booms of forests felled instead of lightning.
The woodland beasts escaped in panic, birds flew their nests —
And where before had been primeval gloom, the sun's rays
Startled the moss. Here men lopped the branches from the trunks,
Stripping the bark and planing even the knotty boles.
The carpenters measured the logs, and drilled dowel-holes
To fix them together, while others carved the rowlocks.
At last, by withes tight-bound, on rollers they dragged their boats
Down to the water. To each of the rafts was affixed
Four wings — the oars, to be swung by eager volunteers.
As bees, when the time of their golden harvest draws near,
Restlessly swarm to and fro from blooming field to hive,
Filling their vaults hexagonal with the sweet nectar
They cull from flowers and kneading the wax honeycomb
And the air is filled with their humming — so was it here:
All in a ferment of labour until all the rafts
Were made ready and borne down to the swollen river.
Then the hasty fleet set out, each craft evenly manned
With armed men — as many as might be safely carried
Aboard, eyes fixed on the far shore, grim and determined.
   Hartung the brave set out first, at the head of thirty rafts
Of Germans, ten on each, four rowers to ply the oars.
Humbold and Gromislav led forth just as many men —
So did Agilmund, Erchenbert, and Ludolf in turn.
In the very centre Britwald gripped an oar himself;
The rest followed him all evenly spaced, oars churning.
Soon all had fought through the current and passed the bank
Submerged. The rough prows bit the silt; into the shallows
The warriors leapt with a shout — all except Dipold.
For his raft, barely having set out upon the stream,
Was struck amidships by an alder swept from the bank
By the flood. It snared the listing raft in its branches
And neither the oars, nor the courage of the oarsmen,
Could push free from the clinching grasp of the tree-branches
Which shortly, like some infernal hand, pulled the raft down
Into the deep, with the men, to an unheroic
Death. Only strong Volkmár and clever Hubert escaped:
For having seen the gnarly threat approaching, they leapt
Into the river, and swimming to the nearest rafts
Clambered aboard with the aid of arms outstretched pulling

Them up safe, though sodden, lamenting their drowned comrades.
  Now, when on the farther bank the troops of Slavimír,
Armed and waiting, beheld the Bavarians take raft,
They splashed into the shallows, wherever was footing,
On fiery colt and swift-legged stallion. The archers
Let fly over their comrades' line their arrows and spears
At the nearing rafts. The air filled with dreadful whistling,
The very sky grew dark beneath the iron tempest,
Which raged in both directions as the Bavarians,
Who'd reached the shallows, strove to link their rafts together
And hurled their own spears and missiles at Slavimír's troops.
Frightful the wounds torn open in men's flesh; horribly
Death raged on all hands. Hartung then bellowed to his men:
  'Now, my brave lads! Now put your backs into it and row!
Group all the rafts together — raft by raft and hold tight;
Then train your fire thick on the enemy's cavalry!
Set up a double firing line, and let them have it!
We'll bury them beneath our arrows! Fire! Bring them down'!
  Such were his words, but they could hear none of his commands:
The roaring of the flood drowned him out. Nevertheless,
They did his bidding, as it were, bringing the rafts in
Tight, out of self-preservation, all instinctively,
And when they'd locked them into one platform, port-starboard,
They trained their weapons on the cavalry with a shout,
Though the river buckled and foamed beneath them, and flocks
Of iron flashed through the air from all sides howling near.
  Grundelfing was foremost to rush against the horsemen.
He brought down seven steeds who stood against him with swipes
Of his alder-club, until he had broken their legs.
Wounded they fell, their heavy chests tilting the pine-log
Rafts they'd splashed upon unluckily. Three of their riders
Undaunted leapt from their writhing chargers and attacked
Their Bavarian enemies with sabres unsheathed:
Zaprislav hacked down Berthold, Subor slaughtered Mundwald,
And Medzidruh slew Volkman, only to fall in turn
Those three: one Rupert, another Grim, and Adelmund
The third sent to the gloom. Then ireful Rozvad rushed near —
Unable to see other succour, he hurled himself
At Grundelfing, whom he tackled, gripping him tightly
Around the waist. They toppled from the raft and vanished

Beneath the waves, stout limbs grappling with limbs no less stout.
Rozvad yet bellowed, resurfacing: 'Just so much muck
Shall you acquire, invader! My dead friends enfeoff you'!
No more — he sank as well, and the flood waters rushed in
To chase his brave soul from his throat, with that of his foe.
   Light-footed Albert, who had no peer on the dry ground,
Had his raft snagged by an oak stump, which once had been
Sacred to Perún, before the pious Rastislav,
Still young at the time, had the god's idol hacked apart,
Splintered by axes and burnt in the flames like kindling:
His men fought to release it with their oars and lance-butts,
But all to no avail, for the raft stuck fast. Nothing
Else to do, they leapt into the waters to free it
By hand. But while at this vain toil, defenceless, Slovak
Arrows rained in upon them — a horrible slaughter
Ensued; the river bobbed with German corpses, the raft,
Spiked as it was upon the stump, spiked still, abandoned,
Swung this way and that, rocked on the reddening flow.
   First among all in strength of limb towered amazing
Všechlap, nourished by his father on the milk of mares
In the deep forest, for his mother died in childbirth.
When he'd been weaned, his meat was game roasted on coal fires —
The fatty marrow of wild razorbacks and fierce bears
Was his most succulent delight. His bed — a cavern
Deep in the naked cliffs. 'Twas he who saw Aribert
Venture near, at which he walloped the earth in anger
With his club — a great log of oak so massive, two men
Of normal brawn could barely lift together. With this
And a large seven-ply shield to protect him from darts
Slung by the Germans he set off to attack. Indeed
A thick tempest of sharp arrows and spears began to rain
Down upon him from all sides as he drew near the rafts.
Not one grazed his skin though, nor made him retreat one inch.
Then, with two hands, he hoisted a large fir tree aloft,
And with a wild bellow, flung it at one raft, sweeping
All from the deck, head over heels. Chaos, cries, jangling
Armour, and splashing — catastrophe for the Germans:
Some were run through by their own weapons, others were crushed
Beneath the massive trunk hurled by the giant, their bones
Mashed into a pulp. When Všechlap's comrades beheld this,

They urged him on with cries: 'O valiant, mighty Všechlap!
Smash the Bavarians! We're right behind you! Our spears
Will finish off those who evade your mighty wallops!'
So they exulted, and so he pressed on, raging,
Sweeping the enemy into the waves with that club
Or tree, rather — mighty Garwald's vessel, and Adolf's
— That sharp-eyed archer's — soon bobbed swept clean of their crewmen;
Cruel Wigbert's, and that captained by great Adelgard
He capsized, and those men who flailed about in the waters
He snatched and drowned. But the great-soulled Marbod, unable
To bear such ruin, grabbed a long, sharp, metal-tipped lance
To thrust at Všechlap from his right flank. Yet the quick-armed
Metislav caught sight of this in time, and with dispatch
Split Marbod's larynx with an arrow. Man and missile
Unlaunched fell harmlessly into the deep with a splash.
Now fear seized Marbod's fellows, as they jabbed uncertain
Lances in a faint defence, withdrawing, wavering
Back to no avail, soon overwhelmed by a like fate.
Once more, as gravid clouds release their loads in torrents
Of hail, Všechlap continued his barrage — raging,
Advancing, hurling at them whatever came to hand
Swamping raft after raft in a frenzy of slaughter.
   Then clever Wilibald again hastened to the fore
Swinging his stave at the legs of the ramping horses.
But Žurovlád, undaunted, cried out to his comrades:
'My valiant friends! Train your arrows on the swift oarsmen,
But let a number attack the rafts with javelins
Forbidding them egress — a further portion, hold back,
With your sharp blades to cover your comrades attacking'!
Thus he commanded; immediately arrows flew
And took down seven of the rowers. A cheer went up;
The spearmen grabbed their arms and eagerly leapt aboard,
Thrusting with lances, hacking with sharp battle-axes,
Although the fierce Germans forced the horses to withdraw;
Sharp Erenfrid took off Lastov, Rajnald —Pustosvet,
While Sebald brought down two men — Chvalomír and Výško —
Raging at them for having slain his brother Gerard,
He took his vengeance. Myslav aimed at greybeard Gotbert
Who sank to his knees, and the blazing spear meant for him
Instead pierced Rudolf of winsome countenance — straight through;

He toppled into the water and found death twice over:
Drowning, and pierced. Gotbert took off Hnevomír, Klodulf
Battered down Zemomysl. Then Žurovlád with sharp axe
Split Adelolf, and clever Helwig, Adelbod, Kempt,
And two flamboyant youngsters named Lambert and Guido,
Fruit of the loins of Radulf by lovely Otilda —
Their brief sun setting. Wolpert and Herman the hunter
Fell too, as did the grizzled Hajno, famed among his folk
For orchard-work, and his great skill in grafting fruit trees.
But here was a different pruning: these wounds close not.
Nor were the other soldiers behind-hand in the scrum;
The shallows seethed with men striving to lay waste their foe.
So much blood was spilled then that the river changed in hue —
The silver Morava ran black with the grapplers' gore.
Oars and other accoutrements floated in splinters,
Spears and spent missiles — and the corpses of both Germans
And Slavimír's men littered the face of the river
Swirling in eddies, now sinking, now floating back up.
   Then, as all were engaged in the slog of attrition,
The waters, so widely flooded, began to recede,
Retreating from the meadows to their accustomed bed,
Stranding the rafts of the Bavarians on the muck.
Struck by the spectacle of the receding waters,
Men from both sides paused their hacking in dumbfounded truce,
But not Sulík — no, he paused not: he spun toward the foe
And hurled his spear mightily. This, Warnefríd, sublime
Swordsman, split just as he'd turned his eyes in amazement
At the bank, that seemed to grow out of the faithless stream.
The bolt caught him between his nape and shoulders, its tip
Slicing his tongue and smashing his lower row of teeth,
To emerge from his mouth like some grotesque appendage.
When Bertwín, his fast friend, beheld that absurd horror,
Riven with ire and sadness, he burned to take revenge
And reached back for his quiver. But before he could set
An arrow-notch at tendon and take aim, he was cut down
By Sulík, who got the draw on him — bow and arrow
Fell harmlessly from his limp grasp as Sulík's arrow
Ripped through his throat. Blood gushing, he fell upon his friend.
   This broke the spell that kept the men stupidly peaceful,
And Slavimír's young bucks and the fierce Bavarians

Set to the battle with anger and vigour renewed,
Although they fought a common foe now: the river muck
That sucked at their feet gone ungainly. Still, the darts shrieked
Through the air, weapons glanced upon armour, spears shattered
With cracks like trees falling; the chaos of war drowned out
All other sounds. Bertchtold raged on with his heavy lance
— He who abided in Passau, whose beautiful home
And stately garden-plots surpassed those of three hundred
Men of great wealth —Žitoslav was the first he laid low,
Then black-eyed Chválboh, Dražka and Hlavsa, but then
When he swung his ferocious spear at Horboj, a flash
Of sharp metal blazed, lopping away its copper tip.
Quickly unsheathing his sword, this he plunged with fire
Into the bowels of his attacker, spilling his guts
Upon the black mire. Then: Istislav, Medzoň and Chvast
He cut down, and more men too would have met their death
At his hands had it not been for great Výboj, outraged —
He shifted his way and hacked off his arm at elbow
As some clever craftsman in a young woodlet might fell
An ash or tall elm for wagon-shaft or wheelbase.
Then the prudent Tatobor aimed his death-bearing reed
At Gumbrecht, from whom he took an arrow to the throat
But not before his own dart tore into Gumbrecht's loins.
Thus both men took each other down at the same moment:
Tatobor falling backwards, and Gumbrecht on his face.
Not far from these, two doughty youths set to close combat:
Dark-eyed Vitohosť and Wolfreg of gallant posture.
These hurled their javelins at one another — on paths
Identical, their sharp heads colliding in mid-flight
Gave off a horrid clatter. At which each of the youths
Lurched forward, enflamed at having sent their darts flying
In vain, to pluck their shafts out of the mire. Once again
They set to the rabid contest without any pause.
Vitohosť was quicker this time, running Wolfreg's brow
Through and through. And thus brave Wolfreg fell, as did his spear,
Useless now, to earth. Hodimír, who hailed from Bóry,
A crafty huntsman he, who brought down each beast and bird
With skilful archery, now let a swift arrow fly
At young Takulf, who with his trumpet fired German hearts
To battle. The sharp missile pierced his Adam's apple:

At once his trump went silent with one wee final yelp,
And its coarse slogans of bloodshed were no longer heard.
Bilbach, enflamed, rushed at the hefty Sirád, who owned
Three hundred hives burgeoning with honey and beeswax.
He flung his javelin, but it flew past, to take down
Swarthy Preslov instead, which mightily envenomed
Sirád, seeing his worthy comrade felled, and swiftly
He let fly from his bow a well-aimed arrow, which plunged
In under Bilbach's eye, just as Hort, his friend, ran up:
He measured mighty Protislav with his javelin,
But missed wide right; the lance's head pierced the grey neck
Of Myslok's poor steed — the evil dart punctured his throat
Emerging through his mane. Mortally wounded, the horse
Reared in his agony and confusion, hooves beating
The vain air frantically, before he fell heavily
To earth, spilling his rider, thrashing his noble head
In frenzied agony, until his soul departed.
   Still Slavimír urged his eager battlers onward,
Giving them heart with fiery speech: 'Forward, my brave lads!
The moment has arrived for us to wrest sweet liberty
With the sword that slaughters slavery and subjection!
Now let us surpass this fragile flesh and hurl ourselves
Upon our enemies with all the might that's in us!
We've whittled down their numbers, and now no cavalry
Will cross the floodwaters to bring them the aid they need:
Why, even Svatopluk the Fierce has not shown his face!'
   Thus Slavimír, to whom his troops responded, rushing
At their foes with hearts even more enflamed. Nezabud
Lay Wolfríd low, who'd towered over all his comrades
Like a tall pine amidst dwarf-holms. Here Vítazoslav
Slew Herwín, there Sumor took down Gutmund, skilled bowyer,
Brought low by the craft at which he'd made his livelihood.
Zemislav busied himself with sallow-cheeked Renard,
Umýl grappled with Klunibert; Sitbor the Bow-legged
Slew Frídman — those two slugging hammers and thrusting spears,
While Sitbor cleft through the archer's bright armour with axe
Double bladed, sprawling him cleft upon the dark mire.
Slavoľub too, the scion of fallen Okta, brought
His battle-axe down upon the crown of sullen From,
Cleaving his helmet and splitting his skull in two halves,

One severed hemisphere, still cradling the brain, falling
To earth apart from the other, helm-feathers bobbing
Above it as if in wonder. Then fierce Hodislav,
Expert in every art of war, began to rage
As fiercely as a frosty hurricano rushing down
From icy northern slopes, piling massive banks of snow;
Thus elemental Hodislav, heaping hills of death,
First with unerring bow bringing down Frídmund, Wolgast
And clever Berechtwald, hearty Rajnmár and Engelbert,
Once the graceful dancer, whose legs then thrashed in spasms
Of agony, and Hartwín the beauteous, whose face
No longer would move a girl's heart to pangs of longing.
This was his first battle, and it was to be his last.
He hadn't even had time to raise a hand in wrath
Against an enemy before misfortune met him.
But Brunhild, despite his experience, was felled too,
And Walrám likewise; so many young Bavarians
Littered the muddy field, so many flights of arrows
He sent in showers upon their hosts. Drawing near,
He cast aside quiver and bow and fell upon them
With the ominous burden of his sharp spear, thrusting —
The first he skewered — clean through the forehead — was Ramulf,
Crushing the skull, and whetting cheekbones intended
To shield, into sharp allies, shards piercing through the brain.
Thus dark night eternal night enveloped him, drawing its shades
Between him and the light of day. Next strong Eberbach
Fell, son of Arnd, who'd taught his fellows the art of herbs,
With throat demolished. At Ajch's shield Hodislav pounded
And pounded until he pushed his spear-point clean through it;
It slid through the chain-mail too, piercing the lung. The loins
Of Ring the Frisian were his next target, but the lance slipped wide
In the rush; still its thrust was not wholly in vain —
It tore through his right thigh and snapped his femur in two.
Then came the turn of two brothers, Gildo and Heinrich,
Who lived together in one room in their old homestead.
Inseparable at rest and when ploughing the fields,
Inseparable they sank into their grave. Unslaked
Still his fury, Hodislav murdered cruel Altman,
Then brought horrid slaughter upon Bernwald, and Volkprecht,
And Stein; insatiable his bloodlust, he paid no mind

To how his own exhausted limbs ached with the hacking,
No, he hurled his mighty javelin at Erchenpald,
Spitting his chin. The lance spread wide the jaws and sliced
The tongue at its root. As a century-old cedar
Picked by some youths for a mill-chute (when nicely seasoned),
Or for a swift canoe to skim over the swift Váh
Will fall with a loud crash biting a trench in the sand,
So Erchenpald was toppled headlong into the mire
And the echoes of his crash resounded from the bankside.
  Britwald burst into great flames of wrath when he beheld
His men begin to lose courage, waver, and, slowly,
Slink backwards and retreat. Envenomed at the skulkers
— Harsh term, for long they'd fought! — He roared at them in such words:
  'Where are you heading, you fools? Back to the deep river
That we've just crossed with so much effort? You'll risk your lives
In its swift current? Are you seeking your own ruin?
The enemy's land lies this way! Is that how you fight?
Is that your even ground? Will you fire his towns from there?
O, how you boasted — from afar — of toppling Slavimír
And routing the Slovak army in a pitched battle!
What are those words worth now? O, how the bold spirit ebbs!
If you've a sense of honour yet, or shame, stop fleeing,
Dig in your heels, control yourselves, and fulfil your oaths!
There Devín lies — the road to it must be hacked open
Through the enemy lines! Clear the path for Svatopluk
That leads to his throne! But if cowardice so grips you
That your heart's shrunken now, and patters in base terror,
Find you someplace to cringe and I'll press on by myself!
Toss down those arms from hands unworthy of wielding them
And wait there, trembling! But when I return in glory
It shall be your turn to die, still crouching shamefully!'
  Such were the words he spoke then, stinging them to the quick.
So now like lions, driven wild with hunger, catching
Scent of fat herds of bullocks grazing on sloping fields
They hurled themselves with violence on their enemies:
Erenhold slew Stražimír, Berwyn Oprislav,
Irmenwald Veľbeh, Giselbert cut down Neustup,
The skilful Zorislav took himself to Hengeswald —
In vain: for first he was cut down by bold Witelsbach,
That strapping warrior. Saved from sure death, Hengeswald

Swept his sharp blade at Milobrat, severing his head
From his trunk — it flew off still helmeted, tufts bobbing
Like helpless, broken wings. Fearless now, Hengeswald spun
To the side, and skilfully ran his sword-blade clear through
Zvesto's left cheek, then sliced through Mirko's nose; he lopped off
Vratižír's fingers, while Witelsbach no less deftly wheeled and spit
Milko's side above the spleen, with his lance
Mauling Vlado's mighty thighs, sending both to the gloom.
He meted like judgement to three other warriors:
Zámoj, Chvál, and Hostislav. Unslaked his thirst for gore,
With force he punctured Pravdoslav's temple — how the flood
Thundered beneath him as he fell! As when some boulder
Loosened by gnawing rains plunges down the mountainside
To crash into the deep Váh, or broad-spreading Volga,
The waters part with shock and violence, in outrage
Seeming to roar before they cover the shattered peak
And slide calmly away from the thundering echoes —
Thus Pravdoslav fell, to be covered by the river.
Pomnislav measured Adelrat, tensing his bow, yet
Adelrat's dart struck Pomnislav first, splitting his larynx,
And stifling both voice and breath at once. Then Bolemír,
Obezd and Všetrap fell beneath his mighty right arm,
As well as Baťán, famed far and wide for his music,
Who ever had new songs to teach to his shepherd friends;
To whom whole flocks and herds would press unto, when beneath
A shady copse, sitting alone, he took pipe in hand
And played — the very rivers hushed their roar, the birds trilled
Not, enraptured — O, how better had it been for him
To remain amongst flocks of sheep and goats, far away
From wars and their ferocious thunderheads of iron!
  Now, Svatopluk, as soon as the waters receded,
Drew up his calvary, dividing them in two halves;
For up till that moment he had not crossed the river.
But then he drew his youthful horsemen aside, to lead
Them by bosky pathway unnoticed by the Slovaks —
Flanking Slavimír's troops, whose attention was elsewhere.
Thus unmarked by their scuffling foe, they forded the stream
Gone shallow, then, on the far bank, he addressed them thus:
'My worthy comrades! Form up now in even ranks,
And advance as one, but as silently as you can,

Then, all at once, we'll charge upon the foe and rout him!'
Thus Svatopluk; the cavalry heeded his commands,
Pricking softly through woodlands, their horses' hooves muffled,
Until they'd nearly reached the edge of the battlefield.
Then horns blared, and with a shout they urged their steeds forward,
Ramming their startled enemy in the thickest flank.
Chaos erupted in the Slovak ranks at this charge
Unexpected, which fell like a bolt from the blue sky.
Bavarians before them, and Bavarians now
Coming at them from the side — swords clashed, armour clattered,
And death reaped a harvest on all hands. Whole hosts were slain,
As panicked men flailed blindly. Those who could escape
Rushed up to Devín, seeking rescue within her walls.

CANTO IX

Having routed the hosts of Slavimír, Svatopluk orders his men to make camp and prepare a great number of ladders for the storming of the city. He alerts the leaders that he wishes to send a spokesman to the Slovaks, to inquire whether they are willing to avoid further battle and accept him as their king, under the conditions specified by Karolman. He takes this mission upon himself and hastens to Devín. Slavimír allows him to be admitted inside, and summons a diet of the elders and the chief commanders of his armies. Receiving a poor welcome, Svatopluk relates his misfortunes to them, and the conditions according to which he is to rule. It is for this reason, he states, that he has come to Devín alone, so as to convince them to accept these conditions. Slavimír responds that he will render his sceptre to him only if he can wrest it from his hands on the battlefield with the aid of his Bavarian troops. Milín seconds this counsel, stating that they would all of them prefer to fall fighting than to accept such a king, under such conditions. For his part, Vseslav proposes that Svatopluk abandon the Bavarian army and join up with his Slovak brothers; in such a case, he reckons, Slavimír would be inclined to transfer supreme power into his hands, should none of the other fathers there assembled be opposed. Indeed, all of those assembled give their assent, even Milín, and Slavimír too, whereupon they urge him to accept the royal authority and lead their troops against the Bavarians, so as to become an independent ruler. Following a very long consideration, he accepts, at which all those assembled elect him their new king, amid great rejoicing. Through Zvestoň, Svatopluk informs Britwald of what has transpired, inquiring whether he is prepared to return home in peace, or whether he is to lead the Slovak troops against him, and drive them from the land with arms. Frightfully infuriated, Britwald fulminates against Svatopluk and all the Slovaks, and, roused to furious action, leads his entire army in an assault upon Devín.

After having routed the army of Slavimír,
Achieving partially the longed-for victory,
Svatopluk ordered his men to encamp on the plain
By the river, raise defensive ramparts, and prepare
Siege ladders for the coming assault on high Devín.
So the men put aside their weaponry, and, taking
In hand tools more peaceful, eagerly set to the task,
Digging three trenches broad and deep, raising salients
Of the excavated soil. The fourth side — was the river.
As the ramparts grew higher, sharp palisades were raised
On slopes made firm with revetments, the men labouring

Without pause, like swarms of bees in honey-harvest time.
Then Svatopluk came before Britwald and addressed him:
  'O valiant voivode, commander of these legions,
He who rules the Heavens has granted us victory
— Our first — over our enemy, who routed, has fled.
We need not fear but the taking of Devín's assured,
Given our mighty arms and your all-wise leadership,
No matter how firm those walls — impregnable, they say —
They're crammed with doubters now, whose minds are wracked with terror,
And so, let's send some trusted spokesmen to the Slovaks
To see whether now they'd voluntarily submit
To me as their king, under the conditions set forth
By Karolman, thus avoiding more pointless carnage,
And so we might bring my forebear's will to fulfilment
Sparing more bloodshed, avoiding more risk to our brave troops.
But whom shall we send? I propose to set out myself
On the well-known road to Devín; I reckon it's me
Stands the best chance of convincing them, and regaining
My ancient favour, while you remain here, making firm
Our hasty defences, lest my mission go awry,
In which case, take up arms again and come and rescue me,
Rushing their battlements with overwhelming legions'.
  Without awaiting a reply, he wheeled his charger
About and galloped off toward Devín, while Britwald gaped.
Barely had he sped onto the plains at Devín's foot
Than Obzor sighted him, who of all men had an eye
Sharp as an eagle's. Obzor had been standing sentry
On Devín's highest point, expecting the foe. Turning
To Polemír, the sentry at his elbow, he said:
'Look there — what splendid champion bestride a white horse
Is galloping towards us? Can that be Svatopluk?
King Svatopluk, whose carriage I remember — just so
He'd urge his charger onward, mounted with just such grace!'
  Then Polemír, whose eyes were no less sharp, made reply:
'It seems to me as well that this is he — but those tufts
Adorning his flashing casque I do not recognise —
And that armour, bright as some golden constellation,
Was never his. That is some foreign shield he bears.
Yet it might well be that in redress of his torments,
The King of the Bavarians bestowed such on him.

Let's wait patiently. Soon enough all will become clear'.
  While they were thus discussing things, with speed Svatopluk
Rode up and reined in his charger at the castle gates.
Ho boldly called out to the sentries 'Ho there! The gates!
I come with a great matter to propose'. Vitoslav,
Skilful, and of all messengers the swiftest-footed,
Then took in his strong right hand his javelin immense,
And sped off to Slavimír with Svatopluk's demand.
The king nodded, and the heavy portcullis was raised.
At once he had a parliament convened of elders
And all the chief Slovak military commanders.
Once all had been made ready the thick gates were spread wide
And Svatopluk was led into the castle forecourt.
The eyes of many men followed him as he cantered
Past to the moot — a crowd of townsmen, both old and young —
The younger warriors were all of them most taken
With rapturous wonder. They gazed at his golden helmet,
At the black feathers that bobbed at its crown, at his shield,
And at the three-ply chain mail and the flashy armour
That girded his breast and limbs — rich gifts of Karolman.
And yet some cursed in silence, hearts brimming with hatred.
Silent too, he passed through the arcaded market square
Until he reached the metalled threshold of the town hall,
Where he dismounted his fleet-footed steed. With dispatch
Milhost' and Privol then led him into the presence
Of Slavimír and the elders, who cast upon him
Wrathful glares, the while angry murmuring smote his ears.
Then Slavimír turned a bitter grimace toward him,
Greeting him in unwelcome terms: 'O you, once our king,
Why have you now come to tempt the nation you betrayed?
Why have you come before us? What is your purpose here?'
  Thus Slavimír. Then Svatopluk spoke in mournful tones:
'O leader most accomplished, and you elders gathered
In diet — my sufferings are not unknown to you;
My sad life, buffeted by so much misadventure!
First was I forced to seek quarter among the Germans,
Who then, suspicious, cast me into a dark dungeon
For no good reason — me, innocent of any fault!
Which, once discovered, I was released, and led back out
Into the sweet light of day, confirmed by Karolman

In my realm, with that of Rastislav added thereto
— Which presently you hold — but under such conditions:
That I be his retainer, sending yearly tribute
Of horses one hundred, oxen double that number,
And like amount of silver; bound too in time of war
To come to his aid with auxiliary legions.
Besides this, he gave me his lovely daughter to wife,
That we might be sealed in bonds tighter than mere pactings;
'Twas he who gave me this powerful army, soldiers
Numberless to lead into war against you, to urge
You to accept my rule — by force, should you be stubborn
And refuse to relinquish my sceptre into these hands,
By your own free will acknowledging me your sovereign.
That's why I stand before you; such is my purpose here
In this stronghold of proud men gathered in parliament —
To convince you to accept the conditions set forth
By Karolman. What sense is there to shedding more blood...?'

  He had not quite finished speaking when the massive hall
Resounded with a loud detonation — in the spring,
When angry winds swoop down upon the thawed river Don,
Crashing ice-floes together, sending a startled wave
Booming upon its bank — like that, the thunderous echo
When Slavimír pounded the floor with his lance, bringing
An end to Svatopluk's oratory; thus the king roared:

  'For long we've known what sort of fortune met you, indeed,
As soon as you abandoned us, preferring to hew
To foreigners, subjecting yourself to German might.
Far better had it been for your honour had you writhed yet
In that blind dungeon, than released, to commit such crimes,
Such foul abominations! To sell your own nation
Into slavery, to rob it of its liberty,
To promise tribute: herds and silver pieces, and troops
To wage another's wars! Is this what you offer? Attempts to suborn us
To treason as base as yours is? Back to your lackeys!
Begone! And ready them for more war, more bloodletting!
For only there — on the battlefield — will I give up
The sceptre you long for! But first you must defeat me.
Then you may rule Slovakia with your German bride!'

  Thus Slavimír. Thereupon Milín arose, than whom
There was no man more eager to make war. Furious,

Chafed to a white heat by Svatopluk's words, he addressed
The king: 'O, leader most renowned! Of counsel no less
Sublime than your lion's heart is courageous! How well
You spoke, rejecting out of hand the base temptation
Tried upon you by him, who would lead you to treason,
And this nation — his own! — to unspeakable ruin!
He would deprive us of our sweet freedom and our rights,
And harness us — willingly! — to human servitude,
Scraping together tribute and silver for Germans
And spilling our dear blood on their behalf! I say no!
Better the bloody battle now, although we may fall;
Better to give our our flesh to our own black soil
Than submit ourselves to such a king under such terms!'
   When Milín had finished speaking, old Všeslav arose.
He was the father of worthy Zemižížeň, once
A great warrior himself, overcome by no man.
He once had been Svatopluk's mentor in archery
And swordsmanship, and the art of hurling javelin,
But now he was no longer fit for war, weak of limbs
And aged, but for all that he was a counsellor
Of priceless wisdom in all sorts of questions, and spoke
With gravity and eloquence. Rising, he took voice:
   'Excellent Slavimír! And you, grave council fathers!
Was it so totally evil, what Svatopluk did,
Abdicating his own freedom, so sweet to all men,
Subjecting himself to a Bavarian liege lord?
Such was the price of escaping long imprisonment
In dungeon dark, and regaining his royal sceptre.
That's what we call extenuating circumstances.
Can there be any here who can state with certainty,
That had the same hard fate been visited upon him,
He would not do the same, but return to his prison,
Abdicating rather his possessions and his life,
Than to re-emerge to the sweet light of day and regain
His honours lost? Even at the cost of serving one
Already set above him? But what if Svatopluk
Should abandon the Bavarian troops and rejoin
Us, his Slovak brethren? And you, O most pious king
Of the Slovaks, who took into your hands supreme rule
So unwillingly; aye, under duress, would you not

Return that sceptre into the hands of Svatopluk
Should he do so? And you, council fathers, is there one
Among you who would hesitate to give his assent
To such a positive turn of events? With one mind
And with one heart would we not all be in agreement?
Thus he would find what he is searching for, yes, and more
Than that. For if he did so choose, would he not free us
From slavery to Karolman with the eager might
Of our army, and rule as an independent king?'
   Thus Všeslav. And all who'd gazed upon Svatopluk
With evil eye now felt their hearts glow warm; thawed, their wrath —
For all felt the old man's counsel to be promising.
The hall erupted with voices — Milín's too — urging
Svatopluk to hesitate not, but accept the throne,
Given that Slavimír should agree to invest him
Once more in the purple. Then pious Slavimír rose.
 'O valiant Svatopluk! You have heard the bold counsel
Of all the elders here, which springs from their deepest core.
Now, if you will not be opposed to what they desire,
And if you should now abjure that, which once you promised,
That foul subjection, wrested from you under duress,
And abandon the war-hungry Germans to join us;
And if you'll have your nation's best interests foremost
In heart and mind, take now this sceptre into your hands;
The army of your nation under your brave command
To lead against the ravening Bavarian packs.
Confound them, and then, rule as our independent king!
Why do you waver? Why wring your hands? Can the Germans
Be dearer to you than motherland and countrymen?
Can it be that you find gloomy servitude sweeter
Than freedom, and unfettered sway over your nation?'
   And though he spoke in a soft voice, Slavimír's voice boomed
Through the hall, and buffeted Svatopluk, who wavered,
Torn by a tempest of contending thoughts. As the wind
Pummels the swallow above the marshland in the spring
Now this way, now that, as with agile wing he battles
The elements for mastery, thus did Svatopluk
Contend with desires that tugged his bosom here and there,
Until at last he found the words he'd speak, and began:
 'This is no trifle, no easy matter to decide.

Should I hold to the Germans now, who first, it is true,
With minds beclouded clapped me in foul imprisonment,
But then returned me to great honours, providing me
With a mighty host of men battling on my behalf
That I might regain my realm and that of Rastislav?
Yet thus would I still be subject to them, as my lords.
So, is it better to return to my own nation,
Bending to your will, receiving anew my old sway?
There lies my oath, but here my love calls me, to my folk.
At last, as every man longs after freedom, seeking
To flee subjection to another — my love wins out!
I shall join you. Here I accept the royal sceptre;
With it in hand I shall lead you against Karolman.
I doubt not but that together we'll see his army
In panic flee our motherland, whipped and remorseful'.

   Thus Svatopluk. At once a loud roar of rejoicing
Erupted, as if from the throats of sailors long tossed
On the deep ocean by contrary winds countless leagues
From shore, which disappears from sight no sooner than glimpsed,
And then, at last, the familiar shoreline meets their eyes,
The strand on which they'd left their wives and children ages
Ago — and they lift a joyous clamour to the skies
As now they pull into the calm roads, their prows gladly
Biting the sand — and leap out to dance upon the beach.
Loud cries of 'Long live the king'! echoed throughout the hall.
Svatopluk stood there, in the midst of the joy, and said:

   'Now that I sit upon this my throne, once more your king,
It seems good to me that we should send word to Britwald
Of what has come to pass, for after me, Karolman
Invested him with supreme power over the troops,
To ask him whether he would not lead them home in peace,
Or will he rather wish to renew the war to force
Us to submit ourselves to a German overlord?
Now, which of you here present will agree to take horse
And bring the unpleasant tidings to the German chief?'

   He concluded, and at once clever Zvestoň arose
And, saddling the swiftest-hoofed stallion in the stables,
Sped off for the German camp. There was no time to waste,
For even so the Germans might opt for war; no, this
Could not be discounted, given the lust for warfare

That marked their forefathers. So the elders planned for war:
Setting all things in readiness, preparing lookouts,
Until the night had rolled to its midpoint. Svatopluk
Then dissolved the moot, and all retired to welcome rest.
   Britwald too, exhausted with toil, fell asleep as soon
As he closed his eyes — which still were troubled with visions.
A strange terror gripped him, for he seemed to see in dream
The copse in which he rested bent low, crowns pressed to earth,
By silent winds — a bloody rain fell from the burdened clouds
Like showers of arrows; birds of prey set to screeching,
Beating against armour, which gave out a rough clangour;
Three times a night-owl fluttered above him, there and back,
Until it came to perch upon his bloodied lance-tip,
With mournful hooting like lamentations from on high.
And then it seemed to him that a gust blew up in camp,
As if an evil chthonic spirit arose from beneath
The earth to howl above, in the upper zones of air.
Such a thick-quick whirlwind erupted of a sudden —
Dust swirled about, leaves, and whatever light was to hand
Spinning in gyres threaded by a snarling wolf. The beast
Vaulted the outer ramparts in one leap — no obstacle
Could slow him down — then he vanished into the gloom
And sent up a dreadful howling, at which sign more wolves
Loped in from all sides — a great brotherhood of bandits,
So many as had never been seen before by any man,
Grouping together, they stealthily neared the tents:
First the perimeter pickets, sentries unaware,
They tore apart — next, all the troops sleeping in their beds.
It was the very leader of the pack that padded
Up to him — with one leap the cruel beast was upon him,
Claws raking at his eyes, fangs clamping around his throat —
With one shake, he severed his head from his broad shoulders
And then tore (the horror!) his gory limbs into shreds
Which he bolted down, smacking his lips — a foul repast!
   In cruel terror, body drenched in sweat, Britwald awoke,
Leaping from his cot to his feet like some prudent stag
Who'd been at rest beneath an elm's shade, when catching scent
Of a hunter, he bounds away through the oak forest
Before the killer might plunge a dart between his ribs.
So Britwald started and, unsheathing his sword from its scabbard,

Ears pricked, eyes peeled — searched the darknesses for any trace
Of the raider of flocks and his hideous pack-mates...
But he saw no bloody-mawed wolf lurking through the night,
Nor any trace of the horrible events of his dream.
Now, was the dream prophetic of some other danger?
All's as it was. While he was still musing on nightmares
Gruff Wilfrid approached his tent with news: 'Some messenger
From Devín seeks admittance to the camp; he would speak
With our commander. He says it's a weighty matter'.
'Lead him to me', Britwald orders — and feels his heart sink —
Why has a messenger been sent to the camp alone?
Why was it not King Svatopluk himself who came back?
What could be keeping him? While he was thus revolving
These thoughts through his mind, racking his brain, Zvestoň approached,
And with such words addressed the Bavarian hetman:

   'Valiant Britwald! First among all warrior-chiefs!
Svatopluk sends me to you with greetings: the Slovaks
Have chosen him king by acclamation — but under
One condition: that he abjure German subjection
To rule his own people, as one of their own brethren,
Independent of all base foreign domination.
And he, moved by the love he bears his dear motherland,
Bowed to their wishes and ascended the Slovak throne.
So now he asks you to weigh the matter in your heart
And send reply: Would you now lead your army back home
In peace, or do you prefer to renew the contest
And try to batter us into subjection by the sword?'

   Thus Zvestoň. At which Britwald, enflamed with great anger,
As when a tigress fierce, returning from long hunting
With her Caucasian prey, be it a stag or great boar,
Arrives at her den to find her cubs missing, captured,
And rages about the cave in great wrath, thus Britwald
Fulminated, until from his bright eyes the sparks flew.
When he could choke out words, thus he roared at the herald:

   'Back to Devín with you, whence you came! Thus I reply:
Your new governor has committed a grave offence
In breaking his solemn vow, abandoning his friends!
We shall not withdraw from here to our sweet fatherland
Until we rest our feet upon your napes, you rebels!
There shall be no quarter for you until I impress

Your necks in shameful servitude to the German yoke —
And pin an iron halter round the throat of your king
Treacherous, who fled us with trickery, to drag him
Before Karolman, to do with him as he pleases.
Such is my vow, which shall not be broken. I'll teach him
By example what it means to give one's solemn word!'
   Thus Britwald, roughly dismissing Zvestoň with such threats.
And then, as soon as morning's bright herald lit the sky
With rose and gold, snuffing the flickering coals of the stars,
He called the troops to arms: 'Take up your weapons, my men!
Prepare yourselves anew for the morning's shock of war!'
And when they'd drawn themselves up in ranks, he addressed them:
   'O valiant heroes — we are now in this together…
Alone. You are under my sole command — Svatopluk
— Ungrateful rogue! — has betrayed our trust; his solemn vow
Breaking, abandoning us to run to the Slovaks.
Basely wheedling a sceptre for himself on Devín
(How well he planned it — how cleverly he won their love!)
Which he pretends now to wield as an autonomous king!
And now *his majesty* has sent a lackey to us
With greetings — "You may go back home now", he says, "or else
Perhaps you'd like to try your luck again in battle,
Subjecting us to servitude by the sword?" Well then —
Have we slogged down so many roads on foot, forded
So many rivers and shattered so many armies,
Sending their remnants scurrying to cover up there,
On Devín, just to shrug now, and turn our backs, and leave,
Our job half done — Nay! Undone! — And return in failure?
What shall we meet with back home but dishonour and shame?
While he, released of Bavarian overlordship,
Reclines sublime on his autonomous royal throne?
Laughing at us, fools that we be for getting him here
Like coachmen, not warriors! Are we such laughing-stocks?
What will our loved ones think? With what face will they greet us?
With smiles or sneers? And what will our King Karolman say,
Should we turn back in mid-road, with victory — so near?
If we go back, it must be dragging Slovaks behind us
In harness, to a shameful gallows for their treachery.
Their shame will cleanse us of our own. My brave-hearted men!
Let us now storm the battlements of Devín, with courage,

And might, and the swiftness of the whirlwind, to batter
Our foes. With sulphur, tar, and flaming arrows, we'll burn
That city to the ground, and trample beneath our feet
Its ashes till nothing is left but an empty name —
A desert curiosity. Death to the rebels!
And off to Karolman with Svatopluk, in fetters!'
   Thus Britwald roared in anger. And his troops in anger
Roared their assent, before setting off to storm the hill.

CANTO X

Swiftly, Zvestoň returns and reports that Britwald has chosen war, threatening to enslave the Slovaks. Suddenly, a cry erupts: the Germans are pressing to Devín in droves. Because time does not permit the army to be led out onto the battlefield, Svatopluk orders the manning of wall and rampart, to defend the city, at least. The Germans pass over the ramparts and set siege-ladders to the walls. Before they have a chance to ascend them, the Slovaks begin toppling burdens down upon them. This causes frightful damage, and ladders are smashed. The line of attackers begins to waver. But not for long: encouraged by Agilmund's speech, once more they advance, bringing up new ladders. But when Agilmund falls, cut down by the arrows of Ohroz, they lose heart and withdraw again. On the other side of the city, Gromislav ascends the wall, followed by the other leaders, including Britwald himself. They bring the Bavarian colours with them. Britwald, having carved a broad swathe through the defenders, arrives at the city gate, which he opens. The Germans flood into the city. As soon as he makes out the Bavarian colours on the walls, Svatopluk rushes there with his commanders and calls to his men. Fired by his speech, they assemble in great numbers. First knocking down the Bavarian colours with a stone, Svatopluk himself rages with his sword: he despatches Gromislav and many other of the enemy leaders. Other Slovak voivodes and the rest of the Slovak youth engage in a pitched battle that expels the enemy from the town. Britwald, battling in a different part of the town, growing weak himself, beholds the Germans retreating in haste, pressed by Svatopluk and the other leaders. However, recognising that the advancing darkness will impede the taking of the city, he calls a general retreat to camp.

   Safe within the castle walls, the council completed,
The Slovak leaders went off to rest their aching limbs.
Only Svatopluk remained awake, on watch that night,
His eyes never resting, his mind ever revolving
With care: will his herald return with peace, or with war?
The warm dawning sun had not yet smiled upon the earth,
Tinging with rose the highest summits merely, when Zvestoň
Sped back to Devín from the camp, his steed's hooves pounding
The turf. His message: Britwald opts for war and threatens
Enslavement to the Slovaks: fetters and iron torques.
The valiant Svatopluk, cheered at the prospect of war
But angered at the threats, responded thus with mockery:
   'Let great Britwald save his iron staples for himself,

To keep his head fastened to his body as homeward
It's borne! No better news could you have brought than battle:
This augurs his end, and our glorious commencement!'
   Hardly had he finished speaking than a trumpet's blare
Met his ears, mixed with the dull roar of soldiers cheering.
Then a louder cry pierced through the chaos: 'The Germans
Have left their camp in massed attack! They're at the ramparts!'
Siege ladders they bore, and the heaviest battering rams;
Slings and catapults they dragged near with ropes slung across
Their broad straining shoulders. Svatopluk seized his weapons,
Encasing first his torso in his three-ply chain-mail
And shining golden breastplate. Soon his helmet-tufts bobbed
Above his flashing crown — at his side a brilliant sword
Was belted. Into the fast thongs of his shield he plunged
His left forearm, while his right fist held an oaken spear.
Accoutred thus, he crashed out of the room with a roar.
Like a lion famished at the break of day catching
Sight of a deer spooked by dogs flashing past his cave's mouth:
So Svatopluk rushed to the windy crenellations
Where he beheld the German hordes at the battlements,
Nearer than he'd reckoned, at which, envenomed with wrath,
He saw that there was no chance now to lead the army
Out onto the plain and draw them up in even ranks —
It was too late for that! Britwald had stolen a march.
And so he ordered his men out onto the ramparts
And onto the walls, to defend the city at least,
Directing the troops with the counsel of his chieftains,
Where they're to be emplaced. How their hearts chafed in anger
At not being sent out to do battle with the foe
On even ground! Yet all, obedient to orders,
Leapt to the walls. Some lugged up heavy stones on their backs
To topple down upon the invaders, along with
Thick logs and wooden beams, which fell a horrid hailstorm!
   Valiant Britwald too clambered up the ramparts, leading
His men advancing in wrathful unwavering ranks.
As when in early spring a black cloud of sad aspect
Comes rolling in from the north, darkening the bright sky,
And winds begin to blow, the sun, blotted out, founders
In the grey, and cold snow swirls down, covering the fields
That had been green, so suddenly Britwald rumbled up,

Shouting out orders to his company commanders,
Where each should set his swarm to attack, where sappers
Should fill the broken fosse for passage, or where to vault
Most easily the earthen bulwarks that ringed the walls,
Which once passed, the assault on the city might commence.
Then each in turn called out to the troops under his charge.
First of all, at the head of large hosts, sped Agilmund,
Straight into the iron maelstrom of arrows that screamed
Against them, battering helmet and shield — deadly hail! —
Lewigild falls, and Fridrich, and Luitbert mighty-limbed,
Ajstolf the manly, and dexterous Egerhard, Sind,
And Heribert too, who had plunged on in the front ranks.
At this their comrades, urged on by the fearsome slaughter,
All the more quickly rushed to the attack, hurling themselves
Upon the earthworks, where Deorpald slew Branimír,
That man of many talents, Engelgast Veľamysl
Felled, Ruprecht Slavihosť and Leszek,
Brave Manhart slew Lubo, Ukrot, Poslav and Hneves,
As well as those two heroic brothers Mileust
And Darek, so similar in face, voice, and armour,
The one a favourite of their father Kolislav,
The other, apple of their mother Žížňava's eye.
Nor was he finished — many a youth fell at his hands!
Just as in autumn the spent leaves of the ash trees fall,
Shrivelled by the sudden frost, when a hard wind strikes them,
So thickly did young warriors fall before Manhart,
Who hacked his way through the ranks of the enemy host.
The German pioneers hastily filled the trenches
To make clear passage to the castle walls, casting in
Earth, and whatever rubble was to hand, making firm
A pathway through the moat. When Ľuboslav the splendid,
Commander of the troops from Velehrad, beheld this,
He called to his men (of all Devín's hosts most skilful):

  'My valiant comrades! Can it be that we shall permit
The Germans to pierce our defences, surmount our walls
With impunity, and pave their way into Devín?
Where is the manhood, where the vanished courage of those
Who once stood knee-deep in gore, hewing down the fierce foe,
Feet firm, unwavering, glorying in the battle?'

  Thus Ľuboslav, at which with skilful aim he let fly

An arrow at stout Manhart, just as he was pulling
His heavy shaft from where he'd plunged it in Načirád;
The arrow flew with an immense wailing, striking home
Beneath his jaw, where the sharp dart slashed the sinews through.
At once the foaming blood gushed forth from the open wound,
And his errant lights spun off into eternal gloom.
His massive trunk tottered and fell to earth with a crash
Like a bastion when its foundations are undermined.
Next, with his heavy spear, Ľuboslav halted Gerold
And Fust in their tracks, skewering the first in his guts,
Crushing the thigh-bone of the latter. Gerold
Fell flat on his face, while Fust crumpled backwards to earth.
To these he added the horsemen Rajnfríd and Lipert,
And Hajnc, who had battled most often with lying tongue.
But then Madulfat rushed against him like the lightning:
A giant, in his hand he gripped a fearsome oak spear.
This he flung, but Ľuboslav saw it and crouched in time —
The angry missile flew past him to pierce the armour
Of Horomysl, that manly warrior, cutting short
His brave and bloody life. His torso dredged a furrow
In the sand. At which Ľuboslav flung off his swift pike
Roaring: 'Let's see which of us two has the better aim!
Sometimes it's the lighter falcon that bites more fiercely!'
The pine-shafted javelin screamed on to its target
And pierced the lower quarter of the seven-ply shield
Bursting through, shattering the femur. Madulfat fell,
And like a stallion in agony, hooves flailing
At the stars, he fell to the earth with a crash that made
The woods to shudder, like a massive fir-tree falling
Under the blows of an axe, or undermined by age.
He roared with the bellows of a great aurochs fleeing
Young hunters and their vicious dogs, who fall upon him
Tearing, this one at his right ear, that one at the left,
Another pouncing on his nape, a fourth at the throat,
And none of them letting go their grip in blood frenzy,
No matter how he roars and tosses his battered poll,
Until he sinks at last and, slaughtered, gives up his ghost.
Ľuboslav the victor, who had flung his javelin,
And whose quiver was now void of darts, unsheathed his sword
— Golden honour-gift presented him by Velepluk,

Which once Zácslav of Nitra fashioned for him, swordsmith
Renowned amongst all craftsmen of the age for his skill —
With such a blade he set to work. First Wolhart he fells,
Slashing his right thigh, then beauteous Malching the left;
He hacks through Firt's brow, helmet and all, and separates
Arfríd's arm at the elbow, hand still gripping his sword.
He ran Trost through the eye, and marred Hildebrand's visage
Once comely with a cruel slash; he severed Máro's
Head, which, still helmeted, flew away from his body,
Eyes blinking in astonishment, to roll far away.
Thus Ľuboslav gave a fierce example to his men
Who, no less ferocious, mowed down their vainly battling
Foes: Cudzikraj slew Wenemár, Utech killed Lenhart,
Múdrohlav Rajnbert, Miluch Witichind, Polihrad
Tunman, clever Dobrochvál slew the swart-faced Lupold;
Nebihosť slaughtered Walbert, and Ekard, and Humel,
Who once in his cups bragged loudly before his war-chiefs
That he would be first to surmount the walls of Devín,
His would be the pitch-torch to set the city aflame.
But even though the Germans were taking a thrashing,
Still they turned their backs on the Slovaks not, but fought on,
Selling their lives dearly as men fell thickly, on both sides.
As when a pride of lions, famished, falls upon a herd
Of bulls, amazed at their stark boldness, and a battle
Rages — these thrusting sharp horns, those flashing fang and claw,
Neither side bending, neither relinquishing the field
As these fight for their lives, those are crazed with starvation,
And blood from both packs flows thickly, fouling the wide field,
While bellows and roars thunder throughout the savannah,
And the herdsmen crouched in the thorns look on from afar,
Daring not to bring aid to their cattle, thus battled
The Germans and Slovaks here, multiplying death
On all hands, sharp blades finishing off the moribund
Who littered the field in great numbers, heaped up thickly
Like lush grasses that once covered the Moravian fields
In spring before the reapers slash through their stalks with scythes,
Laying all low in wide swathes what once had stretched so high.
At last the Germans, blunted by Slovak resistance,
Began to waver and retreat — by small increments,
Steps at a time. When wrathful Agilmund beheld this

He rushed up, bloody, and cried out to his men, striking
The backs of those retreating with the flat of his sword,
Permitting no retreat and berating them for shame,
Then leaping forward himself to grapple with Ľuboslav.
With his mighty spear he cleared his own path through the midst
Of his foes, taking down Vida, Jaslav, Zrín, Omysl,
Hostikraj, that expert swordsman, and Blud, and Laska
Ambidextrous, skilled at hurling spears with his right hand
And left — all these he sent into the gloom eternal.
Soon he was near enough to deliver a mortal blow.
With all the strength of his arm he hurled a massive spear
At Ľuboslav, which slammed into his ear, piercing clear
Through the helm and into the skull. He fell, and a stream
Of bright blood fouled the clean shaft, and his coat once costly.
He toppled to the earth, those limbs so splendid crumpling,
His fair countenance befouled by the trampled soil.
Velehrad mourned her captain; Nitra keened at his fall,
Devín too added her wail to that of the maidens
Of Trenčín; indeed, all of Slovakia bewept
Ľuboslav's death — no less did his victor, Agilmund.
  As soon as his comrades beheld the fall of the chief
Slovak commander, their tired hearts swelled anew with hope,
And with renewed ardour they fell upon their foes.
Many they slew, many themselves went off to the glooms
Eternal, each moment itself an eternity
As victory now inclined to this side, now to that,
Until at last the Germans broke through the defences
Of the outer earthworks, and then flowed up over the top
With frightful impetus swarming over the trenches
And toward the city walls, the sappers tirelessly
Filling the moat with hastily scraped earth and rubble,
While from the high battlements youngsters toppled boulders
Upon the swarms beneath their flimsy shields cowering,
Striving to stem the tide of their approach. Ceaselessly
The storm of stone rained down from the crenellated heights
Mixed with a hail of well-aimed spears and arrows and rocks
From slings that battered the tortoise-shell of linked shields.
As when a dark wind blows in hailstorms that pummel roof
And field, the shot of ice striking the packed earth to bound
High again, battering blossom and budding tree-branch,

Laying prone grainfield and even immature oak-stand,
So did the darts fall viciously, along with splinters
And shards of stone, horridly drumming upon the shields.
But the attackers paid no mind to thunder or hail
However deadly, disdaining Death herself who strode
Among them in the firestorm: their eyes were ever fixed
Upon the city walls, their goal, which, when they had reached
— Those fortunate few unscathed — they propped their siege-ladders
Against. But now came the harsh task of the upward climb!
One unit had overcome the windy road, halfway,
Reaching a spear's length from their opponents on the crest
When the Slovaks toppled a huge trunk of pine, immense,
Such as a team of twice six oxen could hardly drag
Out of the forest — down it tumbled, clearing the wall
And thundering horrid death upon the swarms below.
Just as when the tip of some towering mountain cliff
Split by an earthquake's tremor, or some other fell chance,
Breaks from its base and starts tumbling down the mountainside,
A thundering horror, pulverising great boulders
And crushing whole forests of oak, so this gigantic
Pine trunk fell, clearing a wide path of dire destruction,
Crushing men to a pulp with their weapons and shields
Splintering siege-ladders. And when it pounded to earth,
The city-walls shook from the percussion. Horrid screams
And moans resounded from the escarpment far below.
The quivering pine rebounded once, to leap anew
At the soldiers on the slopes below, where it rolled on,
Causing havoc, catching and crushing all who would flee
But could not into a sticky black paste of sorrow.
Those Bavarian troops who were able to skip wide
Of its path, began to retreat in terror, backwards,
Which, when Agilmund noticed, he cried out in anger:
    'Why are you turning tail? Whither do you hope to run?
O cowardice unmet with in real German bosoms!
You've never yet turned your backs on trenchers of meat or mugs
Of ale! Look! The road to victory is now paved clear!
The horrid roller's come to a stop and lies there dead,
No more harmful than any trunk rotting in the woods,
And they have nothing more of the like to hurl at you!'
    Thus Agilmund roared. His men grabbed their ladders again

And trod the bloody path back, over broken corpses
And their battered brothers moaning out their lives. They pressed
Thickly to the walls to attempt the ascent once more.
Again the air was filled with roaring as toppled stones
And other shot poured down on the thin vaulting of shields.
The helmeted heads of the Germans rang as the hail
Cleared murderous gaps in the line of the assaulters;
Twice the line wavered, twice it approached the wall again
As Agilmund, roaring ferociously, urged them on,
Thwacking the backs of the shirkers who skulked to withdraw.
At the third rush they reached the battlements, gripping fast
Balustrade and crenellation with hands (soon lopped off
By the fierce Slovak defenders hacking in fury).
Those fell screaming, but another wave came, and a third,
Meeting a like maiming horror. Others were dislodged
With spear-butts to the chest, and down they fell to the depths.
The upper reaches of the wall were red against the blue
Sky; below, trench and culvert were awash with red mire
And the air above the battlements steamed with hot gore.
Screams of wrath and terror walloped the firmament
Until the golden stars themselves shuddered in horror.
   Now on the Dobroslavská tower stood young Ohroz,
Skilled with the crossbow, shooting his bolts unerringly.
Nowhere was any sharper-eyed hunter to be found:
No one among the Slovaks could split a reed like he
(Such was his aim) nor launch a stout javelin farther.
A tireless wanderer, from his earliest years
He'd traverse the meadows along the Rudava's banks,
Crossing whole pinewoods, or summiting high Suchánka.
Often in one day he'd hike through Čertová Brázda
And neither bird nor beast could flee his winged arrows.
Ofttimes his darts sped from Baba as far as Ostríž —
Now it was enemy warriors he had in sight,
Whizzing his death-bearing missiles at them from afar.
Ruf he laid low, and mighty-limbed Edmund and Krištof,
And Rajner, whose one cheek (the right) bore a swarthy birthmark,
And pockmarked Gotlib — now pitted more grievously! —
And wise old Sigmar the oracle, who outriddled
The future to his folk — but foresaw not his own doom.
One hundred other heroes Ohroz sent to the gloom;

No arrow missed its mark, no bolt winged aloft in vain.
Then he caught sight of Agilmund raging in attack,
And though no little distance separated the two,
He strung his last two bolts — two, for of such giant limbs
Was Agilmund, big-boned, of massive frame, he would not
Risk wounding him merely, so: two darts from his quiver
He pulled out with nimble hand, tautening the bowstring,
Aiming, but first he lifted his voice in fervent prayer
Before he let fly, pleading: 'O, heavenly Father!
May Agilmund fall by my hand! Please, deign add his name
To the honour of my bow, he who now rages close,
Threatening our city, eager for its overthrow
And our enslavement — readying, they say, the stiff yoke
Of base subjection to fasten round our necks bent low'.
   And the eternal Ruler of the cosmos heard him,
For the allotted time of Agilmund's death was nigh.
Ohroz strained his curved bow backwards with his strong right hand
Until the creaking juniper's ends were nearly touching,
Then he released his arrows, one after the other.
They cleft the air in speedy flight, screaming like banshees.
The first dart pierced Agilmund's throat, the next, his right cheek.
Had they a consciousness, they would have quarrelled, which one
Brought down the German champion! (It hardly mattered:
Each tip plunged death deep into his soul). Great Agilmund,
Whirled by the blows, tumbled heavily onto his side
Making the earth to shudder at his fall. His armour
Clattered, was still, and his joyless spirit crept forth
From his cooling limbs. Great panic spread among his men —
Their hearts sank, and they slunk back, their attack now repelled.
   Then on the other side, Styrians attempted to burst
The iron gate with a battering ram. Gromislav
Was first to scramble atop the wall. He slew Blizkoň,
A captain who by then had two times seven heroes
Sent to the shades below with his battle-axe, piercing
His loins with a cruel spear-thrust. He tumbled head-first,
Splattering his visage against his hard, native soil.
The mightiest of warriors followed him to the breech:
Clever Kraič and Pačemíl, and Grajsa that spearman
Fortunate, while on the other hand massive Humbold
And Irmengard, no less immense, Sigurd, and Waltér,

Terror to look on, each chief followed by his forces
Of valiant soldiers, spilling in after. Britwald
Too, who had circled the city on his swift charger
Seeking a better inroad, an easier ingress
Into the fortress, roused by the attack he glimpsed here
Rushed at the same breach himself, his golden helm flashing,
Trailing its tufts in the sparkling glare, like a comet
That falls from the heavens, thrashing its tail, spitting sparks.
He plunged into the fray, calling Hartung after him
Who followed with his splendid mates Unhat and Otto,
Waninch and Ernest — a terror with the javelin —
Who had under his command the Germans from Salzburg,
For on account of his advanced age and weakened limbs
Adelwin could no longer lead his city's warriors,
Although the bitter man was still blazing in anger
At Bishop Methodius for his institution
Of the Slavonic liturgy in place of Latin.
Then with a raucous voice a blaring trumpet rang out,
And a great cry echoed far and wide, as suddenly
The Bavarian banner was planted high above
The captured corner of the wall. The summiters hurled
Down rubble on the stubborn resisters; others wrapped
Arrows in rags impregnated with sooty resin
And pitch, and setting them aflame, showered blazing darts
Upon the inner rooftops, while others yet battled
Their enemies with sword and mace. Haughty Gromislav,
His bosom swelling with the palpable victory,
Cried out: 'Follow me, lads! To me, you daring heroes!
I'll lead you to the very castle keep, whoever
Will follow me, just as I've led you here, to the top
Of the battlements once bruited insuperable!'
   He finished, and then turned to meet Omyl, who had hurled
A massive lance at him (he would avenge Blizkoň's death,
Who'd recently married his beautiful young daughter).
Him he sent into the next world with one harsh spear-thrust.
Skilful Diva he then took off, young son of Znislav,
Who formerly in prideful and ancient Novohrad
Had been high priest in the largest temple of Perún,
Accorded king-like honours for his blameless carriage,
His wise counsel, and his great piety. The other

Attackers, burning with shame at Gromislav having
Snatched the first glory by mounting the walls of Devín
Before all others, fought all the more fiercely, raging
With rabid ferocity. Pačemíl, unfettered
Of all but wrath, took off Bratroslav, while Irmengard
Slew Lutomír, Sigurd killed Nebovít, and Humbold
Laid savage Pozdrav low, while Waltér slaughtered Loskot.
Kraič laid out Hájislav for the black-horsed cortège,
While Grajsa pierced with his massive javelin angry
Nerád's brow, right between the eyes. His skull-plates shattered
And the shaft passed clear through the head, from tip to lance-butt.
Great-soulled and no less fierce were Unhat, Otto, Ernest:
The first slew Lika, the next laid three brothers low: Mír,
Oprud, and Lúček, while the last measured with Vojtech,
Skilled with the bow himself, but this time it was Ernest
Who hit his mark — straight in the mouth — sending him off
To endless slumber. Waninch slew Hvezdichvál, Hartung
Delivered gigantic Svojslav to the bleak shadows;
Unka met with the same fate next, who'd taken command
Of the troops arrived from the Novohradský region
Following Blizkoň's death; that proved a brief commission!
   Then Britwald with fiery sparks spilling from his eyes
Leapt down from the battlements, as a hungry eagle
Who suddenly spots a fat flock of chattering geese
On a dry marsh swoops down from the heights with sharp talons
To seize a shrieking gander. Thus Britwald raced from the wall
Captured by his brave Slovenes to the high gate, raging.
With flaming sword, in wrath he fell upon the battlers,
Cutting a path through their midst, driving them before him
Like flocks and their shepherds seized by a sudden downpour,
Driven off to where they would not go by the cloudburst
Assailing them from all sides — nowhere a safe refuge.
Thus valiant Britwald mowed down whomever crossed his path,
Herding whole flocks of souls into eternal darkness.
Thus Bolech fell to the dust, Vitomír and Krislav
The swift-footed, Nekol and Voderád fair of face,
Slavozvuk and Rodboj, and Strelut and Trebihosť
Fell, as did great Bolesław, which enraged Nosistrach,
The warrior-chief of the bowmen of Silesia.
With all his might he hurled his heavy spear at Britwald,

But the ashen shaft shattered against rough buckler,
The metal tip biting, but causing no further harm.
Recoiling from the blow, Britwald raised a sturdier
Oaken shafted spear and flung it with still greater might
At Nosistrach. The missile pierced both seven-ply shield
And gilded armour — and his shaggy bosom too.
At once he fell, like some cliff shattered by thunderbolt,
His splendid armour now befouled with gore. Mocking him
Britwald straddled him and laughed: 'Lie there, and threaten wraiths
With your boasts and fulminations now, great warrior!'
So saying, he jerked his knotty shaft out of the wound
And raced to the gate weakened by the ram's pounding.
There he raised his sword and with immense strength brought it down
Once on the bolt, twice, at last, at the third blow he shattered
Its resistance. The oak groaned and cracked, the leaves gave way,
Swinging in with a swift violence that battered both walls
As they groaned on their hinges; the boom echoed afar.
Britwald rushed out towards the Germans, howling fiercely:
'In here! In here! The Slovaks are on their heels! Finish
Them off, set fire to the city, take the castle keep!'
Thus Britwald roared. The Germans swept in like a hailstorm.
Soon the fluttering colours of Bavaria scathed
The eyes of valiant Svatopluk. Like a tiger
In the Caucasus who, in the distance, catches sight
Of some Cossack thief at the mouth of his den, snatching
His cubs, and drops from his fangs the prey he'd hunted down
— Be it goat or deer — and rushes off, bounding through field
Hill and river after the ravisher escaping
Astride his fleet Terek stallion, thus Svatopluk,
An inferno of angry venom within him, raced
Toward that quadrant, his armour flashing, plumes erect,
Like some fierce, wrathful comet streaking through the heavens,
Shedding terror on all hands. Fiery Zemižížeň,
Rozhoň and Slavboj raced on in his traces,
Milín streaked near and mighty Borislav, that war-chief
Most excellent of all. In a loud voice that sounded
Like two times six throats bellowing, Svatopluk cried out:
   'Have you no arms? No strength nor weapons remaining you,
That you permit your foes to inundate your city?
You retreat to defend — what? should you abandon her,

Your capital? Now is the time to be battling! Now,
With all the might that remains you! Forward, to the front!
Batter the wretched Germans! Cast them from Devín's walls!'
   Thus Svatopluk. With hearts enflamed anew with courage
By the words of their king, the Slovaks raced to his side,
Shoulder to shoulder, their plumes waving like a forest
Of ire to seal off the breach, breasting battlements,
At once falling upon the enemy hosts, enraged.
Svatopluk took a massive stone in hand and hurled it
At the Bavarian standard, shattering its pole,
Knocking it from the wall. Then 'twas a stout javelin
He let loose at Gromislav, piercing his skull clean through:
His brains bespattered the dust before his limbs crumpled.
   Svatopluk then bestrode the corpse and exulted, 'O, you!
First atop Devín's walls, and first to fall, threaded through
By knotty lance! Lie there! You shall advance no higher
At the head of your troops to surmount the castle keep!'
   He finished, then addressed himself to Grajsa,
Flinging a missile down at him like a thunderbolt
Flashing past Zemižížeň on the left, who had been
Grajsa's target; he then slew Irmengard and Sigurd,
Skewering the former in the loins, and running through
The latter's navel — neither shield nor chain-mail tunic
Cunningly weft of thickset iron loops availed him.
(These had been given him by his uncle Adelfrid
When he no longer could pull them on over his limbs
Once spry, now trembling with old age). Then Svatopluk turned
To face Humbold himself. He flung his stout javelin
At the helm flashing with martial ardour from afar:
The tip burst through the gilt metal above his right ear,
Smashing through the plates of his skull as well.
Blood gushed forth in a stream, and mighty Humbold tottered
To fall upon his left side in the dust, rolling splayed
Wide on his back, at last, the brilliant light curtained now
By darkness eternal. When Hartung saw this happen
— The Bavarian voivode felled — with blazing anger
He turned upon the Slovak king, and flung a sharp pike
At him, with all his might. It only thumped on the shield
And, wobbling, hovered, to fall to rest between his feet.
Svatopluk spitted Hartung under the chin with dire

Ash-shaft, which split his jaw in twain. Then, a spike he plunged
Into his throat besides. With a jerk, head over heels
Hartung fell, hard, his maimed head striking the earth before
His calves. The earth thundered beneath his fall, his armour
Jangling. Enraged, the Bavarian war-chiefs would avenge
The deaths of Humbold and Hartung: they poured close, frothing
With venom, seeing which Svatopluk unsheathed his sword
— That thunderous weapon! — from its shining scabbard and rushed
At them like lion famished, having torn a sheep
From the fold and ripped into its gut with rabid fangs,
Should shepherds, armed, attack him; ruffling his fearful mane
And sounding a roar ferocious from his maw, lashing
His tail, gnashing his fangs and slashing with claws,
He leaps to battle against the men — ah, fierce the fray! —
Determined to slay all who come at him, or fall himself.
Thus Svatopluk raged, first slashing Otto's face — both sides,
Severing Unhat's left arm at the shoulder (it fell
And with it the shield, to roll away — arm still attached,
Flopping like some shattered wagon axle). Then he turned
Upon the clever Ernest — with one swipe he cut through
The flashy long helm tufts at nape-level — and the nape.
How many more did he slay! How glutted he Hell's maw!
As when a cross-gale whips down from the north, at Trnava
Or Topoľčany fields, tossing about the hayricks
Heaped by the sun-bronzed reapers, scattering the wheat-sheaves
All over the fallow fields: thus raging Svatopluk
Laid out whatever Germans came against him, flashing
His heated blade. Corpse upon corpse lay on the field;
The blood-soaked piles of cadavers rose high on all hands.
His captains were not far behind in rage, cutting down
Their foes: as Zemižížeň skewered Waninch, Rozhoň
Kraič, Milín Pačemíl, and Borislav Waltér.
And then Slavboj laid Alfríd low, who took command
Of the Tyrolean legions upon Dipold's fall;
Nor would Ditmar ever again fire his comrades' hearts
With blasts on a trumpet pressed to his crooked, pursed lips:
The blade entered roughly beneath his eye, and the blood
Fouled the brass mouthpiece as the notes faded, died away.
Zobor, though a young soldier still, laid low great Luprecht;
He fell to earth, a thudding mass of jangling armour

Like some great fir blasted on Fatra by the lightning.
Such younger warriors were inspired to battle hard
By the example of their chiefs, hearts swelling with rage
And confidence. Just like a tall cliff at the seashore
Unconquered, breasting the wild assaults of hurricanes,
Smashing the billows that fall upon it in fury
And laying them low, so did the young soldiers stand firm
As the battle's fury raged against them, beating down
The impetuous hordes of their cruel foes, hounding
Them from the city at swords' point. Higher grew the heaps
Of the slain, and on all hands hot blood flowed in rivers
And the spray of the gore spilt tinted the clouds crimson.
Thus they fought on until night spread wide her sable wings,
Casting a pall of darkness over the hosts, Slovak
And Bavarian. Then did Britwald, his might ebbing
In battle on the other side of town, surrounded
By his enemies' weapons, now in the ascendant
It seemed, and catching sight of the Germans wavering,
The Slovak war-chiefs along with their king pressing near,
And the falling dusk, which makes battle impossible,
Withdrew himself, though furious, sounding retreat.

CANTO XI

Černobog ascends mount Kobyla, which soars near Devín, along with his comrades. Looking down from there, and seeing that it is Svatopluk who is leading the Slovaks against the Bavarians, he falls into a rage and delivers a speech to his mates in which he threatens both him and Slavimír with destruction. Cyril, formerly Konštantín, beseeches the Lord to drive the evil spirits back to Hell. God dispatches Michael with orders to cast them into the abyss. In their church, the Slovaks give thanks to God for the welcome victory. Ojda laments her son Miloslav. Svatopluk would send out a patrol, informing his captains that it would be a good thing to learn what the Bavarians were up to. Zemižžeň volunteers for the mission along with his comrade Slavboj. Svatopluk orders an end to the festivities and has the army go off to rest, so that all should be ready early in the morning for the resumption of battle. Zemižžeň and Slavboj circle the German camp from opposite directions. They find their horses, which the Germans had earlier taken from them in war. Zemižžeň has Slavboj lead the steeds to the banks of the Morava, where he tells him to wait, while he enters the resting camp alone. Overhearing someone's complaints, he learns all that he had come for, and returns to Slavboj. Some Germans, who had been watering their own horses, notice them, and raise the alarm. The Slovaks leap into the water, making for the other bank in haste. Some of their comrades come to their aid on a raft, and help them back. They hasten before the king and inform him that the Germans are resting in their tents, ready for battle at the command of their leader — for they are to draw forth to the battlefield at sunrise.

 Such were the fortunes of war that favoured the Slovaks.
Then the evil black spirit, seeing that his mischief
In conjuring the ferocious deluge went for naught
— For the Bavarians had crossed the swollen river
And chased the Slavimírovci back to Devín's ambit,
Themselves establishing a firm encampment below —
Exploded with untamed wrath. As when a bear, returning
From his foraging in distant glade laden with honey,
Finds his den empty, the little cubs carried off
By daring Pole or Russian, fumes and roars in anger
Terrible, thus the black spirit thrashed about with bile.
Then with his black hosts, no less rabid, he ascended
The summit of a nearby mountain (named Kobyla),
The massive brow of which is brushed by the golden stars
As they pass by. The world spreads out at its foot, below;

That high place provided him a clean view into Devín,
Where he beheld proud Svatopluk engaged in setting
The hosts of the Slovaks into sharp battle-order
To grapple again with the Bavarian armies
Tented now, on the plain adjacent. His fury grew,
The black bile rising to his gorge, his shrivelled heart, hard
And small as a walnut, swelled with rage, and what passes
For blood in foul veins demonic surged wildly, boiling,
And blue flames of wrath licked at his putrid skeleton.
His matted fur bristled, and sparks flashed from his dead eyes
As dark clouds thickened round his forehead and stench billowed
From his flaring nostrils, his scabrous throat belching flame
That singed his dry, splintering horns and poisoned the air.
Nature recoiled, scalded by the black foam venomous
That dripped from his chaps like that of a wild boar thrashing,
Pinned to the woodland loam by the lances of hunters.
Three times he stretched wide his maw, three times he puffed his cheeks,
But could not speak — fierce anger so paralysed his tongue.
He clenched his carious teeth and ground them, the rock-face
Repulsing the sound in echoes of disgust, the vale
Below cringed, but the sharp metal instruments of war
Responded with a lusty rattle, which both Slovak
And German ear sensed. The massive city walls shuddered
And even the hellish brotherhood shrank astonished.
But then bootless despair tamped down the hot coals of rage
And the rabid flux of ire, its allotted bound reached,
Was stilled, impuissant, and cleared a path for speech. He turned
To the deflated hosts of Hell (cast into despair
Again — schemes undermined) and like the River Dnieper
Booming across one of its seven rapids, he spoke:
 'O horrid sight! What a foul vista these eyes behold!
I can hardly believe my eyes — why can they not lie?
Svatopluk, unfettered, now binds himself to the Slovaks
And leads them into war against the Bavarians!
His shield and armour, his flashing helmet singe the orbs
In these sockets — and that blazing sword! Which Karolman
So stupidly whetted to set against his own throat!
What did we gain by heaping up the blind thunderheads?
That hurricane, that flood — what were they worth? All porous
The barricades we piled against too facile a progress!

He overcame the river, no matter how swollen,
He overcame the flooded meadows — no obstacle! —
He abandoned the Germans and ran off to Devín!
He broke his sacred vow, and shredded his faith to bits.
He managed to deceive the first among the Slovaks
And then turned the weapons he'd received from the Germans
— The evil scum! — against his benefactors! And we?
What was it worth, wandering through the entire country,
Enflaming the men with a lust for war? Amassing
A numerous army to do battle against him?
For here — tfu! — that multitude of now-seasoned heroes
Obeys the foul deceiver as commander-in-chief!
For his sake they battle, for him they spill their vile blood
To place the sceptre in his hand and make firm his throne!
Have our powers ebbed so far? Are we powerless?
Must we give up now? Concede the field to that blackguard?
Withdraw in shame, unavenged, to Hell, our plans foundered,
Returning to the horrid dark, to dire sufferings
Augmented by the jeers of our brethren — laughingstocks?
Fight on then, bravely, Slovak king, secure in your might!
Shatter the Bavarian army, exterminate
Britwald himself: we shall greet your victories with joy!
Yet hear this: I swear by the gates of Hell, the river
Styx, the flaming tar, the bellows of sulphurous smoke
That cense the abyss, that I shall never rest until
I see you fall, you villain, the last drop of your blood
Ooze out, and you drop to the putrid muck at my feet!
And should no spearman be able to overcome you,
If there be no other way, I myself shall seize you
By your hollow throat with these cruel talons of mine
And drag your treacherous soul off to the walls of Dis!
There your delights will be of another stripe, good king!
So now rejoice, make the most of your elevation,
From which proud heights you shall soon be hurtled down head first!
Nor shall you dodge these claws of ours, worthy Slavimír!
You too must depart the upper regions of sweet light,
And our last labour will be to turn your multitudes
Away from the Lord who rules in the heights of Heaven,
Returning them to our service, worshipping us again!
Once more the altars shall be smeared with gore and the smoke

Of greasy holocausts once more delight our nostrils'!
  Such rabid words did the hellish spirit out-bellow,
Before issuing haughty orders to his brethren,
Setting each to his task: what evil to wreak, and where,
So as to crown their labour with putrescent success.
  When he who once was Konštantín and Cyril remains,
Who once brought the true Faith to the Slovaks and taught them
To honour God and keep His laws, heard that, he hastened
From his starry abode high above Devín, where he
Keeps watch over his beloved land of the Slovaks
Before the all-puissant Monarch of the universe:
  'Almighty Father! Who reignest omnipotent in Heaven,
On earth, and even in the depths of the underworld,
Behold what foul deception that demon Černobog
And those dark legions of his, that he dragged forth from Hell
Are brewing, with oath made firm by the turgid waters
Of gloomy Styx! He sends such greetings to Svatopluk:
That he'll seize him by the throat and drag him off to Hell!
With no less fierce destruction he threatens Slavimír,
And now has set his plans afoot, Thy Slovak people
To turn away from the true Christian faith, beclouding
Their minds once more to gory altars and the worship
Of pagan idols! That such wrath may be found in breasts
Infernal is no surprise, but still it fills the heart
With horror and awe at such incorrigible pride!
Lord, thwart their plans! Let that foul sprite once more acknowledge
Thy might irresistible! Chasten his brazen pride
And punish him as his evil transgressions deserve.
Cast him and all his rebellious crew into deep Hell,
Into the tarry bogs and depthless abyss of flame!
Let him rage down there! And preserve Thy new confessors
The Slovaks in the true Faith; defend them from lie,
Deceit, and delusion, all plots open and hidden
Deflect! And aid them now in their battle with Thy strength,
Granting them victory in Thy mercy, raising them
To independence, free from all foreign subjection!'
  Thus Cyril pled the cause of those he had converted.
The omnipotent King of the heavens heard his plea,
And in such wise responded from the clouds of glory:
  'My ardent servant Cyril! I shall fulfil your prayer:

Vain is the fury, vain the force of the black spirits!
The destruction they threaten shall fall on their own heads.
Neither lie, nor hidden deception, nor delusion
Can shake the foundations of the pious Slovaks' faith;
Not even should the chief reptile of Hell drag himself
Forth into the light of day to hiss at them; steady,
Firm they shall always be, ever faithful to our Law,
With proper latreia, as you once instructed them.
These sacred customs they shall ever preserve in truth,
Bowing before Me only as their one Lord, the one God
And King of all that is. They shall have their victory.
This I grant heroic Svatopluk: taking the field,
He shall fell the German war-chief himself in battle,
And cast the foreign yoke from off his people's shoulders.
The borders of his kingdom shall extend far and wide;
The kindred Slavic nations shall support his sceptre,
Though like all earthly things subject to vicissitude,
They shall endure the varied shocks of change, and sad falls'.

   Then, turning to the stalwart chief of Heaven's legions,
The archangel Michael, the Lord God commanded him
(His voice thundering from the golden nimbus that cloaks
His throne) to descend to Earth and once again cast down
The evil one, and his black horde, into deepest Hell.

   So St Michael, refulgent in his golden armour,
A shield gigantic on his left forearm, gripped a spear
Mighty and winged, and his flaming sword, and set off,
Soaring to nether earth from the summits of the sky,
With crisp pinions sailing the burly winds of heaven,
Pressing before him terror and cruel destruction.
Soon he approached the high battlements of fair Devín,
His splendour stabbing the eyes of the sooty legions
As in measured flight he whirled above the city walls
At the head of whole hosts of angelic warriors
Riding the bright clouds. Then raising high his flaming sword
He broke from them, shooting downward, an ominous star,
Like a hot coal splitting off from the glowing embers,
Trailing a tail of bright orange sparks. Now they trembled
In terror! And a cry of despair arose from throats
Massed in woe as their destruction swiftly approached them,
Like the lowing of a herd of a thousand cattle.

The very flashing of his sword's blade drove them frantic,
And light, painful light, exploded on all hands round them.
How eagerly they sought the deep, blind crannies of Hell!
Then with a great roar, the earth split wide, a deep fissure
Appeared — a gullet sheer-dropping straight down into Hell.
Here Černobog... fell? No, here the foul seducer plunged
In a panic of flight, escaping with black Cháson.
The giant Svatovít, and the whole ignoble crew
Of evil-wreakers leapt in horror, all to escape
That flashing sword of Truth, racing off to Hell, their home,
In which dire recess they preferred to be, among rock
And sulphur, anywhere dark, dark, that shut out the light
That burned their eyes! When the last had leapt into the chasm
The earth closed up anew — this time forever, that they
Should never see the light of day again, or tempt men
To abomination. All was then quiet, only
A faint, but heavenly aroma lingered aloft
Above the healed meadow, to hang there, as if a hint
Of the delights of Heaven which await the just soul.
Such was the end of the conniving of the demons;
All of their plotting was brought to this — their suffering
Augmented still with fiercer consciousness of their fault.
   The ardent Slovaks took themselves to the cathedral,
Golden and soaring in the centre of the city,
Constructed of massive four-square blocks with pinnacles
That scraped the sky. There they knelt in thanksgiving to God
For deigning in His mercy to raise them above their foes
Repulsed from the walls of their city. Him they besought
To stint not in His loving kindness, but support them
In the battle fortunate, to the final victory,
And bless their lives with peace for long years ever after.
Then, when their sacrifice of prayer had been accomplished
Each went off again to his own hearthside — to rejoice
At table, feasting with their families and neighbours.
Song resounded everywhere, feet thudding the dark loam
In even measure; zither, bass, and pipe sawed and skirled
Pulsing against Heaven's vault. It seemed as if all war
Were finished now, and the threat of all battle vanished.
The name of Svatopluk was on everybody's lips.
All raised a toast to the victor, lauding him with song.

But while the people were making merry at table,
Tapping tun after tun of wine, laughing and dancing,
Ojda alone fed on tears and a fretting heart, good
Helpmeet of Namír, who once led the Belohorci,
Until he fell, with two sons, battling against Karol.
She lingered on the street as the people passed in streams,
Awaiting Miloslav, the one son who remained her,
Sole comfort of his sorrowful widowed mother.
And as they passed, him absent, her suffering increased.
She pulled this sleeve and that, and bowed, apologising,
Begging for news incessantly. Yet none seemed to know
Anything of Miloslav, how he'd fared in battle —
Or if they did, they dissembled, concealing the truth
That would break her tired, tormented heart. Until, weeping,
She beheld Palislav, her son's faithful friend and squire.
At him she lunged, to confront him in the plainest terms:
   'Where have you left your lord? Why do you come back alone?
Is Miloslav alive, or has he fallen fighting?
You are afraid to tell a mother of her son's death!
Stop your mewling and gasping and blubber out the truth!'
But no words were needed. Her hands flew to her bosom
And then to her crown, where they tore at her ashen locks.
Deep moans of sorrow welled up from her bowels, and filled
All the space around her. Then, with a younger woman's
Vigour, she leapt to her ancient feet and grabbed a torch,
And rushed off, with the women of her house following,
Comforting her in vain, to the body of her son.
Vainly would Palislav cheer her with vivid accounts
Of Miloslav's bravery and his heroic deeds —
How many men he wounded in battle, how many
He deprived of light forever, stout Bavarians
All, until the valiant Britwald himself laid him low,
Pierced with a lance. With difficulty she went her way
Among the heaps of the fallen, tripping against shat-
-tered arms strewed about the battlefield, Miloslav's squire
Leading the way. Even amidst the shadows of the night
His rough bier was easy to locate, for Palislav
Had fixed his shield refulgent to the spear at his head.
Then mother Ojda swooned, falling prone upon her son's
Remains, motionless she remained flat on the cold limbs

Until, coming round at last, she raised such a lament:
  'And so, my delightful boy, sole comfort of my age,
You return home to me, and I fall upon your breast?
Thus must I greet you, such our rejoicing embraces?
So cold the face I bathe with kisses, so motionless
The lips that would proudly relate your heroic deeds!
It wasn't enough that your grandfather Svatobor,
That nonpareil of warriors, fell in pitched battle,
Herding into the shadows before him twice fifty
Germans? It wasn't enough that your father, pillar
Of the city, was shattered? Or that your two brothers,
Strong Nebochvál and splendid Rodmíl fell, both laid low
On the borders of Moravia? For now you,
The last comfort and delight that still was left to me,
Lie crushed by cruel war, the last instalment I owe
To greedy Death — paid in full! Martial skill and valour,
The swift response of the courageous heart — these the plagues
That always blasted the bones and withered the sinews
Of our clan. And now I remain alone in the world,
A torment to myself, fodder for ravenous pain.
What shall I do now? Where shall I turn in misery?
What shall I live for now that you are gone, my dear boy?
Twice fortunate you barren wombs, dry-seeded men,
Who never, ever shall experience woes like mine!
Wretch of a mother who watches her babies cut down!
Who's brought sons into the sunlight — lambs to the slaughter!
What now remains me but my own death to be longed for?
Heavenly Father, have mercy on my misery!
Call me to Thyself; O, tear me from this suffering
And lay me in a common tomb with this my sweet boy!'
So bitter the lament the sorrowful mother raised,
— Nor could anyone tear her from the cold limbs she'd born —
That the Ruler of the skies at last heard her complaint
And smiled upon her in pity. From high Heaven's halls
An angel He despatched to receive pure Ojda's soul
And lead her to the mansions sublime. Down then spiralled
In hasty gyres God's servant until he alighted
Beside the groaning mother. Her sorrows grew and grew
Until her snow-white throat was brimming with tears, at which
Her heart burst with a sudden rush of woe, unable

More to bear the strain. Her soul then, released from its brittle
Chrysalis of flesh, unto the blest eternal realm
Of bliss was borne, cradled safe in the angel's bosom.
Her cooling limbs, still entwined round the neck of her child
Like ivy never fading wound round the hoary oak,
Were carried off to a common sepulture with him.
  Still revelled the grateful inhabitants of Devín,
But Svatopluk would waste no more time there, nor wishing
Any longer to give ear to litanies of praise
Sang in his honour, he set off with his chief captains
To that high plateau which looked down upon his foes' camp.
Reaching the summit he encountered Zemižížeň,
The voivode to whose command the sentries were charged.
Incessantly his sharp eyes scanned the deep glooms of night,
Peering towards the Bavarian tents, straining hard
To make out any movement there, where the Germans slept,
But he could descry nothing more than campfires winking
Here and there. And no matter how hard he strained his ears
To fish out any tatter of speech or other sound,
He heard nothing, no clatter nor moaning from the tents,
Nothing but the breeze fluttering now and then to the town
From that side, anointing the sore fields with healing dew.
Then Svatopluk spoke these words to the men there present:
  'It would be to our advantage to learn what our foes
Are up to, what conclusions they have reached in council,
Whether they mean to renew the battle when dawn breaks;
Or maybe they've taken fright and abandoned the camp,
Beating a hasty retreat back to Bavaria?
Those campfires that we see glowing there might be decoys
To keep us pinned here in our defensive positions
So that, unpursued for a space, they might steal a march,
Escaping more safely, without any obstacle.
So now, O valiant captains of the Slovak armies,
Which one of you feels himself capable in his heart
Of stalking among the Bavarian tents to learn
What Britwald intends, bringing back sure intelligence?'
  Thus he. Then Zemižížeň immediately replied:
'I, first of all, should be commanded to such a task,
For always I have been entrusted with defending
The Devín battlements from sudden German attack.

So I shall pay this visit to the enemy camp;
I shall penetrate to the very tent where Britwald
Takes rest and sustenance, and I shall not return thence
Until I've learned for sure: Are they preparing for war?
Or, shocked and numb from the blows of their catastrophe,
Have they determined to withdraw to their own borders?
Unless they've turned tail to attempt some new deception?
Now, who is willing to take up this mission with me?
Two hands will better set to such a bold venture;
Two minds will be quicker to solve a sudden challenge'.
   He'd barely finished when all there present erupted
With ardour clamouring to be chosen his comrade.
Ready-wit Vlastoň volunteered, as did Jaromíl,
And Milín and Borislav, whose might surpassed all men;
Sťahlav stepped forward, and Rozhoň and stout-limbed Slavboj.
Wise Zemižížeň looked upon their fervour and smiled.
'O excellent soldiers! Since so many of you wish
To come along with me, how shall I choose among you
Without offending those not chosen, who might grumble
"Why was *he* taken, and why would he leave *me* behind?"
Such being the case, I think it best that Fate decide.
So let's roll the dice. Who wins will accompany me'.
   He finished. All were pleased with the solution preferred,
Valiant Svatopluk as well. The dice were brought forward,
All rolled, and Fortune chose Slavboj to be Zemižížeň's
Comrade. Then many-wiled Svatopluk spoke to them thus:
   'Off with you, then, godspeed, to discover everything we need
To know. Then hurry back safely with the news you glean.
But see you take the life of no defenceless sleeper:
There is no crime so silent as raises no alarm'.
   Thus he. Then in the place Zemižížeň vacated
He set Milín, clever chief of the troops from Nitra,
Appointing him for the time commander of the watch.
Then he descended from the elevated plateau
And ordered an end to all song and celebration,
Sending his men off to bed to rest their weary limbs
And recoup their strength for the morning's renewed battle.
   Then sharp and great-hearted Zemižížeň and Slavboj
Each took a dull shield and a helmet of black colour —
These a trophy of Ubald and those seized from Gotlob,

German prizes of war — this all their accoutrement —
And off they set for the German encampment, having
First entrusted themselves to their guardian angel:
   'Dear angel to whose care God hath confided our souls,
Who ever keepest us from harm and guidest our steps,
Protect us even now from misadventure, that we
Might accomplish our task and return safely to our homes'.
   With such fervour they prayed. And their guardian angel heard them,
Clearing the path before them of all perils lurking
In the dark of night. Then Slavboj to Zemižížeň:
   'Let's first make for that campfire that flickers straight ahead,
To mark whether it's manned by warriors, or a fraud
Lit only to lead us astray, giving warmth to none,
So that we shouldn't waste our time prowling an empty
Camp of dishonour abandoned by stealthy Britwald'.
   The brave Zemižížeň nodded in assent and straight
They galloped toward the fire, dismounting prudently
To creep near unnoticed. In the silence, no farther
Off than three bow shots, human speech seemed to meet their ears —
So they drew short and listened — were those really sentries?
It was men's words wafted on the faint breeze, but unclear.
So clever Zemižížeň whispered to his comrade,
That valiant chief of the troops from the Trenčín region:
   'And so our enemy remains here in his bivouac!
They've not gone home, since they've set up pickets city-ward;
Now we must learn what they intend tomorrow. Come on —
Let's circle the whole lot. Head that way, and I'll go here:
It will be easier for us to approach the camp
From the rear. We've time enough: a full two-thirds of heaven
Is spangled still with the constellations of the night.
   They ceased their whispering and left, each on his own way,
With quick and silent tread, like two dread lions driven
Mad with hunger, stalking the high wall of some rich man's
Sheepfold, testing with snout and paw each cranny, each chink
For easy ingress to the soft flesh within. Thus these
Two prowled the unfamiliar camp, its whole ambit,
Having slinked past the picket-watch. Then they came upon
A stable of horses turned out on a field to graze —
Perhaps the way in lies there? Where they might come to learn
Something of Britwald's intentions? But no, rather not —

The soldiers were all sprawled out, sleeping deeply, snoring…
They pressed on to a rear gate, then suddenly stopped short —
Catching sight of two stallions, beautiful, strong horses;
The vision held them rooted to the spot — they knew them!
Or seemed to — had they not been their own swift-footed mounts?
Zemižížeň snatched at his comrade's arm and whispered:
   'Those two horses — is the dark playing tricks with my eyes,
Or are they not the ones the Germans stole from us, back
In the last war, when wounded we could not prevent it?
Or are they other ones, just similar to our own?'
   To this sharp-eyed Slavboj whispered back: 'Yes, it seems
To me that the one there with the white mane and front legs
Is my old charger — the other like him, but whose tail
Is all white, is yours. Let's draw in closer and find out'.
   And so they crept nearer. Then each called his horse by name,
The same name they'd use when sitting high in the saddle
They'd put them through their paces with spur and bridle-bit.
The steeds pricked their ears and gave out muffled neighs of joy,
Nodding their heads in recognition of their old friends.
Then clever Zemižížeň smiled at Slavboj and said:
   'These steeds were stolen from us; they themselves bear witness
To the fact. Now, let us take them back from the Germans!
You lead them from their confinement here to the river
And wait there for me until I return from the camp.
There on the bank it will be easier to find you,
And nearer to the city for safe return, in case
The Bavarians should suddenly be roused against us'.
   Thus he. And although Slavboj himself would rather have
Invaded the tents along with his friend, he nodded.
With his sharp blade he slit the thickly plaited halters
And led the gorgeous stallions away. None marked him,
But even if they had, surely they would have thought him
Some squire or stablehand leading the steeds to water.
   Then many-wiled Zemižížeň passed over the ditch
That ringed the camp and made for the via praetoria.
All around was silent, except for the loud snoring
Of soldiers exhausted with that day's heavy warring.
Their lances were driven into the soil so, he seemed
To be threading a wood of blasted oak and ash trunks.
The air reeked of the beer and wine with which the drunken

Legions had dulled their sad hearts. But now and then some snatch
Of speech lured him here or there through the gloomy castrum
In search of information. At last he found a soul
Not muttering in his sleep, but lamenting; awake,
Though he would rather not be. The spy crept near and heard:
  'Ah, how am I to return home without you, brother?
How shall I find the words, slumping before our mother,
To speak of your death to her, who brought you forth to life?
How will these ears of mine, hardened to shocks of battle
Bear up under the thin piping of our mother's woe?
Why did I not fall at your side? Why did fate spare me?
In your grave, all of my delight has been buried too!
All that is left me now is to slake this ferocious
Itching for vengeance that scrapes at my soul ever since
I saw you crumple to your knees, shocked at death's sudden
Approach, fading fast, unresponsive to my sorrow —
And vengeance I shall have this very day, when the sun breaks
The line of the crenellations of that cursed city,
According to our leader's vow — oh, tardy sunrise!'
  This was all that wise Zemižížeň needed to hear:
Britwald had ordered the resumption of the battle.
Assured in this knowledge, he stole back out of the camp,
And once past the perimeter he set off quickly
Toward the banks of the Morava where awaited
Slavboj with the stallions recouped. And none too soon —
For just as he'd reached him and was passing on the news
Of Britwald's intentions, a panicked shouting was heard
From the direction of the stables, as the squires there,
Awakening from sleep and noticing the halters
Slit, hanging empty, the two prized stallions missing,
Raised a chaotic alarm that fairly filled the skies.
This roused their comrades from their sleep. They quickly took arms,
But which way were they to rush? Whom were they to pursue?
Who was it that led away the fleet-footed stallions?
Then the many-wiled chief of the Belohorský youth,
Although it threatened present harm, could not restrain himself
From crowing loud: 'O you valiant Bavarians!
Who keep such careful watch over your steeds at pasture!
If in the camp they were to ask you who it was that
Led from their stables these two fine stallions, tell them

That it was Zemižížeň and Slavboj, two soldiers
Of no inconsiderable fame in their battles.
Tomorrow you'll see these two horses grazing high up
On the fat pastures near Devín. Come there and get them
If you've such a hankering to steal them back again!'
   Thus he; then with a laugh, he grabbed the reins of his steed
And set off chuckling to the ford at the Morava
With Slavboj. Irate, the Germans wound tight their crossbows
And sent a flock of bolts flying after them. In vain —
None hit their mark; their guardian angel saw to that!
   At this time, sharp-eyed Javiboj had been set in charge
Of a unit of soldiers guarding a ferry near
The city; like his men, the brave son of Dúbrovský
Zamysl had been drowsing on the grass until a dream
Awoke him suddenly. He leapt to his feet and rushed
To rouse his sleeping comrades from their rest with these words:
   'Listen, my friends! My sleep has been disturbed by a dream
So real: I saw clever Zemižížeň and Slavboj
Returning from their daring foray to the German
Camp, plashing breast-high through the ford of the Morava,
Making for the ferry, amid a hail of arrows…!'
   No sooner had he finished speaking than a thunder
Of galloping hooves was heard from the river's far bank.
So, with a happy shout, Javiboj and the pickets
Pushed out into the silver current the ferry-raft,
Which bit into the far bank just as the two riders
Where shuffling down on their horses to the water's edge.
Once aboard, while the men heaved at the oars, the two spies
Fell to their knees, folded their hands, and raised fervent thanks:
   'Glory to thee, good angel guardian, from brimming
Hearts we raise ardent words of thanks for hearing our prayer
And leading us safely through the German camp this night;
For thou hast shielded thy two charges from all peril,
Leading us whole to the security of our own.
We shall be ever mindful of the graces received
From thee this night, unstinting in our honour of thee,
To whom we shall raise a carven votive monument'.
   And when they reached the other shore, a crowd of their friends
Had gathered, to pull them in by mooring rope and hand
Following their passage across the burly waters.

Oars locked, they bounded up the incline where, among cheers
And shoulder-claps they were surrounded by well-wishers
As conquering heroes. As when in some thick woodland
A flock of finches flutters round a screech-owl, seeking
Explanations for its hooting, and more and more
Arrive twitching, twittering, crowding in for news,
So were the two men overwhelmed, badgered on all sides
For what they'd learned from their foray into their foes' camp —
Did they mean to escape now, the Germans? Or, rather,
To renew the battle? Others wondered at their mounts:
How did they seize them? And how did they avoid all harm
In galloping home? To these and all other questions
They gave quick answer before setting off on their way
Back to the king in haste. When they were led before him
They told him how they'd crept around the foe's encampment,
Which they found full of sleeping Germans, all at rest
Before the new day's warring, at Britwald's firm command.
For the new day's dawning light would see them in the field.
They added an account of how they'd found the steeds once
Stolen from them, and how they'd stolen them back, at which,
Report delivered, they went off to their beds to use
What little remained of the night to refresh their limbs.

CANTO XII

The sun had barely arisen when Svatopluk had it declared to the troops that they should prepare for battle, drawing up in ranks upon the battlefield. He armed himself and then prayed to the Lord for victory. The old men, mothers, and children went off to the cathedral and lifted their prayers to the Mother of God. Whole hosts approached the tomb of Dobroslava. Here Svatopluk gave them heart with an oration. Emboldened, they set off to war, and the song on their lips, as was their wont, was a hymn to God. The Germans also marched forth from their camp in ranks. A bloody battle commenced: the fight was fierce and even on both sides until Britwald fired the ardour of his men, laying low the strongest of the Slovaks. Then, coming to know that his left flank was in dire peril, he rushed off there to aid them. Svatopluk also added his might and skill to his side. They fought mightily. Having lain low many men himself, Borislav led his heroic troops, dressed in bear-skins, against the Bavarian cavalry. The horses, spooked, reared in fright and flung their riders from their backs, trampling them beneath their hooves. As for Svatopluk, not satisfied with merely managing his troops, he fell ferociously upon the Bavarian army himself. He slaughtered their leaders, but only wounded Radbod, whom he then sent off to Karolman to bring report of the catastrophe of his troops. He refrained from engaging with the other warriors present. Instead, he went off in search of Britwald, wishing to challenge him to a duel. The Heavenly Father addressed Cyril, informing him that Svatopluk would achieve victory and establish the Slovaks as a great kingdom. Cyril offered his thanks. Then, hearing that many of his leaders had fallen, Britwald went off in search of Svatopluk, commanding his army to refrain from the battle, as he would have the two meet in single combat. So the men put up their swords and cleared a place for the duel. The two leaders then set upon one another. It was a long and fierce battle, but at last Svatopluk overcame Britwald.

 The morning star had barely revealed her blushing cheeks,
Dispersing the wispy mists of night from the new skies,
When valiant Svatopluk ordered his trumpeters
To step forth and lift their glistening brass horns heavenward,
With raucous voice to summon the troops to new battle.
And quickly they armed, bold, eager for the battlefield.
Svatopluk himself encased his torso in his sure
Armour brilliantly chased with pure gold, with his sword
Gigantic hung at his mighty hip. And then he knelt
And sent aloft to the sublime Monarch ardent prayers:
 'O Father who rulest the heavens, look down once more

Upon Thy faithful servants, and hasten with Thine aid!
Have mercy once again upon this city, rescued
By Thine almighty arm from the cruel enemy
Whom, thanks to Thee, we repulsed from these walls. Today, Lord,
Aid us again to overcome them in the fierce fray
That looms. Drive them away from here, and from our country,
Expelling them beyond our borders, so that we, free
And independent, delivered from the foreign yoke,
Might wax in peace and freedom. In thanksgiving to Thee,
I vow to build votive churches in Devín, Nitra,
And Trenčín, each with a westwerk soaring to the clouds,
And one hundred other grand temples sacred to Thee,
Timeless memorials of the grace received of Thee.
And I shall establish clergy and canons to serve
Thee, piously lifting the unbloody sacrifice
Of the spotless Lamb to Thee, Father, day after day!'
  He'd barely finished his prayer than he felt his heart swell
With new courage, his limbs lighter and more powerful,
His mind sharper, clearer, more confident in command.
For the great Ruler of the universe heard his prayer,
And in His mercy determined to grant all he wished.
Svatopluk arose with a thunderous clatter of arms.
He donned his helm with the menacing plumes, his left arm
Hefted a shield that glowed like the victorious sun
Flashing irresistible rays of martial power,
While in his right fist he gripped a sharp-tipped oaken lance.
His snow-white steed he mounted, and galloped forth to rush
Upon his enemies with the force of destiny.
  Meanwhile, the old folk, the sad wives, mothers, and maidens
Betrothed, and girls, and boys not yet matured to the fight
Crowded the cathedral built by the pious Oslav
Wherein they lifted their prayers to the Mother of God:
  'O Mother full of grace, O Virgin immaculate!
Deign set our petitions before Thy beloved Child
(For He hears no prayers as promptly as He hears Thine!)
That He should turn a gracious eye upon our men, who march
To ferocious battle today. May He give them strength
Sufficient to expel the Germans from our borders
So that, free from all fear and threat of catastrophe,
We might raise to Him praise unimpeded, as is meet,

And to Thee our incessant thanks for our deliverance'.
   Thus in the temple they prayed, with thricely-humbled heart
Before ascending the high battlements to observe
The ferocious battle that was to commence that day,
Urging their men on as well as they might with their cheers.
   But before the army set out for the battlefield
They drew up in ranks at the tomb of Dobroslava,
That valiant maiden, foundress of the city Devín,
Beneath the shade of the four great linden trees, which grew
From the tumulus where they sprouted ages ago —
Peers to the burial — whose crowns now soared to the clouds.
Milín led the right flank, and stout Borislav the left,
While mighty Zemižížeň and Slavboj, in the midst,
Headed the central corpus, with commander-in-chief
Svatopluk above all. When every man was in place
As appointed, Svatopluk stepped forth before his troops
And with such words enflamed their hearts for the coming fray:
   'Heroic conquerors! Our nation's surest support!
You've nearly shattered the enemy's might, having slain
So many German leaders. Look! thick smoke still billows
From the high hecatombs of the Bavarian dead!
And surely you would have pulverised the lot, had not
The thick glooms of the night intervened, precluding
Further battle, and covering their shameful retreat!
So now I ask you, once more, let your doughty hearts swell
With courage, and what night stole from your grasp, may the dawning
Of this new day remit you! Batter down the remnants
Of the Bavarian army! May your swords ring down
This last of their suns, just arisen — may the daylight
Just piercing the horizon be curtained from their sight
As you drag the gloomy pall of death over their eyes,
Hurling them into night eternal! O my heroes,
My comrades, think upon this your Slovak motherland,
Your wives, your children, and rescue them from slavery
To strangers, split the yoke that has been fashioned for their necks,
So that free, they should never be chafed to blood beneath
Its unplaned burl. Forward, my comrades, and win today
The fame undying of your nation's saviours! And more:
Fight on to free the Styrians and Carinthians,
And our other Slavic brethren from Bavarian

Overlordship, that our nation might stretch whole and hale,
From the deep-rumbling Wisła and the snow-capped Tatras
To where the Dráva rushes to the embrace of the Danube!'
   The troops roared their response, their hearty cheers thundering
Against the vault of heaven. And then as was their wont
Before each battle, they raised their massed voices in song:

   O Lord, Who rulest sky and land,
   Wind, mountain, flame, and wave,
   All creatures Thy almighty hand
   Doth nourish, heal, and save.

   Look down upon Thy faithful band
   Who march unto the breach,
   Have mercy on our Motherland
   We fervently beseech.

   As we unto fierce battle ride
   Support us with Thy hosts,
   Thou, Unbegotten at our side
   And Thou, O Holy Ghost.

   For it is for Thee that we fight
   Against our evil foe,
   Aid us to thrust him from the light
   Into dark Hell below.

   Strengthen our heart, make firm our hand,
   Crown us with victory,
   So once we've healed our suffering land
   We'll live forever free.

   And as Thy people free and strong
   In peace we'll spend our days,
   Lifting to Thee our grateful song
   In sacrifice of praise.

   Thus hymned the Slovaks setting off to the cruel fray.
And then the trumpets blared angrily, swelling their hearts
The more with courage as their slogans echoed from wood

And dale, announcing war. The Germans replied in kind,
Marching from their camp, and soon the ranks stood face to face.
As when the burly clouds mass over Chvalenská peak
Or Siberian winds roar down upon the Black Sea,
Swelling wave upon wave ever higher, crashing down
And pummelling the far shore, with Death lashing each crest,
Thus the Bavarian cavalry began to trot,
Then gallop toward the steady Slovak phalanxes.
The earth vanished beneath the wild thundering squadrons.
All other sounds were drowned out by the drumming,
And the dustclouds kicked up by the hooves obscured the sun,
Which struggled to be seen in flashes from helm and shield,
Its splendour reduced to pinprick stars in murky skies
Below, as all nature was upturned. Spears, like comets,
Streaked through the firmament as the cavalry drew near
And trumpets contended from both sides, bellowing loud,
Urging their colours to slaughter. The darts flew so thick
Their shafts formed a hammerbeam vault above the fighters,
An ever-moiling storm that screamed and whistled, as dart
Glanced against dart and armour, and pierced unlucky flesh.
And then all is a whirl of cavalry and pikemen
As the two sides mix in the deadly scrum: lances, hooves,
Swords, and battle-axes glint and flash as the men hack
And thrust, hack, thrust, and parry. Horrible screams erupt
From man and beast as flesh is slit and punctured, the earth
Becomes one queasy quagmire as blood and dust unite
In a mixture unholy never intended by God.
   Medňan pierces the ponderous Dietrich in his thigh
With his long spear. An artery severed, Dietrich falls
And bites the gory soil. Maloň slays Rudbert,
Adelfat Balša, Kochan Markolf, while Mokuárd
Falls, hewn by Girald. Božislav cuts down Erchenfríd,
Witold overthrows both Nezamysl and Kolboj, then
He himself is taken down by Neplach the bowman.
Medard, the black-eyed son of Burkhard, rips the strong calf
Of Dušek, who hobbles away crippled, while stout Fríz
Has his guts slit open by Un and staggers, trailing
Intestines and the pike-shaft that bit deep, relinquished
By his victor. Briks blinds gallant Nedamír's right eye
With a thick-shafted dart, depriving him of daylight

Entirely, as he'd lost his left eye long ago — Egloft
Burst its jelly when Nedamír fought on the ramparts
Of Devín, defending his city against a siege
Laid by Karolman himself. Now see him plod away
Amid the tempest of steel, oak-staves and flailing hooves
Like a man on a precipice in the blackest night.
Netrask slays Wurm, and is cut down by Ekhard in turn,
Who falls beneath Mažibrad's blows soon enough. Rajnhold
Is slain by Otceslav, Erich slashes dead Výboh,
Who had a fine farm near Bílá Hora's slopes, with three
Flocks of sheep, and three of goats he'd water at the clear
Trnava River — four hundred ewes, three times fifty
Rams and just as many kids in each trip. Then Volkmár
Falls, and gigantic Široslav's trunk topples with a roar.
And you too, Hromýl, fell! Leaving behind your betrothed,
Widowed before she'd known a man! Lovely Malehna
Whom, hunting game with friends, you caught instead, or rather
By her were netted — barely had you brought her home to wed
Than you rushed off — into the arms of Death. Černobog
Blared your epithalamium, egging you on to war.
Leaving Malehna yearning at home, you'll not return
Ever, though you died not unavenged, for Hodislav,
Avoiding Ratfréd's dart (stooping in time, the arrow
Buzzed high, and missed), rushed angrily upon your slayer
And laid him low, cleaving his head in twain with his sword
That flashed bright, until its blade was befouled with dark blood.
Ratfréd barely groaned, crashing to his knees, his great shield
Clanging against the rocky earth where he'd been standing.
Then able Milibor, and no less skilled Hengeswald,
The one from Olomouc, the other an Austrian,
Measured each other from a distance, hefting their spears.
Hengeswald's spear spits the edge of the seven-ply shield
Of stout Milibor, its sharp point grazing his left flank.
Blood spurts, but the Czech falls not, a superficial wound
Only, that slit his skin. But he had better fortune:
His rough spear split Hengeswald's armoured breastplate in twain.
The mighty thrust pierced his left lung, spear-head protruding
Beneath his shoulderblade. Likewise, Požár and Gebhard,
Both heroes bold, hurled their spears with all the strength they had.
But neither Požár nor Gebhard hit his mark, both spears

Untrustworthy whistled past their target's collarbone.
So both unsheathed their blades and moved to clash at sword's-point,
But before they dealt their first blows, both men were cut down
By battle-axes: Gebhard by Vladislav, Požár
By Frodoard, cleft in two by the razor-sharp steel
(But soon enough, both axe-men were slain, and bit the dust
In turn). Múdroslav hurls his fierce spear at Roderík,
Then hears a javelin whistle, but before he turns
To gauge it, the dart's upon him — the last thing he sees
Is the fearsome tip that spits him, and he falls, spewing
A river of blood. Yet his own cast was not in vain.
It skewered Roderík, unspooling his intestines.
   The battle's raging on all sides. Men are cruelty
Incarnate, like bears of the Ural mountains, maddened
With long hunger, who with fierce claws tear apart a tree
To get at their sweet prey — honeycombs — glutting themselves
Before gathering the remnant for their cubs at home.
Legions of men wade the bloody knee-high mire, stumbling
Amongst the corpses; legions of men fall and sink
In the gory thick liquid — a hasty burial.
What dry dust remains soars aloft to obscure the sun
In pinkish clouds of filth. So the battle raged, and yet
Victory neither inclined to this side nor to that.
Like oxen cross-harnessed, each tugging at one burden,
Hunched, muscles swelling, polls snorting at the ground or horns
Jutting to the sky, hooves pounding, but of equal strength
And like determination, neither could budge the load.
The day then rolled on to that hour when herds surfeited
With pasture lumber homeward, their udders to be milked,
Or in late autumn rest in the shade, chewing the cud
(Long not to be plucked from these fields), when Britwald called out:
  'O valiant Bavarians! scrape up from your hearts
The lees of your valour and ferocity of limb!
Today we end this war with our foes' catastrophe!
It matters not that we have lesser numbers than they;
What matters is the girth of one's heart and might of arm!
One forest wolf can tear apart entire sheepcotes;
One eagle scatters entire squadrons of starlings;
One scythe suffices to mow down whole meadows. To me!
And let us fall upon the foe where he is thickest.

There is our open road to glory, there is our reward'!
   Thus Britwald rumbled, like some angry black thunderhead
Falling upon the Slovaks like a sudden hailstorm.
Soon Slavopol is cut down, Mojmír and Bohuslav
From Blučina, wrathful Podivin is sent to death
As well as clever Rušizvad and comely Ozrak
Whose lip and chin had sprouted no whiskers yet; Sarba
And Vitek, able brothers, were the next pair to fall
Before Britwald, with Trojslav their brother, half a head
Taller than both. Then grey-bearded Kazimir and fierce
Malovec, who'd pummelled legions of Bavarians
With oaken mace; then Stach and Marovít and Zábor,
Skilled huntsmen. Nearby fought Pobor, beyond all measure
The courageous battler, hewing down forests of men
With his axe, until Britwald cut him down in his turn.
He was the only son, the only joy of Hrislav
His father — who pastured his great herds at Trenčín's walls,
Ever a generous host to all guests who stopped by.
It was to Pobor that Britwald turned with a mad swipe
Of his axe that bit deep into his side and cut him down,
Ending the father's life by ending the life of his son.
Now Hodislav the sharp, as soon as he saw Britwald
Mowing down so many men, rushed at him in fury,
But anger got the upper hand of aim — the fierce cast
Of the ominous spear went awry and whizzed errant.
Instead of the golden helm he'd been aiming at, tufts
Were all it encountered until it struck Sigebert
— Who'd been standing closest behind — full in his hoarse throat,
Then, passing through, it came to rest in Atunagt's shield.
Now Britwald, cruel by nature, fell into a rabid
Frenzy at his friend's death — for he'd heard the moan of pain
And gurgle of blood-spew behind him — though he dared not
Glance back — the threat was before him. Scanning for the foe
Who'd slaughtered Sigebert, with all the strength he had, he flung
His ashen spear. Catching Hodislav in the shoulder,
It burst the sinews tearing the arm from its socket.
The Slovak crashed to the earth with a clatter of arms.
Upon the helpless trunk haughty Britwald set his foot
And jeered: 'What you would have given me, here I give you.
Take this as recompense for the many men you've slain'.

Blood pumping from his torn shoulder, Hodislav whispered:
  'I've no complaint at bidding farewell to the light now —
I've reached the end of my span, avoiding the burden
Of decrepit age. But you've no good reason to gloat,
For I proceed you by a few paces only. Soon
Enough you'll set off on the same path into the gloom,
Your passage paid by Svatopluk'. These words having said,
He felt the pall of endless night fall upon his eyes,
With his last breath his soul released from his cooling limbs.
  His comrades rushed near, enflamed with vengeance. But Britwald
Stood firm to receive them — indeed, burning with anger
He hastened to meet them halfway, furious, sword drawn,
Like a lion frenzied by herdsman's spear that barely
Grazed his tawny flank, having slashed down their protector,
With fang and claw he tears apart the defenceless herd.
Thus Britwald piled hecatombs of lesser thanes around
The war-chief he'd slaughtered. But as he was extracting
His spear form the ribs of Strojslav, wealthy in stallions,
Radegund galloped close on his charger with tidings ominous:
Milín, ferocious as a cyclone, was laying waste
The right flank, splattering Kučbor's brains with cruel mace,
And laming Mutimír the swift, shattering his thigh.
What's more, Jaromíl carried off Salak, swarthy Borš
Lay dark with gore, slain by Zbíslav; the rest of the troops,
Spooked, had turned their back and were fleeing; it was a rout,
And there was nothing he could to to staunch the blood-loss
Of hearts punctured by terror and despair, reeling, beat.
Ratmír alone delays the enemy's advance,
Slashing the Slovaks as they press, thwacking the skulkers
With the flat of his sword to halt the base withdrawal.
At this news, the venom of wrath seethes in Britwald's veins.
Bellowing at the company commanders to fight on
And give their men heart, force them to manliness, he flies
To that sector of the field like a swift-winged hawk
When, far below him, he spots a flock of water-fowl
On the smooth breast of a calm lake. His eyes flash with sparks,
The sun flares in fits from the boss of his massive shield.
  At this the captains are roused from their funk and turn back,
The embers of their mettle bursting back into flame.
Soon Winfred's slain Skotomír, and Ludolf Sukorád,

Madalhod cuts down Rajka, Wilbert lays Návoj flat,
Ulrich kills Umír, and large-boned Erchenbert Čela,
While Vato sends both Bojša and Ránka to their death.
Then Chocil, Privina's son — pious, but for all that
No less fierce a battler, erupts in ferocious wrath
And takes off Predhora. When the pagan Radislav
Sees the man intended to marry his daughter fall,
He runs in that direction, praying to Svatovít:
  'O god who rulest war and broil, great Svatovít!
Who rainest down panic upon our foes, and smitest
Our enemies with thy strong right hand! Guide now my spear
And send it tearing through the guts of Privina's heir!
Then, should I be given the grace to return home hale,
Beneath the wide-spreading and sky-scraping canopy
Of our oaken glade I shall raise an idol, carven
Cunningly, in thine honour, embellished with copper.
I'll set a bull's horn in the right hand, and in the left
A strong bow and quiver full of arrows; at the side
I'll hang the gilded sword prised from Chocil's cold, stiff grip!'
  Vain words, these — he slings his death-venomed javelin,
But wide it flies, high, to the left of Chocil's shoulder,
At which the able scion of Privina exclaims:
  'O heavenly Father, sole Ruler of the cosmos
Entire, who alone art worthy of divine praise!
Aid me to topple this idolater, just as Thou
Hast helped us scourge the land of their foul idols!'
  That was a proper curse! Which uttered, he sent a-wing
His own spear. True the cast: it plunged straight through the navel
Of Radislav, unspooling his guts and snapping his spine,
The point poking through his back, glinting in the red light.
It spun the skewered pagan, who flopped down on his face —
Such aid might be expected from Svatovít! Such might
Have empty vows! Then Zoroľub strung a sharp arrow
Aimed at Privina's son. It might have wounded him, slain
Him even, had not his splendid son, young Vratislav,
Rushed to his father's defence, and with one swift motion
Lopped off the archer's arm at the elbow. It fell dead,
Harmless, inert, a threat to no man now. Dobroslav
Slew Hodka, valiant Bojmír sent Tur to his grave,
Then able Radbod prevailed over Čudomíl,

Jesutbor felled Ustal, while Dragšo brought down Bazák,
And Zaglav, grandson of Jesutbor, slew Čestislav.
Merisáv's sword shattered on Bodrok's iron helmet.
And so he grabbed a border-stone fixed deep in the earth
At his feet, such as two brawny yokels mightn't lift,
And with one hand he raised it high above him, driving
Off Slavko; hurling it, he crushed his foe's stout ribcage.
So fierce the men battled — like frothy-mouthed boars in rut,
And hill and dale echoed back the shocks and screams of war.
The beasts of the wild hastened to ground, birds sped off,
The local herdboys escaped, whipping their beeves through thorns
To race off the quicker. Meanwhile, on the battlefield,
Who still has sword or axe, slashes and hacks; who hasn't
Tears at his enemy with his fingernails or teeth.
Blood flows in rivers, sweat, spit, and gore befoul the earth,
Fists split jawbones, or are shattered themselves at impact.
Captain and churl mix in the wild scrum — blood-soaked orgy!
   King Svatopluk, in the midst of the fray, urges on
His men: 'O valiant battlers! It lies in our power
To deliver Devín, and all our land, from peril!
Their ranks are thinning, while our valour increases —
And why do we suffer, if not for our liberty,
And on behalf of the aged, our wives and children,
Whose sole defence — besides the prayers they raise heavenward
From the high battlements — are these arms of ours? Fight on,
And save them from cruel ravishment and slavery!
Waver not, my comrades! Fight on with hearts undaunted.
Roll on like billows to swamp these Bavarian scraps —
Cut down the stubborn who will not bend the knee to you!'
   So he cries out, in a voice that overcomes the roar
Of battle. Then, like a wind rushing from black storm cloud
That falls upon old forests thick with oak and ash-tree,
Splitting these, tearing up those by the roots
And leaving ghastly bare wounds where once woods proudly stood,
His troops rip through the German ranks — clatter, shriek and roar
On all hands fill the air reverberating with fear.
The earth thrums like a membrane from the thickly falling
Dead, which multiply in hosts such as earth suffices
Not to bury, buried herself rather, underneath
The ill harvest of Death, thickly stacked in evil sheaves.

Sing, Umka, now, of all those who fell in the mayhem,
For even if I had a hundred mouths, a hundred
Tongues of brass, I could not name them all, those who were slain
By the mighty warriors, or those King Svatopluk,
That many-skilled warrior, sent to the shades below.
The voivode Krup killed the able swordsman Bogdán,
Sťahlav the mighty swept his blade at red Jarohnev
And drove a fatal gash that made his head to totter,
Flopping crazily to the side of his split torso.
The two victors then rushed upon the Privinovci.
Krup wounded father, and Sťahlav the stronger son,
But neither of those wounds were mortal — like a cupping,
Blood was drawn from Chocil's thigh, while comely Vratislav
Felt a trickle at his elbow. But Gotprajz the proud
Was slain by Bor, and Walden fell too, along with Helf,
While Bor's clever son Vlastoň slew Harbrecht and Gunda.
Large-boned Slavboj laid Wolfgang low, Adelrich, Berta,
And two cousins, Landulf and Walda, born the same day,
Now made exact contemporaries in their demise.
He'd now cleared himself a path to Winfríd, who surpassed
All Germans, head and shoulders — of all Bavarian
Heroes the most skilled in heaving the pine lance.
Fierce, Slavboj slashed at Winfred's left ear with his sword.
The blade bit through the brown casque, shattering the skull-bone,
Releasing a spurt of blood and brain. The limbs went limp,
And crashed to the ground, and his shield spun drunkenly
Away. Massive Ludomír, that tower of a man,
Skilled warrior, begored the right cheek of Merisáv
Between jaw-bone and ear. Now, as he was drawing forth
The death-dealing barb, Merisáv's comrade Žarkoslav
Rushed at him, wroth. But Prekrasa, Ludomír's dear wife,
Who would not let her husband go alone into the fray
But followed all his doings, sharp-eyed, from the ramparts,
And — what is more — defended him from harm with crossbow,
Caught sight of Žarkoslav, and quickly fed her weapon
With iron dart, which she aimed and let fly. Whistling sharp,
It shattered the enemy's elbow, severing vein
And sinew, disabling the brawn. Away fell the spear,
Harmless now. Skilled Zemižížeň sent Bystroň to death,
And Dragšo, and two rich mates, Metimír and Divko.

To these he added Zaglav and stout-framed Bojka,
Who along with his brother had rushed to the attack.
Now, when he saw his beloved brother Žalko fall,
Terrified, he sought to beg quarter of the victor.
But before he could form the words in his mouth, his throat
Was pierced by a spear. Zemižížeň turns to Jesutbor,
Massive of limb, a fright to behold even from afar.
The ash-dart flies. Both shield and armour it splits, driving
Deep within his ribs, shattering the breastbone.
Like a large boulder split from a mountain, Jesutbor
Tumbles, shivering the earth with a crash of armour.

   Nor was the German rout any less on the left flank,
Where Borislav, first of all in valour, led the charge.
Frenzied Swojski topples Gunihild, and Bujartúr
Both Detlev and Baldvín; Rozhoň: Ostaš the hunter.
The first fell by arrow, the second by spear, the third
Was battered to his grave by heavy, steel-studded mace.
Deslav the Magnanimous cut his way to Štilfríd,
Horsed, and severed his head from his shoulders. The charger
Reared in panic, terrified at the cooling torso
Still fixed in saddle and stirrup. But it's Borislav
Who rages most among the enemy with slaughter,
For as in the mountains pine and smooth fir are knocked down
Beneath the sharp axe-blades of the Orava woodsmen,
Felling the high growth and casting it beneath their feet,
Thus fell the Bavarians beneath the blows of his club
— Massive thing — with which he decimated the German ranks.
Now Boda falls, now hearty Jeltislav, Častoň, Vít,
Great Budimír and Návoj, along with his father,
And a hundred more. But when he arrived at Svenčar
The war-chief, and gashed a wound on his back to the bone,
He thought a convenable time had come to release
Amongst the foe's cavalry those troops clad in bear-skin
Who up till now had waited, chafing, in ranks, to fight.
Yet just then a rumble met his ears — he turned to see
The giant Izbignev Častoslavovič, blazing
In armour elaborate, cap-a-pie, rush at him;
This clash Borislav could not avoid. And so he cast
A mighty pine-shafted spear at his attacker's head.
No bevor or visor was to any avail here —

The spear passed straight through metal and cartilage, piercing
Nose and mouth to emerge through the occipital. He fell,
And Borislav now turned to the bear-skinned troops, calling
For havoc among the horses, who would panic
When they caught sight and scent of what they took to be beasts,
Frenzied, and cast down their riders, who wouldn't control them.
Indeed, they panicked — here and there they thrashed, knocking a-
gainst each other, snorting fearfully, unwilling to
Obey rein or bridle, and the more the Germans strove
To gain control over them, the more they reared and flailed.
Havoc reigns, chaos, in the ranks of the cavalry.
As acorns in the autumn drum the soil when the wind
Shakes the dried boughs, so the hapless German riders fall
Head-first, beneath their chargers' flailing iron-shod hooves
Which beat them down each time they try to rise: skulls, bones, ribs
Are smashed by the limbs of the great panicking horses
And arms once mighty are hammered into useless pulp.
   Now valiant Svatopluk was not content merely
To gaze upon the deeds of his stoutly battling men,
To direct the action from some safe distance — oh, no:
With his strong arm he wished to do his part to batter
The Bavarian troops, thus to aid his warriors.
So, with impetus fierce, like the Váh when it spills down
From Krivan, when the summit nods under the impulse
Of an earthquake that shivers its spine to Morské Oko
And the lake pushes forth its waters like the ocean
To roar down scree and cliff and submerge the vale below,
So hurtled he to where the battle raged most fiercely.
And as that river, with its massed waters multiplied,
Carries off tree and boulder, and all the things of man:
Dam, bridge, and household, flock, herd lowing in terror
And the hapless shepherds who led them, leaving nothing
In their wake but death, ruin and mud, thus Svatopluk
Raged through the German ranks, slashing down those stubborn ones
Who would not bend the knee to save their lives — bloody waste!
First it is bold Helmut he slays, who had led the troops
With oaken mace, then Érenbert, Urolf, and those two
Skilled bowmen Arimund and Bekman; Gerlach he adds
To accompany them on their way into the gloom —
Gotheft and Brand, who tempted fate in opposing him,

And found it — the first of them caught the spear in his gut,
The second had his larynx drilled by the hefty cast.
Then Švenhild he slays, and then you, Makward, who ever
Sang gaily, strumming your lute at the Germans' banquets.
You ventured off to war because you wished at first hand
To look upon heroes and heroic deeds, to sing
The paeans of war-chiefs all the more truthfully. Now
You've seen what war is! Now you've experienced battle!
That gifted voicebox is forever stilled, torn apart
By the skilful thrust of the Slovak king's lance. No more
Shall your songs be heard to the graceful notes of the harp!
Then eager Ulrich rushed at him from close by, but he,
With one swipe of his razor-sharp sword cut the red head
Off the broad shoulders, which crumpled clumsily to earth.
Then came a sharp whistle, and a thud, as an arrow
Bit into the Slovak king's shield. This was Adelhold,
Skilled bowman, who sent the missile at him. But the joy
Of victory was not to be his: for Svatopluk
Soon turned his steed and set off at a gallop for where
The Bavarian archer stood. Now, when Adelhold
Beheld the menace, he took fright, turned his tail and ran,
Stumbling along the uneven terrain, feet slipping
From the slick corpse's back he'd sought to clamber over,
Then plunging down hard when an expected foothold suddenly vanished, like a man missing a final stair,
Or, in late winter-time, when a person ventures out
Upon the ice too thin to bear his weight, which cracks and splits
With each step, feet plunging through holes punched in the shallows,
Fighting for the firm shore, cursing the traitorous sheet
That promised passage, thus Adelhold with panicked heart
Strove toward shelter — any kind of shelter — in vain:
Svatopluk pinned him to earth with his ash-shafted lance
That punched in beneath his right shoulder-blade, and tore out
His lung. Seeing this, Wilbert turned upon Svatopluk
Seething with venom, set to an even fiercer boil
With the blow that shattered Adelhold, at which he screeched:
   'Be welcome, Svatopluk! Long have I expected you!
How long I've yearned to measure thrusts with your famed right hand!
But come closer, blushing maiden! I've your bridegroom here —
This stiff Bavarian pike! He brings in dowry

A realm impregnable: as many cubits of earth
As you might cover with your corpse on your nuptial bed!'
   So chortled he. But King Svatopluk would waste no time
On empty words. In reply, he sent a spear whizzing
That smashed through Wilbert's teeth, slashing through his haughty tongue.
It was Wilbert whose limbs stretched out upon the sand;
Now his mouth pumped out nothing but enamel and blood.
Only then did his conqueror address him these words:
   'The mate you prepared me, Wilbert, I here relinquish,
Along with the marriage gifts of that wide-spreading realm.
You'll have it, as my gift, with a deed everlasting'.
   He spared him no more time, setting off to other broils.
Soon Vato met his final end, as did Madalhod,
The first struck full in the face, the other in the groin —
Neither their young age, nor their comeliness availed them.
Now, the great warrior had wished to show them mercy.
He'd cried out: 'Put down your weapons, brave lads! And abstain
From further fighting!' Yet the boys, chary of their fame,
Refused to submit, and all the more fiercely rushed him,
Which angered Svatopluk, who then forgot his mildness,
Sending both to their graves on the field below Devín.
When Erchenbert and Ludolf, hastening to their aid,
Beheld their fall, they sped at Svatopluk, empurpled
With still greater wrath, to avenge the death of their sons.
But Svatopluk's arm met them from afar, speeding arrows
At the first, while felling the second with an axe-blow
That shattered his cheek. Then a second slashed his loins
Apart from his torso. Then only Radbod remained
From the Bavarian captains, and him Svatopluk
Determined not to send into the eternal gloom.
Wounding him deeply in his shoulderblade (the blood-spurt
Fouled his armour), he bade him set aside his weapons,
And with such words addressed him: 'O valiant Radbod!
Of all the German war-leaders, we choose to spare you.
Return now to your king and deliver unto him
The tidings of his army: tell him not to expect
The return of his heroes, who have found their graves'.
   These words delivered, he refrained from further murder,
Unwilling to spill the blood of any more soldiers.
But Britwald he sought out yet — for with Britwald alone

Would he measure his sword in a duel, and cut down.
   And so he goes off, riding round the German fragments,
Calling for Britwald, delivering his fierce challenge,
At which the heavenly Father, the Ruler of all
Thus addressed St Cyril in the mansions of the skies:
   'My faithful servant, come! The hour has now arrived
In which you shall behold the fulfilment of your prayers.
For now the capable Svatopluk calls out Britwald,
Whom he shall overcome. The German leader vanquished,
He'll bring all warring to an end, making all subject,
Including the remnants of his foes, to his power.
No one from so large a German host shall return home
Except for Radbod, grievously wounded, to report
On the rout. Thus shall Svatopluk attain victory,
Winning liberty for himself and for his people,
Uniting kindred nations beneath his sceptre, thus
Founding the great kingdom of the valiant Slovaks'.
   Then Cyril bowed low in thanksgiving before the throne
Of the Almighty: 'Thanks be to Thee, O Father, Lord
Omnipotent! For Thou, in Thy magnanimity,
Showest mercy not only unto Thy meek servant
To whom Thou grantest a heavenly abode, but still
Deignest to look with eye benign upon the prayers
Of mortal men, fulfilling their worthy petitions!'
   Now, when Britwald saw his soldiers in flight, his captains
Cut down, never more to behold the light of heaven,
With only Radbod — half dead for all that — remaining,
And even Ratimír wielding his spear — as a crutch! —
While of his Slovak chiefs mighty Chocil was wounded
Along with his son Vratislav, he seethed with anger.
His heart was churning, and steam escaped his lips, as when
Lime rasps and gurgles in a pit during firing, thus
Britwald fumed: 'Am I to turn tail now and run? Return
To my fatherland Bavaria, in shame, to face
The reproach of the mothers and wives of the fallen?
Or should I grapple with the Slovak king, one on one?
If I should fall, it would be better thus — as hero
Amongst the other heroes swept into endless gloom.
Better to face missiles and spears than spittle and jeers!
And who knows but that Svatopluk might fall to my blade?

It is as sharp as his, and has slain just as many
Stout warriors'. At this he turned to his men and cried:
'Leave off your shameful running. Stand aside — I alone
Will fight on, man to man, with the Slovak king. Draw back
And watch us battle'. This having said, he turned to see
The great Svatopluk galloping near. So Britwald turned
To face him, and addressed him in such ominous terms:
'Tell your men to set aside their swords in present truce.
Let us, you and I, enter the gallant lists alone.
Should you emerge the victor, you shall reign in your land
Over a people free of Bavarian lordship;
Just spare these other soldiers, send them home to their hearths.
But should I overcome you, and strip you of your arms,
Your land and people shall revert to Bavaria'.
 Thus he. King Svatopluk was gladdened by the challenge.
He willingly agreed to the terms, yet he refused
To parole the German captives. Still, he told his men
To set aside their weapons, and dismounted his steed.
They heeded him. A large space for the battle was cleared;
They cast their bright shields aside and leaned upon their spears
Fixed in the soft earth. Encircling the tournament pitch
All looked on, eyes wide open, in wonder at the two
Who now approached the mortal combat from either side.
 Like two famished lions, who by mere coincidence
Come upon a doe or stag slain by the hunter's dart
(The hunter himself away racing at the mere sound
Of their roars), who set to one another with sharp claw
And fang, disputing the meal that neither would share,
Demanding it all, so these two approached each other
With death in their angry eyes. First Britwald hurled his spear
At Svatopluk. It flew true — straight at the golden helm —
Almost: it scraped the ear-piece merely, and flew on past,
Unslaked with the Slovak blood it failed to draw. Svatopluk
Then cast his missile — it struck the round shield flush, its force
Piercing the ply and penetrating armour and flesh,
Cutting Britwald to the bone. But he extracted it,
And sharp swords drawn from scabbards, both advanced with fury.
The blows fell thickly then: like two dragons furious
Lashing their triple tongues and breathing fire, barbed tails
Poised to strike with mortal venom, thus they wheeled and slashed,

The flurry of their sword-blows raising sparks like whirling
Tongues of flame when a burning roof-tree collapses; helms
And shields rang most with the fierce percussions, like cliff-sides
Shattered by lightning-bolts falling to earth with a roar
Tremendous, stone upon stone concussing with a crash.
The crowns of their helms were battered. Tufts fluttered aloft,
And armour, once the pride of artful smiths, was dented
And split to uncomely scrap: visors bent and unpinned,
Gorget and bevor hanging split at crazy angles.
Blood seeped through holes punched in breastplate, plackart and cuisse,
Befouling with gore the once pristine metal-plates. Harsh
The echoes of the pummelling filled the air. Both hosts,
Bavarian and Slovak, looked on in awe and fright,
Awaiting the outcome. Whose dish would sink, when at last
Valour and destiny determined the victor?
Soon, both grew sluggish from the blows, breathing heavily,
Their bodies drenched in sweat. Twice a truce allowed them rest;
Twice again they grappled, raining desperate blows
That drum like hail upon their helmets. Yet still neither
Took upper hand. A third time they rushed at each other
Like maddened beasts, with the dregs of their might, cagily
Seeking the inroad that would put an end to their foe.
Their hearts swelled with venom, their eyes glowed with fierce ire,
But then cold Death took her first steps toward the German.
At the edge of his might, once more Britwald raised his sword,
But Svatopluk saw the blow coming and parried it
With the pommel of his own. The blade then shattered
And fell to earth — Britwald now held an empty quillon.
But he had little time to gape in wonder, for soon
Fell his coup-de-grace: Svatopluk's fierce next swipe plunged deep
In the gap between gorget and pauldron — a short cut
For the passage of Death — slicing through sinew, muscle,
And artery, cleaving the neck. Britwald's head then sagged.
His legs, unmanned, took two more clumsy steps forward, then
Crumpled beneath him, as he fell to earth with a crash.
As when some thick oak tree or giant pine, which had climbed
Two thousand years upward from the high Tatra meadows
Falls, hammering the earth, lifting clouds of dust skyward,
So fell great Britwald, sprawling upon the sand, mighty
Limbs broadly spreading as if to embrace his mother earth.

All were silent then. Soon, Britwald's blood ceased pulsing out;
His soul was released from the flesh, and the holy light
Soon vanished from his eyes, ceding place to endless night.

THE CYRILLO-METHODIAD
A Heroic Poem in Six Cantos

CANTO I

In order to support the Christian flock
In his wide-spreading realm with pristine dogma,
And cleanse Slovakia of idolatry,
Rastislav, Slovak king, sends emissaries
To Tsarigrad to beg of the Emperor
Bearers of the Good News fluent in Slavic.
Gladdened at the request, Emperor Michael
Sends Konštantín and his brother Methodius,
Whom Rastislav receives with great rejoicing.
He hosts them at a feast in Devín castle
At which he tells the brothers of the manner
In which the Faith first uprose in Slovakia,
And how it waned to what it was that day.
And then he asks them to relate the ways
In which they introduced the Volgar Boriš
To the True Faith of Our Lord Jesus Christ.

  I sing the Brothers twain from Tsarigrad, Konštantín
And Method, missionaries to the Tatra Slovaks,
Who, overthrowing the empty idols of the land
Instructed all the nation in Christ's truth, and God's law
Established there, so as to lead them to salvation,
And how, when their Slavic *ordo* came under attack,
They triumphed in God's name, at the Holy See of Rome.
  Now You, O blessed ones, residents of Heaven, praised
As the Apostles of the Slavs, hasten to my aid,
Disperse the gloom of black thoughts from my mind, enflaming

My tongue with coal divine, that worthily I might sing
The lauds of your holy labours among my people!
   And you, surest support of my Umka to this day!
Permit me to present my song to you, of the servants
Of God close peer in so many holy things, my friend!
For you have preached His Word too, cementing the true Faith
With wisdom and orthodoxy, lecturing the youth
You raised unto the priestly office, instructing them
How best to lead Christ's people beneath His glorious banner
On their pilgrimage to endless glory in Heaven.
And what is more, you translated the Sacred Word sent
By God's Holy Spirit into Slovak, faithfully,
And other books published — learnéd generosity,
With which you nourished the minds of your countrymen.
Lend me your ear, then, as once you listened to me sing
Of the heroic establishment of Svatopluk's
Slovak realm — hear now how her Christian Faith was planted.
   Rastislav, ruler of the wide-spreading Slovak land,
Great for his valour, still greater for his piety,
Once fell into troubled musing, for he was unsure
Whether the Christian faith, as taught by the German priests
In his land, was unsullied, or faulty, erroneous.
What's more, he was concerned with the meagre successes
They'd had in spreading the Faith among the simpler folk.
And so that the Truth would be better served, his people
Better instructed in the wit of the Saviour's law,
He summoned his princes to parliament at Devín,
And when they'd assembled, he addressed them in such words:
   'My dear friends! We have now abandoned the lying gods
Of our fathers, and justly burnt their carven idols,
Accepting the salvific laver of Christ our Lord.
But how unlearned we remain! How unfamiliar
With the Way of that Truth, which is Life! How can a man,
Whose mind is still wrapped in the gloom of error, take sure
Steps from the darkness, without any light to guide him?
That eye is no better than blind, which sees no daylight!
And who is to blame for this our sad, purblind state?
Who but the Germans? Who've sent such men to convert us
As know our language not, or mangle it in speaking?
What's more, these men are not scholars; they've no wish to whet

The blade of their tongues to address us with precision.
They'd rather make Germans of us! What's more, they are few
In number — and reach not into our outer districts.
And who knows anyway if the faith in Christ they preach
Is the pure faith He Himself taught? Or merely a ruse
To cozen us? So, what are we to do? How are we
To help ourselves in this disorder? Now, word has come
To us of Michael, the pious eastern Emperor,
Who led the Volgars to the wisdom of Christ, sending
Konštantín to them, that famed apostle, inventor
Of Slavic letters, so that all the more certainly
And understandably, the redemptive truths of Christ
Be taught to them, and a liturgy established, whereby
They might understand the mystery of the Holy Mass.
He was followed there by his brother Methodius,
As pious and learned as his brother, devoted
To their mission. And so, let us also send envoys
To that great Emperor, with gifts and like petition,
That of his great kindness he might send to us as well
Such men as might us, and our people, evangelise
In speech we understand, and in which our liturgy
Might be celebrated, uprooting superstition'.
   He finished. At which Svatopluk and pious Chocil
Confirmed his plans with rejoicing. Envoys were chosen
From the men there present — Zemižížeň and Slavek,
Entrusting them with the all-important embassy.
These gifts they were to bear with them to the Emperor:
Three rods of gold of cunning workmanship, moulded as
Stalks of corn with bobbing heads of grain, three golden eggs
Along with a swan poured of the same metal — back then
Native to the Tatra mountains, abundantly found —
The golden head removed from Perún's Devín idol,
Masterfully wrought by Slavyhosť, the clever sculptor
At maiden Dobroslava's court. Along with these things,
A leather overcoat made splendid with ermine fur
Of perfect cut, such as the eastern emperors wore
When the biting frosts of winter were upon the land.
All of this — as the wise reckoned — equalled the value
Of one hundred head of oxen, not counting the oils
Medicinal pressed in the Turčanský vats, which soothe

The sufferings of men, alleviating their pain.
  As soon as all had been prepared, they boarded the craft
Moored at the Danube to set off upon the river
All eager for Tsarigrad. But first they folded hands
And lifted up this whispered prayer to God: 'O Father
Who rulest the heavens, and guidest Thy faithful folk
On the straight path, ever protecting them from evil!
Grant us safe voyage on the waters' bosom, secure
Passage through foreign lands, deflecting from us all harm,
That we might safely arrive at Constantinople,
And fulfil the mission entrusted us, obtaining
Access to Thy holy sages, and return safely
With them, to our sweet homeland, from which we now depart'.
  Such was their prayer. Then with swords they cut the hawsers,
Pushed out from the bank, and set off on the burly waters,
With joy. Soon they arrived happily in the Volgars'
Country, where first of all they took themselves to the church,
Where with what joy they heard the Mass in their own language!
Then through the Balkan mountains where avalanches hang
Until, passing through Thrace, they caught sight of Tsarigrad.
The towers astounded them: myriads of buildings,
Mighty fortresses and walls, which ring the city round.
Then, summoned, they ascended the stairs to the palace
Golden, and as the Emperor received their homage
Of gifts, eloquent Zemižížeň thus addressed him:
  'Renowned Caesar, who reign over three parts of the world,
Governing with wisdom, respecting eternal law!
Surely the tidings have reached your ears that we Slovaks
Have abandoned blind idolatry and accepted
Christ as our Lord and Saviour. Yet here and there remain
Remnants of paganism among us still, for lack
Of clergy to preach the Faith to our folk, and explain
God's Holy Writ to them in their own language. Up till now
The priests who have come amongst us are merely Germans,
And many of our wisest elders are wondering
Whether the faith they preach is pure Christianity,
Or just another ruse to get us in their power?
For this reason our pious Rastislav and the wise
Princes who counsel him have sent us here as envoys
With this request: that you appoint such missionaries

Expert in the Slavic tongue to journey home with us
(For such a boon is in your clement power to give)
Learned in Holy Scripture and the Church's teachings,
Who might instruct us in all that is needful to know,
And teach us piety, translate the Scripture for us,
And celebrate the Divine Service in our language.
We ask you to accept these humble gifts as our thanks
For your magnanimity; receive them as a sign
Of our respect and will to remain your faithful friends'.
   Thus Zemižížeň. The great Caesar was struck with awe.
Not at the rare gifts, but at the men's pious desire
To gain learned teachers by his grace. At last he spoke:
'Your report fills us with a joy inexpressible —
That you have received the Christian Faith, abandoning
Pagan blindness, determining to pay no more heed
To empty idols. We are also pleased that you've come
To us with your pious request for missionaries
Who speak the Slavic tongue. And so, just as we have sent
Such into other lands, we are now pleased to send them
To yours, without further ado. May they instruct your folk
In their own speech, and with much better profit, the pure
Unsullied Faith and necessary teachings of Christ
Than the Germans have proven capable of, up till now.
We thank you for the gifts sent us by your noble king,
And value his friendship, as we assure him of ours'.
   Thus Michael. And then, without a second thought, he sent
For Konštantín and his brother Methodius, who
Had just returned to the city from the Volgars' land.
As soon as they presented themselves, he said to them:
'Dear brothers, greatest ornament of Christ's Greek Church!
Rastislav, who rules the wide-spreading Slovak homeland,
Along with Svatopluk and ardent Chocil, has sent
To us for missionaries to preach the Word of God
Amongst his people. Who better for this task than you?
Their language has been well known to you since your childhood
In Thessalonica; you both spoke it fluently
Before you retired from the raucous world to lead lives
Of holiness, dedicating yourselves to labours
Spiritual and scholarly, perfecting your minds
And virtues. It was you, Konštantín, who for the Slavs

Invented an alphabet with which to teach God's law,
Translating the scriptures and the liturgical books.
You led the savage Kozárs to faith in Jesus Christ,
After which you brought His truth to their Volgar neighbours.
And now we ask you to travel unto the Slovaks
To make firm the Faith they've already embraced, preaching
In their own language, and bestowing your liturgy
Upon them, that their piety should thus be increased
By understanding. Establish the Slavic rite there,
Taking with you, from the Slavic Church you've established
Recently, two learned clerics, eager to aid you
In your holy task, that your numbers be sufficient'.

  In reply, Konštantín responded for both of them:
'The Lord be praised, that in the good hearts of the Slovaks
Such desire for Christian wisdom has been ignited!
So let your will, Caesar, and theirs, be fulfilled! We take
This holy mission upon us with joy, eagerly!
May God grant that our labours soon be crowned with success —
We are prepared even to lay down our fragile lives
On His behalf. Indeed, long have we dreamed of going
Into the land of the Slovaks to preach His Word there!'

  So Konštantín. Then the Emperor ordered that gifts,
Dear ones, of many sorts, be prepared both for the king
And queen (wide-famed for her nobility of manners)
And the princes too, which he would send through the envoys.
Besides this, he ordered that the brothers be given
Gold for their journey, outfitting them too with vestments
And church apparel needed to celebrate the Mass.
Now, when Methodius saw all this, he spoke such words:
'Most magnanimous Caesar! We thank you sincerely
For all the dear gifts intended for Divine Service;
May our Father in Heaven reward your kind largesse!
But we have no need of so great a burden of gold;
We need no more than will get us to Slovakia,
Where we'll arrive all the faster less cumbrously laden.
And there we shall be the guests of all. No virtue there
Enjoys any greater weight than generosity.
The Slovaks are rich in flocks and herds. Nature herself
Keeps their fields burgeoning with grain and fruit; among them
There are no beggars — all are supported, and gladly.

They fit out one and all: countryman and foreigner,
In all that is needed, and travel along with them
From town to town, shortening the long journey with song.
You'll find no other folk more welcoming than the Slavs.
In Sláva's lands all doors are open wide; each table
Is laden with food and drink against the arrival
Of any chance wanderer in need. The modest hearth,
Unable to keep a stranger alone, may apply
To the wealthy to aid them in hospitality.
Indeed, the law of hospitality is revered
So highly amongst them, that should one slack one's duty
— Which doesn't often happen — refusing to admit
A guest, or shooing him from his door at evening,
His neighbours, aghast, deprive him of all his chattel,
Combusting all he possesses to the foundations
Until all the wealth that he had so jealously guarded
Is reduced to ash. Cast out from the community,
He becomes a despised laughingstock until his death.
And also, should it occur to any traveller
To suffer any loss to his health or possessions
While in the care of a Slovak guide, whether because
Of said companion's neglect, or any other fault,
The whole community is up in arms against him,
Believing that it is a holy deed to punish
Such an offender. So, no traveller through Slovak
Lands need take anything with him at all, for they
Are so eager to help and so gracious to their guests,
To serve whom is their greatest joy. So let this treasure
Fund, rather, seminaries for the training of priests,
Or for the erection of churches for the people!'
   Thus he, at which the Emperor bade them both farewell,
And they set off for the Slovak lands with the envoys.
When they had reached the valley of the Volgars, drawing near
The city of Preslav, King Boriš, new to the Faith
And teachings of Christ's law, set out to greet them with joy.
Learning of their mission, immediately he sent
For six clerics well tutored in plainsong, to aid them
In the celebration of the Mass, and other works
Pious, as needed. After imparting their blessing
Upon the king and queen and all the land of the Volgars,

They set off on the route to Belehrad, and from thence
They crossed the border to Slovakia. Here at once
They knelt and lifted up a petition to Heaven:
 'O Christ, who once commissioned Thy disciples go out
Into the whole world preaching salvation, upending
And overthrowing falsehood, aiding them in their task,
Deign to look down upon us now! Guide us Thy servants,
Strengthening our weakness, confirming us in office,
That we might make perfect among the Slovaks Thy wisdom,
And from their land eradicate all superstition.
Grant them Thy grace, dear Lord, to live Thy law, and the strength
To cleave unto it, living unto Thee as Thou wilt'.
 Such was the prayer they lifted on high. When finished,
They journeyed on through ploughed fields, orchards full of grafted
Trees, and vineyards on the sunny slopes of the hillocks,
Where healthy flocks and herds grazed on the pasturages.
On each side of the path a row of lime trees expired sweet
Aromas through the air, providing a cooling shade
To footsore traveller and beast alike. How gaily
The people set to their daily tasks with song upon their lips!
Each copse and hillock resounded with song, each meadow
With sweet piping and chorale. The people greeted them
With good cheer and gratitude as they drew near Devín.
At the moment, by chance Rastislav was on a mound
Named Glavica, meaning Headmost, where Dobroslava's
Father lies buried. There he caught sight of their approach
(First it was Zemižížeň he recognised by voice,
For he'd been singing too), then Slavek and the younger
Clergy in the foreign train, leading near the two priests
Garbed in vestments liturgical. With unbounded joy,
Like an old father, poor and whittled thin with pining,
Who catches sight of a beloved son returning
From foreign parts, he raced near and, extending his arms
In greeting, called out: 'Oh, welcome! Be welcome, Fathers!
Oh, holy men! For whom we have been yearning so long!
And so our embassy was not in vain, as our dreams
Have now become reality. Most beloved guests,
Sages so needed, explicators of the Lord's Word!
Come now into our palace, take your rest after so
Arduous a journey'. And with such words, he led them

Toward his castle, ever plying them with questions
About the Emperor and the court imperial,
And what they'd seen and undergone on their long journey.
He had his servants make their quarters ready, and called
All the boyars to greet them. But the pious brothers
First took themselves to Rastislav's cathedral, to give
Fervent thanks to God Almighty, for He had seen them
Safely to the Slovak realm, protecting them from harm.
They prayed next for the Slovaks, that the Lord might defend
Them from all danger too, blessing their sacred labours.

   Meanwhile, the envoys made their report, concerning how
The Emperor received them and gave ear to their suit;
How at once he summoned the missionaries, and sent
Them here, with gifts, such as they then displayed. 'This scarlet
Cloak, this golden sceptre, golden cross, and chalice
Are for you, Rastislav. This golden chain, these jewels
And vestments are for the queen, and all the other things
He asks you to distribute fairly, as you see fit.
But first Chocil and Svatopluk must have their portions'.

   While the envoys were speaking, and the king inspected
The gifts, the leaders of the people sat to table.
The nimble servants carried 'round the fare: silver bowls
Filled with meats, shining silver jugs brimming with wine.
The brothers twain were seated at the place of honour.
Then all gave ear to Janko, that sweet-voiced baritone,
Who sang the lay of Sláv, the hero who bestowed his name
On the whole nation, and of the maid Dobroslava,
Who raised castle Devín on its star-scraping summit.
But as they feasted, all eyes were upon the brothers,
Wonder-struck at the piety and wisdom fixed there:
Such virtue and modesty, probity and measure!
When the debt exacted by hunger and thirst was paid,
Rastislav broke the silence, raising a toast with wine
From Zobor. Lifting the krater, he spoke in these words:

   'Your health, Konštantín! And yours, brother Methodius!
I drink the health of your Emperor as well, who heard
Our pious plea and sent you to us; you I thank most
For undertaking so long a journey to our lands
To explicate the Scriptures to us, teach us God's law.
May this date be recalled and held sacred ever more!'

These things said, he drank from the krater and passed it on,
To them first, but they merely lifted it to their lips,
Not sipping the drink they'd set by in their early youth.
They passed it on to Zemižížeň, and then to Slavek,
And he on down the line. The guests relaxed with prattle.
But when the second cup had passed around the table,
Pious Rastislav rose once more, and all grew quiet.
   'Beloved brothers, missionaries of our Lord's Word!
Perhaps it's known to you how deep the roots of the Faith
That clutch the Slovak earth, though scanty... Legend has it
That full four hundred years ago, still during the reign
Of the Marcomanni in these parts — rough taskmasters
Of us Slovaks — Queen Fritigil accepted Christ's Faith,
And led her husband King Rozemund to Baptism.
Then, so as to spread the Faith throughout the whole country,
Confirming it amongst the people, she built a church
In Nitra, which became our episcopal see.
But then our folk lifted their heads, and the Marcoman
State was shaken. Shortly thereafter those impious
Cruel Huns fell upon us, slaughtering the people
And overthrowing cities in their wax; all learning
Was extinguished here, and the land ravaged to desert,
And both the bishop and the Christian Faith disappeared
Till Charles the Great became Emperor of the West,
Then, once more Christ's wisdom broke over our horizon.
Pribina established a church in Nitra, and here,
In Devín, another was founded by King Mojmír,
Each with a bishop. In Nitra, worthy Alevín
And here Method, were ordained for the Slovak faithful,
Two bishops beyond measure pious, to tend the Church.
But when they'd passed on to their meet reward, cruel wars
Broke out upon our having repudiated the rule
Of the Bavarians, casting off the servant's yoke
Which they had lain across our backs — some Christening gift!
That harness was the last we've ever suffered. Alas,
Except for the clergy that was here already, none
Dared to venture among us, on account of the wars
Waged frequently. And those who are here are unlettered,
Unable to instruct our people in the Scriptures
As they speak not our tongue, nor are eager to learn it!

And for that reason we saw fit to send our envoys
To the Emperor, with a request for learned men
To preach to us in Slavic, and celebrate the Mass.
That he inclined a favourable ear to our wish,
Your worthy selves are proof positive! For here you are:
Having journeyed to the land of the Slovaks, coming
Immediately, to take upon yourself the labour
Apostolic, to teach us the true Faith unsullied,
To root out blind idolatry, to found new churches,
To be spiritual fathers to a new clergy
For the good of our nation, celebrating the rites
And preaching to our people in their native Slavic.
We too shall be to you as obedient children.
You shall have nothing at our hands save love and respect'.
   Thus he. To which Konštantín made reply in such words:
'O valiant King! We are familiar with all you've said,
About the first dawn of the Faith amongst your people,
Its sunset, and its dawning to a new day. About
The ferocious battles here, we've heard some news: how you've
Struggled for liberty from Bavarian lordship.
But how is it that the Germans, first baptising you,
Sought next to drive you beneath their exploitative heel?
When we brought the Chersonese Kozárs to the Lord Jesus,
And washed away the stain of original sin
From their Neighbour Volgars, instructing them in the Faith,
The furthest thing from our minds, then and now, was conquest!
It was not for such that the Emperor of the East
Sent us among them, to use the bonds of brotherhood
As imperial fetters! But as for us, we'll spare
No effort to instruct your people in the proper
And pure teachings of Christ. There shall be no admixture
To our prayers, and we shall ever be eager to found
New churches in which Christ's Holy Mass will be sung.
May God above bless our labours, and the government
Of men support us. Then no obstacle shall avail
To hinder the spread of the Faith among the people.
For gladly to your pious request we acquiesce:
All preaching and rites will be carried out in Slavic'.
   Thus Konštantín. At which Rastislav once more took voice:
'Since you speak of the warlike Volgars, we would gladly learn

How it was that you converted their monarch Boriš.
For we have heard that he stood firm in pagan error,
And fought against the Christian faith with intransigence'.

CANTO II

Methodius commences then the tale
Of how the king, terrified by the image
Of the Last Judgement and the Day of Wrath,
When all the world shall be combusted, cliffs
Dissolved like lava, nations perishing
In mortal terror, sun, and moon, and stars
Crashing to earth, where all's reduced to ash,
Accepted faith in Christ upon learning
Of how the trump will sound, summoning all
To the Last, and Eternal, Assizes.
For then, the resurrected dead shall rush
Unto the Vale of Kidron to behold
The Judge Supreme, enthroned high in the clouds,
Sending his angel servants forth to pare
The damned from the redeemed, herding the first
Unto the everlasting pains of Hell,
The latter into glory everlasting.

All present then looked expectantly to the brothers
At Rastislav's request, all eager to listen to
An account of the conversion of the fierce Boriš.
Methodius scanned their faces before commencing
— In ardent words — such as would satisfy the pious,
And jolt the hearts of the sluggish to penitence:
  'By that time, nearly the whole nation of the Volgars
Had acknowledged the true, salvific revelation.
Boriš alone wavered. Both his sister and Kufar
Never left off urging him, to win him for the Lord,
Yet neither the one nor the other proved capable
Of overthrowing the idolatry in his heart
And leading him from the deep darkness of paganism
Into the light of Christ. I myself strove frequently,
But all in vain, until this idea came to me:
To paint him an image of the Final Judgement,
Which should represent, in order, all that will occur

Here on earth on the great day of the Almighty's wrath.
Now, King Boriš is a hunter beyond all measure,
Who loves not only to pursue wild game through forest
And meadow — especially great bears and foam-flecked boars —
Armed only with a spear, but, when at home, takes great joy
In gazing at images of woodland animals,
Above all the fiercest, whose glances inspire terror —
Such are the images of wild beasts that please him most.
He was then occupied with building a splendid home,
And wished to decorate its walls with like ornaments.
I took the task upon myself, sketching first burly
Lions and tigers ferocious, and vile hyenas
Who dig up with their nails human remains.
I dreamt up gigantic dragons thrashing barbed tails
And belching flame, nor did I overlook sea monsters.
I left out no such beast as would inspire terror
In the beholder, nothing of aspect horrible.
Above all, though, I set high in the clouds the strict Judge,
Among His myriad angelic hosts, the Father
Upon His flashing throne in all His awful glory.
His face I painted as bright and unsupportable
As the sun, while from His angry eyes there seemed to dart
Bolts of terrible lightning as He surveyed the earth
Upon the face of which great multitudes of people
Were gathered all together. While some of them, the saved,
Had shining countenances and brilliant crowns of gold —
Victors they seemed, rejoicing with dancing hearts, raised up
To their eternal reward of heavenly delight —
Others there present: the damned, godless, those resistant
To God's law, were quaking in despair, tearing out tufts
Of hair and scratching their faces, as if they desired
To become unrecognisable. The earth gaped wide
At their feet, spewing forth rank smoke, and fire, and sulphur
That rose from the bogs of Hell yawning to receive them.
In this way I sought to nudge the stubborn-headed king
Toward Christ and salvation. Nor was my toss in vain:
For as he gazed upon the frightful scenes (depicted
With all the skill a man might muster, the stakes being
So high), in his mind he made his calculations
And so his heart was moved to ask for enlightenment:

What exactly did all this mean? I was more than glad
To explicate the pictures, and thus did I commence:
   "The last day shall arrive, on which the wrath of the Lord
Will fill the world with terror, as all will pass away
Amid havoc, and much wailing and gnashing of teeth
For — like it or not — all generations will be called
Before the judgement seat of God to give an account
Of all they've done, both good and ill, during their lifetime.
Now — all evils are permitted in this world of ours:
Laws can be broken, the plain truth consciously denied,
Virtues trod underfoot, morals shredded, religion
Mocked... Cruelties of all sorts are permitted to man:
One may oppress the weak and deprive helpless orphans
Of heritage and sustenance; one may loot and kill
In the most hideous manners, find satisfaction
In wading through blood; one may take girls by violence,
Tearing through their chastity without any remorse,
Wallowing in shameful acts as swine tumble through filth;
One may even blaspheme God, sinning against the Lord,
The Supreme Ruler of Heaven and Earth entire.
But in the end, the wages of such delights is Hell.
   The Judgment Day is coming. As it nears, strange wonders
Shall be seen: the sun's face will darken as black as coal,
The moon will turn blood-red, and the shattered stars will lash
Their tails about the heavens, pouring plague upon earth.
Streams of lightning will weave deadly spider-webs, to snare
All of creation. Flaming marvels will fill the skies;
A bloody rain shall fall, a bloody dew smear the fields,
And clotted blood instead of sap will ooze from tree-bark.
   An awful wind will rage over the face of the earth,
Knocking down what man has built, and flattening forests,
Heralding a downpour such as no man's ever seen,
With bucket-sized drops pummelling the landscape, until
All the clouds of Heaven have been wrung dry. The rivers
Will overspill their banks, the oceans and seas will boil
And storm over their former limits, engulfing shore,
Plain, and mountain; angry billows swamping everything!
Floods will rage below, and in the sky the storm won't cease:
The world will be a spinning maelstrom of destruction
With sea and sky joining hands in a frenzied chaos.

Whatever cliff pokes above the flood will be shattered
By strikes of Heaven's fire laying the mountains low.
Some of those then living shall be slain by the onslaught;
The remainder will either perish from pure terror
Or crawl about what scrap of earth is left them, blinded
And deafened. But all the pillars of the world will split,
Crumbling and casting the splendid edifice of Nature
Into the maw of the depthless abyss yawning wide
And belching forth smoke, and sulphur, and infernal flame.
Cities destroyed, fastnesses pulverised, mountains
Levelled flat and everything on fire — clouds of smoke
And flame stitching earth and sky into one weft of fright
As the air is consumed, all things shrivelled to cinders.
Like snow in late spring, densest rock shall melt to lava
And spill down in scalding streams. People and animals
Shall choke on the acidic air that singes their lungs.
No glee will be found anywhere that day, only Death
Will rejoice at such spoils, unheard of before,
Until her turn comes at the end of the general
Annihilation, and she shall follow the last man,
Vanishing into the depthless, dark abysses.
   The very air that sheathes the globe will burst into flame;
The sun, sick with its dull fire, which had grown dark before,
Will spew from out its innards its half-digested store
Of flesh and vegetation consumed in expansion
— A mass greater than the Balkans taken together —
And fall from its perch with a horrible commotion.
Wrapped in a flaming shroud, the moon, become like the sun,
Will disgorge its pale core to its own demolition
And receive a like funeral. Panicked galaxies
Will whirl about the seething sky in frantic chaos;
All, slipped from its harness, colliding blindly, one star
Knocking against another, shattering some, others,
Smaller, will be sucked down screaming, trapped in vapour trails
Of larger suns, dead, as they fall into the chasm.
And just as fruit is dashed to earth when tornados howl,
Splintering branches, the planets will fall like thick hailstones
Booming through the vacuum of the ruined universe,
As they jostle each other, rebound, and crash again.
   When all's burnt down, and the world lies in cooling cinders,

And no voice is to be heard, not even a whisper;
When no light gleams, not the merest flickering ember,
Nothing but deadly silence and the deepest darkness —
When the globe's as smooth as a ball, all hillocks flattened,
Then shall a trumpet blare out, a tremendous clamour
That shall fill the skies and all four corners of the world,
Resounding even through the depths of Hell, end to end,
Crying: Arise from your graves, you dead! Present yourselves
For judgment! And then once more a great clatter shall be heard
Like shattered cliffs tumbling down from high mountain summits
To crash on the valley floor and rebound — so the earth
Shall be fissured at the sound of the angelic horn
And send forth from its ashen womb the many millions
Of generations of man, all who had ever lived:
Ash, bone, dust that once was flesh. Then, fragment to fragment,
Ball to socket joins, limbs; once more the immortal soul
Finds its accustomed dwelling, and as it enters in,
The sheath of skin knits anew, the muscles swell and harden,
Lymph and blood course once more through their network of canals,
Golden filaments of hair sprout and grow on their scalps
As the bodies glow, perfected as never before.
Motion returns: they arise and stand on their two feet
Immortal now, and free of all blemish of the flesh;
Thus all those resurrected — but with one difference:
These have faces that shine like the bright morning star,
While those have countenances darkened with cold shadow.
   There is a broad plain that lies between Jerusalem
And the Mount of Olives, known as the Vale of Kidron;
Some of the Jews call it the Vale of Jehosaphat.
There gloomy Gehenna and Tophet lay, at one time
The scene of foul sacrifices raised by the ancients,
Where, to the blare of horns, men — fiercer and crueller
Than wild animals — would sacrifice small children
To Moloch's idol. There all the nations shall be gathered,
All the renewed, from every direction: chilly north
And warm south; from the rising of the sun to its setting,
Unto the Final Judgment. Emperor, king, and earl,
Lady and churl, the industrious and indigent,
But — Caesars without their brilliant imperial cloaks,
Kings without crowns, mighty magnates stripped of their power,

Peasant without his landlord, beggar without his crutch.
All naked, no distinction there at all, no symbol
Of office nor preference of place, gold, nor treasure
Abundantly heaped will be of avail to any —
Idols to testify against their old worshippers
Rather! We shall have nothing there except the report
Of all the good and ill we'd done during our lifetime:
Those who had done good will rejoice; the evil-doers
Will be in a pother, quivering like elms shaken
By a strong wind. The cruel who'd made others to shiver
In fright will now be made to quake themselves in terror,
For among the multitudes gathered at the Judgement
Devils will prowl, eager to haul off the souls condemned
To everlasting torment in Hell. For a trumpet
Shall suddenly ring out, and the maw of Hell shall yawn
Wide to receive those judged unworthy of God's mercy.
The dark mobs of the damned will then be swallowed by Hell
Amidst the dreadful shrieking of lungs renewed to breathe
Stench and smoke forever more; nerves and sinews reweft
For torment eternal, everlasting consciousness,
With no hope of pause, mercy, or obliteration.
  For after all have been gathered there in the valley
Of judgment, and are standing side by side, suddenly,
Like a bright dawn breaking, dispelling the glooms of night,
That sign of victory, that most glorious banner,
The Cross, shall flash forth in the sky with a flaming glow.
The just shall greet it with great rejoicing, but the bad,
And all who had fought against it before, as its foes,
Will be thunderstruck, and fall into great fear.
They shall turn their eyes away, and seek with fists to block
It from their sight, but the more they turn away from it,
The more they shall see it before them. The more they shield
Their eyes with their hands, the more that fiery, bright image
Will strike those eyes, as if those hands were boneless, fleshless,
Transparent. Behind the Cross, angelic regiments
Will march, bearing the instruments of Christ's Holy Passion:
The reed and the pillory, the nails, the crown of thorns,
And amidst these princes, more comely than the morning star,
His face as bright as the fiery sun, His eyes flashing
As if they darted lightning bolts, terrible in might,

The Judge Supreme shall be revealed in supreme glory.
He shall take His seat on His throne, shining from afar,
Set high in the clouds above the place He'd prepared
From all time, for the redemption of the world entire,
With His death on the Cross presenting us all with life,
After He had been falsely judged, like some criminal
Crucified, exposed to shame, jeering, and mockery —
While all the heavenly hosts adore Him, all earthlings
And all the rout of Hell perforce, bend their knees in praise.
   At that moment, some gigantic tomes hanging before
The throne of the Most High will be unsealed. They'll open wide
By themselves to reveal all that anyone's ever
Thought, and said, and done, from early childhood to his grave.
All that was recorded by the scribes divine, at work
Both day and night — all the days of man, set in order.
Nothing can be denied. All will be clearly exposed
To the light of day: all acts concealed, done in the dark,
In hidden corners — all these things shall be read aloud
For every angel, and every earth-dweller to hear.
O how the once-powerful will cringe and wring their hands
In anguish when the veil they'd poorly woven is rent,
Exposing all their lies meant to conceal their evil,
As those counterfeiting goodness are shown to be wicked,
Those hypocrites of virtue exposed in all their shame!
   Nor will there be any lack of accusations there
From the mouths of those who were wronged during their lifetime.
One will charge: 'O most Glorious Heavenly Judge!
That godless wretch standing there, with face dusky, despaired,
Worse than a raging lion, worse than a savage tiger,
Did nothing during life but foment war, slaughtering
Men like sheep, destroying cities, burning villages,
Consuming all to cinder and ash in a moment —
All that had taken centuries of labour to build,
Believing that the world belonged to him, him alone!
He even wished to make of himself — God! Divine praise
And worship demanding from those he made to kneel
Before him! Lord, mete him the punishment he deserves!'
And then another: 'That inhuman torturer there
Burdened me with such labour as no slave might endure!
But when I once pleaded with him to lighten my load,

He pinned an iron collar around my throat, fetters
Around my ankles, and chaining my wrists behind me,
Thrust me into a dungeon foul, fixed to a post
Of oak. And so he murdered me, in torments of thirst
And hunger! Lord, mete him the punishment he deserves —
One equal to mine!' And then a third: 'That savage man
Hunted me down as if I were a beast, enchaining
Me slave. Above my supplicating wife's outstretched hands,
Above the heads of my orphaned children for mercy
Wailing, he raised a hangman's broadsword — and brought it down!
Beforehand, my elder daughters, already betrothed,
He raped, vending them to voluptuaries for gold!
Me and my son he harnessed to a plough like oxen,
Whipping us on, treating us worse than he did his dogs!
Now deal with him, Lord, judge him according to his merits!'
Then an impoverished widow shall cry out: 'That foul
Bandit! No sooner had my valiant husband fallen
In war on behalf of our homeland, than, like a wolf,
He pounced upon me, stealing all I owned, home and goods,
Expelling me, a widow, along with my orphans,
Into the cruel world, to beg and die in misery!
But now, Judge Almighty, measure him a meet reward!'
A host of voices shall cry out in accusation:
'That one there — puffed up by the devil, the godless wretch! —
Boldly seduced our progeny, piped them off to Hell
With teachings of the worst sort: heresies and errors
Inimical to the Faith! They might have lived in joy
And glory eternal in Heaven. But he tore them
Away from the one, true, redemptive Faith in this world,
Leading them on to plunge, along with him, into Hell's
Chasm. For all that measureless ruin, Lord, smite him!'
   When all the accusations have been aired, when the Judge
Supreme has heard through all the charges, seated on high,
He shall command His angelic servants to sort out
The impious from among the pious, setting each
Group apart, to the left, and to the right. The angels,
Like experienced shepherds on high mountain pastures,
Shall cull out of the milling creatures each his own flock:
No hard task, though the heads there seem innumerable —
The peaceful flocks set on the right hand, the freakish goats

To the left in a shameful herd — O, sad division!
For father shall be split from son, mother from daughter,
Brother from brother beloved, sister, scared, from sister;
Husband his wife, and friend dear friend will abandon —
Led away, forced to the opposing fold! Ah, how many
Who had been famous during life will be infamous
Forever! And how many despised, forever praised!
What great weeping here, and there: dancing! And rejoicing!
When the great multitudes have been thus separated
Into two camps, the all-righteous Judge shall first incline
His merciful countenance unto the righteous souls,
Smiling with measureless sweetness. All shall become still,
Awaiting the verdict of the strict Lord of justice.
Then shall His voice resound far and wide, speaking such words:
  'Come, blessed ones, and receive the eternal reward
Prepared for you from all ages, for which you've hungered!
Reign from your thrones with joy, for all your sadness and tears
On earth; enjoy abundance, who once pined impoverished;
Receive everlasting honour for the mockery
That lashed you below; come — take your chaplets unfading
To crown your steadfast virtue; for you loved your Lord
And brethren — take now your just recompense of glory!
For all time now, you shall gaze upon my face divine'!
  Thus shall He address the just, before bending His brows
In flaming ire upon the damned, eyes flashing in wrath,
And in a voice more terrifying than lightning bolt
When it shatters the granite cliff, He shall lay prostrate
The cringing mobs with a thunderous, terrible roar:
  'Away with you, godless ones, into the flaming pit!
Away, proud spawn of Satan, to everlasting fire,
Along with all his rebellious crew! For you no less
Waged war against your Maker, seeking to be gods
Yourselves, demanding the worship due the Lord alone!
Now, lord it over Hell, foul realm won you by your pride!
Get you gone, blind idolaters, base mob of pagans!
Who bowed before deaf images, worshipping kindling!
Away with you, too, cruel hatchet-men, foul ravishers
Of peace! Who for the stupid splendour of fame, or name,
Or pleasure perverse, at the bidding of the serpent
With godless blades butchered human beings like cattle.

The blood you've spilt courses like the mightiest river;
The bodies you've piled high out-top the highest summit!
You've done nothing but spread pestilence around the world,
Burning cities, destroying sacred tabernacles,
Turning happiness to woe, rejoicing to wailing.
Your minds ardent with nothing but love of the vacuum,
You would have exterminated all if you could have!
Be off with you, monsters cruel, who tortured your brothers
Innocent with dungeons dark and dank and cold fetters,
Or sold them into slavery as if they were beasts.
Ignoble men! Who forced yourselves upon captive maids,
Pillaging them of the garlands of their maidenhead.
No tears, no pleadings, such as might melt the hardest stone
Could move your flinty hearts! Be off as well, you proud fools,
Heads swollen with the vain winds of self-adulation.
Be off, you misers voracious, who sought to clamber
Higher over the backs of the fallen, heaping up
Wealth in dull piles for the good of no man; rust and mites
Had joy of it, while beggars were beaten from your door.
Away with you, bloated drunkards and gluttons, all you
Who served not Me, but the idol of your own stomachs.
How many times would a wretch, clothed only in tatters
Approach the threshold of such haughty skinflints as you,
Begging for crumbs fallen from your groaning boards, or drops
Of water, only to be shooed off, just as hungry,
Thirsty, and naked as when they first dared to crawl near?
And your closets: bulging with linen, silks — who wore them?
Who had use of them save clothes-moths? And though you wouldn't
Feed your hungry brothers, still you feasted and swilled wine
To vomit the excess, and burnt beasts in holocausts
Of vain sacrifice, spilling libations to the dust!
Away with you, rank lechers, goats, shamelessly rolling
In sties of filthy rutting! Be off to Hell with you
Envious ones, swollen with the venom of your rage,
Enemies of virtue, hostile to the laws of Heaven!
Away with you, who once abandoned the narrow path
Of piety and led your brothers to commit acts
Rude and shameful, in the cause of error, heresies,
And teachings black; away, all of you evildoers
Opposed to My law, you, who sought to pervert others;

You of all sinners might have repented, with sorrow
Cleansing yourselves of the filth of your guilt no matter
How foully you were besmeared, and yet not one tear fell.
Go now, be off, follow your iniquities to Hell,
Where, deprived of My presence and heavenly glory
You'll be submerged in abysmal lakes of endless fire.
There, the worm that burrows through your conscience will sleep not,
And the serpent of guilt will ever strike at your heart
Full of despair — suffering without hope of redemption!'
   Thus shall He speak, and then shall the chasm open wide
To swallow the damned, who, squealing, tearing at their hair,
Shall call unto the hills 'Come and fall upon us now,
And bury us here — anything but endless torment —
Grind us to powder unfeeling — annihilate us!'
But no, the maw of Hell will gape, and all plunge
At once into the fiery abyss to wallow
In seething bogs of flame, where pain is everlasting —
Nothing but wretchedness and suffering, the hard fate
Of the Lord's enemies, weeping and gnashing of teeth,
The greatest pain of all, perhaps, is their consciousness
That their own guilt — their own impiety brought them there;
Of their own free will they chose endless imprisonment,
Eternal torment, measureless, no end to their pain —
As many hells there shall be as there are damned souls
Seething in the isolated woe they chose themselves.
   Meanwhile, the chosen shall ascend to their heavenly
Reward, to the joyous blares of happy fanfares
Into joy upon joy, beauty upon beauty,
Glory upon glory, their faces bathed endlessly
In the delight that streams from the countenance of God".
   Thus ran my lecture on the last day, the Last Judgement,
Heaven, and Hell, at which Boriš, terrified, his eyes
Ever fixed on the painting, trembling throughout his limbs,
Swore to abandon idolatry and the errors
Of his ways, and accept the sacrament of Baptism'.
   Thus in plain words Methodius addressed those gathered
At table, while the steeds of the night raced on, and the men,
Both the comforted and the shaken, went home to bed.

CANTO III

First, all the souls that hasten in from hamlet
And village far removed, the brothers teach
In Devín proper; then they travel out
Into the Slovak backcountry. The Lord
Sends them an angel to serve them, and aid them.
Konštantín takes the Váh route to the north
Where soar the Tatra mountains; everywhere
He preaches the true Faith and baptises
The folk converted from idolatry,
Toppling the lying idols' carven figures:
Letnica, Černobog, Chásoň and Baba
He grinds to kindling, knocking down Rarášek,
Triglav and the whole band of Leš, Rusalka,
Vila, Pochvista, cruel Stríbog, comely
Živa along with Veles, battering Perún,
And three hundred others: Zmok, Pikulík,
Black visaged Morena, Vesný, and the like,
And finally, he batters Svatovít.

   The news spread fast throughout all the neighbouring regions
That new missionaries from Tsarigrad had arrived
The nation to instruct; that the Holy Mass is sung
In the Slavic tongue, in which Heaven's law is explained.
The influx of people from all places was unending.
Like bees, who had remained in their hives for a long while
Due to a fierce storm, are roused as soon as the bright sun
Uncovers its smiling face from behind the livid clouds,
And rush off to the fields, all the swarm gaily buzzing
To the flowers, refreshed, strong stalks drooping no more,
One after the other, in a crowded, eager throng,
So gathered the Slovaks to Mass: first Belohorci
Arrived, flooding in from the nearby Morava's banks,
Then those from the Danube and Váh came, and those who sip
The Nitra; indeed, whole legions pressed in from the Hron,
Wave after wave, filling full street and square in Devín,

Eager to hear the Word of God preached in their own tongue.
And as they listened to the pious brothers in church
Preaching and teaching truths of the Faith before unknown,
Celebrating the Mass and singing their praise to God
In the vocables of their own dear maternal tongue —
How their hearts danced for joy! How the tears welled to their eyes
And ran down their cheeks in streams! Thus they lifted on high
Prayers of thanksgiving to the Lord who reigns past the stars
For showering upon them such blessings, allowing
Them to come to know His wonders in their common speech.
But as their seventh month in Devín rolled to its end,
Seven full months of teaching the citizens, and those
Who'd flocked unto them from afar, the truths of the Faith,
Wise Konštantín turned to Methodius and spoke thus:
   'Dear brother! We've spent enough time here teaching the folk —
See the progress they've made so far! Let us turn elsewhere
Now, where our instruction is more needed. For still,
As you well know, there are some regions of the country
Sunk in the blind depths of paganism. To them then,
Let us go, preaching, baptising, and toppling idols'.
   To these words Methodius responded in this wise:
'Your sage suggestion, brother, is fitting and timely,
Not only as the foundations we've laid here are firm,
But also — if credence is to be given to talk
Recently bruited — Ludvík, the King of the Germans,
Is having fierce weapons forged, and gathering soldiers
With which he plans to wage war against the brave Slovaks.
The fortunes of war being impossible to guess,
It may be so that he will draw here and lay long siege
To Devín, surrounding the town and bottling us up.
And if such were to be the case, a people shaken
With clashing arms, cries, and uncertainty, bellies pinched
With rationing, and minds occupied with but one thought:
"When will it all end"? will have little use for sermons!
So let us not pursue a redundant office here:
Let us move on to where our preaching is more needed'.
   Thus Methodius. At which both brothers knelt to lift
From glowing hearts such petitions to the Almighty:
'Heavenly Father! Fount of all mercy, who wishest
To lead all people to salvation, extracting them

From the gaping jaws of ruin, look down upon us
Now, as we have set out to bring Thy sacred truth to men
Still stumbling in darkness. Strengthen us, weak, with Thine aid,
Make firm both mind and sinew that we might accomplish
Thy holy will. Enlighten the minds of the people
Still blinded by paganism, that their eyes behold
The shining Truth, receive the Christian Faith, and abjure
Idolatry to become, and remain, forever Thine'.
The great Lord of the universe heard their ardent prayers
And granted them, summoning two comely messengers
And thus commanding them: 'Go now, my swift-winged envoys,
Unto the Tatra regions, where the Slovaks reside.
There, where the fish-stocked Morava encircles the broad
Cliffs upon which Devín is set, soaring to the stars,
You'll find a pair of brothers of Greek parentage, named
Konštantín and Methodius. Their sacred mission
Is to spread the Christian Faith throughout the pagan towns
And batter down all shameful heresy and error.
Protect them with your might, and when their vigour flags
Freshen their limbs with strength renewed, that they might pursue
Their holy calling to its triumphant conclusion.
Be at their side with prompt assistance, both day and night,
And move the wills of those who hear them preach to embrace
The law of Christ, abandoning their fathers' errors'.
   Thus spoke the Lord. Then, obedient to their Father's will,
Like two swans sent forth from the cliff-summits towering
Above the Danube or the banks of the River Prút,
Awakened by the distant honking of their comrades
A-wing already, hasten to catch up with the flock
Departing, hurtling down from on high on cleaving wing,
So the angels skimmed swiftly through the clouds. And soon
They caught sight of Devín in the near distance below,
Just as the dawn began to break over Kobyla.
The brothers twain were up already. The angels saw
Them pass through the city gate, each to take his own path.
Zephon glided to Konštantín's side, while Raphael
Joined his brother Methodius. And so they set off,
The angels, with the men, just as God had commanded,
Eager to do whatever needed to further on
The holy task set by their missionary office.

Before they parted ways, the brothers warmly embraced,
Entrusting each other to the mercy of the Lord.
Konštantín took the road north following River Váh,
Convincing all the folk he met of the foolishness
And villainy of paganism, and the blessings
That await Christ's faithful. He headed to the Tatras,
Preaching the true Faith, expounding all the articles
Of the law of God, all such as is necessary
For salvation, and all those who accepted the Faith
Were baptised, cleansed of the stain of original sin.
Idols toppled everywhere, in Trenčín Letnica,
Rain-god Mokosla in Rajec, in Púchov Černobog,
In Ílava Diblíkov, Chásoň in Čátca, evil
Baba on bare Babia hora, on Magorka
Rarášek, Čurov on Tvrdošiň, the guardian
Ninva in Námestovo, and gigantic Triglav
In the Krivan foothills, that had puffed its foul cheeks
Above Morské Oko — toppled, reduced to grey ash,
The flimsy remains of the ferocious god playthings
Now, left to the whim of the capricious mountain gusts.
He hacked apart Kúpala in Hybe, Nemissa
In ancient Lupoč. The idols of the Lešy spirits
On Fatra he knocked down, and in Turiec — Rusálky.
On Dúpna and cloud-veiled Mažárna swarthy Vily,
In Pravna he shattered Prov, and Semeník's idol
In delightful Mošovce, on roaring Volovec
Stormy Pochvista and Stríbog on the windy cliffs
Of Lomnica. Zemarglo along with Koleda,
Both in snow-white wraps, crashed to earth in Brezno, like Ďas
In Bystrica, Dažbog in gold-yielding Kremnica,
Ohlas of mocking echoes in Hliník, Lútice
In dreary Ban, near Zvolen black Poludnica
With the Besy, her sprites, and besides these, the altar,
Flashing and sacred, in Ješlava. Merot tumbled
To earth in Halíč, Korša in Lučenec, wide-famed
For craftsmen; Veles fell in Synec, and on Matra
The fair Živa, whose idol in ancient days the Slavs
Brought here from India in search of a new homeland.
Likewise, Parom, the ruler of thunder and lightning
In Novohrad, fell — that god above all other gods,

Brought here, like fertile Živa, from India, as Žnislav,
His eldest priest, held. He, before all others, the folk
Worshipped alone as the ruler of Heaven, the winds,
The earth and the entirety of being, while himself
Resting above all on his splendid throne, wielding
Thunder and lightning, cared but for the upper regions,
Giving no thought to the realms below. Human reason
Peopled the elements with divine beings, who lived
Eternally, ruling the nether regions for him
As children of his loins, those closer to their father
In appointed office held more worthy of honour.
But he stood, an awesome figure, on a high column,
In his temple surrounded by an oaken woodlet
Never scarred by hatchet. In his right hand a ploughshare
He gripped, while in his left a threatening javelin,
From which hung a banner, covering his broad shoulders.
But neither that warlike spear, nor his dread lightning bolts,
Nor his flashing crown availed him in the face of Truth;
Konštantín shattered him, the sacred flame that ever
Flickered before him to his honour both day and night
Then roared, reducing him to ash, following which, doused,
The soggy embers were trod into the mire. After that,
Without a moment's hesitation, Konštantín left
For upper Ostrihom, where River Danube kisses
The Hron with silver lips, to take away Devaňa,
Mistress of groves, along with Chvor the god of the winds.
In Komárno he exorcised the evil Poronec,
And Water-Man, who had once been set up in the heights
In the midst of the city. So long ago — no man
Could recall when his wooden idol had first been carved
From ash-post and established for public beseeching.
Now, not two years had passed before he began to drown
A great number of people, overturning their crafts,
And in the darkness climbing out on shore, horridly
Shrieking. Such are the results of foul demon worship!
But soon he was to be submerged again, along with
Seja Pohoda, goddess of tillage, and whole mobs
Of lesser sprites: Drakes and Tasany, Succubi, all
Heeding the harsh command. Then to Pukanec he went,
Where Henil met with his deserved fate, knocked prostrate.

Thus everywhere — as when a ferocious windstorm howls
From the west, tearing up stout trees by the roots, sending
Whole woodlands crashing to the earth in calamities
Of havoc, Konštantín shattered forests of vain idols.
Lesser beasts — Zmoks and Pikulíks, three hundred Mornas
Of swarthy cheeks, Vesny, and Škráty, who lurk near graves.
Imps and demons, Kykymor, werewolves and goblins, all
Chased back to Hell, votives ceasing, monuments shattered.
   Yet one four-faced god of war and conflict cruel
Remained, whose idol reared upon cloud-scraping Sitno:
Svatovít, in honour second only to Perún.
Konštantín drew upon him just at the holiday
Most sacred to him, when, each year at the harvest's end,
First-fruits would be brought him in offering. From all lands
Surrounding, throngs arrived to sacrifice bulls, heifers,
Sheep; tuns of wine and mead to be spilt in libation,
And baskets of round sweet pastries — koláče — all brought there
With happy song and music snaking along the paths.
Each meadow and mountain and vale echoed the praise of Svatovít.
Now, when he arrived at the temple, which on eight stone
Pillars rested, surrounded by a stout palisade
Of smooth beams of oak and spruce, its thatching painted red
To mark the holiday, all the people were gathered
There already, resting in the cool shade of the limes.
The beasts had been slaughtered, fat was melting on the flames,
Joints roasting on the coals, plumes of smoke rising aloft,
And the sacrificial banquet was nearly prepared.
When the worshippers had circled the altar three times
And thrice intoned their praise of Svatovít, the music
Rang out to the end, at which the arch-priest Vitoslav,
With beard thick and long, reaching to his waist, hair untrimmed,
Wearing a white robe embroidered by skilled Kreslava
Stepped forth, leading a steed from the stables by the reins.
This was a sacred horse, produced for all there to see:
How spent he was, and his coat, whiter than snow, befouled
With mire, for this was Svatovít's steed; mounted on him,
The war-god battered down the gates of his enemies.
Baloň himself (for such was his name) appeared eager
To testify to that: he reared his head and loudly
Neighed from the depths of his powerful lungs. Vitoslav

Turned to lead him back to his stall, but then Zemislav,
The first among warriors gathered there, halted him
From his place on the verdant grass among the war-chiefs:
  'Most pious father, first among Svatovít's servants!
You who alone among men are permitted to feed
And handle the colt of the god, and mount upon him,
Tell us, your people, if we are to be met with war
This year, and what our fortunes in such battling might be?'
  Thus he. Then Vitoslav the elder said in reply:
'Although this is not the meet season for prophecy,
Still, because war's never leaden-footed on the march,
And you have ever been first in defence of this folk
And this sacred precinct, having battered the Germans
Ever eager to fall upon us, and, Zemislav,
Because you've so generously awarded the god
Out of your war-spoils, I'll query the god's white charger,
Though out of season, and what he announces, I'll say'.
  Thus he, at which he bade the profane crowd draw aside
And leave an empty space between fane and palisade.
Three priests stepped forth, and in even sequence, plunged three rows
Of iron-tipped spears into the earth, twain staffs athwart.
Vitoslav then, facing the temple with left hand raised
(For in his right he held the horse's bit) prayed thuswise:
  'O god of Sitno! Supreme governor of combat!
Who knowest all things that are soon to be, deign reveal
Through this Thy steed the fortune that is to befall us,
Thy people, in the coming war. Be propitious!'
  Thus he ends his petition. Meanwhile, the other priests
Who had made all ready, the area purified,
Called the sacred charger out of the foul enclosure
Where death was worshipped. The horse, proudly arching his hooves,
Stepped forward at a solemn measured tread, approaching
The spears driven into the earth. In the sight of all
He drew near the first obstacle with his left leg raised
And surmounted it, with a quick leap. Backing up some,
He passed over the second, and the third, both these times
Leading with his right leg. The onlookers, wonder-struck,
Took this for a bad sign. They stood there with hackles raised,
Frozen and silent, until the priest set them at ease:
  'Be not afraid that the charger augurs misfortune

In war, approaching the crossed staves from the sinister
Side; after all, he addressed the last two from the right,
Untutored by man. This is a good omen! It means
Triumph for the Slovaks, catastrophe for their foes!'
   With such words he overcame the fears of his people.
Then, before leading the horse back to his stall, the priest
Himself entered the temple — going where only he
Was allowed to go. Indeed, it was he that had cleansed
The sacred precinct on the day before the yearly
Holiday, taking great care not to breathe while inside,
So as not to infect the god with the contagion
Of mortality. (So, constantly he'd hasten out,
Again and again to the threshold, blue in the face,
To exhale and draw a fresh breath before going back!)
Now, entering, he took the crooked horn with silver
And gold chased, from the idol's right hand. Then, he peered close
Within it, gauging whether the wine poured last summer
Had lessened any. It hadn't, which he took to mean
An abundant harvest and full-swelling granaries.
Returning to the crowd outside, he bade them rejoice
Even more fully, having spilt at the idol's feet
The old wine in libation, refilling the horn with new,
And raising draught after draught in toast benedictive
To his own good fortune, to the weal of the people,
And finally, in hope of victories in battle,
Before returning it, refilled, to the idol's grip.
This done, he returned to the people waiting outside,
And, taking in his hands a large koláč, bigger
Than a tall man, baked in Žarnovica expressly
For the rite, he placed it between himself and them.
He knelt down, calling out in ceremonious tones:
  'O god four-faced! O Svatovít our god! Who seest
All things, on every hand, and to the ends of the earth!
Who for the sake of thy people dost ride upon steed
Of white into foreign parts, terrifying thy foes
In the night! Victorious in battle ferocious!
Look down upon us now in mercy and deign accept
This sacrifice of fields abundant from us, grateful,
And may each prophecy of future harvests be as rich
As this one, indicated by thy wine-horn, shall be.

Strengthen us too, in war, against all our enemies,
Sealing our victory, defending our land from harm'.
   Thus prayed the hoary priest, at which he rose, and turning
A solemn face (though still hidden by the great koláč)
To the crowd, asked: 'See you me?' They cried 'We see thee not',
In a massed voice, 'We can see nothing but the koláč'.
Again he took voice: 'That is good. My sincerest wish
Is that next year as well you shall not see me, hidden
Behind such a gate of plenty. Stint not in worship
Of our god, lift up to him your endless petitions,
And fail not to offer him generous sacrifice.
Seek here his aid in times of trouble, and in despair
His wisdom will resolve your doubts; in lean times
His stores will support you; victory in war shall be yours
For the pious worship and meet praise which you bring him'.
   He finished, and then sliced the koláč into portions.
He left the best piece for Svatovít in sacrifice,
And shared out the remainder among the gathered crowd.
Each there took a piece, and then once more broke out in song,
Raising a hymn of praise and thanksgiving, in accord,
To their god, in antiphons, along with lyre and lute:
Strings humming, flutes piping, and trumpets bellowing loud.
But when the song had reached its end, the rites over,
Konštantín stepped forth to stand where the old bearded priest
Had stood, and greeting first the gay throng, began to preach.
At once, all eyes were fixed upon him, gasps of wonder
Sounded. Konštantín raised high his right hand; all grew still.
   'What can you expect, you, gathered here from near and far,
From a man who would have you worship a piece of wood?
For Svatovít is nothing but a log, which once grew
In some forest, before it was hacked down and borne off
By some woodcarver! What was your god before that one
Shaved off his bark and planed him smooth, plugged up the bore-holes
Of termite and woodpecker? Can a craftsman craft a god?
And give him the might that he himself does not possess?
And so he shaped this gigantic idol. But tell me —
Did he breathe the spirit of life in through his nostrils?
Did he animate wooden limbs — with a wooden soul?
And those eight blind eyes poked under four brows — can they see
Anything, not to say "all, to the ends of the earth"?

You can jam an arrow in to that doll's left hand — sure.
But can you endow the right with might to stretch the bow?
Away with such gods of lumber, fit only for bonfires!
To cleanse your temple, first cleanse it of this dry kindling!
God eternal, the true God, has neither beginning,
Nor shall He ever not be; it is He who sees all:
What was, what is, what shall be, before it even is;
It is He Who created all there is, with a word
Creating heaven and earth; in the wink of an eye
He could bring all things to nothing, once again, the earth,
The firmament — with one nod of His, all would vanish:
The moon — blotted out, the stars would cease shining and fall,
The sun would explode and become once again... nothing.
That is the God before Whom you should kneel in worship,
The Almighty God, who seeks not the slaughter of beasts,
But rather the sacrifice of a pure heart, pure mind.
Serve Him! Only He can grant you everlasting joy!'
   This said, he took the razor-sharp sacrificial axe
That had felled the animals to hideous Svatovít.
Thrice to the right side, thrice to the left, with all his might
He hacked until the foul idol tumbled to the ground,
The garlanded cap it wore rolled to the side, the horn
Emptied of the wine — ending all such divination —
And the whole temple filled with loud chopping, as chips flew.
Then Konštantín turned to the crowd: 'A mighty god, that!
Flat on the ground, his mouth — one of them! — biting the dust!
Well, get up then, Svatovít! Why are you so lazy?
An enemy invades the land; he's running riot,
Threatening dire destruction to your dear worshippers.
So, grasp your sword that hangs there on the post, strap it on,
And mount that fiery steed of yours — rush upon the foe!
But look! He moves not — why, he can't even help himself!
He's down, and never more shall rise. O, brave god of wood!'
   This said, he summoned pious Slavyhosť and Ranka,
Two brothers who ministered at the altar of God,
And had them carry the foul thing out to the fire-pit.
They gladly obeyed, dragging the log that was the god
Outside the fane to fling it upon the eternal
Flame that had glowed in his honour. Now, the greedy fire
Licked at the idol, then caught, and soon the god was naught

But flimsy ash and smoke that soon vanished in the wind.
   The idol consumed, he set once more to teaching them
About the Son of God, the Father's eternal love,
Who was sent forth into this fallen world to save it,
Suffering a cruel death on the wood of the Cross
In order, through His death, to spare us death unending,
Redeeming the lost, and rebuilding the destroyed. He taught
The Faith needed for salvation, its chief articles —
Above all, how membership in the Church Christ founded
Leads him who keeps His laws and commandments to glory
Everlasting in Heaven. But as for stubborn souls,
Those who reject His Word and deny Him, who remain
True to a shameless creed, walking in pagan error,
Those shall be deprived of every heavenly joy,
Thrust into the black, ever burning marshes of Hell.
   Thus Konštantín preached. A great uproar ensued among
The throngs there, a portion of which accepted the Faith
At once, while others rebuffed it, enraged with dull wrath
At the felling of Svatovít, the extinguishing
Of his eternal flame. But when they saw that Slavoš,
Revered for his piety, and wise Víťažoslav,
Žárko, renowned for his riches, even Zamysel,
Steeped in black sorcery, Vojzvuk himself and Zastav
(Who had the honour of bearing Svatovít's banner
In war, and with his trumpet firing the hearts of men),
And even the high priest — in short, every man of note
Accepted the law of Christ, eagerly casting off
Their ancient errors at the urging of God's servant
Konštantín, unwearied by his labours on behalf
Of God, they also withdrew from idolatry
And processed to the laver of Holy Baptism.
Once all had been cleansed of their sin, the gates
Of Heaven, which had been shut, swung open before them,
Konštantín departed to spread the salvific Faith
In further regions still sunk in glooms of unbelief.

CANTO IV

With no less devotion, Methodius
Set to his mission, following the stream
Of the Morava, teaching as he went,
Toppling idols horrid. In Bzenec Tras,
As in Velehrad he battered Oslad,
Koštej and Porevít, foul Radogasť
On his Radhosť, Div, Ďonda, and Bobák
And Lel his brother, Belbog and Láda;
After these Krt along with Nocena,
Tur, and the Sudičky he sent to Hell,
Upon which he returned to Devín, where
Along with Konštantín anew he preached,
Translating texts into the Slavic tongue,
And ordaining new servants unto God.
And then they set off once again from Devín
Founding new churches in city and village;
Konštantín then remained alone in Nitra,
While past the Danube went Methodius,
Selecting Velehrad for his new seat.

   And thus did Konštantín convert the eager Slovaks
Of the Tatras to faith in Christ. His younger brother,
As if his mirror image, did the same in other
Regions, toppling idols and winning the people
To Christ, converting them from their hideous errors.
Of him now I sing, and may that same Holy Spirit
Enlighten me, with His rays banishing all dark clouds.
  With no less dedication, Methodius set forth,
Following first the Morava to its headwaters,
Preaching, instructing the people, and overturning
Their idols: Tras in Bzenec, Oslad in Velehrad,
Koštej in Hranice, in burly Kotúč Porevít.
Arriving at Radhosť, which soars nearly to the stars,
Where reared prophetic Radogasť crowned with his garlands,
Atop whose head a bird spread wide its speckled pennons,

While to his breast the idol clutched a blackish bull's poll,
Steadying it there with powerfully hewed right arm,
While in his left was placed a sharp double-bladed axe.
It was there great hosts of people gathered from all parts
For a grand celebration of the day when the sun
Takes longest to complete its diurnal orbiting,
The day on which most sacrifices of beasts were made.
When the rites of praise to Radogast were completed
And the worshippers were spread out upon the lush grass
For the feast, with great honeycombs drying in the sun;
When their first hunger had been satisfied, their minds turned
To gaiety and sport. Some tooted horns, others
Scraped their fiddles' catgut or pumped their bagpipes to skirl —
Whoever could finger a stop or press a clean fret
Made music; the great member of the multitudes sang,
Whirling their partners, dancing on the meadows,
Stealing a kiss, pressing flesh upon flesh, to applause
Of oldsters beating palms in time to the spry music,
Remembering... Meanwhile, in the sacred grove, elders
And high priest passed judgement, reconciling the wroth,
Reuniting in concord those sundered by squabbling.
The youngsters were at play, turning somersaults, standing
On their heads, vaulting stuffed saw-horse or piled-up kegs,
Racing round, matching wit and dexterity in games
Or spreading hide-targets, and vying in archery.
Higher and higher soared the revelry on all hands.
It was the summer solstice, and many chafed towards
The night, keeping hot embers glowing in readiness
To light the bonfires as soon as the lazy sun set
For the lines of bold youths to surmount, leaping in turn.
But then they caught sight of Methodius approaching
The temple at a solemn pace (they recognised him
By his priestly vestments; many had heard of his deeds,
His fame preceding him). At once they all grew silent,
Abandoning their games and dancing. They approached him
And, grabbing hold of him, would lead him to their banquet,
Their raucous jollity interrupted. But he signed
For peace, for a space, and when he saw them step away,
Expectant, eyes trained upon him, he began to speak:
    'I haven't journeyed here to join your festivities

Or banquet with you; rather, I would lead all of you
To such a feast as your eyes have never seen, your ears
Never heard — if only you permit me; a table
That surpasses your powers of imagination,
A feast that lasts forever, but never cloys, with food
That sates the partakers, who'll never hunger again!'
   Thus spoke he. At once they began to beg him warmly
To tell them more about that feast, where it would be held,
And to take them there, all of them, if he were able;
Or at least to allow them to taste some bit of it, now.
When nearly all had gathered around him, he began:
   'Whoever would arrive at the glory of Heaven,
Where that banquet awaits, full of the sweetest delights,
Free to all, following whatever their heart desires,
With splendid music to delight the ear, choruses
Of song, never-ending dance, freed of all black worry
And anxiety, must first foreswear vain Radogosť
And all his vile crew, which leads only to ruin —
Spurning all idols, and serving the Lord God alone,
The only true God, Source and Creator of all things.
To Him he must confess, Him alone worship as God.
And in His only Son, the Lord Jesus Christ place faith,
Who, in the flesh, announced unto the world the pure Truth,
The only Way that leads unto the Life unending
All those who walk in His righteous ways all their life long.
Those who do otherwise will fall into the abyss
Of Hell. He must also believe in the Holy Ghost,
Who proceeds from both Father and Son, the Comforter,
Who strengthens the limbs, enlightens the intelligence,
Here and now pouring grace upon grace upon all folk
Who love and believe in Him. Therefore, O dear Slovaks!
If ever you wish to taste such true happiness, arise,
And give yourselves wholly to Christ, accepting His law'.
   So taught Methodius. They wavered in unbelief
A while, like cattails sprung from marshy soil when breezes
Agitate them, now to this side, now to that bending,
Until at last their hearts were touched by the grace of Christ
And renewed, like a new creation, chose to follow Him,
Calling Him Lord and choosing Him Guide. Then, for three days
(For such was the amount of food that they had with them)

They listened to God's Word preached them by Methodius,
Mastering the articles of the Faith, upon which
They were cleansed of their guilt in the laver of Baptism.
The temple they destroyed with their own hands, the idol too
Of Radogosť was toppled over, fed to the flames,
And the people jeered as their ancient error crumbled.
   From there Methodius travelled on to Olomouc.
He neared the town as the sun began to set, the glooms
Of night to thicken. Then a mournful wail met his ears;
A short space later, his eyes beheld a funeral
Conduct, with blazing torches. There then approached the bier
Of Milko Hodislavovič, once a stout war-chief,
Borne in great woe toward an oaken copse, where a pyre
Had been prepared to reduce his cold remains to ash.
The crowd of mourners grew as they entered the oak grove,
And when they were at the place where the pyre was readied
For the cremation of so mighty a conqueror,
The people grew silent at the edge of the wood-pile,
The keening women as well, dressed in their mourning robes
Of white, their hot tears dripping into lachrymal vials.
Hodko, the golden-tongued bard, intoned the hero's praise,
At which all there present joined their voices in lament:
How splendid he was, they moaned, how strong and beautiful,
How kind and generous, a father to all in need,
Defender of the weak and avenger of all wrongs;
Who multiplied the weal of this people, his nation.
What a sharp mind he had! — they sang — how wise his counsel,
In bravery and might of arms surpassing all men,
His glory eclipsing the greatest heroes of old!
Of judges the most skilled, whose sage determinations
Untangled the knottiest gnarls of contention.
In war, 'twas nothing for him to slay one hundred foes;
'Twas he who felled those two giants Langebrecht and Rajno
Who, in battle, like mowers, had cut down whole armies,
Extending their haughty sway over Moravia.
   As the laments wound down, the body of the hero
Was set upon the pyre. The torchbearers then lowered
Their firebrands to the oil-soaked wood, and black smoke billowed
Aloft with the flashing sheets of flame soaring skyward,
At which the painful sacrifices were underway:

Bulls culled from amongst the best of the herds were slaughtered
Along with rutting rams and the fattest of the sheep
And — at last — his favourite charger, who'd carried him
Boldly into battle, a conqueror returning,
Was led once in a circle about the fire, bearing
All his master's gold-chased armour and richest garments
To be tossed upon the flames. Then the procession resumed
Around the hero's flaming bier — everyone weeping,
Everyone rending their garments in woe, tearing hair
And cropping beards, tossing all onto the roaring blaze,
Sending toward the heavens unceasing cries of woe.
Now, when the procession of mourners had thrice circled
The pyre, with the armourers and soldiers parading last,
Before the games commenced (bright shone the moon, the bonfire
Provided light enough), to display their skill in arms,
His splendid helpmeet Luboslava — than whom there was
Amongst the Slovak women no one fairer of face —
Keened loudly in great pain, expressing thus her despair:
  'O my most splendid husband! Why have you gone away
So early, abandoning this world for the black shades?
Did you tire of it so quickly? Were you not happy
Amongst us here? What joy, what delight were you lacking?
Possessed you not riches exceeding all other men?
Were you not held in honour above all your fellows?
Was your glory not the greatest among all our folk?
Unmanly, shiftless types, who have no name to boast of,
Drag out their drab existence for two times fifty years!
But you, manly, mighty, lauded for heroic deeds,
Had hardly witnessed three times ten harvests of the fields
Before you fell, like a bloom slashed by a careless scythe,
Leaving me here, alone, abandoning your children!
Who shall be father to your little sons? Who will cheer
Svatoslavek? Who will now instruct your Prekrasko?
You might have lived at least so long as to train them in arms
And teach them the paths of virtue, and truth, and justice!
Yes — and who will now be mother to them, poor orphans?
Who now will clothe them, comfort them, wipe their tears away?
For having followed you here, I shall not return home
Alive, again; I shall now hurl me into these flames!
This one pyre shall consume us both; beneath one kurhan

Our ashes shall be raked; there our love, changeless, will bide'.
  Finishing thus, she made to walk into the bonfire.
Upon which seeing, Methodius cried out: 'One moment,
Lady! Allow me a small space to appeal to you,
O most mournful widow! What good will it do your spouse
For you to join him on his fiery bed? Can mere ash,
Can embers deaf hear anything you say? Does charred bone
Care anything for the dread sacrifice you would make?
And if your husband could hear what you say, would he wish
You to follow him, through death, into an endless dark?
Live, rather, for your little children now, care for them!
If only he could speak to you, would not your spouse urge
Exactly as I, exactly as your Creator,
Who sets His ban against us taking off from this life
Until He call us from it Himself, the penalty
Otherwise: eternal suffering in Hell. Turn then
To Him, the Ruler of all, accept His Faith, and He
Shall soothe your pain in time and comfort you in sorrow,
And grant you a glory far greater than your husband's.
And you, the rest, who've come to mourn these crumbling ashes,
Accept the Christian Faith and the promise of Heaven!'
  Thus he, at which her faithful friends blocked the path at once,
Forbidding her to cast herself onto her husband's pyre.
But the host there assembled received the pious words
Of Methodius unwillingly, shaking their heads.
Then Milko's father, the capable Hodislav, spoke,
That mournful man, directing such words at the Christian:
  'Praise be to you, stranger, from whatever land you come.
But let it suffice, that you have saved dear Luboslava
From a horrid death, plucking her from the very flames.
Divert us no longer from these sad rites with your speech;
Disturb this funeral no more. Indeed, there will be
Time enough for you to speak about your religion
Back in the city; as for now, deign assume the place
Of honour at our sad repast, and refresh yourself'.
  Such were his words. Then, according to ancient custom
Passed down the ages by our forefathers, they set to
The rites of hospitality, with thighs of oxen
And other loins and ribs of the beasts there sacrificed
Shared out to all, with ever-flowing goblets of wine

And honeycomb to sweeten the tongue. Hunger sated,
The rites funereal drawing to a close, once more
They bade a last farewell to their dead hero, tossing
Over their shoulders stones, earth, sticks, whatever they had
To hand upon the crumbling ash-pile before leaving
To head back to the city. There, at the fervent words
Of Methodius instructing, day in and day out,
They left behind all pagan error and turned to Christ.
Both splendid Luboslava and her father-in-law
Converted too, although she gave not off visiting
Her husband's grave for twice times fifteen days, to mourn him,
Upon which his bones were gathered into a glass urn
And lain to rest beneath a high-piled funeral mound.
   Now, when Methodius had converted all to Christ,
And shattered the idol of Div on the river-bank,
He pressed on with his mission, overturning Ďonďa
In Bystrica, and Bobák, that terror to children,
In Boskovice, slicing him clean into two portions.
Then Lel and Polel, brothers, the first the sprite of love,
The other ruler of marital bonds, both equal
And unequal — both of them he smashed in Jihlava
And sent off to perish forever. And then Zbíslav
Kladiva, the Czech, beyond all measure of his clan
The foremost in battle, the wealthiest in riches,
Most sincere in all his dealings, being at the time
By chance in Jihlava and hearing Methodius
Preach to the people and celebrate the Holy Mass
In Slavic, at once converted to the Christian Faith.
Having accepted baptism, he begged Methodius
To come into his land and instruct the people there
On the same truths, overturning the crumbling idol
Of Belbog that stood in a sacred oaken woodlet
At the border, as well as all those in his homeland,
And in the kindred region of the Moravians.
He smote them, they tottered, bearing off to Hell with them
The spiritual plague that had infected the folk.
Moved by his ardent pleas, Methodius continued
To press through the Czech lands. News of his arrival soon
Spread among the folk, of some teacher from Rastislav's
Land arriving, to teach some new rites and religion

In Belbog's grove. They gathered there in large numbers,
And in great haste — not from enthusiasm to give ear
To Christian wisdom, but rather out of novelty.
For, as wise-headed Zbíslav himself had called him there,
He must be a worthy man — otherwise, he would not
Have bothered! So, there Zbíslav led Methodius
To preach the Faith to his folk, and urge them to convert.
At the time the high priest of Belbog was one Oslav:
White-haired and whiskered, dight in a white cloak of weasel.
Grandson of Pravomil, of all his fellows in age
And strength of sword-arm excelling all — one of the Czechs
Who, along with his father, had led his people there,
To the land of Bohemia. Oslav would slaughter
Goat and white-feathered cock to the idol of Belbog,
Begging it long, striking his own pate with his left fist,
Then touching the idol's lips and his own with his wand.
Thrice he would bow low, and three times embrace the figure
Until his hackles rose and the eyes rolled in his head,
Whereupon he would tremble and shake until at last
He fell upon the ground to utter through froth the words
Sent him — they thought — from the god, to predict the future.
Still, he could not foretell the destruction of his god!
And now, beholding Methodius in foreign garb,
Before the gathered crowds, and learning why he'd come there,
He raged in fury before greeting him with such words:
    'Now what, new stranger, was it tempted you to these lands,
Our homeland, to upturn our fathers' ways, and with force
Whip us in to some new religion? Perhaps you wish
To ruin our state, enslaving us to another?
Why, two times seven Czech lords have already opted
For Baptism in Rezno — three of them I knew quite well.
The German king himself, Ludvík, grandson of Caesar
Karl, was present — it all went off with great rejoicing.
But what was that Baptism worth? What good was that faith?
No sooner had they returned home from our neighbours
Bavarian, than the whole country was up in arms,
And drove them from their inheritance by force of arms.
They were afraid, and they were right to fear this new faith
That, shared with the Germans, would league them with the Germans,
And soon lead the Germans to press them beneath the yoke!

Indeed, that's what happened! No sooner had Ludvík heard
Of his neophytes' exile, than he gathered a great force
And with it rushed upon the land unprepared for war
With mighty arms, subjecting them to heavy tribute,
Indeed, subjecting their land to cruel slavery.
Twice did he fall upon them so, yes, three times, when they
Uprose to struggle free of the tight German halter.
Is this what you would bring us, too — just such misfortune,
Imposing this your foreign faith upon us, and driving
Us from our homes to knock about foreign parts, begging?
Would you like the Moravians to die for your faith,
Bringing the Germans here too, to make us into slaves?
Take your own folk in hand, rather, and bind your Slovaks
With your faith'. Thus did Oslav the idolator speak.
  Methodius replied to this, calmly, but warmly:
'Dear brother Oslav! I have not travelled to this land
Unthinkingly, nor to bring any foreign teaching
Unto you so as to drive the folk with violence
Beneath the heel and halter of the German nation,
Or enslave them to anyone! I've come to set you free.
My aim is not to destroy this people, but to lead
One and all from the threat of eternal destruction
Into happiness everlasting! Such is the Faith
I preach — the same Faith our Lord and Saviour
Jesus Christ, Who descended from the Father to save
All men preached, who at His ascension into Heaven
Bade us to go into the world converting all men,
Gathering unto Him all His chosen ones. Is it
Not a good thing then, to set before them who wish it,
So great a good? Is it not right to suffer all pains
Here on earth for that Faith, to receive as recompense
A reward greater three-hundredfold beyond the stars?
Each prince then, deprived of his dukedom on this account,
Receives in recompense an empire everlasting,
And woe to them who lift a weaponed hand against him,
Thrusting him from his homeland on account of the Faith.
And should you be deprived of all you have on behalf
Of the Christian Faith, you should consider yourselves blest,
Receiving a treasure that shall never pass away.
For what are earthly possessions, lands, or great riches

Holed up in fortresses, where moles and rust consume them?
What good is an excess of bodily luxury,
And beauty that fades and wrinkles? What good one's own will
Should that will lead but to everlasting slavery?
For the life of man is like to dust blown in the wind.
It lasts a moment before vanishing, and should one
Make poor use of the time allotted him, what awaits
Is torment eternal in the everlasting flames
Of Hell. What a vain bugbear you make of the Slovaks!
That I should use the Word of God to overthrow you,
As if joining them in the bonds of Christian brotherhood
Were tantamount to binding the wrists of your stout men
In slavery to them! Such may have been the Germans'
Manner of progressing, but these are Slavs! Your brothers!
They share your blood, you come of one father! How could that
Be to your disadvantage, even should you unite
In one realm, and of your own free will, with Rastislav?
All the more easily would you win back your ancient
Freedom, splintering the German yoke impressed on you;
All the more mighty would be your forces united —
How easily you are routed when you stand apart!
Streamlets can be leapt over by a child, but when they
Unite into a sounding river, like the Lába,
Or the mighty, foaming Vltava — that can't be crossed
With a hop! Flow together then! For when you're in flood,
Your waters will wash your foes away to the Ocean!
You think this wasn't the way of your ancient fathers?
Perhaps you've listened to your elders' tales of Avars
Cruel, who ravaged the lands hereabout, pillaging,
Slaughtering, carrying off — how they oppressed your folk,
Imposing the harsh yoke of slavery on their necks,
Until an army was mustered thirteen times greater
Than theirs — this happened some five times fifty years ago —
And they regained their freedom, choosing as their leader
Sám, great in wisdom and in strength of arm, electing
Him chief of brave Lusatians and Slovaks both, who whipped
The Avar hordes with forces united, expelling
Them from these Czech lands, and all regions held by the Slavs.
And how, in fierce, pitched battle, these same arms together
Drove Dagobert and his valiant Franks from the land.

O, united, they always returned from their battles
Rejoicing, in glory. As long as Sám led the Slavs,
The borders of these lands were secure, no enemy
But respected his might. Such power's in unity!
But how dare you, Oslav, speak of the Faith that I preach
As something ill? For what I teach comes of Truth itself,
The Truth that eternally bides with God in Heaven,
The Ruler of all, the Creator of everything,
The beginning and end of all that is good! From Him
No evil can come — especially your pagan lies
And errors that come of man's own frail inanity,
Through which you steal the praise due to the Ruler of all,
The one and only God, on behalf of rotten timber!
Your wooden idols are incapable of lifting
A finger in aid of anyone! Dead wood, brass, stone,
Which time will gnaw away should they stand long; like the Greek
Zeus, the great Jupiter of the Romans, Tuiško
Of the Germans —where are they now? And a thousand more?
Toppled all from their pedestals, perished, specimens
Doltish of man's folly. For lies, however clever,
Cannot last; myth and fable all will pass; God alone
Is eternal, the one and only true God, Ruler
Of all the universe, immutable only that Lord,
To Whom, if you have any sense yourself, you will bow
Down, prostrating yourself before the one Deity.
Now, cast aside idolatry, shameful holocaust
To wood-shavings! — and accept, rather, the Christian faith
Salvific, as that nation more renowned, the Slovaks,
Have welcomed it; as in Jihlava Zbíslav, that great
And wise prince received it, who has brought me here with him.
I tell you — I see it already — the Czech nation
As a whole is soon to embrace the Lord Christ. The prince
Whose seat is Prague will be first to accept Baptism —
Why don't you beat him to the finish line? O, knock down
That god of rubble, Belbog, and with his splintered shards
Cobble the path to salvation for your countrymen!'
   Such were the words of Methodius. The host was moved,
All except Oslav, yet his once-glaring eyes grew soft,
And then he spoke anew: 'Great glory and praise to you,
Learned in the most ancient history of the Slavs —

More learned, perhaps, than we ourselves, though a stranger
From distant lands. You speak true of our brother Slovaks,
And of the unity we once shared, and still ought to.
True is it too, it seems to me, that you intend us
No evil in your coming, but rather good fortune.
But, can you guarantee that our kin the Moravians
Will not themselves oppress us, freed once from the German
Yoke, but permit us our own free will in that common realm?
You know yourself that not all alliances are good.
To give just one example (so as not to bore you),
That Rastislav of yours — is he not deeply guilty
For having entered into an evil alliance
With the Germans? And why is it that you so boldly
Call down our religion as stupid, erroneous?
And fulminating so, prophesy its destruction?
You praise this great God of yours, I reckon, overmuch!
And in exchange for accepting His faith, you would urge
Us to relinquish all we possess — and that gladly?
Now there's a reward for you — suffering in meekness!
We are to praise a God Who deprives us of our goods!
But know this — even if He be true God, the Ruler
Of Heaven itself, dispenser of all happiness,
I still won't accept Him, until, as you prophesy,
The whole nation and all its princes do accept Him first,
Casting down all the gods that our forefathers worshipped.
Then I'll accept Him, and that won't be too soon, I reckon!
And until that happens, in this sacred grove of oak
Belbog shall have his praise, Belbog shall protect his folk.
Why was the clever Zbíslav so quickly off the mark?
Now, rumour has it that you sing no hymns to your God
Nor restrain his anger with prayer as the Germans
Are said to sing and pacify Him with petitions;
Show us what you do in your sacred churches, the rites
You perform. For we all like music, and would gladly
Hear new songs sung in our tongue, so we might understand!
   Thus Oslav, to which wise Methodius responded:
'If you wish to remain stubborn in the face of truth,
Remain so. You run the risk of no one's damnation
But your own. However, that you and all these gathered
In this oak grove would like to hear our pious music,

I tell you this cannot be until that shameful thing,
That stump you honour with divine latreia, Belbog's
Idol, be hacked apart and in place of his sad lies
You accept the Christian teachings and the one true Faith
Granted you from on high, washing away all your guilt
With penitence sincere. Only then might your wishes
To hear God's holy service as we celebrate it
Be fulfilled. Now, if your hearts swell with redemptive joy
At the chance of salvation offered you, come on now,
And overthrow this horrid pillory of your shame!'
   No sooner had these words passed through Methodius' lips
Than all the men gathered there, greatly moved, with a shout
Rushed upon the idol. At their head, Zbíslav, enflamed,
With all his might buried a hatchet deep in the brow
Of Belbog, cleaving it to the nape. The wood-grain cracked,
And off the head tumbled, thudding dully to the earth.
The next blow, no less mighty, landed on its swelling
Stomach. This knocked it off its angular pedestal.
It toppled to the ground with no little clatter and
The whole copse trembled, the oaks echoing the ruckus.
Zbíslav fell upon the idol, hacking at its limbs,
Smiting the trunk again and again. Thick flew the chips
Until there was little left of the image but small
Fragments and the shattered stone base. When, frozen in shock,
Oslav beheld the furious destruction of what
He'd called his god, he was filled with a rabid anger.
He called to the rest to rush to the aid of his Belbog,
And to avenge the great insult done him by Zbíslav.
But none moved. He glared around, speechless at the manner
In which his fiery urging was met… with apathy.
Furious, Zbíslav he cursed, and brother Methodius,
And all the onlookers, threatening torment in Hell
For their actions, and their omissions. Tearing away
From the temple profaned, he hurried from the copse
Of his own free will, impelled by no angel's command.
The pious Methodius proceeded to instruct
Those who accepted Christ all that day long, explaining
The chief tenets of the Faith, the initiated
Baptising, absolving through the sacrament all guilt.
When the sun began slowly to set, Methodius

Sent all the people home until it was time for Mass.
  The next day, when the dawning sun's cheeks blushed in the east,
And the raucous voice of the watchman's trumpet echoed,
The neophytes hastened back to the hoary oak grove.
In the midst of the woods reared an ancient linden tree,
So thick of trunk that two times five grown men of widest
Arm-span might scarcely embrace it; its crown brushed the stars.
Beneath its leafy brow and outstretched branches the crowd
Gathered, with room for half as many more. It was there
Methodius ordered the sacred altar prepared.
Four posts were driven in the even ground, topped by planks,
Planed smooth, covered by an immaculate altar cloth,
Beneath which he'd set the altar stone with its relics;
Branches cut from the grove's trees formed a fresh canopy.
Eagerly toiled the men, pressing on till all was done
And Nature formed a new basilica for God's praise.
When all was finished, when all had been set in order,
Methodius, vested, took his place at the altar,
And before commencing Holy Mass, explained the rite.
Following this proper teaching, he proceeded
To celebrate the Offering in Slavic, the tongue
Native to the Czechs, as he offered to the Father
The sacred Sacrifice of the Son so dear to Him.
The bread he transformed into the true Body of Christ,
The wine into His precious Blood, nourishing his soul
By communicating. He recited ardent prayers
And then intoned hymns of thanksgiving, heartfelt, response
Antiphonal sung by his clerics standing in groups
To each side. Intricate the melody, delighting
The ears of the new flocks gathered now unto the Lord.
All the more ardently their thoughts were turned towards Him;
All the more glowingly burned their hearts in gratitude;
All the more sincerely did they love their new-found Faith.
When pious Methodius had dismissed them in peace,
And after he'd instructed the rest of the Czechs who'd come
To embrace Christ and be baptised, he set off again,
Bidding the Czechs farewell, returning to Jihlava.
  From there he travelled to renowned Brno, where a grand
Temple stood flashing with gold, and in the cella there
Láda's idol, shaped like a beautiful young woman.

Upon her forehead she bore a chaplet of roses
From beneath which in thick locks her hair flowed to her knees.
Her coral lips were parted in a comely, gay smile;
Her eyes shone bright with flirty welcome, sending a warm
Glow forth, afar, from the torch that burned in her bosom.
In her right hand she bore three apples of purest gold
And in her left a decorated buckler, on which
Were figured the heavens, the sun, and the fecund earth
With mountain and plain, beyond which spread the ocean broad.
This female idol, naked, the work of that craftsman
Most skilled with chisel and maul, Vlastislav, was shattered
By Methodius, who then convinced her worshippers
Of their senseless error, converting them to the Lord.
He then progressed to Slavkov and Znojmo far-afield,
Where Krt and Nocena, those judges who'd ruled the folk,
He shattered in shards. On and on he went, proclaiming
The merciful law of Christ throughout all the region,
Knocking down every idol he chanced upon there
And feeding it to the flames proper to such lumber!
   Then, as he went on his return route to Breslava
He found no pagan idols left, except for warlike
Tur, worshipped by the people of the Turán region,
Which proudly derived its name from that false deity.
There first he hastened. When the crowds who had gathered there
From all around to offer annual worship
To their god circled the sacrifice three times (each oak
Bound in streamers) and three times lifted their voice in song,
He spoke to them, proclaiming the heavenly truths. Some
Believed at once, but the greater portion rejected
The new Faith, standing stubbornly in their old error.
Methodius only strove the more. Nor would he leave,
Abandoning the labour once begun, until all
Had been turned away from their shameful practices,
Accepting Christ, and cleaving unto His holy Church.
Only then did he smash the idol, and furthermore
Hew down the sacred grove, clearing the land for true praise.
   Once he had accomplished this, he returned to Devín
Where, in the cathedral, he met his beloved brother
Konštantín preaching — such had been their plan: after two
Years apart, to come together again. They spoke,

After embracing, of their missions and adventures:
How God had led each one, imparting strength and wisdom,
Shepherding each of their slightest tasks to fulfilment.
They told of how He had brought light to those in darkness,
Enflaming the iciest hearts among them with Love,
Until everyone had cast off idolatry,
The true Faith to embrace. In Devín again they preached,
Translating further sacred writings into Slavic,
Multiplying hymns and prayers for liturgical use,
And teaching the young men who would take Holy Orders.
Nine months they spent at this, after which once more they went
Out into the countryside, preaching without pause
And building churches where they were needed by their flocks.
Then Konštantín, worn with age and wearied by the road,
Took up residence in Nitra, while Methodius
Crossed over the broad Danube into Pannonia,
Returning to Velehrad, with its cloud-piercing towers.
There, Chocil, of measureless piety, Pribina's
Son, received him into his court with great rejoicing,
Entrusting his people to him for their instruction.

CANTO V

Envy enflames the Bavarian clergy
— Especially Richbald — against the brothers.
He leaves at once for Salzburg to report
The doings of Methodius, and Adalvín
Summons a synod, calling for good counsel
In the face of what he takes as evil tidings.
The synod posts some messengers to Rome
To make their case before the Holy Father
Against the Greeks: for trespassing their pasture,
Poaching their flock. They charge them, furthermore,
With spreading error through the land, imposing
A Slavic ordo on the liturgy.
The Pope, at these complaints, summons them both,
Konštantín and Methodius, to his presence.
They bid farewell to Rastislav, ordaining
Young priests to take their place, and go — bearing
With them the relics of St Clement, found
Miraculously in the sea — to Rome.

   In such wise, four full years passed by. The seed they'd planted
On their arrival from Tsarigrad grew healthily
Into a sturdy sapling. But their success aroused
The fury Envy, that evil hag of skin and bones
And spleen, whose only happiness is men's misfortune.
She could not brook their holy success, so up she rose
To poison the minds of the Bavarian clergy
Who, up till now, had full run of Rastislav's kingdom;
These she pricked with the bile of ferocious anger —
Even those such as Chocil, pious beyond all measure,
Had introduced into his land, founding their churches —
Especially Richbald, most powerful of them all.
Him she struck first, badgering with such venomous words:
   'O otherwise pious Richbald! Superintendent
Of Chocil's Church! Where has it vanished, your paternal
Concern for the arch-priestly office entrusted you?

Have you not heard about those brothers from Tsarigrad
Spreading disobedience and disorder among
The Slovaks of the Tatras? Can it be you see not
How one of them has made his way as far as this land
Where, against the divine laws of the Church, he says Mass
In Slavic? Leading the people astray with deceit?
How in their great numbers, bedazzled by novelties,
They abandon the Roman *Ordo*, and flock to him?
Yes, only his chants, only his hymns sound sweet to them,
And no more will they heed the pastors set over them —
They will not come to your churches, hear the Latin Mass…!
He dulls your blade, comes out against all things — there's no hope
That your flocks, scattered, shall ever return to the fold
As long as that stranger, that seducer, walks these fields!
And yet you sit here and do nothing? But tell me — Why
Do you permit so great and cruel an evil as this
To multiply? Such is your conscience, such your care —
O vile unconcern! — for the lambs entrusted you?
Sit then, you wretch, until that comely misbeliever
Knocks you from that chair, and drives you forth from the city,
Chasing all the German priests after, back to Salzburg!
Or — arise now and go report the threat to your lord.
Let him thunder a curse, a mighty anathema
So strong that it will blow them back to Greece, whence they came!
Chase away those tramps, and put an end to disorder!'
   Thus screeched the hag, after which she huffed her putrid breath
Into his nostrils. It penetrated bone and flesh
And coursed like flame through his arteries. Mission fulfilled,
She once again withdrew into the deep, black shadows.
Richbald's heart swelled so with her venom it nearly burst,
Pumping the searing toxin of black blood all through him.
He roared with anger, like some tiger sorely wounded
By huntsmen, pacing his chamber in agitation.
Then — in rushed Gerold from Vitomírovce's region,
Of Roman stamp, he — after him, Ludolf, with the same —
A complaint against Methodius: all improper,
All unjust. And all against him, all fired with ardour
To stamp out what he saw as evil, Richbald decides,
Consumed by the witch's flames, to set out for Salzburg
Where pious Adalvín had his rich cathedral chair,

Being at the time the head of the see of Salzburg,
Who had sent him forth and established him in office.
When he had heard through the report of the misfortunes
Of Chocil's Church, long familiar to those residing
Amidst the Tatras, Adalvín remained silent long,
Weighing the mournful news, considering what to do.
How might he put an end to the destruction? At last,
It seemed best to him to summon a priestly synod,
At which to determine a proper response. At once,
The clergy of the see of Salzburg, bishop and priest
Obedient to the archbishop's command, gathered
At his cathedra, from which he addressed them such words:
'Dear brothers, pastors of the flocks who believe in Christ,
Ever burning with concern for the heavenly truths!
Be not surprised that I call you here out of season.
I am impelled by harsh necessity! The pious
Bavarians, ever eager to aid their brothers
To come to knowledge of our glorious Creator,
Strove to preach His Faith to the Moravian Slovaks.
Who knows not of the deeds of Urolf, of diligent
Runhár and Adalrám, who led this see before us?
And Luitprám, and the heroic clergy sent there?
Nor did the Lord God decline to further their labours,
Making dark hearts to glow with the light of love kindled
By those great missionaries. How many did they save!
How many did they turn away from idolatry!
It was their labours that brought them to our Mother Church.
The seed there planted flourished well — up until today.
For now two Greek brothers, inventors of alphabets,
Have crept into our sheepfolds, trespassing on our rights.
They're spreading heresy, leading the people astray
Into a crooked error — celebrating the Mass
In the Slavic tongue, boldly casting Latin aside!
Destroying the Roman *Ordo*! And now not only
In the realm of Rastislav do they commit such crimes;
Now, one of them has brashly dared to cross the Danube
Into Pannonia, where Chocil is the ruler
By due descent, secure on the throne of his father,
Whom, when banished, Ludvík generously supported.
And now this Greek is upsetting all in that realm, too,

Teaching the same errors, setting the same obstacles
Upon the path that leads to salvation, deceiving
The people, who flock to him in their sad delusion,
And those who once loved the Latin rite, abandon it
For his partisan ritual. The faithful clergy
Resist this dire lawlessness, but they are powerless
To move them, whether by strong words or gentle advice.
Blind, the people progress along that ignoble road,
Repaying the counsel of their priests with derision.
Should we find no remedy, should events continue
Down this same path, all the country, including Chocil,
Will turn to him, and we'll be turned out of the churches,
Driven from the land, banished, back to Bavaria!
Our rights abrogated, all the good we've done upturned.
From here the pestilence will spread along the Drava,
Indeed along the Sáva, until it reach the sea
Where Slavic nations also live, arriving at last
Among the Volgars, where the infection of error
Already taints whole realms with corruption. If only
The Ruler of the Heavens would hear our frequent prayers,
And enlighten the dark minds of the Slovaks' brothers,
The Czechs and Poles and Ruthenians! For otherwise
All too clear a path to them would error have as well.
And then what profit to the infernal powers!
How many souls to prey upon in such widespread fields!
And so we must put an end to this while there's still time —
Stamp out the smouldering brands before the fire catches
To rage beyond our control, consuming everything.
For this I've summoned you, to discover the best way
Of dealing with this danger. Brothers, what shall we do?'
   He ended, and at once the nave was filled with murmurs
Thick and whispers echoing from the vault — as when flocks
Of starlings or of ravens twist about the heavens
In swirling swarms that dart now here, now there, the swift blades
Of their wings whistling loudly, or as when, alit at Mlíč,
Before settling down to sleep, their chatter fills the air,
Sounding from each elm-bough straining beneath the load.
And now it was that Envy — that revolting monster! —
Began to flit about the nave on foul, sticky wings,
Alighting — now here, now there — on the brows of the priests

There gathered, soiling them with the vile stains of her filth.
For as soon as she'd envenomed the blood of Richbald
With her infected stinger, she'd hastened to Salzburg
On the winds of misfortune, to spread her poison there.
And so she did: the men there sickened with contagion
That churned their minds with hectic, souring blood and marrow —
Which sickness vented with their breath gone putrid: all cursed
Methodius as innovator and seducer
Of the faithful to heresy, calling for sharp saws
To hew the stubborn trunks of weedy, invasive growth
Sown by him amidst their healthy Slavonic orchards.
Some of them called for him to be cursed by the synod
According to his just deserts, banished from the bounds
Of the authority of the Bavarian Church.
Another portion urged the complaint be sent to Rome,
Before the Holy Father, that both brothers be called
To account for their deeds, their faults to be examined,
Condemned and extirpated. Once more Adalvín spoke:
  'To me as well it seems best that we send our complaint
To Rome, instead of banishing the misbeliever
Ourselves by force, lest those whose minds have been led astray,
Blinded by him, should raise a ruckus, turning on us
A fiercer anger, a yet more ferocious hatred.
And anyway, simple exile would be nothing worth.
Whether he took himself back to the Moravian king,
The ignoble preacher, or into any other land,
He would not cease his spreading, once begun, of errors
And heresies maleficent, which lead straight to Hell'.
  Thus he. And the synod, acknowledging the wisdom
Of his determination, elected wise Baldo
And Godolév spokesmen, to bear their complaint to Rome
And beg the Holy Father's aid against this evil,
The support of the Pope against this foul heresy.
The synod then closed, and the fathers departed home,
Except for the envoys, who, without hesitation,
Set out on the road for the famous city of Rome.
Upon arriving, they requested an audience
With the Vicar of Christ. The leader of Christ's faithful
At the time was Nicholas, a man great in wisdom
And virtue, and all that belongs to that high office.

Admitted to his presence, the first of the two spoke:
  'Holy Father most renowned, who guides the Church of Christ
— Firm Rock, that the gates of Hell shall never overcome —
As head infallible in defence of law divine,
Guarantor of true doctrine, hammer to heresy!
We are sent to you by pious Bishop Adalvín
To reveal to Your Holiness and the Curia
The great misfortune that has befallen the faithful
Of our lands — a noxious plague that we fear may spread wide!
It is well known to you, how our great predecessors,
Yearning for the redemption of our pagan brethren,
Long ago sowed our Christian Faith among the Slovaks.
They reaped an ample harvest, for that soil is fertile!
The mightiest of the princes of the land, Mojmír
And harried Pribina, Chocil his son, powerful
Rastislav, along with his grandson Svatopluk,
Confessed to Christ. But then, pride-swollen King Rastislav,
Growing bored at last with the doctrine of our preachers,
Turned to the Eastern Emperor, sending to him gifts
And begging missionaries from thence to teach his people.
Indeed, he did send such wise and diligent brothers,
But wise as serpents, two stirrers-up of blasphemy!
For they have been so bold as to wholly overthrow
The Roman ordo, long cultivated there with care,
Imposing in its place a Slavic liturgy, Slavic
Prayers unsanctioned, celebrating the Holy Mass
In that vulgar tongue, so as to entrap the people
And submit them wholly to their will. And see: nearly all
The nation has abandoned their true pastors to follow
In the footsteps of this heresy. They now refuse
Obedience to the Church. The Latin Rite, that once
They gratefully received, they spurn, unwilling to hear
Celebration, sacrament, or sermon in any
Form other than that new, unauthorised, Slavonic.
They've become stubborn-necked, and hatred of their hearts
They openly display to us, late their benefactors.
Indeed, they harry our priests back to Bavaria,
As guests unwelcome, men no longer necessary,
While the banished clergy seek a remedy all in vain
Against so great a lawlessness. Such being the case,

Since we can do nothing, our powers being so small,
To put an end to these harmful villainies, we come
Before your Holiness, chief pastor of Christ's people,
Who alone can put a stop to these saucy brothers,
Forbidding their ruinous propagation of ill,
Damming the current of this raging river in flood
That it not overspill the fields of nearby nations,
While the fertile cornfields of Slovakia may yet
Be weeded of these tares of ecclesial chaos'.
   Thus Godolév. Baldo confirmed the truth of his words,
Which surprised the Holy Father not a little, for
Up till then he had heard only good of the brothers,
How tireless they in apostolic labour, how
Far they'd stretched the borders of Christ's realm, spreading the Faith
Among nations sunk in paganism. His reply
To the envoys' request was as follows: 'Glory be
To Bishop Adalvín, and all the priests belonging
To the Bavarian Church. Indeed, great your merit
For long years bringing the Christian Faith to the Slavs —
You shall find meet reward in the mansions of Heaven.
Right it is so to plant the Faith, and holy the zeal
To keep it pure and free of error's taint. As for me,
I shall be tireless in its defence, forbidding
All harm of error to Christ's Church, and her faithful ones'.
   This said, he dismissed the envoys to their homeland.
At once they left the city to return and repeat
To the Bavarian Church what they had heard in Rome.
Then, pious Pope Nicholas, so as to be certain
In his mind that what the Bavarians said were true,
And if so, what the proper remedy should be,
Immediately summoned the Greek brothers to Rome.
All of their doctrine, all their reasons for using
Slavic in ritual, he wished to hear from their lips.
Now, as soon as the brothers received the Pope's summons
They made their way before the pious king Rastislav
To render an account of why they were called to Rome.
The king pondered a long while in silence. Then he said:
   'Go then with God to stand before the Holy Father
As quickly as you can, obedient to his summons,
And clear your names of the false charges hurled at you.

The Lord God Himself will testify on your behalf
That you have preached nought but sound doctrine, no error.
As I see things, the Bavarians are behind this,
For they can't bear the use of our language in the Mass.
But mostly they're afraid of losing the rich profits
That they've amassed amongst us; of control of the Church
Slipping out of their hands, or, more nefariously,
Their chance of subjecting our crown to their government.
If ever through their machinations Germans become
Our lords, they'll hardly let us out of their grip again.
Now, hold your ground there before the Vicar of the Lord —
Argue the case for retaining Slavic for the Mass
That our tongue forever be allowed in our churches.
Tire his ears with petitions: a Slavic Mass, Slavic
Liturgy, and above all, that in this our kingdom,
As in all other Christian realms, our Churches be placed
Under the care of our own archbishop, with his seat
Amongst us here! May the Holy Father send to us
A bishop unbeholden to the Germans, in all
His doings and determinations autonomous
In his own Slavic see, with suffragans to aid him.
What a great joy it would be should he send you back here
With crozier and pectoral, bishops ordained of Rome!'
   He finished, but before they set out, twice, nay three times
He held them back with ardent instructions. Then at last,
Entrusting them to Zemižížeň and Slavek,
The boyars who had first brought them here from Tsarigrad,
To lead them to Rome, he outfitted them with all one
Needs for such a long journey. Konštantín said to him:
'Renowned King Rastislav! We shall do as you command.
Indeed, we shall not overlook the slightest detail
In our plea to be allowed to celebrate the Mass
In Slavic; that our rites be in the Slavonic tongue.
We'll also urge a Slovak bishop be appointed
A Slovak diocese to shepherd, autonomous
Of the Bavarian Church in all things, with brother
Suffragans to aid him in his labours in those lands
Settled by Slavs. Yet I know that until that happens
The Germans will not cease to put stumbling blocks along
Our path, opposing us in our office, stirring up

The people against us, turning them away from us.
But now our time is running short. And so, most pious
King Rastislav, all here present, and the absent, too:
Receive our deepest gratitude for all the kindness
We've experienced at your hands, for all your friendship
And support. Cling to the Faith we've preached with all your heart,
And never grow tired or flag in performing good works.
May the Lord bless you, may He prosper all your labours
As you carry on the work we've begun amongst you'.
   At this, the brothers bade farewell, taking unto them
The greater number of the most learned men they'd taught,
The most skilled in liturgy and sacred song, for these
They would have accompany them on the road to Rome,
That they might be ordained to the priesthood by the Pope.
The first man chosen was the most pious Slavimír,
A none too distant relative of King Rastislav.
At one time he'd possessed great wealth and wide-spreading lands
Which he'd inherited from his worthy ancestors.
Besides this, he was wise, and powerful of arm, skilled
And eager in battle. But when he heard Konštantín
Preach of the poverty of Her, who gave birth to Christ,
Of the need to raise churches to honour God, of love
To one's brethren, at once he divided all his wealth
In two halves. One he devoted to building churches,
The other, with generous hand, he gave to the poor.
And then, himself he dedicated to the service
Of the Most High Monarch, electing the priestly state
And spurning all earthly care and glory. But flee it
He could not, for the Slovak people, wrongly convinced
Of the death of Svatopluk the valiant in battle,
Elected him their leader in his place. Slavimír
Opposed this with all the vigour of his manly heart,
Setting before them all the most valid arguments:
That such a worldly calling did not befit a priest.
Yet they refused to hear, refused to accept his pleas;
Indeed, they threatened him with death should he not accept!
Following him, Mrakšo was chosen, and very pious Nebochváľ,
And Dobrovesť, Bratoslav, Jaromíl and Zorek,
Who earlier had been a seer, while the others
Gay musicians, who had played on all the gods' feast days

And celebrations, weaving song from tightly-plucked strings.
There were one hundred others — the son of Vitohosť
Especially, clever Pomnislav, who on the colt
Sacred to Svatovít would race through marshy barrens
And shingled waterways at night, till, sweat-drenched, foaming,
The horse he'd display to the awe-struck crowds at morning.
But when his aged father had accepted Christ's Faith,
And Svatovít, cast down, was consumed in his own flames,
He too became a student of the godly brothers
And never wished to leave their side again. Gorazd too
They chose to take with them — one of six young acolytes
Whom selfless Boriš once sent on their way, for that grace
When ardently petitioned. Renowned for his morals
Gorazd, and not last in wisdom, still he was not fain to leave
His homeland for the long journey, for what would become
Of the people, were they detained a long while in Rome?
He'd rather stay and instruct the youth in all needed
Christian wisdom and song, for which labours, above all,
He was most suited. Methodius would not hear of it!
And later, when Konštantín, who had taken the name
Cyril in Rome, had gone off to his reward in peace
After a short illness, struck down by the pestilence,
Gorazd returned to administer the Slovak Church,
Ordained and appointed to the see by the brothers,
Though later he was wronged and made to depart, replaced
By Vichýn, who, although Methodius had made him
His suffragan, still rebelled against the kind bishop,
Openly, constantly opposing him, the Slavic rite
Especially suppressing, driving into exile
Whenever he could, the priests ordained to serve the Slavs
In their own tongue, converting their churches to Latin.
   Besides these seminarians, they took a treasure
More precious than all gold with them to Rome: the relics
Of St Clement, who had been St Peter's disciple,
And then — against his will — succeeded him as bishop:
The fourth Vicar of Christ. He led so many Romans
To Faith through his great learning and piety, that proud
And impious Emperor Trajan had him exiled
To Taurus. There, he preached among the idolaters
Inhabiting Crimea, converting so many

That he was martyred by the proconsul, who cruelly
Hung an anchor around his neck and had him tossed
Into the depths of the sea. Later, when Konštantín
Was preaching the Faith to the people of the region
In Kherson — in the Slavonic tongue — a miracle
Occurred: the martyr's relics were revealed unto him.
These he collected, and carried always with him; now
He wished to take them back to Rome, where Clement was born,
And where he'd led the Church of God as Vicar of Christ,
That he might intercede for him, and his holy cause.
When all had been made ready, they set off on their road.

CANTO VI

Pope Adrian, the Vicar of Our Lord
(His predecessor, Nicholas, had died)
With great pomp translates Clement's saintly relics
Into the church, then asks the two brothers
How it was that they found the sacred treasure.
The elder tells him how, preaching in Kherson,
He found them, directed by a miracle.
The next day, the supreme Pastor of the Church
Calls them into his presence, where they give
Their witness to the articles of the Faith,
And explanations, why they saw fit to craft
A Slavic ordo. When they have finished,
A voice from Heaven sounds, at which the Pope
Without delay decrees permissible
The Slavic Rite's use in the Catholic Church.
Both brothers he ordains as Bishops, then
Commits them once again unto their mission.

Soon they drew near the walls of Rome, at which all the bells
Of all the churches in that famous city rang out
Their greeting. And then the Supreme Pontiff of Christ's Church
Adrian (for by then Pope Nicholas had gone off
To his eternal homeland) came forth to receive them,
At the head of a procession of priests and people.
In this way they translated St Clement's blest relics
Into the Church: with ardent sacred song, horns blaring,
Drums thumping — a magnificent celebration.
After the martyr's relics had been placed with reverence
Upon the high altar, and the solemn rite wound down,
The Holy Father of all Christendom turned to them:
   'Dear brothers! Who so far have spread the Faith of Our Lord!
I praise the Most High Bestower of all good, that He
Saw fit to augment His praise through servants such as you!
To you I offer deepest thanks as well, the great joy
Of a heart leaping and dancing in delight at this

Return, through your hands, after two times four hundred years,
Of this beloved countryman of ours, St Clement,
To rest at last in the Church raised unto his honour.
But how did you find this dear treasure, so long submerged
In the depths of the sea? Tell us, please, from first to last!'
   At this Konštantín arose, because he above all
Was concerned in the matter, and thus made he reply:
'Most Holy Father, prime Shepherd of the flocks of Christ,
And all you present, pious hosts of priests and people!
Since you would hear the story of how it came to be
(And who dislikes to hear accounts of God's great wonders?)
That He allowed us to discover these blest relics,
I'll tell you, briefly. I had been sent by the pious
Michael, our eastern Emperor, to preach Our Lord's Faith
To the mighty Kozárs, who themselves had sent envoys
To him, requesting missionaries. Obedient
To his command, I immediately undertook
The mission and set out on the journey to their far land.
I crossed the smooth waters of the Black Sea happily,
Reaching the Crimean shore, the limits of Kozár land.
Then, first of all I travelled to the walls of Sarkel
To engage in the mission to which I'd bound myself.
First of all, clearly, I needed to master the tongue
Of the Kozár people. I chose the town of Kherson,
As most convenable to my purpose: a city
Wealthy in gold, and respected by all its neighbours
Of every nation. Residing there for that reason,
I asked the inhabitants: "O faithful citizens!
Where, may I ask, can be found the grave where St Clement
Reposes? For he was exiled here by the cruel
Trajan, and later martyred, being thrown in the sea,
With an anchor fixed round his neck". At first, in wonder
They gaped, unfamiliar with the tale. And then they said:
   "O most noble father! Why do you ask us of this?
We cannot provide you with the answer that you seek,
For we ourselves are new arrivals here. Our fathers
Came to this place not long ago, from lands far distant.
This is the first time that we've ever heard this story".
   Thus their startled response. Then an aged, white-haired man,
The only descendant of the ancient ones who lived

First in the city, rose, aroused, and said in a weak voice:
"Long ago, I heard my grandfather, an old man
Who lived twice one hundred years before he left this light
Of day behind, whose clear mind preserved fresh memories
Of many notable events, speak of a certain
Priest of high station, banished here from Rome (his name I
Can't recall). Since he ceased not preaching the Christian Faith
Here, a rusty anchor was shackled around his neck,
And he was cast into the depths of the sea and drowned.
He also testified to the strange rumours he'd heard
Of a beautiful church that would appear on the spot
Of the man's martyrdom, covered by the deep waters
It was, invisible to all, except when the day
Of his martyrdom would roll around each year. For then,
In his honour, the sea would withdraw, and for eight days
Reveal the church, permitting access to all, dry-shod!
The people might approach the relics then, but after
Eight days had passed, the waters once more engulfed the shrine.
Grandfather said that he'd never beheld the wonder
With his own eyes, for by his time all marvels had ceased.
Besides that, though, he spoke of another church, raised high
Upon a hill in praise of God by that same martyr.
The story goes, that, while it was being built, a lamb
Showed him a well of living water, when he lifted
An ardent prayer to God to slake the thirst of the poor
Stonemasons labouring under the pitiless sun.
That temple exists no longer, looted and destroyed
It was, when those savage tribes the Huns fell upon us,
Pillaging so, that no stone was left upon another.
I reckon that this is the same man of whom you inquire".
  Thus did the ancient man relate to us, between spells
Of coughing, all that he had learned from his grandfather.
Lifting his cane, he pointed at the hill where the church
Had stood, and then at the cliff on the shore, whence Clement
Had been tossed to his death in the sea. From none other
Of the people present there could I learn any more.
I set myself to a strict fasting with ardent prayer,
Begging the Lord in His grace to deign reveal to me
What man could merely indicate. Then, at the sunrise
Of the fifth Sunday, after we had celebrated

With joy the advent of the Son of God among us,
After the Holy Sacrifice had been accomplished
And I'd led a large host of the faithful to the shore,
I knelt there, and the others fell to their knees as well.
Folding my hands, I lifted this petition to God:
  "O Lord, great Ruler of all things, Who once didst permit
Thy faithful St Helen to discover the True Cross
And retrieve It from the shameful pit where vile hands
Had cast It, to raise It on high, the victorious
Standard of Thy holy Church, deign now reveal to us,
Thy ardent servants, the place where Thy servant Clement,
Who once administered Thy Church as Thy Son's Vicar,
Teaching the nations, unlocking the Gates of Heaven
Broadly, and closing the same with the keys of Peter,
Hath left his mortal remnants in these depths of Ocean!
Direct our steps to this most glorious, blest treasure!
Show us a sign, Lord, illuminate our intellects!"
  I'd barely spoken these words, when lo! Strange as it seems,
A great roaring was heard, as when in spring the north wind
Howls and lays whole forests prone with its rending blasts,
For the sea rushed far away, its billows retreating
From the unfaithful shoreline to the flat horizon,
Revealing the abyss, the wide seabed spread with sand.
There, where none might pass unless safely aboard a ship,
A dry plain now stretched, inviting us to cross on foot!
I set out at once, and multitudes of men followed,
Hastening in the direction where my thoughts drew me.
For soon I saw, as if a mausoleum of stone,
A church in ruins, or some building darken afar,
Above which wheeled a flock of dancing seagulls, screeching
Gaily. 'Tis there I raced, the old man's narrative fresh
In my mind. I clambered up the steep temple ruins
— And with what unutterable joy my heart was filled! —
For peering deep within, I caught sight of a pavement
It seemed, cobbled of evenly-squared flags, amidst which
A sepulchre stood, and within it — a skeleton!
An anchor lay near the skull, barbs arching over the bones.
Immediately, dissolved in tears, I fell prostrate,
Weeping out joyous prayers of thanksgiving to the Lord,
The Ruler of all, for having fulfilled our ardent prayers,

Miraculously discovering these blest relics
To our unworthy eyes. I got up then, and approached
The tomb, to venerate the martyr's relics. I kissed
Them, wetting them with my tears. The others did the same.
And after all had passed by the saint in reverence,
I gathered up each bone, taking great care not to leave
A single shard behind. We took the anchor as well
Upon our shoulders, gaily, and hastened back to shore.
No sooner had the last man set his foot on the dunes
Above the tide-line, than with a roar renewed, the sea
Rumbled with a horrid pounding, like some fierce storm wind
Racing down from the summits of the Tatra mountains,
Engulfing the world in its booming black cloud-cover.
Terrified all, we spun around to look on, awestruck,
As the waves, released from their chains, swelled higher than Alps
Before crashing to the exposed sea-bed, once again
To cover all with their turquoise, lapping peacefully.
In such a way did the Lord lead me to the saint's relics,
And thus I've brought them here to Rome, where he was born,
From whence he had governed as Vicar Christ's holy Church,
That they might rest here in the honour that is his due'.
   Thus said Konštantín. From the very start, the saint's tomb
Was crowded with ardent petitioners — all in need:
Those seeking relief from suffering lay down their cares
Before him in trust. And lo, the Ruler of Heaven
Glorified His servant through many a miracle.
For whatever the ailment, the weakness, the hardship,
Should the sufferer but approach the martyr's relics
With piety, touching them with reverence, at once
The ailment disappeared, he regained his wonted strength.
The speechless tongue burst out in song, intoning with joy
Praise to the martyr, which the deaf ear suddenly heard.
The blind returned home without anyone to guide them,
Their sight restored; crippled limbs were straightened, in joy
Crutches and canes were cast away as the once lame gaily danced.
All wept for joy, all raised their thanks to God Almighty,
And testified to their healing by the blessed martyr.
To the brothers too they offered thanks, for having brought
So holy a physician to cure them of their ills.
   Now, on the second day, as soon as the sun arose

And banished with its bright beams the cold shadows of night,
Pope Adrian summoned Konštantín and his brother
Methodius before a great synod of clergy
And curia, and with such words did he address them:
'O brethren unstinting in spreading the Faith of Christ!
With what great joy did our heart dance within our bosom
When news arrived of your labours amongst the Kozárs,
Your conversion of the Volgárs, and, at last, your deeds
In bringing the Slovak nation out of the darkness
Of idolatry into the sunlight of Christ's Faith!
How you have enriched the Church of God, and how quickly!
Yet this same heart of mine is troubled at the complaints
Brought before the papal throne by the Bavarians
Accusing you of spreading heresy and error
Shameful, and for having concocted a Slavic Mass.
What good would it be, having loosed men from their bondage
To ancient heresies and witless superstition,
To bind those just freed with fetters of novel schisms?
Thus now we wish to hear the confession of your faith,
So all might plainly know if what you preach is wholesome
Or harmful. What is the reason for your suppression
Of Latin and Greek, so long used in our rituals,
Shunting them aside for Slavonic in your churches?'
  Thus Adrian set the matter before the brothers,
At which Konštantín arose and responded in such words:
'Most pious father! To whom the Church has been entrusted,
And all you, Fathers gathered in holy synod.
I believe all that the Roman Church of Christ teaches,
Founded as it is upon the rock, which never lies.
What She commands us to believe, this is what I teach,
And what I teach, I teach as She bids us to teach.
I preach no heresy, I bring no harm to any!'
  Thus spoke he, after which he professed the Church's creed.
Methodius did the same, departing not a jot
From the Catholic creed, just as his brother had professed.
At this, Pope Adrian's heart rejoiced. He said to them:
'Empty then was the complaint the Bavarians brought us,
For everything that you have taught the Slovaks accords
Entirely with the faith of the Catholic Church.
Praise be to you for these your labours! May your reward

Be great, that with God's aid and graces begged from His throne,
You've led the Slavic nations to endless felicity
In Heaven. May success always crown your blest labours!
But as to the second matter, explain that as well.
What was the reason for your introducing Slavic
Into the Mass, and the other divine offices?'
   Konštantín answered with a sigh: 'O supreme Shepherd
Of all the flocks of Christ! If you ask me what led me
To so many extra labours, to establish
A Slavic rite amongst the newly converted,
I will explain my reasoning, but first I beg you:
If you find my argument sound, deign confirm its use
In those churches where it has been of service.
I had some success preaching the law of Christ among
The valiant Volgárs; wherever I set my foot
Great crowds gathered, and heard the Gospel preached with great joy.
But none showed much interest in the Divine Service;
Indeed, disinclination and distaste could be read
On their faces at my use of a foreign language.
At last they came to me and beseeched me to say Mass
In their church in their tongue, so that they might understand,
Clearly, the holy mysteries, and love them fully.
A long time I resisted, a long while I held back,
Presenting them with all the valid arguments
That might dissuade them from their request... They'd not be moved,
No more than would a rock-face in the Tatra mountains,
They have such a devotion to their spoken language.
Then, one day, as I was out on a long, hot journey
On foot, I came across a meadow near a wellspring:
There was cool shade there, thrown by the tall trees, and birdsong;
The air was filled with the pleasant perfume of flowers.
All this invited me to repose. My mind still churned
With thoughts about what they sought of me — could I really
Abandon the rite to which I was accustomed, and
Introduce a Slavonic liturgy for them
Who begged it so earnestly — enkindling in their hearts
A greater piety thereby? A love for the Mass?
The lazy buzzing of the bees, the quiet whispers
Of the light breezes, and the gentle purl of the stream
Wafted me off to sleep. No sooner had my eyes closed

Than I seemed to see the blue firmament part in two
And a dove descend on golden wings, gently circling
Until softly alighting here, on my left shoulder.
And then I heard it say, in pleasant, soft murmurings:
  "Konštantín, have done with these meditations of yours
Which you turn and turn, endlessly, through your tired brain.
Boldly establish the Slavic rite in your churches
So that the people know what's happening during Mass
While the Holy Sacrifice is taking place upon
The altar; that they should understand the petitions
Raised to God by the priest, and along with their pastor,
All the more warmly present their thanksgiving to God
For His graces bestowed on them. In this way, more men
Will turn from idolatry, and be drawn to the Faith.
In later years, your Slavic rite will spread throughout the world,
For which you shall be remembered as well, and honoured".
  Such did the dove whisper to me. Then, gently, three times
He fluttered above my head before disappearing
Again into Heaven, borne on those golden pennons.
Then came a rushing, as of a great wind from afar,
And a thunderbolt rumbled through the pristine blue sky,
At which I awoke, and the first thought that came to my mind
Was that, which Jesse's son was used to sing to the Lord:
"Let every spirit glorify God!" And Paul, too:
"Forbid not those who speak in tongues". At once I thought that
If praise in Armenian, Syrian, and Coptic
Be raised to the Lord in Church, why not in Slavonic?
The Slavs are a great nation, numerous and widespread.
At this, all doubts on the matter vanished from my heart,
Which burst into flame at the thought of a Slavic Mass.
No more would I oppose the wishes of the people.
I set to work without a moment's hesitation,
Translating the *Ordo*, songs, and all things else needed
For the proper, solemn, celebration of the Mass;
Indeed, as to the music, I had such tropes to hand
As I had already translated in Tsarigrad.
  With all this now prepared, I sought out Methodius.
I learned that he was in the old city of Ternov,
Instructing the people there in the truths of Heaven.
And so I hastened there, and explained all this to him,

What had come to me in that dream, what I intended.
His heart afire too, he wavered not a moment,
But vowed to celebrate the Slavonic Mass himself
And introduce the Slavic language to the churches.
How the hearts of the Slavic faithful then leapt in joy!
Never more willingly had they ever pressed to the Mass;
Never higher had their souls ever soared in ardent
Praise to God the Omnipotent raised from glowing hearts!
When the stubborn pagans who had held back from the Faith
Heard what was happening, they too at last converted,
Abandoning the dark errors of idolatry.
Like tongues of flame the news spread through their kindred nations,
And soon Rastislav, mighty ruler of the Slovaks,
Sent emissaries to our emperor requesting
Like missionaries to labour amongst his people.
And so Michael, our Caesar of the East, whose sceptre
Rules many lands, eagerly agreed to their request.
He chose us two, and sent us to instruct the Slovaks.
They wanted the Slavic Mass. They yearned for priests who spoke
Their tongue, and they gladly sent us here with the request
That you, Holy Father, not forbid their tongue in church!
That's the whole truth; now, judge me: Have I done any wrong
In establishing the Slavonic rite, which has helped
So many? Shall it be forbidden, or authorised?
   He finished, and soon murmuring spread throughout the nave,
First, as softly as the whispers of young couples gathered
To bill and coo in a secluded copse in springtime,
But then it grew in force, like strong gale winds against which
A boat can make no progress; no matter how they gasp
And sweat, the oarsmen, straining toward the other bank
Of the river from which the adverse wind is blowing.
Quite simply, there was no consensus, for too many
Were opposed to the introduction of the new rite,
And neither side could sway the other. When he saw that,
The Supreme Pontiff of Christ's Church addressed the synod:
   'My brothers gathered here, locked in difficult debate!
Those who stand against our Thessalonian prophets
And do not wish to introduce their innovations
To the Church — pause to consider the circumstances
In which the Church finds herself today, threatened with schism.

Then, I reckon, you'll see matters differently.
Although the Patriarch of Constantinople once more
Enjoys the fulness of the authority due him,
Acknowledging our primacy and preserving unity —
How long will that last? Let us say Ignatius should die.
Might Phocius not return to usurp the vacant see,
Exploiting the will of the people, which is ever
Unstable in turbulent times? What should happen then?
He would never cease his efforts to pry away,
In his overweening pride, the Eastern Church from Rome,
Abjuring obedience to the See of Peter,
Declaring himself supreme. For he is a schemer,
And a clever one, too, who will never rest until
He's wheedled both the Volgárs and the Tatra Slovaks
Into his hands. And what better way to do that
Than to authorise the Slavic rite? All the more so,
Since the Eastern Church allows the use, alongside Greek,
Of Syrian, Armenian, and Coptic in Mass?
Indeed, long have those peoples enjoyed that privilege.
So let us as well permit the use of Slavonic
In the realms of both Rastislav and Chocil, so that
Neither have any reason to separate from Rome
And cleave unto the Eastern See. Now, let us grant
The brothers' petition, and allow the Slavic rite
Which, after all, in no way harms the Catholic Faith'.
Thus Adrian's advice. But still the synod dithered,
Back and forth, chewing over the same old arguments
Until, at last, a loud, strange sound was heard. All grew still.
Then a mighty voice resounded from the heavens, thrice
Filling with awe the nave where the priests were assembled:
'Let every spirit praise the Lord! Every tongue
Echoes His glory!' At once, all their doubts were resolved.
No more *sic probos* or scholastic oratory;
Everyone voted 'Aye!' And thus pious Konštantín
Was granted all that he requested: the Slavic Mass,
The Slavic lectionary for use in the Slavic
Churches. His heart overflowing with joy, Konštantín
Poured out words of thanksgiving for this grace, then added:
  'Since now you have authorised the Slavic ritual,
Grant Rastislav this one more, righteous, request he sends

Through me, Holy Father. He begs you to establish
A new see in his realm — as is the custom elsewhere,
Amongst the other nations — a see autonomous
Of the German Church, with a Slavic bishop to guide
The Slavic flock, a brother among brothers, no more
Under Bavarian tutelage and German sway.
This will put an end to all temptations to excess
Pride and banditry. In this way Rastislav wishes
To take his place before you, Father, as an equal
Amongst equal rulers, your ever-obedient son'.

   Thus Konštantín. After a short pause to consider
This request, Pope Adrian turned to him with these words:
'I am prepared as well to grant this wish of pious
Rastislav's, expressing too my gratitude to him
For turning for aid to the Holy See of Peter,
And placing his trust in our fatherly protection.
Now, who might I find more prepared to lead that new see
Than you two? Thus, in the church of St Clement Martyr,
Three days hence, I shall ordain you bishops, appointing
You both to shepherd the Church in the Slavic lands'.

   This was his determination. The synod agreed,
And when the third sun had dawned over the seven hills
Of Rome, they were raised to episcopal dignity,
And the seminarians they'd brought with them ordained
To the priesthood, with all the rights pertaining thereto.
After their ordination, the Holy Father said:

     'And now, dear brethren, return to the land whence you came,
No longer dependent on Bavarian overlords.
You, Konštantín, we appoint as metropolitan.
Methodius, be obedient to him in all.
Celebrate the Mass in Slavic, give glory to God
In that tongue, and cleanse those lands of any remaining
Error of paganism and foul idolatry.
Erect new churches, administer in order
Calm and consecutive, appointing to parishes
These young disciples of yours, now your priestly brothers.
Above all, teach the people, and lead them to virtue,
Shepherding your great nations to eternal glory.
May the Lord bless you, and crown your labours with success.
We, on our part, shall always keep you close in our prayers,

Unstinting in fervent petitions on your behalf'.
 Thus spoke Pope Adrian, after which, with his blessings,
Embracing them, he sent them back to Slovakia.

SLÁV
A Heroic Poem in Six Cantos

CANTO I

Bondor the daring, hearing that the Tatrans
Had smashed the army of the Chudes sent there
For pillaging, calls all men capable
Of bearing arms to gather for revenge.
First of all, lifting prayers of praise to Ár,
The god of his fathers, he begs the advice
Of all the more renowned of the Chude elders,
How best to strike the Tatra lands: as one,
In sudden blow, at one place, or in three
Dividing the large host? The council leans
To casting all their lots on one bold rush.
Bondor then visits the warriors assembled
In great numbers, exhorting them to fight
In vengeance for their comrades' shameful rout,
At which he leads them on swift-footed steeds
Against the Tatra Slavs. While on their way
They meet Dízabo, who once had set out
Against the Slovak lands to ravage them.
From him they learn of the catastrophe
That cruelly smote their brothers. Bondor then
Sets out again, with no more hesitation,
For the Slovak homeland, which he condemns
By solemn oath to thorough desolation.
Wherever they alight, they raze and ravage
All structures: homes of men and sacred temples
Burning to ash along with the gods' idols.

I sing of Sláv, who shattered the savage invaders
Set on pillaging his realm, and slaughtering his folk,
Thus liberating them from a horrid destruction.
Umka, who high upon thy Tatran throne dost preserve
The deeds of thy folk, unerring chronicler, who best
Rememberest each episode of thy nation's past,
Speed now unto my aid, who seek to plumb the dark mists
Of battles past and long forgotten, who most of all
Would our most ancient father conjure before the eyes
Of present generations, for they derive their august
Name, the Slavs, from him, our most worthy protoplast!
A hard task — difficult! But if Thou come to my aid,
Teaching me what I know not, enflaming my cold heart
With inspiration, strengthening, sharpening my sight,
My song shall flow lightly, coursing onward to success.
Indeed, I feel a strong rush of light flush through me now —
Dost Thou sing, Umka? Am I bathed in thy bright kenning?
I feel my bosom swell, my thoughts flash with sacred fire,
I see it all now, clearly, my reason enkindled,
The great deeds of Sláv, our hero, accomplished of old!
   And you, who most gladly give ear to tales of ancient
Exploits wrought by our forefathers, who sing of them, too
Most willingly — champion yourself in the battles
Against all who tilt against the glory of the Slavs,
You, always victorious! Friend dearest to my soul,
O most brilliant ornament of our Tatran nation!
Incline a kindly ear to this my song, of Umka
Inspired, as I recall the deeds of our great voivode,
Heroic Sláv, who, at the head of his doughty hosts,
Cast aside ploughshare to take up the sword, and after
Entrusting themselves to Svatovít with sacrifice,
Rushed upon the invading enemy and routed them,
Slashing to pieces the cruel, abominable foe.
   Bondor the daring, lord of the empty expanses
Held by the Chudes, was awaiting his raw marauders
Sent off to pillage the Slovaks of the high Tatras.
With what unfettered luxury did he salivate
At the thought of the slaves, and the herds, and the riches
They would be bringing home from their rampaging, and ah!
The fat share of the booty that would fall to his lot!

But then Rumour, that strangest beast of one hundred eyes,
One hundred ears and just as many tongues chattering
Endlessly, whose legs scamper more swiftly than arrows,
Flitting here and there, to brood in settled places
And spawn, like countless roe, her progeny among men;
Who prattles all things, the true, the false, and the uncertain,
Leading men to see bulls where are nothing but rabbits,
And rearing Plešivec hill up past Kriváň's steep tip,
Swelling Blava streamlet into the River Volga —
Rumour came to him now — but speaking truth — of the rout
Of his men at the hands of the tame Slovaks, unskilled,
Supposedly, at war… There was to be no booty;
All his men, whipped, were enslaved by those they would enslave.
Only a small fragment had escaped slaughter or chains,
And these were skulking terrified through the mountain wilds,
Starting at every twig-snap, despairing of return.
As soon as Bondor heard this, he swelled black with venom.
As when a bear returns to his den and discovers
It empty, his cubs stolen by a daring Cossack
To train them to leap and dance to the strains of fiddle
For the entertainment of the crowds at village fairs —
So rabid flames coursed through his arteries, scorching flesh
And bone. Sparks of wrath filled his eyes; his limbs were trembling
With ire. Amidst howls of rage, he fulminated thus:
   'So this is the booty you bring home from your raiding?
Where are the slaves you promised? Where, the herds of cattle?
What a great name you've made yourselves! What sublime glory
You've won for your arms and your nation! What has become
Of the valour of the Chudes? Their great power, their speed?
What's happened to the hearty bravery, undaunted,
Of the rulers of the steppe? Now you have been thrashed, whipped
By villainous bumpkins unaccustomed to the sword,
Who never up till now have been victorious in war —
Such as these you've allowed to run roughshod over you?
Shame! Horrid, never to be lived down! Brother Ednek,
Where are you now, otherwise valiant, now so tainted,
Foul with disgrace! The enslaver enslaved, the slayer
Slaughtered! The predator become the prey of trembling small-fry!
The dogs and ravens of the Tatras will glut themselves
On your dishonoured flesh. But still I will avenge you;

I shall not let your bones be scattered and made sport of
Without wreaking sharp revenge upon my enemies.
I shall wipe clean the blemish of your cowardliness;
I shall obliterate the deep shame you've brought on me.
Enjoy your victory while you may, warlike Slovaks!
For it shall cost you much — O, a salty price you'll pay!
Life for life and man shall pay for man in strict reckoning.
However many warriors you've killed, so many
Shall we offer in sacrifice, their blood slaking
My throat now parched with the bloodletting of my Chudes.
And when the tally-sheet is even, the rest I shall
Bind in heavy fetters of cruel slavery.
Each house I will burn to ashes, leaving in my wake
Scorched earth where once were towns, desert wilderness of soot'.
   Thus did he rant and fume. Then he decreed that all men
Who might bear arms should gather at once. As in winter,
When winds like wolves race howling over the Tatra meads
And never cease their clamour until all the sheep-flocks
Huddle in fright, bracing together for warmth, so he
Pummelled about the Chudes with ranting and rough bluster.
Thus the startled Chudes, as soon as the order was given,
Drew near from all parts, galloping on fleet-footed steeds
Jostling against one another in panicked haste, until
They'd gathered at the place allotted to hear further
Commands — as if anything could be heard! — rough voices
Out-shouting each other, impatient hoof beats drumming
The earth; but then the king approached his forefathers' god,
The warlike Ár, in his gloomy brambled den. No ray
Of clean sunlight ever pierced the dank miasmatic air:
Eternal darkness reigned within that copse, and nothing
But horrid, cruel wails were heard there, and the clashing
Of blades at midnight. No grass grows there; no fragrant blooms;
The humid soil rots and exhales a poisonous stench.
Even werewolves, who terrorise men, avoid the place,
Shuddering to enter the terrifying thicket.
No gentle Veles there toots love-songs upon his pan-pipe;
No Vila's gentle foot taps the earth in wheeling dance-steps;
No Rusalka adorns her hair with such reeking weeds —
They like not sluggish streams choked with reptiles, nor cavort
In filthy bogs. No bird winds her nest in pestilent

Umbrage, nor brightens the mournful wilderness with song —
Only the raucous croak of scavenger crow is heard,
And the hooting of owls, which makes men's skin to crawl.
Should any forest beast stumble near, the fur bristles
Along his spine, and in panic he shuffles backwards,
His tail between his legs, until he can spin and flee.
Even the wolf, who fears nothing else, shuns the blasted
Thickets. Only man strides boldly in where the wise beast
Will not venture. For here the Chudes offer sacrifice
Bloody, of fellow and foe, whoever has no right
To law or respect in such hearts as respect no law —
Humans in sacrifice to their god preeminent!
As if God were pleased with murder and cruel torments
Imposed upon men by man — brothers soiling their hands
In brothers' gore! Insane thought — would He not be the more
Aroused to anger by such unhallowed crimes? Alas,
Man's understanding determines his acts, and reason,
Corrupted by sin, spawns only deeds of bloody crime.
On the other hand, rarely did they sacrifice stallions
Now, only emaciated jades, and furthermore
The gods had to be satisfied with lapping horse-blood,
As the Chudes reserved the paltry gristle and marrow
To themselves. Into such a foul enclosure Bondor
Entered, fuming with wrath, to offer his praise to Ár.
He held a lad of beauteous face and strapping limbs
Named Tirák — booty from a raid in the Tauris lands.
Three times six years he'd barely aged, the fluff on his chin
Was just beginning to stiffen into a man's beard.
Not only Bondor loved the boy — all and sundry there
Amongst the savage Chudes were drawn to him at first sight.
Although that raw nation couldn't bear any stranger,
But looked upon all non-Chudes with fierce wrath and loathing,
Whenever the Chude maidens happened to catch a glimpse
Of the boy, their untamed hearts fell prisoner to love;
Broken and softened, they sighed after his great beauty.
And now, just such a lad Bondor orders sacrificed!
The cruel priest had never before hacked at such a face,
Though more than two thousand men he had thrust from this world
With cruel axe-blows, but then — his arms grew limp, the blade
Thudded to the floor of the filthy grotto, harmless.

Seeing this, Bondor was not moved to pity; the black
Flames in his hard heart but bellowed to wilder raging.
He unsheathed his own sword and plunged it into the breast
Of the youth, to the very hilt. The child's blood spurted,
Outraged, crying to heaven to be revenged. He fell,
Like a tender violet snapped by a sudden wind,
Down on the moist earth, his lovely limbs crumpling helpless
Onto his own gore. His eyes grew dim, his rosy blush
Ebbed to blank pallor, his cooling corpse stiffened in death's
Freezing embrace, while his soul fled to eternity.
Suddenly, the savage killer cried out in loud voice:
  'Ár, god of battles! Who ever enflamest our hearts
With manly courage, and never permittest our swords
Bent like sickles to wallow long dormant in their sheaths,
Who leadest us in war, and prickest us on to slaughter
With pitiless rage the strangers upon whom we rush,
Shattering their forces; who regalest us with trains
Of cattle and human chattel to nourish, enrich,
And serve thy people, for which ever the best portion
Is reserved unto thee; for now, be satisfied with this
One sacrifice, the dearest I might ever offer!
But if thou givest us to rout the Tatrans in war,
Corralling all the scattered who avoid the first slash
Of battle-sword, to lead them here safely with the herds
We wrest from them, I swear to thee, that not only one,
But one hundred souls of the most renowned Slovak youths
Will fall before thee, to glut thee at bloody bever
Along with one hundred stallion foals prancing with vim!'
  His horrid prayer finished, the cruel murderer withdrew
At once from the gory copse and returned to his tent,
There to debate long in council with his folks' elders
How best to attack the Tatran land: in one fell swoop,
Forces massed? Or, dividing his horde into three troops,
To invade at three points before pushing in to meet?
The council split in two, each party pressing its point.
Long smouldered the quarrel, neither side the upper hand
Gaining. Like jackdaws in the treetops yammering
At one another they sounded, until Losid, rich
In spoils of old (when successful raids yielded pillage)
Uprose and directed these words at the assembly:

'O great king, and all you elders gathered in council!
Were we to fall upon the Tatrans with massed force,
It would be easier to slaughter their forward ranks
Than to bind them in withers and carry them off as spoils,
While the ranks to the rear would scatter. The highlanders
Would seek shelter in the caves among the mountains there
Out of reach, as once I learned from Výboh, whom Bundok
Had taken captive, when he'd wandered into our land
Ignorant of Chudan law, which condemns each stranger
Who arrives here to be taken prisoner at once,
To be slaughtered, his flesh to serve at a solemn feast —
Though he himself skirted that fate, for just as the priest
Was prepared to strike, with uplifted axe, to assuage
With his blood the anger of Ár for a three year-long
Neglect of raiding, a sudden gale blew up, thunder
Boomed, and from the skies some god descended, armed with spear
Of flaming lightning to snatch him, into the dark clouds
Returning on his chariot of fire. The lowland
Folk, on the other hand, will disperse into thicket
And marsh — Yes! into the very depths of lake and stream
They'll hide, escaping us by sorcery, like Výboh —
I've heard that they can live underwater, for whole days
On end! And who among us will plummet through such pits,
Or stumble about sharp summit, or wade through foot-sucking
Bog, or thread though thicket, sound the lakebeds — we are not
Lynx or pike, but men! — searching in vain to locate prey
Elusive in den enchanted? Better to divide
Our force, then, into three, and to attack from three sides,
To round them up in a circling net, confused, as we
Herd them panicked from side to side, in constricting web
Of horse and man. Less bloody battle, less risk, more spoils
Of man and beast shall fall into our victorious hands'.
   Thus Losid. At which aged Lotand, on creaking knee
Uprose, trembling, his face furrowed by Time's deep harrow
And scarred in battles of yore by blades long rusted now.
Tottering unsteadily on a thick staff, he spoke:
'It's true enough that we should obtain richer booty
If everything turns out according to Losid's boast:
We should also come across more nourishment — stallions
And people — for future expeditions of pillage.

But when force is divided, that force becomes weaker,
And smaller parts are less effective than one great whole.
It's hard to snap three rods joined. By themselves, they're flimsy.
Consider the booming Don or the broad Boristen:
When they push out their waters into narrow fingers
Of side-channels dredged through silt, they lose all their power.
But when they roll on along one single riverbed,
And undivided storm their way to the broad ocean,
How they roar! How they foam! Unstoppable energy!
Even the canniest find it difficult to cross
A mighty river in flood. But shallow channels? Why,
Ponies can ford them, hardly dampening their fetlocks!
What if some scout — only one! — on fleet-footed charger
Should catch sight of one softened regiment and rush off
To announce their advent to the Tatrans? Would they not
Storm up in force and overwhelm that portion? And so:
We're one-third weakened, they've grown one-third more confident,
Emboldened by that victory, and thus they set off
To smash our second, and third, companies, one by one!
Strike with one force, I say! Let us overwhelm the ranks
Of those who first oppose us; there will be time enough
Thereafter to sweep up the remaining scraps and orts.
And what is more, you'll have the advantage of surprise
Over the unsuspecting, unalarmed countryside
Before news of the invasion reaches there, to pluck
And lasso the unwarned Slovaks. You'll have your booty —
You'll fairly depopulate all of Tatrania!
O, what a curse old age is! If not for droopy brawn
And palsied vigour, how I should wish to go with you!
If only I still had the might of my youthful days!
When the hard-pressed Mízi nation called to us for aid,
Struggling against the valiant Thracians in fierce battle,
How many did I slay! Including Bisto, of all
The mightiest in their ranks! He had lain low hundreds
Of Mízi in the first scrums before rushing on us,
Thinking to wreak such havoc in the ranks of the Chudes.
But his bloodlust was in vain. He had but taken aim
At Bikindo when I rushed upon him like a gale
Blowing down suddenly from the peaceful blue heavens,
Unlooked-for, spitting his throat with my lightning-bolt spear.

He fell to the sand now wet and befouled with his gore
To thrash about a while on all sides, crazily,
With futile battle-axe, burbling curses through a voice box
Shattered, chords loosened like the catgut of a smashed lute.
And later, when the Mízi drew back at the sharing
Of spoils, withholding the portion we demanded,
I called them out — "Come on, the strongest there among you —
We'll settle our accounts right now, one by one, just me
And you, and you, and then you!" O, how they trembled then!
They wanted nothing to do with me! Meekly, rather,
They handed over all that we asked for, and then some!
If only now I were the lad I was — with that speed,
That might — I'd gladly meet my end in Slovakia
Rather than here, with sluggish blood and limbs ungainly,
Feeble and palsied, broken with age, withering
In a cold and silent tent, against my will my shield
And spear rattled by the mocking breeze that giggles through
As they rest against the tent-post, gathering dust! Go,
Set off to pillage, fortunate ones! And if you do
As I advise, you'll have success. All will turn out well'.
  So saying, he slumped back down, wiping away a tear.
The men gathered in council were convinced by his words:
Each and all present, including the king, thought the same,
And without a moment's hesitation more, set off
For their quarters to incite all capable of war
For murder and pillage in the land of the Tatrans.
Soon time matured unto that fateful hour when the horde
Should mass, as ordered, on the limitless rusty sands
Of that desert oceanic, stretching endlessly
On all hands, pitiless and barren. As in autumn,
When dry leaves numberless cover the Trenčín vales,
Or blades of grass the meadows near Nové Zámky
In springtime they crowded, and at their head was Bondor,
Coursing the first ranks on his spry, fleet-footed charger.
Such a great host would never press upon Svatopluk,
Sláv's scion, three hundred years later, though whole thousands
Of Magyars would gather, on the other hand Germans
With Volgárs allied; nor would such great armies gather
On the plains near Leipzig to dam with their breasts the flood
Of the overflowing Seine, which sought to submerge Europe.

Impossible it would be to reckon up that horde
Of the godforsaken Chudes, so thickly gathered, the earth
Sagged sighing beneath the burden — a forest of spears
With their angry metal tips flashing in the sunlight
Like the ice-capped crowns of soaring pines in winter-time.
The clamour of the massed men's voices and pummelling
Hoof beats roared like a distant sea when stark hurricanes
Suck from the sand-beds astonished mountains of water
To hurl them upon the rocky shoreline. Ah, woe, woe
To the fertile fields that lie before them! Woe to man
And beast, upon whom such swarms of locusts should alight,
That plague of banditry set on slaughter and rapine!
From prancing mount, the king regarded his marauders:
'O great-hearted Chudes! Who sow terror and black despair
Amongst the surrounding peoples; who every nation
Against whom you set your hand you grind into the dust,
Overcoming them not only with arms unvanquished —
Overtaking them too, escaping, on swift ponies!
You have been waiting long on the return of brothers
Sent into the foothills of Slovakia, waiting
Eagerly upon the looted wealth, the fattened herds,
The fruits of their pillaging with eager, greedy hearts!
But know: that vile nation, who have neither war-chief
Nor noble weaponry, who know neither battle, nor
How sweet it is to ride to war and return with loot,
Expert at nothing but slave-labour, at war with dirt,
Incessantly hacking the tired earth with horse-drawn blade,
Stabbing it with their hoes and battering with shovels,
Heaping as treasure whatever loot — in vegetables! —
They tear from her womb — well, just such a wretched rabble
Have shattered those brothers of yours, including Ednek,
My own! That force decimated, the meek survivors
Led off into shameful slavery! A mere handful,
It seems, have avoided catastrophe, and these now
Wander about the high mountains there, quaking in fear,
Unable to find their way back to the Chude homeland.
Now what will men think of the power of the fierce Chudes
After such a humiliating, shameful defeat?
Well, now we must wipe our disgrace from the memory
Of man, by exacting our just and bloody revenge

Upon the people of the Tatras. Death to the Slovaks!
In one massed force we shall invade their land, enslaving
Those who shiver defenceless before us, binding them
In the tight fetters of cruel subjugation, while those
Who should dare raise a weapon against us in defence
Of their land — who should dare toss a pebble our way,
Who should dare raise a finger against us! — we shall slay
With our pitiless sword. We shall not leave a soul there
Alive: all shall be slaughtered, or led away as slaves,
Along with their fattened cattle, and anything
Combustible there, we shall give over to wild flames.
Let there be no Tatrania left after your passage,
But all that's worth anything, we'll bring back to our land.
Our god has promised us this victory; he himself
Revealed this to me, when in his oak grove I fed him
The most precious morsel that I could offer to him'.

   Thus he, at which their hearts were set aflame, the venom
Within them overflowing at their lips like the foam
Of rabid dogs. Horrid cries assaulted the air, in ire,
As they screamed out for vengeance, the extermination
Of the people of the Tatras. All lusted to strike,
All swore to lap the hot blood of the slaughtered Slovaks,
The godless mob! They vowed to stitch new cloaks of skin
And hair, and turn empty skulls into drinking cups.
Then, just as a cloud that has brooded long on Bílá
Hora tumbles down the slopes, urged by a savage wind,
Cloaking the world in darkness howling with gloomy gales,
Shaking bolts of lightning like crossed swords, thunder booming
Throughout the valleys cringed beneath the assault of hail,
Thus did the bloodthirsty horde surge forth with wild hoofbeats
Screaming with lust for the loot of the Tatra highlands.
The dust kicked up by their horses' hooves darkened the sun
And plunged the whole world into eerie, early nightfall.
They paused not in their savage rush through the empty steppe:
Like an angry river in flood, they followed the sun
And not only — they kept up the march even at night,
Until at last they reached the lofty brows of the Tatras.
While they were on their way to pillage, they came across
Dízabo, whom they led before the king with wild shouts
Of rejoicing. From him they had a harsh report of woe:

The catastrophe that met their marauding brothers.
But when he saw the wretch led near, Bondor spurred his steed,
Galloping up before him, to address him thusly:
   'Where is my loot? Where is the pillage you promised me
Upon setting out for this land? How did it happen
That such bold warriors adept at wielding weapons
Where whipped by unmanly rabble untrained in battle?
How could such overcome you? And why are you not dead?
Did you preserve your life through shameless flight? Turning tail?
Speak! Tell us now what happened to you and your brave mates!'
   Dízabo gulped, and then began his tale in order:
'We arrived in the Tatras safely, losing no man.
It is a land most beautiful, full of all good things
Necessary to life; no land there lies long fallow:
Grain fields burgeoning, orchards full of maturing fruit.
The lush meadows there are clothed with blossoms and thick grass
Adorning vale and hillside. Innumerable flocks
And herds wander there at pasture; music fills the air,
Trilling from copse and field too, for birds and people
— Industrious, working their plots with joy — seem to vie
With one another, the latter making light their tasks
With song. As for us, all was looking propitious:
Massing our force, we rushed upon them in one fierce wave;
We met no resistance, no obstacle in our path.
But then the fifth sun had barely cracked the heavens
And we had gathered all our booty for transport —
A fine taking! Men, youths, boys, women of splendid face,
Maidens whiter than driven snow — a whole host of them!
Seven whole herds of stallions and mares, along with foals,
And three times as many head of cattle and rich flocks:
Six of sheep and goats and swine — an exquisite treasure!
And I'm not mentioning the wealth we might have pillaged,
Had not our leaders put an end to our looting, saying
That we'd had enough to keep us busy on the road
With this take, driving it all to our Chudan homeland.
And so we prodded forward our captives and the herds,
While we rode on behind them, always on the look-out
Lest the Tatrans, enraged, should fall upon us in turn.
And this they were to do, to wreak their bloody revenge!
There was a longish plain in the midst of scattered orchards;

Narrow-throated, though broad enough to the rear, a swollen
River flowed through the mid-plain, roaring with mighty voice.
On both sides of the vale soared high, star-scraping mountains
With thickets of beech at their feet, and here and there cliffs
Like impregnable battlements. So rocky the soil
That the chargers had to pick their way through the rubble,
Clumsily. It was on the third evening, in that vale,
That we stopped to offer our thanksgiving to great Ár
For providing us with such magnificent pillage:
Seven black-maned steeds, seven bulls, and three youths, slaughtered.
We shared a portion of the butchered sacrifices
Amongst us, regaling ourselves with the fatty meat
Which we'd roasted on our campfires far into the night.
Then, after we'd satisfied our hunger, we lay down
To sleep. At dawn, when the ruddy cheeks of the new day
Blushed in the sky, chasing off the dark shades of the night,
We saddled our horses and moved off, quick-pace, for home.
We had barely left our campsite when, from a distance
Of three arrow-shots — should each archer let fly his dart
As soon as the earlier reached him — we heard a shout
From the rear that a mob of Tatrans was drawing near.
We turned and lashed our steeds, and soon enough met with them:
They were not many, but each was as stout as an oak
Of the mountains, as lithe as a water-loving ash.
Their weapons were axes and shafts hardened in the fire
— And some had spears too! — though none among them carried swords.
A fierce battle commenced. On one side and the other
It was our young heroes, expert in arms, who fell slain.
But when great-soulled Ednek, roaring like a wild tiger
Wounded, cut down whole heaps of the fierce foe, they withdrew
A space — but this was merely a lull in the tempest.
For soon a horn sounded, and they were upon us again
In closed ranks, and the ferocious battle recommenced.
As we were cutting down the boldest of those farmlads,
A roaring blizzard of stone began to pelt our lines:
A new swarm of Tatrans emerged from the thick cover
Of both slopes of the valley, hurling flint and rubble
— Though they had archers too, who sent death whistling from afar —
Whizz after whizz, crash upon crash, like a thunderstorm
That suddenly blots out the light, and as our men sheltered

— Or tried to — from the barrage of missiles, their army
— For such we must name it! — rushed upon us in renewed
And furious attack, while some of them slipped past us
To free their brothers whom we had earlier taken.
Those set there to watch over our booty abandoned it
Before the Slovaks enraged, who had rightly divined
Our murder of their men. Ours raced into the mountains
Where they found refuge. The Slovaks then freed our captives;
Some they delegated to drive the cattle back home
While they outfitted the abler amongst them with arms.
These rushed upon us with all the fury of the wronged.
Ednek, caught off balance (he was struggling in the midst
Of a swarm of foes) bellowed ferociously "Cut off
That path!" so hard-pressed were the troops, this new irruption
Was sure to overwhelm them. Like a pack of famished
Wolves who come across a flock of sheep without shepherd,
We fell upon the Slovaks at the pass, cutting down
Many. I myself sent to the gloom two times seven
Of their boldest in the front line. Ednek, like a reaper with scythe
Slashing flat the dewy grass, mowed down all attackers,
But then the leader of the mob, a valiant man
Named Sláv, slew him with a cruel thrust of his ashen spear.
In vain we strove to avenge our leader's death; in vain
We sought to cut a path now through the milling
Crowd of our enemies — there were far too few of us,
And far too many of them. We were so sorely packed
We could neither raise our right arms to deliver blows
Nor our left to lessen the impact of theirs, falling
Upon us constantly — or the quick bolts of arrows
Or the stones that fell like hail from the cliffs to the sides —
Soon they were taking prisoners: binding from the back
Their arms exhausted and immobilised. I, half-dead
With blood-loss, was lifted from the ground and borne away
By a certain Jaroslav. He extracted the dart
That had punctured my back, and then, rinsing clean the wound
With water and herbs medicinal, made a poultice
Of ground roots, which he changed often. In less than two months
I was completely healed. He then compacted with me,
That I should serve him for the space of fifty moons,
And when my indenture should run its course, I could choose

Whether to remain amongst his folk as a free man,
Or return to my homeland. I didn't wait so long!
When he and all his household departed for a feast
Of their god Perún, I took to my heels; I escaped.
And now I beg you — take revenge upon the Tatrans
For their foul murder of our men. With bloody slaughter
Liberate your brothers from their cruel slavery.
I'll lead you to them, as I know the roads there by heart'.
   Thus he. At once the king gave the order to set out.
As soon as they were well within the Slovak land
Bondor, enraged, directed such speech at his raiders:
'Now it is ours, revenge; now shall we avenge the shame
Of our brothers! Amass great booty! Rub out the men,
Fire their buildings — make a wasteland of Tatrania!
Thus did he bellow — at which they responded with howls
Of bloodlust, rattling their swords, before galloping forth
Like a flooding river in springtime that bears away
Even great boulders. They ruined all that lay athwart
Their path — a grand conflagration that turned the sky red
And black with the billowing smoke, the earth — to ash.
Everywhere panic reigned, everywhere terror, the gods
Themselves were not spared in their fanes; their altars awash
With the blood of their priests, each temple burnt to the ground.

CANTO II

Živa, in dread, flies to father Perún's throne
To save her dear Tatrans from catastrophe.
He vows that evil will not go unpunished,
And to provide his faithful with the strength
To crush the cruel invaders. Svatovít
He then dispatches from the heights of Heaven
To lead the Slovaks, roused, in the fierce battle.
Meanwhile, Oslad he sends into the camp
Of the raw Chudes, them to regale at feasting,
The while the irate Slovaks draw upon them.
These gather now at Sláv's command, inspired
By the father of the gods. The Chudes are fired
With lust for pillaging and savage deeds
By Oslad, who appears in dream to Bondor
With Ednek's face. He begs him celebrate
His rites funeral on the Oborín Plain.
This Bondor vows, but only when the land
Entire has been annihilated. Still,
Upon rising he calls his horde together
So that an offering might be made unto
The great god of the Chudes — intent upon
Fulfilling all the rest of the false Ednek's
Commands for wreaking bloody retribution.

The while the merciless Chudes were wreaking savage ruin,
Živa, the mother, whose image had been burnt to ash
By the invaders along with her temple (adorned
Inside and out with clever carvings), and furthermore
Her servant Čestislav, burdened with years — clapped in irons
Along with fair-faced Dobruslava his young daughter, led off
Into harsh servitude — hastened unto the starry
Hearth of Perún. Her hair undone, loose, and unadorned
With the garlands of wheat and blossoms that so often
Graced her white brows, she fell before the god's golden throne
And formed this urgent plea with her most pious lips:

'Sky-ruler, O father, wielder of the lightning bolt,
Governor of the tempest, supreme lord of the laws,
And agriculture, and truth, avenger of the wronged
Who always punishes unrighteousness with justice!
Since the earth's fertility was entrusted to me,
To provide all nourishment, both daily and festive,
It was my desire to lead people to batten on
Beechnuts and acorns, both sweet and bitter windfalls,
Fresh leafy vegetables and crisp nutritive tubers
And roots, rather than — as savage beasts — to feed on meat.
I wished to incline them to a gentler husbandry!
And thus did I teach them to yoke the plodding oxen
And groove the sillion in even rows for planting.
Thus I presented them with the seeds of varied plants —
I taught them to sow and reap when the crop matures;
To winnow the chaff and to mill the health-giving grain,
And how to prepare the yield in succulent dishes.
Of all the nations, the Slovaks are dearest to me,
For eagerly they heed me, wholly devoting themselves
To the soil, which rewards them ever with abundance.
No other people is so wedded to sweet tillage!
They know no weaponry, they are not a warlike tribe.
Rapine and pillage are terms unknown to them, who earn
What they enjoy from honest toil. They need no war-chief!
Far from vice and harm, they live in peace. Fearing the gods,
They raise our images amidst their broad, fertile fields,
And on wooded hills they erect us splendid temples.
They honour us with annual holidays and rites
Of frequent feasting — for all these reasons, I've chosen
To live amongst them particularly, protecting
Them specially, bestowing my favour upon them.
But now, the horrid Chudes, who serve only their god Ár,
Who raise no monument nor fane to any others
And hold our gifts in contempt, working no furrow,
Preferring the flesh of horses, beasts — and even men! —
To consume from filthy trenchers, nor have they cities
Or villages as do the cultured peoples, but roam
From grassland to grassland dragging their flimsy tents
Behind them as they wander on in search of murder
For which they lust no less than booty — O, foul bandits!

Now such a savage mob has fallen upon my folk!
The ripened corn in the fields, the grass of the meadows
Is trampled down by hooves, and everything that serves man
And beast for nourishment is overturned in ruin.
Flourishing city and populous village alike
Are pulverised — indeed — ah, the godless horde! — temples
Of the gods are reduced to ash; billowing black clouds
Obscure the sunlight — how close to your throne they rise!
They rustle herd and flock, and bind in fetters whole crowds
Of people, yoking them enslaved. With their cruel swords
They run through the innocent, and what they have in mind
Is nothing less than the annihilation the whole
Land of Tatrania, and the subjection, as slaves,
Of the Slovaks. And then where shall I go? What new folk
Must I search out to live among? Who will honour me?
Who will nourish me with the incense of sacrifice?
For my own tabernacle, where I lived, is now ash —
Fired by the Chudes. Now, when they drag off to slavery
My fervent faithful, this whole land will lie desolate,
Depopulated! Can you endure such injustice?
Will you permit such godless, evil ones, the sworn foes
Of our godhood, to deracinate our worshippers?
Turn your eye thither, O father omnipotent!
Incline your ear to my pleas, and the prayers that arise
From a people who cannot raise fettered hands toward you
In supplication. Deflect this evil from their heads,
Enflame Slovak hearts with courage and enable them
To overcome, with strength united, these marauders!
Grind beneath your heel the heads of those who deserve it.
For why should such a nation infest the earth, whose aim
Is pillage, who ceaselessly slash with their shameful swords
At the innocent, murdering them, devastating
The earth like a plague of locusts, leaving nought behind!'
  Thus Mother Živa. The great ruler of the cosmos,
Perún, then directed such words to her: 'Sweet mother,
Great goddess of the earth's fecundity! Be at peace;
Chase from your heart those black fears, and once again be gay.
I shall avenge all the wrongs done to your worshippers;
I shall not leave such cruelty without punishment;
I should cease to hurl my lightning bolts of justice

Were I ever to forget the merits of your folk
The gentle, good, hardworking Slovaks, who offer harm
To no one. Know then, that I've grown tired of the Chudes,
And so I have allowed them to invade Slovakia
In such numbers, only so as to bring them to ruin.
For now they shall serve as an evident example
To other bandits, who the patient work of ages
And other hands would ruin in one frenzied moment,
Who find their joy in murder and rapine. They shall die
To the last raider unless they abjure pillaging
And settle, to live by law, like the Tatran people —
Yes, they shall all perish by the sword they wield themselves.
The Slovak heart shall swell with courage, the Slovak arm
Too, with the might of my thunderbolt. I shall strike down
This plague of murderers and liberate their captives,
Returning their cattle, their flocks, which were torn from their hands,
And in short order make the ravaged land lush once more.
Your monuments despoiled will rise anew, your temples
Shall rise again from their ashes in all their beauty,
And you shall live again in honour there, enjoying
The daily sacrifice raised by your most pious Slavs.
What's more, their nation shall spread far and wide, the people
Multiplying in peace, waxing in power, until
Their holdings stretch from the Northern to the Southern Sea.
They shall occupy the lands where others dwell, including
The Chudes', which lies fallow. Such desert wastes they shall cause
To flourish with abundant culture. The Slavic folk
Shall swell into the most numerous of all nations,
A realm immense! And as they are now, so shall they be
Forever your faithful worshippers. Never the plough
Shall be far from their calloused palm, which shall never reach
For the sword, unless it be in need, when strangers attack
As now, when in defence of their land they shall be fierce:
A terror of inexorable, mighty warriors!'
   Thus spoke Perún. Then, as a token of his promise,
The clear sky flashed with his thunderbolt, which echoed long,
Its sharp point spitting the astonished land of the Chudes
In bitter omen. At this, Mother Živa, appeased,
Took heart, refreshed as the parched fields baked to grey powder
Beneath the pitiless sun sigh with gratitude

When, slaked at last by the steady, gentle, cool rainfall,
Each stalk rises supple for having drunk to the roots,
The meads, clothed in fresh green again, turn a smiling face
To the serene blue of the heavens. Thus Živa smiled,
Her beauty returning in all its wonted splendour,
A sheaf in her right hand, in her left a bright bouquet.
   Then the first of all gods and the governor of men,
In order to fulfil all the more quickly the vow
Made to the fecund goddess of the harvest, summoned
Svatovít, and spoke thus to him: 'Because the Tatrans,
Dear to my heart, have always led a peaceful life,
Knowing no conflict, to say nothing of cruel war,
They have never needed to worship a martial god.
But ever since they shattered the fierce Chudan bandits
Who had invaded their land for pillage, valiant Sláv
Has added you to the pantheon of the Slovaks.
With great urgency they are raising a splendid fane
In your honour, carving from linden wood an idol,
Four-faced. A priest has been ordained, and a milk-white steed
Vowed unto you, so that you might lead them in battle
Against each evil foe, unto final victory.
If ever man needed your mighty arm, it is now,
For a massed horde of Chudes has once again invaded
The land, spreading terror and harm. And so I bestow
Upon you might in warfare, to lead them to blest peace.
Be also an oracle unto them, predicting
Future times to gird your worshippers in readiness.
Take now this sand-whetted ploughshare as your sword, and sling
This longbow from your shoulder, this quiver of arrows
Tinct with my thunder, each of which shall return at once
To its case after striking its target in defence
Of the oppressed, O new god of war of the Slovaks!
Now, hasten to the aid of those threatened with ruin
And liberate their brothers groaning in slavery.
Increase the power of their brawny arms; fill their souls
With courage as they plant their feet firm to the onslaught
In which you are to fight as well. And if the Chudan god
Should stand in defence of that rabble, rush against him
And batter him with your sword of thunder, making him
Fly the battlefield. Grind that foul horde into the dust

And lead your Slovak side to victory. The grateful
Folk will call upon you when in need of your great might
To defend them against their murderous enemies.
I shall consider you first among all Slovak gods;
You shall enjoy great honour and splendid offerings'.
   Barely had the ruler of the cosmos uttered this
Than he called into his presence angelic Vestoň
— So aptly named, the three swift messengers who bided
Near his throne, eager to make his wishes apparent
To earthlings and other spirits — him he sent to Oslad
With the command that he visit the fierce horde of Chudes
To distract them with lavish entertainments until
The Tatrans were prepared to draw against them in force.
Quicker than any arrow, from the heights of heaven
The Vestoň sped on his way, with wind-swift wings at back
And ankle. Soon he alighted on a star-scraping
Palace, splendid with marble walls, smoothly carved columns
And all else that this wide world, or man's craft, might provide
Of the beautiful. From this height he beheld gardens
Of varicoloured blooms that never fade, and orchards,
The trees of which push forth new fruit as soon as one's hand
Can pluck them — all respiring a delicious fragrance —
Beyond which plain upon luxuriant plain stretched, none
Less rich in all that the most capricious heart might desire.
Three delightful streams purled before the palace, and a lake
Teeming with life; amidst its pure waters an island
Stood, with elders and elms providing a pleasant shade,
Their boughs alive with birds of varied plumage, bearing
Fat meals to their nesting chicks, or simply admiring
Their pied reflections on the crystal pane of the deep,
But all sending up the sweetest harmony of song.
Thick were the copses, and the nearby springs: warm and cold
Providing ease of limb and slaking the thirst of beasts
— All tame, no wolf lurked near in search of murderous spoils —
Above all rose hills robed with vineyards, tendrils bursting
With grapes, and further, at the horizon, blue mountains,
Toward the feet of which fields of grain were swaying gold.
There it was always spring, fragrant zephyrs whispered sweetly;
There it was Vestoň flew, thrilling with wonder. Upon
Entering the splendid hall, music overlaved him,

And cooing, led him to a dining hall where Oslad
He beheld, seated upon a gem-encrusted throne.
Before him a board was spread with a white tablecloth
Of damask, upon which steamed in bowls all that forest,
Or stream, or high larder of the sky had to offer,
With all that earth brings forth in foison. Nor wine goblet
Nor jug of mead was lacking either. Seeing him approach,
Oslad pushed plate and cup aside and spread wide his arms:
   'Welcome, fleet of foot! Welcome, messenger of father
Perún! It's been far too long since you've visited us!
What is it urges you to our palace? The matter
Must be great — But first, sit you down and refresh yourself!'
   'Greetings, Oslad!' Vestoň replied, 'great lord of wassail!
I thank you, but right now there is no time for feasting.
I have an urgent mission to impart to your care.
Perún, the ruler of the universe, sends me here,
Commanding you to hasten to that pestilent rout
Of Chudes, who sour the air of the Tatras with their rage
Against the Slovak nation. Distract them for a space,
Especially their king, with a thirst for revelry,
That they might pause in their devastation of the land
Until the Slovaks have had time enough to arm themselves
And surprise the cruel invaders with war's sharp tempest'.
   No sooner said than done, for Oslad, swift as lightning
That falls from the clear sky, rushed off to the Chudes encamped
Upon the hills swiftly to do his father's bidding.
Meanwhile, Svatovít, from on high, scanned the Slovak land
For Sláv, whose heart now swelled with bravery and wisdom,
Virtue and war-skill, till he towered above his men
Like a spruce among birches. For he'd already licked
The savage Chudes in a just war, slaughtering legions
In battle, recovering the booty they'd stolen.
For such deeds he was held in great esteem by his folk,
Who lauded him with praise verging on adoration.
Him he would inspire to assemble men from the lands
Yet untouched by the foe, setting them in ranks to lead
Them into battle. Svatovít had barely begun
His second ambit when he caught sight of Sláv
On a high elevation (so sharp the eightfold eyes
Of the god) where had been raised a stone altar and idol

Splendidly carved in honour of Perún, ringed by groves
Of oaks newly sanctified to the purpose, since when
The place has been known as Perún's Mound, whatever name
It previously had, forgotten now in favour
Of the new appellation. Svatovít descended
There, and when the sacrifice had been completed
To the accompaniment of hymns of praise, and Sláv
Had raised his petition to the gods in the quiet,
From the depths of the grove the god let his voice ring out:
  'O pious Sláv! And no less valiant in the defence
Of your nation! As you have raised this sweet sacrifice
Of praise to our glory, continue still to worship
The gods, who incline their ears to your supplications,
For they who give more to the holy ones, take in turn
More from them in recompense. But now, alas! You know
Not what new misfortune looms above your prostrate land!
What blows are about to rain down upon your people
Staggering yet from the late pummelling they endured.
The savage Chudes burn to revenge the catastrophe
Lately wreaked upon their looters. Numerous as the sands
Of their distant wastelands, they invade Tatrania,
Firing its villages, trampling down its ripe harvests
Beneath the hooves of their steeds. Nor will the foul flood ebb
Until they've raped the land of all its wealth, and enslaved
All its folk, scourging your homeland till it lies barren,
Accurst. Arise therefore, and gather together all
Men still unvanquished, lead them back into the cruel fray,
And as you once shattered them on the plains of Obrín,
Once more — and finally — smash those ungodly bandits.
I shall be there with you, leading you to victory!'
  He finished. At once, the grove echoed with the clatter
Of arms, as he manifested himself to the eyes
Of Sláv. Immense of stature, and like unto the form
Of the idol newly raised in his honour, four-faced
And bearded, over his left shoulder a bow was slung,
A sharp blade dangled at his powerful thighs, massive
Beneath his kirtle — in all manners identical
To his carven image, except that in his right hand
He held no horn of wine, but menacing javelin.
Thus having appeared to his wonder-struck worshipper,

Svatovít turned and marched off into the darkling copse.
As soon as he'd heard these words, as soon as he'd seen that
Wonder, horripilating, Sláv cried out suddenly:
'O Svatovít, new god! All that you command, I'll do!
But in your mercy, you too accomplish what you vow!
For that your altar shall groan beneath rich offerings,
And after Perún, you shall receive our greatest praise!'
Then, like a sharp-eyed hawk launching from the highest branch
Of an elm, when he sees a rustle in the tall grass,
And swoops off after his prey on swift wing, thus did Sláv
Set off racing homeward from the sacred grove at once,
To summon the swiftest-footed young men of his clan
And send them off to all the regions of the country
(Appointing each according to his speed: nearer goals,
Or farther afield), to call all his brethren to arm
And gather, quickly, ready to wage cruel warfare
Against the savage Chudes, who threatened the motherland
With ruin. Their muster-point was to be the new temple
Of Svatovít. As soon as they'd received his command,
Each envoy hurried off to those regions of the land
As yet unscathed by the ferocity of the Chudes,
Spreading the word of the threat that loomed over their folk,
Of the need for all to arm and to gather for war.
At once all able-bodied Slovaks abandoned plough
And tillage, their hearts swelling with rage against the foe,
And gathered before the temple newly sanctified
To Svatovít. Meanwhile, Sláv roused the neighbouring folk
For the bloody task pressed upon them, preparing all
For war — taking counsel, and commanding the craftsmen
To fashion stout lances and arrows sharp, iron-tipped,
And swords too, and javelins, clever copies of those
That were seized from the Chudes following the first scrimmage,
So that, this time, they should be armed with like weaponry.

   And meanwhile, the lord of wassail, Oslad, had entered
The camp of the Chudes unnoticed. At once, all the men
(But especially Bondor) were seized with a happy
Panic of feasting and drink, their cruel savagery
Abated a while, their horrid lust for booty ebbed,
Their thirst for blood transformed to a frenzy for wine, mead!
Benches they mounted instead of steeds, and plunged their knives

Into roasts, gluttony chasing out of their minds all
Thought of war. Oslad, satisfied at having fulfilled
So well the task entrusted him by Father Perún,
Diverting the Chudes — for a while — from looting and rape,
Allowing the Slovaks time to arm and march against
The bandits in crushing force, now took on the aspect
Of Ednek, cut down by Sláv on the field at Obrín.
At midnight, when Bondor had passed out on his bed
Spread with soft goat-hides after the Bacchanalia,
Oslad stood before him: the image of his brother,
His throat seeming to bear the mortal wound that felled him.
He thus addressed the king in dream, feigning Ednek's voice:
  'Sweet brother! now set on despoiling Tatrania,
Hunting cattle and slaves, regaling your heart with loot,
Glutting your every desire and merest whim! —
While we stumble about in pitch darkness, the foul mire
Of endless marshes sucking at our feet, our flesh seared
By the scalding waves of lakes of liquid fire that crash
Upon us from their restless depths with flame, our scalded
Lungs choked by thick clouds of the sulphurous smoke we breathe —
From which there's no escape! For as soon as anyone
Espies some stretch of land beyond the reach of this pit,
An oasis cool and green, and flies there, by luck,
At once those cruel unsleeping harridans —Lútice —
Swoop down upon him with their scabrous claws to drag him
Back to these wastelands of torment and fling him again
Into the caustic filth. Our flesh is furrowed by scourge
And whip, and we must bear it all, who lie unhallowed,
Our bones unsanctified by funeral. I beg you,
Brother, look down upon us suffering, take pity
Upon us wretches! Now that you've amassed great plunder,
Slaughter some of your fattest cattle (but not humans —
We know now that such offerings are useless,
And only serve to augment our woe) and with their flesh
Burnt in holocaust, stuff these Ghouls and Gorgons, appease
Their wrath against us, that the She-dragons, satisfied,
Might let us pass safely through the gibbering turnkeys
Of our harsh prison to some place of sweet refreshment!
As soon as you lay our tormentors' ire with those gifts,
I swear that you will accomplish your every aim:

Tatrania shall be transformed into a wasteland
Like unto this hell — you shall be enriched with pillage
And men enslaved, all lashed securely to your homeland!'
   Thus Oslad feigned his lament, which, having heard, Bondor
Replied to thus, still deeply submerged in slumber:
'As you have suffered so far, and as they have been vexed
Who fell along with you — so ignobly! — at the hands of peasants,
Suffer on still in your lakes of flame and searing bogs!
Indeed, your punishment is not half what you deserve
For your shameful massacre by villainous bumpkins,
Which brought the whole Chudan nation into disrepute!
Away with you now — you muddy my joy with whining.
But when I have reduced Tatrania to embers,
When I have gathered all my herds together, and bound
My slaves in tight fetters, I shall return to the place
Where you fell, and there I shall take pity upon you,
Performing the rites funereal for you wretched cripples.
With black offerings of cattle I shall satisfy
The Ghouls, and spitting upon the bones, raise a marker,
Sealing the cavern of your shame with a stout boulder'.
   Thus Bondor. At which Oslad, as Ednek still, pressed on
Unappeased: 'Sweet brother! Bury my body later,
But perform the sacrifice now! For if you do not
Accomplish the rites that are due us, I swear to you,
You shall meet with the same harsh fate that is our portion!
For valiant Sláv — that heart of oak! — shall cut you down
And hurl you into this eternal abyss of woe
Along with the remainder of the Chudes — to these glooms
Where we crackle with torment in swelling waves of flame
Shuttled helplessly, raised up on high only to crash down
Onto jagged cliff and sands abrasive. What is more:
Know that our gloomy god, Ár, grows impatient with you,
So long in the land of the Tatrans, and so sluggish
In service: his altars unbloodied, unsmeared of gore.
Should you hesitate longer, denying his nostrils
The sweet stench of groaning victims' blood, in his anger,
Bursting with venom his heart, he shall abandon you,
Forsaking your army overwhelmed by the Slovaks.
Quite all shall be slaughtered! If you would avoid this fate
That looms above you, leave off now further pillaging

For a more convenient hour, and gather your army
Together — now! — to perform the solemn sacrifice!'
   Thus Oslad, as Ednek disguised, cast before the king,
Threatening ruin. Then, withdrawing to a corner
Of the tent, and perching himself upon a tripod,
He disclosed to his sight images of fallen Chudes
Screaming in pain in Hell, begging for ensepulture
Ritual to deliver them from the Mátohas
Fierce, who tore at them. Bondor then beheld Černoboh
And Pikulík feasting with cruelty on the men
Of his nation; hordes of Rarašky and She-dragons,
Tarany with sharp axes, Lútice with pitchforks
Vivisecting the souls of Chudes unhallowed with rite
Funeste, who bellowed with suffering, vomiting fire.
   Then Bondor, like a wolf surprised in his inner lair
By hunters, sprang from his cot in terror. His nostrils
Flared at the stench of sulphur in the air, his flesh cringed
As if seared by the white-hot irons of Hell's fetters.
In his one ear his brother's voice still rang, the other
Was filled with the cracking of whips, as if the demons
Were herding the sufferers back to the depths of Hell.
Terrified, his mind raced: should he pillage the Slovaks,
Lassoing all the more swiftly the people
Before they had a chance to scurry off to refuge
In mountain and cavern? Or should he rather give heed
To the frightful threats and pleas of his brother Ednek?
And so (not even waiting for the dawn) he summoned
His war chiefs to his tent for counsel. Thus his address:
   'Renowned conquerors! Able leaders of our heroes!
Before quite half the night had fled, the wretched Ednek
Appeared to me in a dream. His throat still bore the fatal
Wound that felled him, and in a voice heavy with sorrow
He told me that he, along with his fallen comrades,
Now stumbles through the darknesses below, their flesh seared
By the seething bogs of sulphur, which they cannot flee,
For as soon as any scramble out onto a bank
Of cool grass, the Lútice snatch him, and hurl him back
Into the caustic mire or liquid flames, with pitchforks.
Their backs are flayed with whips and scourges, which they must bear
Since they have not been buried with the rites due the dead —

Negligence, he claims, of ours, which we must rectify,
And that immediately, satisfying the ghouls
With fat sacrificial banquet. Now, if we do this,
He promises us a successful expedition.
My response was such: "Until we gather our booty
From all these regions and scorch the earth of Tatrania,
After which we may return to the place where you fell
To carry out the libitine rites, glutting Tasan
With blood, and piling pure sand upon your bones picked clean,
Capping the deep pit with great boulder, suffer on!
For this your present punishment isn't half as bad
As that you deserve for permitting such clowns with staves
To slaughter you, thus bringing shame upon our nation!"
At this, he revealed to me the merciless abyss
Where — so he vowed — should we not perform the ritual
Properly, and now, we were to join him, suffering
The same aimless anabasis through the searing plains,
Marshes, and lakes, lashed by the same demonic scourges.
Beyond this, he admonished us all for neglecting
The offerings due great Ár, who, should we not feed
With gore, and soon, he might abandon us, impious
Laggards, permitting Sláv to shatter us in war.
   Thus our pathetic brother threatened us. I beheld
(O, horrid sight indeed!) an immense number of Chudes
Covered in blood, their hair aflame — those who fell back then
On Obrín plain — wallowing in a lake of acid,
Suffering flames that engulfed them whole, but consumed not,
Begging for ritual funeral, release from pain.
Many the monsters of Hell I saw then: Mátohy,
Pikulíks and horrible, black Černoboh himself,
Ďas and Rarášok emerged from the stench-choked abyss,
But most of all: abominable hordes of Tasans,
She-dragons and Lútice wielding three-pronged pitchforks;
Their eyes all spitting sparks, they belched fire from yawning gobs —
Frightful the clamour: screams, and a hissing like serpents —
And all of these tormenting cruelly the fallen Chudes.
   Such was my horrid vision — you yourselves can still smell
The rank smoke in the air, and feel the heat make your skin shrink.
It still lingers after this visitation from Hell!
So now consider, and tell me: should we continue

With pillaging? Or fulfil the demands of Ednek?
First performing the ritual burials, glutting
Impatient Ár with gore, having summoned all our troops,
That all be present at the rites, and we thus skirt the doom?'
   When Bondor finished speaking, the savage Kondok rose,
The greediest ravager, avid seeker of loot,
But all the same a capable warrior, too.
Aghast at Bondor's suggestion, he bellowed in ire:
   'We go on burning and pillaging, as long as loot
Remains and slaves are to be plucked from the villages —
As long as fortune favours the bold — herself our slave!
Reck not of dreams, nor the thin sprites that squeak in nightmare!
What a man sees in dreams, in the light of day never
Crosses his mind, nor will such things ever come to pass.
Let all those ferocious Ďas, Pikulíks, Mátohas,
Rarášky and what other bugbears say "Boo!"
In minds tormented by nightmares terrify small girls'
Hearts — and not those of Chudes, heroic manly livers
That guest no ghosts! What if it were some Slovak godlet
And not Ednek's soul that came to frighten you this night?
So that — Your Majesty — while we'd be busied with bones
And priestcraft, time would be gained for the Slovaks to run
And burrow deep inside cranny and defensive crag?
Our comrades suffer? They should not have lost the battle!
First let us reduce all Tatrania to cold ash,
Burning and slaughtering all that we can't carry off.
When we've snatched our fill of slaves and riches and cattle,
When we've all the gleanings of this land in our clutches,
Then we'll have time to pipe laments and spatter the slab
Before Ár's image — I shall be first to do, gladly!'
   So Kondok roared. Then Endeb the brave rose to his feet,
Whose counsel was the opposite of Kondok's. He said:
'Our god marches before us. And those fallen in war
Deserve a proper burial. I say — first things first!
A wake for our fallen comrades, a heaping sacrifice
To Ár. Let us heed well your brother's ominous words,
For once it so befell Kemend, mighty in battle:
He belittled the warning sent to him in a dream
By his father, when he was intent on pillaging
The lands beyond the Don: "Bury my body, my son",

The wraith uprisen at midnight urged him, "and to Ár,
At once offer sacrifice — or else..." But he, trusting
That fortune, which heretofore had propped him, ignored that,
Putting off both ceremonies for another time,
And set off with his men. What happened then? A handful
Of Don Slavs knocked him on the head, slaughtered his army.
When the trembling Tatrans notice that we're at feasting,
No longer plundering the regions hereabout, why,
They'll reckon that we're celebrating our victory,
Preparing to set off for home. Some of them will think
We've gone already, having disappeared from their sight;
They'll see no need then to abandon their villages
For thicket and cavern. And anyway, why not go
Now, with what we've already pillaged? What need have we
To strip the land desert? Would it not be well to leave
A seed of slave and chattel here, to spread and burgeon
Into a future crop for our harvestings to come?
Let's give them some space to multiply, to stock the larder,
And replenish the loot that we take off with us now!'
   All who were there were pleased with his advice, for Oslad
Saw to that, kneading soft — no easy task! — hearts as hard
As flint. Their hunger for further looting was sapped,
And all that they thought of now was feasting, sweet repose.
And so the king called back to camp the bands that were still
Raping the land of the Slovaks to the funeral
Of Ednek's men, and the great holiday of their god.
At once they gathered, like flocks of starlings, once summer's
Basking has matured the fruit in the swelling vineyards.
Whole woods fell to their hatchets — of ash and elm and pine;
Two pyres immense were piled of resinous lumber, one
To Ár, the other to the fallen men of Ednek.
With fat-smeared torches they set alight these great wooden
Kurhans, and soon two pale infernos were raging high.
A great host of colts, both white and black, fell to the knife;
A great host of sheep and goats and fatted porkers, tossed
Onto the flames (only men were spared — so admonished
Ednek in dream). The butchers' forearms dripped with beast's blood
To the elbows. Around the two pyres then they circled,
Mounted on steeds, ululating and screeching shrilly

In their harsh Chudan tongue. Day after day they feasted;
Mug after mug swilling mead. Oslad kept them at it:
Despite bulging paunches, they were never satisfied.

CANTO III

Before the newly-built temple he'd raised
To Svatovít, Sláv hastens now. The hosts
Of Slovaks he'd summoned await him there.
The god himself prepares for war, advising
Sláv to split the mass in smaller fragments,
Each with their hand-picked war-chief. Besides this,
Sláv he instructs how they're to be disposed.
There will be ten units, each to its flank,
Each led by voivode. Arming then these ranks,
And each group having chosen its commander,
Sláv takes supreme command over the whole.
They honour Svatovít with sacrifice
Before the fane. Then Sláv leads forth the horse
To take the auguries of the steed prancing
Before the troops. Success is prophesied.
Sláv raises thanks renewed, establishing
This rite forever to be celebrated
Each year, a solemn feast, by all the Slovaks.
At this, he sets off with his men to war,
Svatovít marching in the army's van.
When they arrive at the Ľubovín mounds
Toward evening, Sláv ascends a high hill
To gaze upon the battlefield to be.
Meanwhile, Perún sends Vestoň to Oslad,
Commanding him the Chudes now to abandon,
No more them to regale. At once the horde
Sickens of feasting, in astonishment
At their long luxury, and fall to squabbling
For having wasted so much time, so softly.

    Sláv, having roused his people to the homeland's defence,
Directing his men to gather before the temple
Newly-raised to Svatovít, and cruel arms to be wrought
By the craftsmen and delivered quickly to the fane,
Hastened there now, to take command of the great army.

So far, so good — but then his mind was troubled by doubts
Of how he was to dispose the massed legions for battle.
Then, suddenly, upon his way he met Svatovít
(In the guise of Výbor, his brother-in-law, husband
To Bojboha, Sláv's beautiful sister, a man famed
For his good counsel, renowned for his great wealth, renowned
The more for selfless generosity. He gloried
In manly sons: full six, and each as eager for war
And fit as their father; indeed, from Výbor's home hearth
All rushed to the defence of the motherland, leaving
Behind with their sweet Lady none but those unable
To bear arms. In such guise then, the god appeared to Sláv
And, with shining, confident countenance, addressed him:
 'Sláv! What a great peril has swooped down upon our land!
From cloud-wrapped Branisko to the lands past the Tisa
Which swallows the waters of the River Bodrok — Chudes,
Savage and cruel, have ravaged it to desert wastes!
How many cities, how many villages thickly
Bordering each other in abundance are no more,
No trace left behind to mark the place where once they stood;
Consumed all, to ash and dark stains upon the charred ground.
And even that ash is swirled afar by the mocking winds!
Whatever cattle — whatever men! — have dodged the sword
Of slaughter have been crowded into pens in the camps
Of those bandits! Indeed, as I learned of the envoys
That we've sent out, their camps are spread on the Malovské
Hillocks, where now they busy themselves with great feasting,
Having paused their depredations for the nonce. And so,
Now is the time to distribute weapons among us,
Both those on the temple walls, and those you have had forged
Just now by the craftsmen. I would advise you yet, thus:
Because no one man can direct so great a battle
While swinging his own arm in the fray, appoint other
War-chiefs to aid you, each in command of his own men,
To dispose of them and give them heart, subservient
To your overall command, leading by example.
So, divide your massive force into smaller units
And have each regiment elect their own commander
To whom they would hold, fulfilling his every decree.
And what is more: in order for us to overcome

So great a mob of savages, brute force suffices
Not — one needs wisdom and prudence, and that which most serves
Victory: a readiness ever alert to take
Advantage of the best opportunity. And so
I would advise you, should you deign grant me your ear:
The broadest mesa at a safe distance from the camp
Of those villains is Ľubovín — as distant from them
As the idol of Láda from Svatovít's temple.
A great plain stretches at its foot, enclosed on both flanks
By rocky cliffs of great height. Between both these walls
A marsh impenetrable spreads to the very camp.
Emplace there, upon both sides, your army, keeping to
The high ground. When the cruel Chudes see us, they shall move
Against us, but will not be able to outflank us.
They shall be funnelled into a narrow defile:
The only scratch of land they'll have to stand on. And there,
The bandits' great numbers will be of no help to them!'
   Thus Svatovít disguised. As Sláv hastened to respond
The god turned and vanished among the gathering ranks
Of men heading for the temple. Stunned with pious awe
At what he recognised to be the hierophany
Of a blessed one, Sláv stopped in his tracks and exclaimed
'Thanks be to thee, O great Svatovít, for thy concern
For thy people, and for this profitable advice
Imparted to me now! Pray, abandon not thy folk
In the coming battle, but aid us to crush our foe,
For which the gifts we will offer thee in sacrifice
Shall be all the greater!' Having lifted up these prayers
He pressed on, ascending the crest of the temple hill
With eager stride. Before him, he beheld the great host
Of heroes numberless who had gathered at his call,
With yet more pressing in from all sides. Like the rippling
Expanse of a dark ocean flooding its bounds they came.
Arriving before the temple porch, Sláv knelt and prayed:
   'O warlike god, defender of the Slovak nation!
Hold it not against us, that in this our pressing need
We strip these sacred precincts of the weapons heaped here
In offering, which we must borrow, but rather aid
The arms that shall wield them in battle, that they should strike
Unerringly, thunderously, in defence of our home!

And when we march back from battle, we shall return these,
With trophies new, wrested from our enemies, to thee!
The votive gifts shall fill thy temple to bursting,
The oaken grove surrounding to adorn with glory!
Enlighten now the minds of this thy faithful people,
That they be heedful of thy directives in this war,
Electing such men as will deliver them thy will
In battle, leading them to victory in thy name!'
Thus prayed he, then, turning his face toward the gathered
Hosts, he addressed them thus: 'Valiant comrades! You have heard
What a calamity has befallen our sweet land!
The godless Chudes have ravaged with fire no small portion
Of this our motherland, despoiling men of their lives,
Their property, and their freedom. Nor shall they withdraw
To their land, it seems, until they reduce Tatrania
To a barren wasteland, carting off all our chattel,
Our wealth, and those of us they reserve for slavery.
We shall not let this happen! Let us arm ourselves now
To attack them and deliver our land from ruin!
Here are the arms we need — take them; with might unflagging
Destroy the evil Chudes! And may our German neighbours,
The haughty Thracians and even the warlike Greeks see
What brave and excellent warriors we Slovaks are!
What terror we might sow ourselves were war our custom;
What realms we might upend, what nations we might enslave
Were it our way to exist by pillaging others
And not — as is our nature — to till our own soil,
Our only wish to live at peace in our homeland!
Now, because valour alone leads not to victory,
But only when coupled with discipline, and because
I cannot oversee myself all this great army,
Let us divide into ten equal portions. Let each
Elect the most capable man as their voivode,
Him to heed in all things, obedient to his commands,
Fulfilling each task he allots without wavering'.

   Thus he addressed them. Then, reserving Ednek's armour
For himself, he had each of the warriors approach
And take a buckler stiff with goat's leather, a sharp sword,
Two javelins fleet, light of heft, a bow planed of yew,
A quiver full of arrows, and a spear sharply tipped

With iron for thrusting. They all crowded near, like to
Oxen long labouring beneath the summer's swelter,
Led to the River Váh at last, to plunge their muzzles
Into its cool stream — so they snatched the weapons, eager,
But struck with wonder all the same, for many of them
Had never held real arms before. With enthusiasm
They thrusted and swiped before them, testing their weapons,
And boasting how they'd strike the enemy, cutting him down!
Those with crossbows inspected them carefully for flaws:
They had not been damaged in the earlier battle?
The wood won't split, the tendon was still supple, won't break
At the first strain? Some of the men received the helmets
Stripped of the fallen Chudes, but they were so numerous,
Those eager for war, that the arsenal soon ran dry
Of forged-metal arms. Some were outfitted with axes,
Or massive, gnarled maces and sharp fire-tempered staffs.
Besides such arms, ox-horns were passed out among the ranks
To blare in the fray both signal and encouragement.
When all the troops were armed, the host divided at once
Into ten units of more or less even numbers.
Each regiment picked a captain to lead them in war.
   First of all was the regiment of Matranci,
Whose name derives from Mount Matra, which their forefathers
Named in honour of their ancient Indian homeland,
So that their children should never forget whence they spring:
That ancient land where the Indus and the Ganges flow.
Those doughty troops elected Namír to be their chief,
A strapping man of great stature and brawn, and wisdom.
   From the Tisa regions, from the fields laved by the king
Of the Slavic streams, the Danube, from the steppes immense
Where herds of lowing cattle stretch out across the plain
So numberless, the human eye can't overtake them
To the horizon, where fresh calves skip on wobbly legs
Adding yet to the press, came the regiment who'd chosen
Proslav to lead them, of skilful hand, expert in herbs
Medicinal, that heal all illness of beast or man.
   The men from the banks of the Rímava, from Hnilec
And the moors through which the River Slana swiftly flows,
Whose boundaries the Chudes had already poked around,
Joined into one troop and chose Dobroslav to lead them,

The wealthiest among them in herds of sheep and goats,
Which swelled each year with new sleek lambs and mischievous kids
Of which the gods received part in grateful offering:
Dobroslav the clever, the mighty, the courageous!
   Next, those from the muddy banks of the cloudy River Iseľ
And those from the fields cut through by the lesser Žaďva,
From the highlands where the brows of mountains brush the clouds,
These chose virtuous Ľubomír as their voivode,
High priest of the temple of Perún in Novohrad,
For which reason his locks were ever bound in oak-leaves,
His beard ever untrimmed. In the sacred oaken grove
He sat in judgment, along with the other elders
Of the folk, took auspices, and gave good counsel,
Often foretelling the end of things to come, mostly
Though, assuaging the anger of the lord of thunder
When offended by the vice of men, through sacrifice.
   Those from the banks of the Hron, and those from the cities
So rich in gold that one often wounds the sickle
Swung at harvest on the scattered ore: most numerous
They, Ponislav the great hunter they chose to lead them,
Who with his arrows laid a hundred wild boars low
That had been trampling the ripening fields of grain;
And he'd no fewer gloomy bears — perhaps even more! —
Felled with his sharp lance; such things were a trifle to him,
Who as a little boy would venture into their caves
And carry out their toddling cubs to play with. These men
Swore to obey his orders (so courageous of heart
Was he — a trustworthy mate!), that they boldly vowed
To shatter the Chudes by themselves under his command!
   Then those who drink of the Nitra and the Žitava
That gently flows through the fields they furrow with curved plough,
Elected Milko their chief, the son of great Prekras,
Who founded wide-famed Nitra, which was soon entrusted
To Milko, when implacable Morena snatched Prekras
Before his time. Over the space of three hundred moons
Milko raised the city high on the firm foundations
Prekras had lain. On Mount Zobor too he'd raised a fane
Splendid to Perún, whom he regaled with offerings.
   Nor did it take the men of the Váh long to elect
Leaders for their troops. They had divided in two halves.

Those from the lower Váh, where the river rages untamed,
From the Danube islands, and where the gentler Dudváh
Rolls, from the edge of the Tatras to the great city
Founded by Vratislav all the way to Komárno,
Called the wise Pravomíl to be their leader, of whom
There was no man more courageous, saving Sláv himself.
Those of the upper regions deliberated longer.
The swift-footed Turčani, from the mountains soaring
On the far bank of the river, would choose Hájislav,
Beloved among them, who taught them how to brew herbs
That keep death at arm's length; the Leptáci, however,
And the host from Orava, supported Zamysel.
A mighty man he, of great stature, who first rafted
His people's crafts, the products of skilled hands, down the swift
Váh, returning from his peddling laden with herds, flocks,
And other wealth, with which he enriched his motherland.
They batted the vote back and forth, unable to set
Their choice upon one or the other. Then Hájislav
Of his own will withdrew his name from the lists, at which
Zamysl was chosen without further dissension.

   The stout Belohorci and their neighbours from the near
Morava River elected pious Istislav,
The shaman-bard of the pine woods, whom they vowed to heed.
For he was held in high esteem for wise soothsaying;
A deft carver too, he was, who sculpted uncanny
Images of the gods, erecting them on hillock
And in shady linden grove. To these he offered songs
Of his own crafting, before the splendid cheeks of Dawn
Blushed in the heavens, to sacred music he'd composed.

   The final group — those who obtained no forged weaponry —
Chose as their voivode strapping, able Bohumíl,
Who towered over all by a full head, like an oak
Amidst shrub-growth, a proud lion among flocks of sheep.
In his right hand he bore a shaft of elm so massive
That any other man would be unable to heft
To his shoulder, though he use both hands. And this he'd fling,
Recoiling but one step to wind up, which when he hurled,
It never missed the target at which he was aiming.

   Then all the chosen presented themselves before Sláv,
Whom Dobroslav addressed on behalf of them all:

'Sláv! Accept supreme command over us, elected
Leaders of your people's hosts. Lead us to the cruel strife
And rule us in wisdom. We shall heed you like children
Obedient to their father, fulfilling every task
Commanded us. Your courage shall be an example
To us, as we strive to emulate you in battle,
Spilling our blood to the last drop for our motherland!'
   To this Sláv responded with such terms of gratitude:
'On behalf of our motherland, for our nation's weal,
I gladly accept command over all her forces.
As best as lies in my power, with the aid of great
Svatovít our god, I shall govern this massed army
In battle, swinging my sword in your midst without rest
Until we smash the might of our evil enemy.
Gladly, too, I should give my life, gladly leave this world
Fighting on behalf of the Slovaks, O my brothers,
Secure in the knowledge of your loyalty and trust'.
   Thus proclaimed Sláv, after which he ordered sacrifice
Be made unto Svatovít, offering one hundred
Fat oxen, one hundred goats, as many sheep, the same
Number of roosters black, all flung upon the heaped pyre.
Then Veslav the priest, robed in vestments as white as snow,
Folding piously his hands, thus petitioned the god:
   'O mightiest of all the Slovak gods, Svatovít,
God of war and peace! Look down upon your worshippers
Who in their pressing need offer thee sacrifice
Flaming upon thy altar, and deign incline an ear
Benevolent to petitions that rise from ardent
Hearts! Turn back the tide of catastrophe from our land
That it may fall upon the heads of our enemies,
Engulfing those who swell the flood of war against us!
Help us to shatter the might of the bandit Chudes
— Cruel ravishers! — in battle! Grant us victory,
So we may live hereafter in blessed peace, forever'.
   So prayed the priest, so prayed the countless hosts behind him.
So many were they, and so near the hour to set out,
That only those closest processed around the pyre,
Lifting their voices in shouts of praise to Svatovít,
The rolling thunder of their clamour echoing far.
Three times they circled the sacrificial pyre, three times

They sent up resounding praise to the glory of the god.
When the hymn had run its course and the folk fell silent
Along with the musicians, when the fire had burnt down
After consuming the victims, more inspiration
Broke upon Sláv. Taking six hefty spears from the chiefs
Standing nearest him, he plunged their iron barbs deep
Into the grass in three even rows, placing three staves
Athwart. Then he ordered that the god's steed be led out
Of his stall and set before the spears for augury.
Obedient to Sláv's will, Veslav the priest brought him forth,
Caparisoned, onto the courtyard of the temple.
Then, raising both arms high to the heavens, Sláv thus prayed:
   'O Svatovít, our new god! Thou hast manifested
Thyself unto me twice — first, when we routed the Chudes
Who had forced our borders for banditry, and second,
Revealing the looming catastrophe that threatens
Our land at the hands of those who would avenge their loss
By scathing our realm to desert, slaughtering our folk.
'Tis thou hast commanded me to assemble these hosts
From all regions yet untouched by their depredations,
To lead my countrymen into the horrid battle.
There, with thine aid, we shall shatter our enemies' might;
Thou shalt then lead us to victory as thou'st promised.
But send now a visible sign to us thy faithful
Through this thy charger, confirming thy blessed promise
That all these hearts be over-brimming full of boldness
And enter the cruel fray all the more eagerly'.
   No sooner had Sláv finished praying than the stallion
Was loosed by venerable Veslav before the spears.
Arching his hooves, he approached the obstacle, prancing.
He stepped over each row, his right leg ever foremost,
In such a way signifying victory in war.
Sláv was elated at the augury delivered
By the sacred animal. He raised such ardent words:
'For this token of thy promise confirmed, Svatovít,
Accept thy grateful people's thanks! This ceremony
Of taking auspices by thy fleet-footed charger
We here establish for all time to come. Whenever
The Slovak people are threatened by some grievous harm
At the hands of a foe intending war, whenever

Their sons are called to stand to the defence of this land,
After due sacrifice is offered thee, three such rows
Of spears will be set up before thy horse, to augur
The fortunes of the coming fray — whether good or bad —
But, lord, grant us in thy mercy only good fortune,
And bring to real fruition what the steed prophesies!
And when in fierce war we've ground our foes into the dust,
We shall return to this high temple to sing thy praise
With even greater celebration. Our descendants
Will hold the day of victory in perpetual
Honour: a yearly holy day in praise of thee, lord,
To whom fat offerings shall be sacrificed before
They set to feasting. Thee, Svatovít, they shall revere
Second only to father Perún, O Slovak god!'
   Thus Sláv. After which he turned and addressed the people:
'Now that we have offered meet sacrifice to our god,
Come forward yourselves to the feast. Strengthen and refresh
Your limbs at the pious banquet. Partake of the flesh
Reserved for you, grilled on the coals, and raise the flagons
Filled with mead'. Then, when their hunger had been satisfied,
Their hearts and their limbs swelling with joy and boldness,
He rose again, and called them to march off on the road
Leading to the battle, addressing them in such words:
   'And now we turn our knives toward the Chudes in their camp
Spread on the Malovské hillocks, where they still wallow
In drunken feasting. Let us set out at a quick pace
For the Ľubovín plateau, which rears by old Chválkov
Reduced now to ash. It is there we shall do battle,
There in the narrow ambit of the valley, where they
Shall be constrained by marsh and wetland; there we'll force them
In a sudden rush. Their forces are numerous, but
Crowded thus on a mere tongue of firm land, their powers
Will be constricted by lack of space. The advantage
Will be ours. We shall fight to the limits of our strength
And overcome our foe in bloody strife, or die there
Ourselves. Far better would it be to die, than to serve
Those Dogheads as fettered slaves! But why should we fall there?
Who shall enslave or overcome us, since Svatovít
Himself has promised us — as we have already witnessed
Through plain augury — that we shall destroy that horde

Of bandits, in victorious, glorious battle!
Onward then, friends, in haste! And those who will not submit,
Kneeling before you, casting their arms aside, cut down!
We shall overcome the Chudes, liberating our friends,
Recovering our goods that these raiders have stolen,
And delivering our homeland once and for all time
From the threat of catastrophe posed by those wild-men'.

   He finished, and then, led by their voivodes, eagerly,
With manly hearts and bosoms swelling with confidence
At his words, they set off on the path leading to war.
Svatovít marched at their head, enveloped in thick mist.
None of the soldiers saw anything save that pillar
Of cloud, but all heard the clatter of arms from within.
He himself infused their legs with vigour and spryness
So that they seemed to fly, rather than to march along.
Before long they arrived at the Ľubovín plateau,
Where they were to rest their weary limbs and spend the night.
The prudent Sláv, waiting for the rearguard to arrive,
Ascended a high point, taking along with him
The leader of the Belohorský youth — and behold:
The whole immense camp of the Chudes was spread out before
Their eyes. It was a jolt, but it did not frighten him,
And turning to his wise companion, he spoke these words:

   'Tell me why such immense hosts should not remain at home!
And earn their living from the soil, harvesting the wealth
Of the honest toil of their own hands, as our folk do?
Why must they rape and ravage the lands of their neighbours?
Can it be that we were created but for this,
To batten their appetite, our lives at their command?
Why must the good man suffer, and the evil prosper?
Is it that the gods have made them our nation's scourge,
For punishment of some offence, of which we know not?
But shortly their brigandage will end! Soon they'll leave off
The looting of strangers' goods! The dogs will gnaw their bones'.

   He spoke, and then he lifted his face to the heavens:
'How good is Perún! How patient to bear such evil
So long, restraining his bolts of justice, which might have
Blasted these murderers to deepest Hell long ago!'
Then he inspected the two wings of the rocky cliffs,
And the marshland in their midst. Long did he gaze, sharp-eyed,

At the future battlefield before leaving the chief
There on guard, lest some rout of the Chudes should surprise them,
And went down the empty mesa to address the troops:
   'My brothers, gathered together here for the defence
Of our wounded motherland! Once you've supped frugally,
Lay yourselves down to rest. For when half the night is through,
We shall move off to both sides of that distant defile
To be ready for war as soon as the new sun dawns,
Before those villains in their camp take note of us here,
And have time to ready themselves for the cruel fray'.
   They heeded his advice, and after eating, lay down
On the thick grass for some short hours of restful sleep
Though the sun had not quite sunk past the horizon yet.
At which Perún, the governor of the universe,
Called near his messenger to impart to him his will:
   'Wing-footed Zvestoň! Get you to the Malovské hills
And tell the god of wassail who long has bided there
To bring the splendid feast of the Chudes to an end.
Let him get out of there, abandon that horrid camp,
For now the Slovaks are emplaced upon Ľubovín
Awaiting but the dawn for the rout of their cruel foes'.
   At once the messenger winged his swift way to the camp
Where, in the king's tent, he found the god of feasts seated.
Appearing before him, he addressed him in such words:
'Oslad, supreme governor of joyous carousing,
I'm sent to you by Perún, who commands you to cease
Regaling the Chudes with feasting. Abandon this place,
For now the Slovaks are gathered near, awaiting dawn
To crush these villains in defence of their motherland'.
   Oslad needed no convincing. Yearning for his home,
He'd long tired of the company of these boorish louts.
With happy heart, relieved, he hastened to his palace.
As soon as he'd left the unpleasant tent of Bondor,
And set off on the road leading home to Radostov,
The black bile once more coursed through the veins of the raw Chudes.
Astonished, they blinked around at the feast in disgust.
Again 'twas blood they thirsted for, not wine; not music
But screams and the groans of the slain would they gladly hear!
Once more the cold lust of rampaging set them aflame.
They grabbed their arms and nearly fell to blows then and there,

Irate at having wasted so much time in softness!
They'd have set out at once to pillage the nearby towns,
Were it not for the fact that the sun was then setting,
And darkness spread beneath the outstretched wings of the night.

CANTO IV

Sláv exhorts the Tatrans he'd emplaced
Upon the farther ridge for the coming fray.
As soon as the Chudes see them there, they rush
Down from their camp, sending tempests of darts
Whizzing toward the Slovaks, at which Sláv
Sends up a prayer to Stribog, god of the winds,
Who bends their course in flight, hurling them back
Upon the Chudan bowmen, and of those arrows
None of them miss their mark. Even the great god Ár
Is impotent the carnage to avert.
The ranks then close, and fierce combat ensues:
Weapons swing on both sides cutting men down
At close quarters. The Slovak men with crossbows
Pour down a crackling fire from both ridges —
Fierce bolts upon the Chudes — then grab their blades
And rush upon them too as infantry.
The Slovaks wreak great slaughter upon their foes
Trapped in the valley; most of all great Sláv
Piles heaps of Chudan corpses. Savage Kondok
Himself, raging against him, he cuts down,
Hurling him from this world. Then Svatovít
Rips Ár with his sword, sending him with whimpers
Hobbling home to Chude-land. Nevertheless,
Below, amongst the men, the Chudes rage on:
Bondor especially, laying great waste
To the Slovak ranks. But Svatovít flies near
To strengthen Slavic thew with might refreshed,
And soon they press their savage enemies
Into the fatal maw of the narrow vale.

The speedy chariot of the night, brilliant with stars,
Had barely crossed the midpoint of the sky. Prudent Sláv
Awoke his warriors, refreshed with sleep, and sent some
In haste to the farther ridge. Obedient to his will,
They moved off to occupy the designated heights,

In utter silence stealing there, foregoing song
With which they otherwise made pleasant every road.
Not a sound passed their lips, so stealthy they, lest the Chudes
Catch wind of their near approach. Skilled bowmen on both sides
Of the valley were thus emplaced, while along the slopes,
From summit to foot, the rest of the Slovak army
Was ranged in battle order for the contest to come.
When they had renewed their strengths with a hearty breakfast
Against that day's fierce labours, Sláv addressed them thus:
   'My valiant comrades! The great hour has now tolled, when Perún
The god of righteousness and truth will exact vengeance
Upon the horrendous ravishers of our homeland
For the wrongs we've suffered! And their catastrophe
Will be an example to all, who would be bandits,
Of the punishment that falls upon such as would rape
The goods of others, destroying their cities, pressing
Free men into the cruel fetters of slavery.
Parasites! Growing fat on the fruit of the labours
Of other hands! But we must not just beg our rescue
Of Perún, nor leave our revenge in Svatovít's hands.
We ourselves must now set to the task, weapons in hand,
And rush upon the Chudes in mighty force to crush them!
For the gods help those who help themselves, and with the aid
Of Svatovít, we shall shatter our foes in battle,
Liberating our sweet homeland, defending our wives
And children from shameful ruin, to win for us the name
Of a nation valorous, fierce on the battlefield!'
   Thus Sláv, just before the dawn tinted the eastern sky,
Just as the Chudes were saddling for a new day's wicked
Depredations. Then, just as the sun broke the ridgeline
To pour down its light, Sláv commanded his trumpeters
To blare blasts of praise to the glory of Svatovít.
The heroic roars rolled through the valley like thunder,
Reaching the Chudes in camp, and stunning them, making
Them stumble, feet at stirrup, struck by masses of air
Rolled their way. Recovering, they scrambled a-saddle
And peered, wide-eyed, toward the regions whence the roars came.
The light was still too dim for them to clearly make out
The armed Slovak heroes with whom the ridges bristled,
But the well-known summits seemed more wooded than before…

At just that moment savage Forkond and Nemoltok
The bloodthirsty, who had set out beforehand, itching
For rapine, burst into the camp with the shocking news
Of the Tatran force. Anger inflamed the savagery
Of the Chudan ranks. So great was their raging black bile,
It was like the venom of adders, of which men say
Their poison swells so that they sometimes burst into two halves
That spring upon each other then in vicious hatred.
Thus did the Chudes rage, their veins swelling, their teeth grinding
In umbrage at the very thought that the Slovaks dared
Stand against them, massed, and bring the battle to them!
Like wasps or hornets seething for revenge, when boys
Probe the deep chambers of their hives with sticks, angrily
Spilling forth in massed legions, or when men in the fields
Drop rein and plough-handle from their startled grasp, and race
Back to the village from all sides as soon as the whiff
Of smoke meets their nostrils, their eye catches thatch aflame,
In just such a chaos of shock and anger the Chudes
Raced out toward the Slovak lines with savage bellows
That quite drowned out the blare of trumpets, the hymns of praise
Raised by the Slovaks to Svatovít at break of day.
And as they charged into the vale, they sent a tempest
Of arrows upon the Slovaks waiting to meet them.
So thick was the barrage that the very sky itself was dimmed
As if a plaited wooden roof had been raised above
The battlefield. Svatovít, unable to deflect
Such a great deluge of death from the heads of his folk
By himself, inspired Sláv to raise a prayer to Stribog,
The god of the winds, beseeching him with fervent plea.
At once the champion folded his hands, crying out:
   'O Stribog! Thou great governor of the whistling winds!
Hoary progenitor of those who ride the billows
Of gale and hurricane, before whose might all truss
And beam is powerless, who canst level with the earth
The proudest edifice that man's feeble strengths can raise,
Who elm and oak that stand one thousand years treadest down
Like puny blades of grass, who rulest the waterspout
And whip'st inland the sea-surge so that man must abide
Thy pleasure before he loose the hawsers of his craft
And set out from harbour calm, bring thou here thy whirlwind

And blast away these arrows from thy folk, twisting them
Back upon the heads of those who unleash them at us!
And carry too our arrows and our bolts with power
Upon our enemies, so that each dart drive sure death
Into the bosoms of those proud, lawless invaders!
For this I shall raise thee a splendid fane upon these heights,
At which we shall celebrate an annual holiday
In thanksgiving of our liberation at thy hands!'
   Hardly had Sláv finished this prayer than Stribog himself
Flew near to aid the Slovaks. For in his cave of winds
He had no subalterns to send, having ordered them
Off to the north, past the Tatras, to dry the Pripet
Marshes, toward the day when the Slavs should multiply
And bring that wide-spread black earth under cultivation.
So the lord of the winds, to the rear of the Tatran
Forces, filled his gigantic lungs and blew tornados
From his own mouth against the Chudes — a contrary gale.
Their missiles paused in mid-flight, turned, and then hurtled back
Upon the hosts who'd sent them, each arrowhead plunging
Deep into Chudan flesh. Twice, and again Stribog blew,
Then paused. The Chudes, thinking that the freakish storm had passed,
Sensing no breeze now ruffle whisker or pennon thence,
Once more strung dart on bow and launched anew. But Stribog
Was waiting just for that: he huffed again, and sent them
Whistling back, down upon the Chudes, who fell in thick heaps
Of groaning maimed, and slaughtered, felled by their own archers.
Then, Stribog paused no more. His hurricane-like windstorms
Sped on the arrows and bolts launched by the Slovak troops
With twice the speed, and carried twice the distance. The darts
Pierced whole hosts of the Chudes, drinking deep of their black blood.
None of the arrows missed its mark, each missile bore death
To a Chudan murderer. As their bosoms bristled
With killing arrow-shafts, as they belched forth blood in streams,
Pierced by the Slovak missiles directed by a force
Uncanny, they began to call upon their god Ár
For succour — most frantic, I reckon, was King Bondor:
   'O mighty god, victorious Ár, who hast ever
Received of us the best portion of our war-booty!
If truly thou carest for the Chude nation, if thou wishest
To fill thy belly full with fat offerings from us,

Come to our aid now, in this hour of mortal danger!
Stop up the mouths of the winds that now rage against us
And deflect the arrows of the Slovaks from our flesh,
Directing ours to fall upon them unerringly!'
   Thus did he pray in his ignorance, knowing not
That his god, before then, had been trying to do just that —
Oppose the winds, deflect the darts, direct the arrows
Of the Chudes to their targets, but all in vain: the god
Was powerless in the face of the will of Perún,
Supreme here, and he willed that Stribog be hindered not.
In a panic, astonished at his might grown feeble,
Ár bellowed, his voice as loud as lightning smashing cliffs:
'Set by your bows and crossbows! Rush upon the Tatrans
And hack them down with your swords and axes, toe to toe!'
At once they hurled themselves upon those whom Svatovít
Chafed to the fight, standing firm like an oaken forest.
The first ranks clashed, a bitter fray ensued, as with sword
And spear they hacked and thrusted, close quarters: first to fall
Was Rastek slain by Elel, Protislav by Rondok.
Bolkolt felled Omysl, while crosseyed Kolondor laid low
Javimír of towering stature. But the Slovaks
Gave as they got, dexterous in battle, too.
Not in vain they struggled, animated as they were
Not by mere fury alone, but according to plan,
Synchronised, disciplined, the wildly flailing Chudes
They slaughtered with ferocious sword-swipes, but ever keen
To mind the battle plan. Vlastislav slew Endeklen,
Prostoľub Esk, Dobor felled black-haired Zezabender.
Lubko slew Ferend, Volborovič Zaslav slaughtered
Gajulák, who free-ranged four herds of fleet-footed steeds
Along the Ingul when he was at home, but of course,
Most of his days were spent in foreign parts, pillaging
And murdering innocent strangers. Mighty Proslav
Brought down Kelezarden, and Turel, and Itind too.
He battered down the three Búzovič brothers: Astag,
Gob, and Fared, along with their powerful father.
Even Dúzab he slew, who formerly had been prince
Of the Gerský nomads, overburdened with booty.
   As thus they battled beneath the high shadowy vault
Of arrow and javelin, ferociously hacking,

And neither Slovak gave an inch before Chudan foe
Nor Chude relented from savage attack, wave on wave,
Ár noticed death winging down most thickly from the tops
Of the rocky ridges that embraced the narrow valley
Where the Chudes were crammed in a packed and sluggish mob.
Just as in autumn, when leaves singed by the frosty air
Cover the meadows in thick rustling heaps when north winds
Blow strongly, shaking the oak boughs barren, snapping twigs,
So did the hapless Chudes fall beneath rhythmic waves of darts.
The mightiest warriors fell there: Thom, Ehd, and Trul;
Packed in so tightly there, they neither could raise their shields
To fend off the bolts, nor did spryness of limbs avail
Where was no space to nimble; their might was nullified
Which otherwise might have felled one hundred stout Slovaks.
Thousands of horses, trapped there, reared in panic, flailing
With hooves that cracked the skulls of their riders unsaddled,
Pashing their prone corpses to jelly as they escaped.
Ár ascended the left ridge, endeavouring to snap
The tendons of the Slovak bows. He too would shatter
Crossbows, but in vain he strove — they were the work of hands
Immortal: Svatovít himself limbered the strong wood
Fresh and flexible, quite impossible to splinter.
Then he raced to the right, in hopes of better success,
But failed again: the Slovaks immediately stringing
Their supple bows with fresh tendons, firmer still, and so
The arrows flew more swiftly for Ár's intervention!
Now while he was struggling with the bows, he chanced
To cast his eye down at the scrum, where the battle raged
Most fiercely, the two sides battling hand to hand. There too
With terror he beheld the slaughter of his troops,
For, as when a pride of lions, out in search of prey
Since early morn, falls at last upon a flock of sheep,
And tears them apart, their hunger magnified by rage
At the long, impatient delay, so the Slovak men,
Their mettle augmented by the god who favoured them,
Hacked at the Chudes with their blades, spearing dead the fallen.
Matran Nemysel slew Kad, while Father Perún's fire
Burnt Bundok to a sudden crisp for impiety:
He'd planned to reserve Výboh for gory sacrifice!
Able Dobroslav proved worthy of the name he bore,

Slaying Losidek, a churl grown wealthy on thieving.
Solid Milko, captain of those who sip the Nitra,
With his mighty sword ran through Endeb, best counsellor
Amongst the rough Chudes. Before this, pious Lubomír
Laid low on the trampled earth Borkol and Karimáj,
The beastly bellowing of the latter now silenced.
The former was hated of Perún for having hewn down
Two of his idols and stealing their golden chaplets.
Karimáj was no better! Having plundered Živa's
Fane of its opulent wealth, he consumed it to ash
With pitchy torches, and carried off in harsh fetters
Her priest and his daughter. But now he paid for his crimes!
Istislav, voivode of the Belohorské legions
And prophet, sent to the shadows three Chudan seers:
Gen, Úz, and Tomeb, who'd earlier picked through the gore
Of entrails and bone-shards at the funeral service
For augury, and then ate the filth, ululating
Hymns incomprehensible in their Chudan jargon.
But prophets though they were, supposedly, they foretold
Not their own ruin, nor their army's catastrophe.
   Now, like to a stallion galloping over field
And verdant plain, trampling all beneath his mighty hooves,
Sláv raced about, always where the fight raged most fiercely,
Felling both enemies and the steed that bore them. Mon
He sent to his death with a spear-thrust, Randol, Balsor,
And Honed he slew with the sword of Ednek, slashing
Baldok to pieces, and Ug, and Turtul, and Farek,
While with his battle-axe he hurled both Áz and Terel
And giant Zarokender into the black abyss,
To coup-count adding Bodohender, son of Lotond,
Who, aged now, against his will, had to remain home
Childless and thankless, refraining from sweet pillaging.
Bodohender was slighter than his father, and yet
In might and battle-courage his equal. Sláv slew him,
The last of the sons of Lotond, all of whom were hewn
To death by the Slovak leader in the Obrín vale
Save the last, here. And all their wealth, stolen from others,
Would now pass into other hands. So many men fell!
When Cendor and Etkel, comrades-in-arms, who ever
Fought side by side, beheld the torrential carnage wrought

Amongst their ranks by Sláv, with seething hearts both men rushed
Upon him. But they fell in first mid-stride towards him,
For he awaited them not: ripping through Cendor's throat
With a swift arrow, and crushing the other's ribcage
With boulder catapulted from his mighty right arm.
Empty-saddled steeds, escaping from the fray, trampled
In panic their corpses, face-down into the dark mire.
   When Ár beheld the slaughter of so many raiders
He left the heights, descending swift as a lightning bolt
To the thick of the fray. There he sought out the wild Kondok
And hissed at him thus: 'O mighty Kondok! O battler
Beyond all others! If only the Chudes had heeded
Your wise counsel, the shattered remnants of the Tatrans
Would now be crouched upon their ravaged land, bewailing
Its ruin! And long since, with all our slaves and booty,
We would have been back in our homeland, fully glutted
With fresh luxury! Alas, there's nothing for it
Now, but to repair the errors of others. Look there!
Rush upon that foul ravager who's thinning our ranks,
And add one more heroic deed of slaughter — his death! —
To your exhaustive reckonings. His the chief command
Of all the Slovak forces — cut off the head, the limbs
Will crumple harmless to the ground! Go now! It is he
Who has lain low so many of our best warriors.
When he falls by your hand, the tide will turn, the others
Will in a trice be overrun, hurled into the dark
Abyss of eternal desolation. Kill him!'
   Thus Ár, and Kondok, recognising the voice he heard
To be the god's, although he saw him not (wrapped in mist),
Made this reply: 'O mighty warlike god! Where've you been?
Why have we waited so long on your aid? Tardily
You come among us, having allowed so much carnage
To befall your people! What of our sacrifices?
Have we been stuffing your belly full of gore in vain?
I've been in many wars, but I've never seen the like!
— So many Chudes lain low, sent to their deaths bellowing
In agony, as I have seen this day — so many
Fallen beneath the angry swipes of but one sword, his,
That wicked doomsman! Think not that I've not attempted
To lay him low! So many times I've hurled javelin

And spear at the rabid Sláv, now at his eyes, and now
At his midriff, and even at his shanks, to topple
Him to the earth, where I'd finish him off: all in vain,
Whereas my darts have otherwise unerringly bit
Deep into Slovak flesh. There must be some god in this
Protecting him, whisking away all missiles whistling
Near his favourite. But I shall try again. Now you,
Do your part! Speed on this angry spear and drive it home,
This hefty barb, into the brawny flesh of our foe!'
   Thus he. At once the great iron tip of his spear flashed
In the sun, and he hurled it with all his might at Sláv,
Aiming for his belly. The spear flew swift as lightning,
But struck wide of its target, not to taste of Sláv's blood,
Svatovít deflecting the ashen shaft. However,
It pierced the calf of Bohosť, the most excellent
Of the hero's six sons, who'd been battling by his side,
Felling their foes. Reeling under the blow, he fell down,
Striking the earth with his face. Sláv, infuriated
At Bohosť's injury, grabbed an even greater spear
— Like the shaft of a mountain pine — and cursing, hurled it
At savage Kondok. This sped truly, plunging through shield
And breastplate, and flesh — its head emerging through his back,
Between the shoulder blades. Ár, though he tried to defend
His favourite from harm, whom he'd goaded to the task,
Proved powerless to parry the blow, unable now
To aid his men in the cruel fray. For Svatovít
Had sniffed him out, as only a god can recognise
Another god, although he'd never seen him before —
He'd seen who'd sped on the spear cast at Sláv just as soon
As he'd deflected it from the hero's broad midriff.
At once he flew up to Ár and as swift as lightning
Brought Perún's sword crashing down on his head. Horridly
Ár screamed in pain — so frightfully that both armies paused
In horripilating truce for one uncanny moment
Before plunging anew into the strife. The Chudan
God, recovering from the blow, thrust his hefty pike
Straight at the throat of Svatovít, but missed, for nimbly
The god of the Slavs dodged to the right, and the missile
Lurched wide. And then once more he delivered a mighty
Blow to the head of Ár. Nor did he leave off: thickly

His blows fell, battering ear and brow and face entire,
Slashing and pummelling the savage god on his chest
And his arms, and smashing the stout hull of his ribcage,
Like a thresher at work with his flail ever swinging,
Blow after blow he rained down on the defeated god
— Now but a quivering mass of aethereal flesh
Crumpled upon the dusty plain. Then spoke Svatovít:
  'Cruel god of bandits, governor of war! Slink off now
Back to your Chudan homeland to rule your gory plot
Bespattered with the blood of innocent offerings!
For if you don't hightail it from the Tatran homeland,
And leave off aiding the Chudes — who get what they deserve! —
I'll give you such a thrashing that it will be a year
Before you recover enough to sniff holocausts!'
  Thus Svatovít. Ár meanwhile, stretched out upon the ground,
Could not even raise his right hand to defend himself.
Nor was he fain to endure more such harsh walloping.
And so he struggled up on aching legs, and sped off
— As much as panicked hobbling can be so termed — for home,
For peace, for safety, with Svatovít in close pursuit,
Giving him nary a moment's rest, urging him on
With thwacks whenever his bruised muscles cried respite
And his pace slowed — all the way to his hideous grove
Did Svatovít harry him, before heading back. There,
At last, Ár stretched out in one sore, throbbing pulp of pain
In the dark shades, steaming, and bathed his wounded body
In the rank mire of the black marshes that fester there.
  Meanwhile, with the gods now absent from the cruel fray,
Left to their own devices, the two armies fought on.
The Slovaks continued victorious, casting down
Their foes to the bloody soil. But when the sun's cart
Rolled near the midpoint of its daily journey, fortune
Switched sides. Fresh hordes of Chudes unscathed as yet in battle
Rushed forth, wave upon wave, against the wearied Slovaks,
Like to a pulsing windstorm that lays oak-forests low.
Bord took down Slavomíl, and Kudor slew Pomstislav;
Embo killed Namír, while the gigantic Edendor
Swept away both Velohosť and Jarek. Eldo's son
Alirendo, whose horridly scarred face was often
Presented to Ár in his bloody grove, slew Burák,

Pinning the agile warrior to the earth, at last,
With a spear-thrust to the throat, just as he'd drawn deep breath
To sound a clarion on his horn (for he was both
Bugler and warrior — in one hand he held his trump
And in the other his sword, with which he mowed down the Chudes).
But now he fell — spun by the impact — upon the grass.
No less raged those two bandits, always lusting for spoils
And always found together: the ferocious Forkond
And Nemoltok, seething for revenge. Forkond slew Lub,
Born brother of Chválok; Nemoltok slaughtered Kalín.
To such prey they added the hunters Zhor, Mír, Tolok.
Zen wounded Tech in the ear, Irok crushed the mighty
Arm of swift Zvestoslav, while Sibo slashed Žarok's calf
And Dojko's hand, Seberád's firm jaw. Then Tulbol, prince
Of the Chudes, clave Zorimíl's head to the collarbone,
Collapsed Bucok's lungs, crushing with spear-thrust his ribcage,
And punctured Budhihosť squarely in the loins. And then
His eyes caught sight of Bolemíl flattening whole crowds
Of Chudan raiders with his club, as if with hawthorn
Staff a boy battling thistles on the field swipes them down.
At him he hurled his unerring ash-wood javelin
Which rushed straight through his navel and snapped his vertebrae,
Its angry trip emerging through his back. Paralysed,
He fell to the meadow grass with an immense rumble
Echoing doubly: his great frame and elm-club falling.
Ordogelek, on account of his might and courage
Spared by his uncle King Bondor from the sacrifice
To Ednek — the cruel fate of his foremost servants —
Wielded in the battle, as always, a fierce hatchet.
Nedo, Kraslav, Božok, and the fair-faced Hostibrat
He severed, hacking, from the light. His blade bit into
Bolek's nape, and splintered Dobromysl's shoulderblade,
Adding these to his bloody list: Bratroslav, Vitek,
And Plaveš. Swarthy-grey Omlok, a sorcerer foul
And hideous of countenance, who'd taught his people
How to mix fatal venom from the gore of hissing
Reptiles and human blood, with which — the godless scoundrel! —
He'd tinct arrowhead and spear-barb, so that the slightest scratch
Grazed by them should fester into an unhealing wound,
Ever mumbling his spells, poked Zemorád in the thigh

With his corrupt arms, wounding Borok thus in the throat,
Domomysl in the ribs, and Laslav, Branek, and Rašín,
Who'd always been a first-rate hunter of the wild boar
And mountain goat. And then, the base villain set his sights
On Lubomír, aiming to cleave his head, but Perún,
Supreme ruler of the universe, would not have his
Pious servant felled. Barely had he smeared the arrowhead
With venom than it turned upon itself — corroding
The barb and splintering the shaft still in the wretch's
Vile hand, falling to pieces, leaving him weaponless.
  Rabid Bondor not only screamed, not only bellowed,
Urging men from the rear; he too fought tirelessly.
Like to a sharp-eyed windhover striking at sparrows
Chattering blithely on a fence before flapping off
— Or trying to — in panic, thus he swooped down upon
His rivals. His unforgiving spear toppled Stojmír,
Then Vid, Kreslav, Dražok, and the two valiant brothers
Radomíl and Posvoj. To these he added Surovec,
Than whom Detva boasted no shepherd richer in flocks,
Who'd trained the ever-proud herdsmen of Brezno to fight
With spear and to reckon in red — like counting their flocks! —
The Chudes they culled to the gloomy pens of Hell. Lain low
He was by Bondor in the midst of wreaking havoc
Amongst the Chude ranks. Then Bodor cut down Ľubohosť,
And after him Zorovít, Horín and Rodkovič
Múdroslav, Pochval, and Darek, brothers swept away
To the shadows of death by his curved battle-axe.
Neither valiant Ranko, Nor Výš could stand against him,
Nor even Jarmíl, great of stature, renowned in war.
Volimír fell before him, as did swift Radoslav,
The former run through the loins, the latter through the chest.
And you fell too, Milín, you best of Namysel's sons;
You, the greatest delight of a nation enamoured!
You too bit the earth, coming to rest on the black soil.
Not even your great beauty could coax the flinty heart
Of the cruel savage to pity. Neither tender years,
Nor heroism in arms, nor your father's great wealth,
Nor even your piety was to any avail.
Not even your parent could deflect death from your side.
Seeing you crumple, sick to death with sorrow, he leapt

To your cooling frame in one bound. Seeking death himself
— What reason had he to live on? — he flung a great spear
Of oak at the Chudan king. Ineffective the cast:
It flew wide of its target, harming the villain not
Though it grazed his cheek and drew some little blood, before
Flying on, its impetus unhindered, to impale
Bodofork through the spine. For Sláva reserved the fame
Of felling Bondor to another: Sláv. Seeing this —
The spear meant to fell him now protruding from the side
Of Bodofork like a stiff third arm — Bondor raged thus,
Taking to hand a death-dealing javelin of pine:
'Let's see if my aim is better, you hapless spearman!
When I cast my darts, they fail not to find new quivers
In the bone-cages of my enemies!' He sent it
Screaming through the void. Crushing like destiny, the head
Plunged through the shield of Namysel, stiff breastplate, cartilage,
Bone, and flesh, to puncture his lung and soil his back
With gore as it passed out. Blood pumped in streams from his wounds
And his mouth. 'Lie there now with your son, tender parent!'
The cruel villain cried. 'Such is the price that all shall pay
Who boldly dare to rise in armed revolt against us!'
   Roaring thus, Bondor rushed upon others with his spear.
And just as heavy apples clinging on their thin stems
Will drum upon the soil, should one shake the bough stoutly,
So fell the Slovaks as their foes raged, fiercely hacking.
They were within a trice of overcoming the men
Set on both ridges, the archers, and would have slain them,
Slashing their way to a total victory, if not
For Svatovít. As soon as he had chased Ár, limping,
Back to his foul grotto, he returned to the Tatras —
Two leaps, and a third, brought him back to the army's side.
And there amongst the hard-pressed Slovak ranks, limbs aching
And near exhausted with long battling, Svatovít flew
In the guise of an eagle, calling down the thunder.
Before the face of Lubomír he swept, passing near
Milko, Zamysel, Ponislav, calling each by name
In a booming voice: 'Fight on brave lads! Destroy the foul beasts,
Those savage marauders of our land! Take the vengeance
Your folk deserve! Waver not, Slovaks! The day is ours!'
Thus did he hearten all the men, making their breasts swell

With courage renewed, refreshing the limbs of fighters
Weakened with the toil of war who, emboldened anew,
With thrice their wonted power, thrice their sword-arm's vigour,
Fell on their startled foes like a sudden thunderstorm.
Blows rained on the shocked Chudes from all sides, battering them.
Deft Tur brought down Sib, Nábož slew Zen, Hostivod Emb.
Pravdoslav slaughtered Bord, Koják laid Alirend low,
Prudent Výbor, whose countenance Svatovít borrowed
When he wished to counsel Sláv how to emplace the men
Before the battle, catching sight of Orgodelek
Flailing about with horrid battle-axe in fury,
Rushed upon him and with his razor-sharp sword severed
His forearm at the elbow. Down to the blood-soaked mire
The limb fell detached, followed by the massy trunk,
Slipped from the saddle, fainting dead from the loss of blood.
Hajisláv crushed the bosom of Forkond. When nimble
Nemoltok beheld that, his own breast churned with venom,
And quickly he flung his ash with murderous intent.
Its evil barb would surely have been glutted with gore,
Shattering Výbor's face had not clever Zamysel
Intercepted the shaft in flight, cleaving it in twain
Before it caused his Turčan friend any salty harm.
He rushed upon Nemoltok then, and with one fierce thrust
Skewered him through both armpits with his spear, shattering
The humerus upon exiting. Writhing in pain,
Nemoltok crumpled to earth. Not far from him, Veslav
The pious stretched out the godless Omlok with a thrust
Of his spear. The sorcerer's treacherous concoctions
Were of no avail to him then! The wicked Omolt
Fell under the crushing blow landed square on his chops
By Ponislav, who also punctured Irtiš's groin
And Edenbor's loins, sending all three crashing down low
To gnaw the filthy soil in their final agony.
Kudor then fell at the hands of Pravomíl; cruel
Čereksor, Zud, and Irok were slain by him as well,
Like Bentold and Ombol, gigantic of frame and greed,
Who'd slain his own brother to steal his portion of loot.
    Incensed with rage, Sláv set off to chase down cruel Bondor,
That shameless villain, whom he'd long wished to batter down.
But Svatovít, fearing that at their leader's demise

The Chudes, despairing, might turn their backs and flee the field
Upon fleet-footed chargers — he wanted them all dead! —
Deflected Sláv, rather, at Tulbol, the Chudan prince,
For he was nearer, cutting down crowds of the Slovaks.
At him he urged Sláv then, addressing such words to him:
'O Sláv, turn your vengeful arm upon that murderer —
It shall be your great glory to bring him down, I vow!'
Heeding the god's advice, Sláv took himself to Tulbol
And laid him low, shattering his copper-clad forehead
With one powerful blow of his mighty oaken spear,
The point of which pierced helmet and skull, both front and back,
Passing clean through in its flight, squelching the wicked brain.
Tulbol fell to earth with a crash, as did many Chudes,
Like fir trees upon the Magorské Hills, all aflame
In a wildfire sparked by a lightning burst and billowed
Into a roar by the whistling wind, sheets of fire
Leaping from trunk to trunk, gnawing through the wood, which snaps;
They topple to the ash-strewn forest floor, live embers
Consuming them at length to shave thick-wooded hills bald.
Just so one heard the skeletons of the Chudes crackle
And burst beneath the mighty blows dealt by the Slovaks.
Not much time passed before the earth was black with shattered
Chude corpses. The gore of men and stallions flowed in streams
Of nauseating filth, like black rivulets of ash
And blackened treebark sent spilling down the bare hill slopes
By a torrential rain quenching at last the wildfire.
So were the hills, once thickly bristling with Chude warriors,
Swept clean from summit to foot by the raging Slovaks.

CANTO V

Svatovít counsels Sláv, with all his force,
To strike the centre of the Chudan horde,
And then to press the wings into the marsh.
At once Sláv and his men attack; immense
The blow, immense the panic of the Chudes.
The Slovaks penetrate the very midst
Of their foes' ranks. Meanwhile, god Svatovít
Hovers above the right flank, urging on
The Slovaks there to push their enemies
Into the chasm below. With strength renewed
They do so, and the Chudes fall, helplessly,
Into the dark abyss, where they are drowned
By Water-Man, who presses them beneath
His feet into the mire. On the left flank
The Chudes, made more resistant through despair,
Cling on more fiercely. There, the marshland god,
Obedient to Svatovít (in turn
Moved by the pious Veslav's urgent prayer)
Summons the rivers to swell close in aid.
He sets his conch aside and grabs his trident,
With which he loosens spring and source to give
An unimpeded path to the rushing streams.
At once the rivers overswell their banks,
Submerging quickly all the vale. The Chudes,
In terror, at the urging of Oland,
Would swim their horses to the farther bank —
In vain: both steed and man sink into the reeds
That tangle hoof and foot. They scream for Ár,
But he's unable to rush near with aid,
And in the black depths of the river mud,
That flank too founders, drowned in agony.

With no less speed the Tatrans, valiant beyond measure,
Harried the pummelled Chudes across the plain, stumbling,
Their panicked legs enmired in sucking mud. Svatovít,

Ever a-wing, added strength to Slovak arms, urging
The troops to battle. To doughty Sláv once more he came
And in such words, he offered his strategic advice:
   'Most capable Sláv! Wisest voivode! With all our might
Let us now train our forces at the very centre
Of our reeling enemies. If we are successful
And hurl them backward into ruin, then on each flank
We'll press them from both sides into the swamp, drowning them
In murky bog and dark abyss of water; then the few
Who cling onto some scrap of land, we'll mop up swiftly'.
   After saying this, he hastened off to the front lines
Where, sweeping a grand arc with his sword and brandishing
His shield, he roared loudly, giving heart to his army
And filling his evil foes with sore trepidation.
Sláv too was pleased at his counsel, and immediately
Plunged into the very midst of the repulsive hordes,
Calling his men to follow him and strike the centre
Of the wavering Chudes, except for those on the flanks —
Those he had remain where they were, with swords drawn, to block
Any route of escape to those herded to their doom.
   And all the Slovaks, obedient to him, eagerly
Fulfilled their allotted tasks. Meanwhile, as an eagle
Will swoop upon a flock of linnets pecking at grain
And tear them into meat with savage beak and talons,
So Sláv fell upon the Chudan villains with a roar.
First Tuhut fell, then Rebendol of majestic frame,
Lizul and Hondolk, and Gumbor of fierce countenance.
Next, he cut down Tum, Uktol, and Irdo,
Bolto's sons, mighty all; he also slew Ud, brother
Of Zondol, and later brother Zondol in his turn,
Who had the savage custom — fearsome it is to tell! —
Of slicing off the noses of all he took captive.
Now it was his face demolished by the fir-shafted
Spear that passed clean through his nose, emerging at the nape.
It was that Tatran javelin that hurled him to Hell
Where he would cut off no stranger's nose ever again!
Big bellied Etobelt fell beneath Sláv's blows, like Kondul
His father; the first with a spear thrust through his visage,
The latter, through the Adam's apple. Wealthy Ellak,
The future son-in-law of Bondor, who had paid court

To the king's eldest girl; Bondor smiled upon the match,
Meaning, once the Slovak incursion had run its course,
To organise a joyous marriage with much feasting.
Over-anxious, the lad hurled an oaken spear at Sláv,
Yet it flew amiss, passing over his right shoulder,
Though it was a narrow miss, the shaft scraping the scalp
Above Sláv's ear, leaving the bare mark of its passage.
Stunned at the brief impact, Sláv slowly turned toward him,
Then hurled his own missile, which passed through his shield, breastplate
And breast, entering at his left nipple, passing through
To exit beneath his shoulderblade. Ellek crumpled,
His wounds out-pumping a black torrent of blood. So much
For wedding plans — the gift he brought his bride-to-be: woe,
Endless woe, for a maiden widowed before her vows.
Then Sláv turned to others: Tod, and Oktol, and Bondo,
Kut, and the capable Tobovec brothers, Sorok
And Odolondo soon were lain on the gloomy bed
Prepared for them by Sláv for the night that's never ending.
To these he added Dolokonto, Zizoktel, Remb,
And Alnok — and others beside them, the catalogue
Of heroes sent by Sláv to the caustic chasms of Hell
By sword and spear — what tongue, what pen might enumerate?

   The others followed him. As hearty reapers at dawn
In the fields along the Dudváh or the Rímava
— Gorgeous streams! — set out behind their leader at the front
To mow down the grasses, heaping sheaves in growing piles,
So did the Slovak warriors follow Sláv, scything
A bloody path through the very centre of the Chudes —
Felling their ranks. Thus Hostislav mowed down Kodolán
And Telibond was lain low by Javor, the former
Struck by a sword, the latter run through by javelin.
Milko punctured Zorod's jutting jaw and Čerkoront's
Guts, which spilled out of the ghastly wound, a flood of fat
And unspooling intestines. The massive-brawned Proslav
Speared Korikond in the groin. The shaft transfixed his horse
As well through the muscled back; the poor beast stumbled on
Without falling, though the shaft, driven deep to the bone,
Waggled on until Proslav drew it out from rider
And mount, whom he'd transformed into a grotesque centaur.
Deft Vitohosť, younger brother of the voivode Sláv,

His equal both in height and power, though in wisdom
And cleverness Sláv exceeded him, took off the head
Of wild and savage Onotolk and then, spinning 'round,
With one powerful sword-swipe cleft Zundúr in two halves.
His trunk first thudded to the earth, while his hips and legs
Were borne about still in stirrup and saddle until
His frenzied charger bucked the half carcass from his back.
Brestislav shattered repulsive Karadúr's skullbone,
Though his helmet fended the first blow, while with right hand
He measured a swipe at his assailant. Brestislav
Parried this with raised shield, then punctured Karadúr's jowl —
Which blow knocked him from his steed; dead, he tumbled to earth.
  No less fiercely did Výbor and his sons set themselves
— Skilful battlers! — to the task of vengeance on behalf
Of brother and uncle slaughtered. First did Haleton
Fall before Výbor, then Ilton, Oktul, and Zardo,
And hideous one-eyed Otulm, who'd used that right eye
— As long as it could see — to cast evil spells on men.
Výbor's sons, meanwhile, like to juvenile hawks who sense
Their claws harden beneath them, and, borne aloft on wings
That rejoice in the novelty of flight, leave the nest
To swoop down from the sun on defenceless prey a-wing
Below them, tearing with talons, hammering with beak,
So did these rush upon the Chudes, wreaking dire havoc
With sword and spear, maugre their young age — fresh, and mighty!
First they cut down the three Tolbovič brothers, and then
The three immense scions of Dibol, who once had been
The largest man whelped of Chudan parents. Three further
Brothers — Olmovič — were sent to the shades by Výbor's
Bold lads, urging Tololm soon after to be their guide
Through the dark alleys of Hell, Tololm, who'd seized four wives
And a fifth might have taken, had not death now seized him,
Putting an end to his widow-making and his lust.
They slew Ulikán, they slew the bard Kopolt as well,
Who made a lute of two larger and two shorter bows
— For no other music was known to those savages —
Which he bound together and plucked with flying fingers,
Wailing the savage battle-hymns of Chude banditry.
And as mature fields of grain will blacken to stubble
When a chance fire catches the stalks to rage, fed by winds,

So the ranks of the invaders crumpled suddenly
Wherever the Tatran forces ravaged in their midst,
Strengthened by Svatovít fanning the flames of their wrath.
  But when they'd cut a deep path through the very centre
Of the Chudan army, pressing deep into its core,
Svatovít left them and hurried to the right-hand flank
To inspire the Slovaks there with like battle-ardour,
Making their hearts swell with courage, strengthening their limbs.
Here and there he raced along their lines, calling to them:
  'O valiant comrades! To arms! Grip fast your weapons now
And tense your muscles, strain with the last ounce of your strength
To push the bandits, bloated with loot, into the bogs!
Cut down the Chudes! For if you waver now in warring
And sink them not in the bottomless depths of the marsh,
With ease they'll encircle our men who have pressed deep
Into the centre of their ranks, and cut them all down!'
  With this he drummed against his gigantic shield and swung
His battle-axe. At this sudden thunder and whistling
In the air, the Chudes felt cold terror course through their veins.
The steeds beneath them reared, snuffing the air with horror.
The Slovaks sent up a cheer, recognising their god;
At once they charged upon their foes like an avalanche,
Hacking them flat and pressing them into the wetlands.
It was here that Uzob fell, and brave, splendid-faced
Ondomelek, along with Čendol his father, both
Chased from this world. The first of these was slain by Borboj,
Mojmír took off the second, and Prislav slew the third.
There Kompol lost his life. Júz, Tember, and Olontob
Fell, along with Bolomtondolk. Satanic Bendol,
Who had wielded such weights as no other man might lift,
Sprawled now upon the ground himself, an inert burden
Slowly sinking out of sight. Unoslav slew the first
Pair, Zamysel the rest, although it was the last one
Who caused him the most trouble. Twice he lunged at the wretch
With his Oravan ash, which twice snickered off the shield;
At the third thrust the evil champion hacked away
The shaft, leaving but a splinter in Zamysel's grasp.
The Slovak then unsheathed his sword and, closing fast,
Slit a gash in his fat midriff, cutting a deep wound.
Bendol tottered in agony and fell with a crash.

Jaroslav, welcoming to guests beyond all measure,
Slew Dízabo, who'd once escaped him in his absence
To lead his raw countrymen into Tatrania
By ways familiar to his ungrateful traitor's feet —
Lugging away the loot he was never to enjoy.
But first, to get at him, he had to cast to the earth
Zolob and Cindo Hurdovič, who had blocked his way.
These he despatched with his curved blade. On approaching near
His erstwhile servant — and patient — he addressed him thus:
   'Ah, you bandit! You scoundrel! That I once carried you
In my own arms, sorely wounded, from the battlefield
And healed those wounds, yes! wresting you from the jaws of death
With medicines and tender care, to introduce you
Into my own home — not as a slave, as you deserved,
But as a brother, or a son! Thus I treated you!
And what was the reward for my kindness? Treachery!
You robbed me of my goods, stealing even the chalice
I'd used for the liturgies in praise of Radogost.
How impious the paws that dared such desecration!
Now you come at me again, astride my very horse,
Who plants his forelegs, bucking against your foul urgings
To charge his master! Traitor! You'd come at me again?
Once trampled prone, half-dead, into the mire, one would think
You'd learned what the rewards of pillaging are! Pardoned
Once from punishment you deserved, now you seek more?
The hand that once delivered you from death now deals it!'
   Thus Jaroslav, to whom cruel Dízabo responded:
'What man would live meekly in foreign parts, in comfort
Even, if that meant living as a slave, though pampered?
Should you capture an eagle and keep him in a cage,
Fattening him on the choicest meats, he will escape
Still, to life more arduous, but life in liberty!
Let but the sharp-eyed captive king of the mountain crags
Espy the slimmest fissure in the gilded network
Of bars that confine him — he won't hesitate, but fly!
How can you then be shocked that I would escape your grip,
However soft and caressing? Yes, now I return
To pay you back for my brothers fallen in Obrín —
So much for words of gratitude. Take them or leave them'.
   While uttering these last words the villain hurled his spear

At Jaroslav. But great Radogost himself, mindful
Of Jaroslav's piety, who had raised a temple
In his honour on a proud hilltop, and his kindness
In welcoming all travellers to a richly spread
Table — never was man in need shunted from his door —
Deflected the cast with a sudden billow of wind
So that the ashen missile buried its vicious head
In the grass to the side, rather than Jaroslav's skull,
And there it shivered long after the mighty impact.
Then Jaroslav tossed his javelin — more skilfully,
For it missed not its target, smashing Dízabo's teeth,
The sharp point of the glinting spear exiting the nape.
He tottered to the ground like a silver poplar felled,
At which Jaroslav the deft called out to him once more:
'Run off to your Chudan homeland now, with such booty
Hanging from your chaps, as a dog bears off his morsel,
Proud of such takings, though alone, with no slaves in train'.
  Now, as the Slovaks were pressing the Chudes to the bogs,
The Water-Man, craving a great haul of such pillage,
Lifted his head above the water's surface to gaze
Upon the fierce battle of the opposing armies.
He cried: 'Here! Push them here, those cruel killers, to the marsh!
I'll help you, pulling them into the watery depths!
No more shall they return thence to loot the Slovak land!'
  Having said this, he hastened to the lip of the marsh
To drag whatever Chudes were in the reach of his hands
To a horrible death by drowning. Many there were
In the sucking shallows already, the Tatrans so
Herded them, with Svatovít pounding his buckler,
Driving them mad with panic at the shriek of his axe.
So packed were they on the shrinking firm ground still left them,
So maddened with fear, that they flailed blindly with their weapons,
Friend wounding friend, comrade felling comrade, son father,
Father son, brother slaying brother. Some in despair
Sought to flee the carnage by leaping into the deep
Black water themselves. And soon, just as the strong spring wind
And stronger waxing sun loosens the great sheets of ice
That had clung to the granite boulders in the Dnieper
To speed downstream and smash into shards in the rapids,
So the horde splintered, man and horse alike all plunging

In chaos from the melting tongue of land to wallow
And sink in the dark depths of the bog, the Water-Man
Treading them down beneath his webbed feet, making more room
For new larder-stock. Thus they perished on the right flank.
  On the left shore of the wetlands it was tougher
Going for the Slovaks, though nimbly and strongly they fought,
Bringing down four of the mightiest Chude warriors:
Belotond, Aldul, Tomolondor, as well as Prince
Endebelel, and other battlers without number,
Still they couldn't press them all into the black waters.
They might easily have escaped death in the dark flood
Had Veslav not received new help from the river god.
Downstream, a wide, open plain spread beyond the marshes,
Where the bank suddenly plunged to the height of a man.
It was covered in fat grass and all sorts of bushes
And always, in springtime, when the mountain snowmelt rushed
Down the channel, or when the river swelled with rain,
It so filled with the runoff as to become a lake.
But under the strong summer sun, when hot breezes blew,
It would dry, and however pasture might be lacking
Elsewhere, the cattle would find here the richest grazing.
At the time it was dry beyond all measure; indeed,
A full thirty years had passed since it had been so firm
Underfoot and empty. And here on this bald meadow
The Chudes took a stand, putting up a fierce resistance.
'Twas there that Svatovít directed Veslav's eye. He
Immediately lifted this urgent petition
To the god of the waterways and the black marshes:
'O mighty spirit, who rule these wide-spreading wetlands!
Come swiftly to our aid now! Let loose a rushing flood!
Submerge the lower valley, and with it, the cruel Chudes!
Should you do this, and sink our enemies in the depths,
I promise you the richest annual sacrifice!'
  Such was his prayer. And the god looked out upon the plain,
Upon the fiercely warring armies, from the height of a lone
Poplar tree, which grew upon the summit of a hill
In the midst of the flood-plain, where Ponislav once waged
A fierce battle with a river monster, who'd emerge
From the depths to creep upon dry land and carry off
The cattle that strayed near — even throttling the herd boys.

To this high perch, then, the governor of the marshes
Had betaken himself at the strange clatter of arms
— Odd in that peaceful place — to gaze out upon the fray,
Unseen himself. The venom of wrath coursed through his veins
At the sight of the bandits hacking down his guiltless
Countrymen, in hopes of despoiling them of their goods;
And so, having heard the prayer of pious Veslav,
He scrambled down again and roared upon the marshland.
He blared a summons upon a mighty horn, which rang
Far and wide, summoning there all the streams and freshets
Which spilled down at once from the mountains to congregate
Upon the plain. Then the god himself seized his trident
And, plunging it swiftly and deeply into each spring,
Each bubbling water-source, broke through all the barriers
Regulating their measured flow, loosening all
The powerful flux to swell forth in a mighty flood.
The waters burst out from underground caverns roaring,
Rolling into dark billows as massive as hilltops.
Freshets and streams, meanwhile, no longer streams and freshets,
Rushed down the mountain slopes and through the flanking meadows
Like new-born rivers, deep and wide, surging toward new seas:
Those wetlands, and the dry lakebed where the vile Chudes knew
The waters would soon begin to swirl about ankle
Knee, thigh, waist — and soon engulf the high banks above them.
Soon the vale was inundated, to their horror —
Only the mighty Olond was unperturbed. Sneering
At the panic of his comrades, thus he called to them:
   'Well then! What the great minds to the rear were unable
To concoct — a way out of our dire situation;
What the king himself, as clever as he is, couldn't
Devise — our rescue — the marsh itself offers us. Come!
We'll save ourselves from the slaughter by swimming away!
Come on! Let us breast this flood to the other shoreline!
Have we not swum across broad River Don on horseback?
Have we not braved, and conquered, the Danube's growling waves?
Have not our horses carried us over the eddies
And deep pools amid the Dnieper's current? Let's go, then!
All the more easily shall we cross these waters — still,
Though deep; they lack a current — what's a lake to our steeds,
Even though they will have no firm ground beneath their hooves?

We shall swim these waters and then, once on the high ground
There, we'll gallop back and strike the Slovaks from the rear.
What seems an obstacle will be our path to glory!'
   Thus Olond, at which the Chudes set out on the waters,
Thinking to save themselves, and to destroy the Tatrans
As he suggested. So they spurred their horses forward
Onto the suddenly risen bosom of the lake.
Their steeds churned the flood with pumping legs, barely keeping
Wide-open eye and snorting nostril above the waves
That swelled around them. And they might have made the far bank
Had not the Water-Man, when they'd reached the deepest part
Of the lake, mid-point between near shoreline and farther,
Stretched out (at the god's command) a net thickly woven
Of long grasses and cross-stitched reeds beneath the surface,
As wide as the lake itself. In this their hooves tangled;
The more they struggled against it, the more it bound them;
They tired, they cramped, they sank along with their riders
Who pushed them down the more, kicking with panicking feet
Against the saddles below them sinking out of sight.
And when their horses were drowned, they drowned one another
Pulling at comrades' arms, clambering on the shoulders
Of those nearby, who pulled them down themselves by the legs,
Trying to shinny up the sinking bodies, gasping,
Gulping, cursing with their last breath before they vanished.
The last ranks, just approaching the fatal trap, cried out
In terror at what they saw, and, jerking at the reins,
Tried to reverse their flailing steeds and regain the shore
Where the Slovaks waited — better to die in battle,
A warrior's death, than to drown in a bog! And yet
Such was to be their fate as well, for the Water-Man
Circled beneath the flood, dragging the plaited grasses
Closed like a purse-seine around a shoal of shocked small-fry.
What were they to do? Their horses spun and spun, panicked,
Searching for firm footing, and finding none. They cursed Olond then,
The drowning hordes, and cursed themselves as well for heeding
His fatal advice. Spluttering, they called to their god:
   'Almighty Ár! Such is the aid you send your soldiers?
That you let us drown like groundhogs in flooded warrens?
Were we ever lax in smearing your grove with fresh gore?
Were we ever behindhand in sacrifice to you?

Why then do you not aid us? Lead us to victory!
Why, at the least, do you not pluck us from these waters
That we might die like soldiers, facing our enemies,
A death heroic? Deserve we not at least such grace?
O, turn your eyes upon your people, and hear our prayer!'
   Thus did they cry. Ár did hear the screams of the dying,
But he was powerless to help them, though he would:
Three times he strove to lift himself to his feet, groaning,
Pressing upon his staff, tensing his muscles to rise,
But three times he collapsed, tottering on splintered gams
So many times bruised by the battering Svatovít's
Sword. Meanwhile, the Chudes were still wallowing toward shores
They'd never reach. Their swimming steeds' strength gave out; they sank
Beneath the waters' surface, out of sight of their foes
Who looked on from the firm ground: here some drowned man's back bobbed
On the waves, there a head rose, to sink again. Nothing
Floated long, save the shields, whirling flat on the eddies,
Spun round and round, and the spears released from hands gone limp
Floating horizontal, though here and there barbs glinted
Upright, still gripped by the panicked men as they foundered —
And some, before sinking, still menaced the men on shore
Though unable to fling their missiles — glaring with hate.
But at last they too sank from sight. The surface grew still:
No more bubbles or rings disturbed the glassy pane. Then
The marshland god once more blared upon his twisted horn,
Sounding the waters' retreat from the cluttered lakebed.

CANTO VI

Through Zvestoň Perún orders Svatovít
To withdraw from the battle, and Stribog
No longer to impel the Slovak darts
With blasts of wind. The Chudes are in despair:
Should they escape? Or carry on the fight?
Lobontol blares retreat, but wrathful Bondor
Refuses to withdraw. So they war on,
Heaving their swords with the last of their strength,
With equal fortune on both sides, till, at last,
The archers race down from the flanking heights
To aid their brothers. Thickly fall the Chudes;
So thickly that Kelentol near succeeds
In bending Bondor to rethink escape.
And he might have convinced him, had the One
Who rules the cosmos not dispatched Neustup,
Who hardens more the hearts of all the Chudes,
Those evildoers! and so they fight on,
Refusing to withdraw deceitfully.
The Tatrans, heartened by their leader's words,
Press on their enemies with great slaughter,
Until Sláv meets up with Bondor the cruel
And calls upon him to surrender. No —
Still he rejects peace with contempt, urging
His mob to battle yet, to the last man.
So Sláv imparts his will to his soldiers:
Since they will not submit, cut them all down!
And this they do — save for the king himself —
Sláv faces him at last in single combat,
And with his axe, sends him into the gloom.

From his throne in the clouds, the ruler of the cosmos
Gazed down upon the progress of the battle. And then,
Seeing that the Tatrans had repulsed the Chudes' assault,
Helped by their god, in battle and in the waters' depths
So many warriors to destroy, summoned Zvestoň

And bade him hurry swiftly earthward, bearing his will:
  'My fleet-footed messenger! Hasten now to the gods
Who aid the Slovaks in the terrifying battle
And say — to Svatovít first — that as the Tatran troops
Have beat down the main forces of the Chudes, and forced them
From both flanks to their deaths in the dark bogs and waters,
So many slaughtering! withdraw now from the fray. Ár,
Licking his wounds and moaning heavily in his grove,
Will never return, never again aid the bandits.
Have him withdraw to that summit and follow the war
As it winds down without him. And then go to Stribog.
Tell him to calm his winds and no longer bear the darts
Of the Slovaks upon his breath. But have him remain:
In case the Chudes once more should dare to launch their missiles,
Readied to blow them back upon their heads. Otherwise,
Let the bold Slovaks fight without the aid of the gods
So that they might attain their victory on their own'.
  Thus said the supreme governor of the universe.
At which Zvestoň sped off to the cruel battlefield
Piercing the blue sky. First, he alit near Svatovít,
And greeted him: 'O martial god of the Tatranians!
Great Svatovít! Perún sends me here, commanding you:
Withdraw now from the fray, seeing that the bold Slovaks
— Strong beyond measure! — with your aid have battered the Chudes,
Driving deep in their midst, laying them low with their arms
Impelling them into the black depths of the wetlands
From both flanks, so that the great number of savages
Have been destroyed. Enough: retire to that hill to watch
Your people win the day now, to their own great merit.
The Chudes will have no more aid from Ár, who lies pummelled
After his thrashing at your hands. On their own, the Chudes
Will perish alone now, without any aid divine'.
  When Zvestoň finished, Svatovít thus replied to him:
'Although Ár, broken, can no longer aid his people,
Still am I anxious, lest I withdraw from the fray and
The bandit Chudes yet overcome my much-loved Slovaks.
I still would rather fight a little while longer
Lest their courage flag, their limbs grow sore and exhausted.
But since such is the will of the supreme lord of all
That I withdraw, withdraw I shall: mine is to obey.

I trust that he will not abandon my Slovaks now!'
   Thus Svatovít. And at once he took himself away
From the cruel battlefield to ascend the hillock
Where Stribog waited, and sat down by his side. Zvestoň
Arrived there quickly too, to deliver the command
Of Perún to the mighty lord of the booming winds:
'Stribog, who rule the raucous company of the air!
The ruler supreme, first among all the deities,
Perún himself has sent me to you with this command:
Inflate your cheeks no more to send blasts upon the Chudes
And carry the Slovak darts that cut down so many.
But take yourself not back home just yet. You must remain
Here in readiness to act, should the vile enemy
Take up the bow again, which, if they do, he'll bid you
Return and blow and send their barbs back down upon them'.
   Thus Zvestoň. Then, his messages delivered, mission
Fulfilled, he soared back into the sky and returned home.
Stribog closed his lips and the gale winds ceased their raging.
Now, when the Chudes beheld how many men had fallen
Both in battle and in marsh, their hair standing on end,
They began debating: Escape? Or continued war?
Had they strength sufficient to engage in more fighting?
Might fortune turn and favour them again? Common sense
Urged: *Run away!* Shame scolded: *Remain and struggle on!*
Divided thus, the Chudes quarrelled and wavered within
Until Lobontol, aged and wise, able to judge
Whither all foreboding tilted, addressed King Bondor:
   'Seeing as no more happy fortune awaits us here
In this land of the terrible Slovaks, let us go,
Avoiding further defeat, so that our fate be not
The same as the wretched catastrophe that befell
Our brothers on the plains of Obrín. For this people
Is a strange one: tough and mighty; what if they had trained
In arms since early youth, and led a warrior's life?
There would, I reckon, be no folk as might withstand them
In battle, since, unschooled, they fight so ferociously!
Let us leave off then, and retreat. That is my advice.
Let's leave this cursed land. Wise is the man who'll balance
The fortunes of looming war, and when the black dish sinks
On the scales of calculated reckoning, withdraws

To fight another day — when the auspices are good.
The world is wide; we'll find easier pickings elsewhere'.
 Such was the advice that Lobontol offered Bondor.
Enflamed with rage, the cruel king replied to him thus:
'Shameless old man! First you urge others on to slaughter,
And then, when the battle rages near, you would escape,
Showing your heels and back to your foes as you hobble
To safety? Villain! You seek your nation's infamy!
Be glad that I restrain my arm from bringing slaughter
Upon your doddering head here and now, thus putting
A swift and bloody end to your cowardly advice!'
 It was at this moment that the strong winds ceased to blow
And carry the arrows of the Slovaks with added
Force upon the Chudes in tortoise huddled, seeing which,
Bondor cried out in a booming voice: 'The damnéd god
Of the winds has coughed out all that he had in his lungs!
Our fortune is turning! Soldiers! We've endured the worst —
Take up your crossbows once more, the bows from your shoulders
Unsling, and pour new fire upon those villains up there
On the rocky summits! Let them receive payment due
For all the arrows they've generously sent our way!'
 Thus, at Bondor's urging, the men rushed to seize weapons,
And soon from Chudan tendons a tempest of missiles
Flew toward the Slovaks on the heights. But then Stribog,
Beholding the withering fire from his hilltop perch,
Recalled his heavenly father's command and, rising,
Released once more the whistling gale-winds and reversed
The arrows in mid-flight, pouring them upon the Chudes
Who'd sent them aloft. Once again many archers fell,
Spitted by their own darts, catching sight of the rebounding
Terror with no time to raise bucklers in defence.
The ground was littered with fresh gore — so many lay sprawled
In death as earlier had stood, feet firmly planted,
Sowing the fletched whirlwind. There'd be no retreat for them!
Those that survived the pitiless tempest shouldered bows
And, unsheathing their swords, rushed again to the attack,
Furious with a violent despair. The Slovaks,
Though exhausted with the slog of war, breasted anew
The ferocious assault of the fiends with balanced strength:
The battle wavered, fortune favouring now this side,

Now that. Rodoktol slew Radomír, Potech cut down
Colobond, Bendeb of little worth slew the doughty
Pošlislav, Myslibor Onda, Valiant Čerekel
Marovít, Div rubbed out Ondol. Lombod first hewed down
Chranok, then Hosťboj, Žislav, and Radka, Nestrach too
— Youth of splendid countenance — was slain at the threshold
Of promising manhood. But Lombod would rage no more
Through the Slovak ranks, though seemingly without measure
Warlike — for Topolčanský Božislav soon sent him
Tumbling to the grass in death. Božislav then shattered
Kalazúr, Elimb, and Kiktol, while savage Oltor
With a spear-thrust brought down Zorok, whose homestead stretched wide
At the foot of high Žibrica, where his tillage spread
As far as the eye could see. Immense his herds and flocks —
No wealthier man was to be found within the ten
Neighbouring villages. Dobroslav pierced Tol's temples
And ran Zeb through the back, Ilm through the neck, Olutolm
Through his stout rib-cage. Short work, this — their spirits flitted
Through their gaping wounds with their final groan. Aladúr
The cruel crushed the hunter Byster's Adam's-apple,
Running his spear through the bowels of Lubomíl next.
   Like a wolf long pinched with famine catching scent of fresh
Goat's milk on the wind will rush upon the helpless flocks:
Kids and does bleating in the underbrush, and ravage
The lot with rabid jaws and slashing claws, so Proslav
Raged through the ranks of his startled foes: Zolotelmen,
Arfak and Tordo fell before him, then Elutolm
And Čerok, once nimble both, crumpled now at his feet.
Ozod, who'd ravaged his countrymen, raged no longer:
With skilful thrust of ashen spear Proslav rudely stopped
Him in mid-rush as a javelin jerks from the air
Some speeding fowl. Thus Ozod fell suddenly inert:
A clumsy dead weight, his bosom transfixed by the shaft,
Spinning head over heels to the ground. Nor did he leave
Among the living the ambitious Kaskad, who erst
Had sworn to his bloodthirsty brethren he'd lay him low —
Proslav himself! So much for the oaths of the wicked!
Alas! He ran you through too, valiant sons of Tulbol:
Alazún the beautiful, and Zolond, soft of hand!
The elder's breast was punctured, while the younger: the spear

Spitted his stomach. Panting, Proslav then rushed the skald
Orodarzen. When Elgúr and the massive Ondolt
Caught sight of that — to these Orodarzen had betrothed
His daughters: dark-eyed Cidobeldena to Elgúr,
Kadorka to Ondolt — they were paralysed with fear
A space. Then Elgúr snapped out of it and said, 'Brother!
Let us strike that murderer both at once; for the ribs
I'll aim, while you go for the jaw'. Thus, just as raging
Lions, driven wild with hunger, will rush at a bull
Split off from the herd on the slopes, so these two attacked
Just as Proslav was pulling his spear from the body
Of Orodarzen, prone in death. Both pine javelins
Hit their mark, and Proslav fell with a clatter of arms.

   Thus the two troops, evenly matched, raged with balanced skill,
Neither side quite able to overcome the other,
Dealing and parrying blows, the front line wavering
Back and forth, but neither advancing much to or fro.
Sometimes a flock of well-fed rams, tramping through a wood
Of ash or elm will meet with another flock, tending
Opposite. Neither wishing to give way, they'll rear up
On hind legs and bash their hard skulls together, re-
bounding from the blow to rear and strike again, and re-
bound and strike — so the ranks of Slovaks and Chudes battled,
Evenly matched, with equal success and loss: Slovaks
Battering down the evil Chudes, battered down in turn,
Each winning a few feet of earth, just to lose it again.
But then the Slovak archers — sensing the wind that had
Carried their barbs afar die down, so that they fell short —
Rushed down the slopes with swords drawn to help out the front ranks
At the end of their strength from the hand-to-hand combat.
It was this push of fresh, most welcome Slovak reserves
That turned the tide of the horrid battle at close range.

   It was these who felled Elgúr and the massive Ondolt,
Who together, in crooked fight, had just slain Proslav,
The first cut down by Nechvál, the second Ranislav
Battered into the nether shades, smashing through his skull.
Bezmír, that stunning warrior, met with Kardolen,
Savage scion of Kelend, whose hollow windpipe he pierced.
Swift-footed Žnislav took himself to the haughty Uldo,
To whom the great usurper Boltor, his son-in-law,

Sped to aid. Uldo had just one daughter, Tebaja,
And her he had given to Boltor — who had pleased him
With how he'd fought in the battles beyond the Azov —
With all his flocks of goats and numberless herds of steeds
Too, as no sons remained him. Boltor added this wealth,
His wife's dowry, to his own, grazing them together.
But he was late in arriving. His father-in-law
Lay stretched out on the ground — his wounds all behind — kicking
His legs in spasms. All the more enveloped with ire,
Boltor flung his oaken spear, which flashed through the air, but
Missed. Rabid at having so clumsily thrown, in haste,
He sent another dart whistling like the wind, but this
Buried its barb, too, in the marshy earth: wrath casts wide!
The great-souled Žnislav then turned slowly toward his foe,
And hefting his spear, with shaft of Tatran fir, called out:
'Unskilled, I see, your right arm, bandit, twice-flinging wide.
Take this then, your first, and last, lesson in javelin!'
He said no more, but flung: the spear ripped through Boltor's guts,
And he fell, like a toppled pine, upon his wife's sire.
   Miloslav, that mighty lord, rushed at cruel Orond
Who'd wronged him with his comrades, snatching his three brave sons
And just as many beautiful girls carrying off;
Besides which, he'd driven off his fattened herds to the camp
Of the Chudes, and set aflame Miloslav's fair homestead
Nestled among the hills. Him too Orond would have grabbed
— The greedy villain — had not Miloslav been absent
From home, along with his sweet helpmeet Vitohosť,
Preslav's daughter. For they were in lovely Novohrad,
Visiting their nephew Horimíl, whom they'd not seen
For ages — a happy occasion: he was wedding
The beautiful Zora, granddaughter of great Príspor.
'Twas there the news reached him of the vile Chudes ravaging
His country, looting and laying it waste. He returned
Not to his own children, but rushed unto the battle
Still clothed in his festive garments, along with nephew
Horimíl, newly married, at his side. Rejoicing
Turned to mourning once he'd learned what had happened at home
During his absence; that mourning turned to fierce vengeance
Upon espying the villain who had so lashed him
With sorrow. With one fierce spear-cast he took down Orond,

His dart plunging through the Chude's breastplate and emerging,
Soaked with gore, beneath his shoulderblade. Horimíl
And Príspor himself, though grey with age, battled fiercely
As well — the former brought down massive Bolotelmen,
The latter Elold. Milhosť, raging, pierced Dizúr's skull:
The brass helmet shattered, as did the tough bone, and blood
And brain gushed forth in a smoky torrent. Mighty Zvol,
Who'd founded Zvolen on the banks of the River Hron,
Slew with spear-thrust the massy-framed villain Etold.
Through the bone-cage straight it passed, piercing his liver through.
As a sudden torrential rain sends cascades of mud
From freshly-ploughed hillsides streaming into a valley
To befoul the fair pastures below with sticky mire,
So the valiant Slovaks sent the Chudes, suddenly caught
Up in their rush, tumbling head over heels to the plain.
Kelentol, prime sacrificer to the warlike Ár,
At a loss what to do at this swift turn of events,
Wounded in the leg himself, cried out to King Bondor:
'My king! This curséd place is a vale of misfortune!
Either some shaman, or evil sorcerer from Hell,
Has spell-cast this land with morbific song — word-spinning
Charms that corrode our powers, impede our victory!
Our vicious minds seem fogged, and even Ár refuses
To aid us here, as he has done elsewhere! Let us save
What men we can by sounding a retreat, escaping
To the rear. Perhaps we may find some better footing,
Some fitter place to regroup and rethink an assault
Such as would shatter those Slovaks and carry the day'.
   Thus he advised, and King Bondor was nearly convinced,
And might have ordered the strategic retreat had not
Perún, the ruler of the universe, read his mind.
Summoning Neustup, the genius of stubbornness,
He quickly commanded him: 'O, you who fill men's minds
With angry paralysis, who seal their hearts against
Rational argument, when cool deliberation
Is most needed, blearing the eye that it no longer
May discern truth from falsehood, sure foothold from void chasm,
Quick! Descend now among the army of the cruel Chudes
And flummox them all, so that they not retreat, but stand
As a forest of stubborn oaks flouting the gale winds

Until they all lie toppled at the feet of their king'.
  Command received, Neustup withdrew from Perún's throne,
And like a star detached from Heaven's heights, trailing sparks
As it falls to the earth, sped to the chaotic fields
Of fear and slaughter. Disguising himself as Olmol,
The prince of the Crimean Chudes, husband to Onda,
The youngest of Bondor's sisters, he approached the king
Just as his vile lips were forming the call to fall back
And slipped between intent and execution, saying:
  'O Bondor, who govern us with your iron sceptre,
The day is not yet lost — there is no such hasty need
For us to swivel our chargers and escape rearward!
We have yet men and horses fresh enough, who have not
Been worn down in the fight. Let us tense our muscles still!
The Slovaks are as weary of the fighting as we —
One more push, Sire, and we'll overthrow the Tatranians!
The wheel of fortune ever spins. If now we're below,
That means that we're about to ascend! We need but wait!'
Such were the words he spoke to King Bondor, and with such
He hardened the hearts of the remaining Chudes: *Fight on!*
Just to fight on in pitched battle — only this they desired.
And so they raged on, seeking to shatter the Slovaks.
Oltolomol slew Vitomír, Bolod strong Povlast,
Olutor the immoral killed Silorád, while Zib
Battered down Osvet. Kundobulol ran Bohumíl
The tall straight through the crotch, while Buzdok pushed his sharp spear
Of ash through Trebomysel's stomach, Boltok hacked through
Sojok's spine with an axe-blow from the rear. Slavihosť
Had his face shattered by the spear of Zod, who stabbed Bor
Through the right jaw too — always aiming high. However,
The most destruction was wrought by Satanic Lombo,
Who delighted in no food more than the flesh of men;
Whose drink of choice was human blood. First he felled Svojok
The mighty, and then Pribral and Stanok, and the two
Most manly heroes Samovít and Tešok — the first
Was Nemysel's good son; the second, wealthy Istok's,
Whose homestead was set there, where later Trenčín would arise.
Others raged likewise, till the plain was strewn with corpses.
Then great Sláv arose, and addressed his men exhausted
With long and ferocious fighting in such heated terms:

'My valiant comrades! What worth would it be to have slain
So many Chudes, were we to submit to their might now?
Now we must tense our aching limbs once more, with our last drops
Of strength to beat them down! Their numbers are much smaller —
If they will not surrender to us, cut them all down,
The murderers, and deliver our beloved land
From the catastrophe and vile shame they offer her!'
   With such words Sláv fired the Slovak forces to the fray.
Now, Svatovít, watching the battle from his hilltop,
And seeing that it was not playing out as before
When he was fighting in the front ranks along with them,
Could hardly restrain himself from aiding his people.
Three times he arose, determined to rejoin the scrum;
Three times the hand of Stribog restrained him, reminding
Him of their father Perún's injunction. He heeded
The wind-god's counsel, and remained in his place; he feared
To be disobedient... yet there could be no harm,
He reckoned, in pumping new vigour into the tired
Slovak arms, their legs with renewed swiftness, and their hearts
With valour — that would not infringe the will of Perún!
   So, flush with the rousing words of Sláv, their strength renewed
By the inspiration of Svatovít, all the more
Fiercely the Slovaks fought, mowing down swathes of their foes.
Capable Siloslav lay Hundoktol flat, Olomb
Was slain by Neplach, Dobrochvál beat down Etelelm,
Lubor killed Telefard. Ponislav, from Bystrica,
Voivode of the mighty troops of the Hron, slew Tolom,
Who rode the fleetest-footed charger of all the Chudes
Excepting only Bondor. Him Ponislav bashed out
Of the saddle with a thunderous blow of pine-shaft spear
That skewered his breast, passing out near his shoulderblade
While the panicked steed ran on riderless. Tolom crashed
To the earth with a booming rumble, as if Perún's
Lightning had split some high crag, sending granite tumbling.
Hájislav, son of fair Pravno, where stood a temple
Of no mean size raised to massive Prov, in which the rites
Were daily sung, split Zomolt's skull with knotty spear,
Thrusting upward, knocking out the teeth, slicing the tongue.
It was pious Lubomír who stretched long cruel Lombro —
Running his ashen spear right through his paunch, those guts

Grown fat on men's flesh and black with perverse gore-sops:
'Bloated with unhallowed meat!' he cried, 'You quaffed men's blood!
Now the dogs your flesh shall eat, ravens pick clean your bones!'
As he was speaking, Endel sped an arrow at him
But missed his mark: sailing low, it grazed the arm,
Lodging in his sleeve. Calmly, Lubomír pulled it out,
Strung it on his own bow, and winged it through Endel's throat.
Massive-framed Luboslav, who once in the wide meadows
Of the White Mountains came across springs of fresh water,
Some warm, from which the untamed Blava roars, making sport
Of the toughest winter frosts, its current unfrozen,
Which region charmed him so, he built himself a homestead
And settled the region — Dobrá Voda — Good Water
He named it, sent his spear whistling at savage Eldek.
Straight it punched through the groin, shattering pelvis and spine.
As the winds from the frozen north sweep over the plains,
Whipping the grains of sand up from the road and sending
Them spinning in chaotic dust-devils where it lists,
Thus the Tatranians swept the Chude troops before them
Till few were left standing. 'Twas then that Sláv encountered
Bondor. The Slovak voivode addressed him with swift speech:
  'Submit to us and preserve your lives. What sense is there
In perishing? You can see for yourself how it goes:
The battle's almost over — you can't take any more.
Remain here with us in peace. Learn to work on the land,
And make an honest living in the sweat of your brow.
When you have learned the ways of living off the good earth,
When you have left off savagery, you shall be our friends.
Then, should you wish to return to your homeland, you'll go —
But you'll go as better men, polished, no longer vile.
Come, learn to plough the fields, labour in honest toil,
Swear off murder and pillaging now, and for all time!'
  At this, Bondor only swelled the more in wrathful bile:
'Submission is for cringing villains like you, you wretch!
For Chudes, the terror of the wide world, submit to none!
Teach your thin-blooded sons to scratch the earth with harrows —
Teach them, born slaves, to wallow in manure like insects,
Not us, inured to grand, heroic warfare since childhood!
We wish to live the life of our forefathers, a life
Of victories, despoiling the lands of other men,

Wresting their wealth and cattle from their hands. Thus we toil!'
   Thus bellowed Bondor, urging his men to battle on,
And chase the shameful thought of turning tail from their minds —
Thus did Neustup harden his heart in stubbornness.
Upon hearing this, Sláv turned to his Tatranians:
'Dear brothers! The Chudes have spurned our offer of mercy.
Since they refuse to withdraw from a fight they can't win,
And rush into their grave, madly choosing to war on,
Help them to it! Cut them all down, the godless villains!
Tread them underfoot! Spare nary a single one!'
   Thus Sláv, at which the Slovaks rushed into the battle,
Their wrath redoubled, making short work of the raiders.
But two of the Chude villains, Berkeld and Etelmen
Of ghastly strength, did not let themselves so easily
Be shoved into the shadows. Savages both, the clothes
They wore were woven of the hair of men, which they scalped
From the dead on the plain, collecting in sacks the skulls
Of the fallen. From skins thus sheared they stitched their kirtles!
The crests that waved as plumes atop their helmets were not
Horsehair, but the black locks of men, nodding frightfully.
More than one sought to bring them down — in vain. Pribislav,
Hostichvál, and Kolboj of gigantic frame himself,
And even Výbor, up till then fortunate in war,
And one hundred others — but each came to grief, their blows
Paid back with bloody interest by those two, who raged
Among the Slovak ranks, wreaking carnage and maiming
Sláv's comrades, until at last both were brought down at once
As if felled by a lightning strike. The first by Pravomil
The prudent was taken down by a blow to the breast,
The second by Istislav, not the least among bards,
And a fierce battler moreover, who punctured his crotch,
Both javelins spitting their targets clean through and through.
Thus Berkeld and Etelmen fell to earth with a crash
And with these taken down, the Slovaks found it smoother
Going to overthrow the rest of their enemies,
Strewing the plain with their corpses. But little time passed
And from so mighty and splendid a host there remained
But a handful of wretches, struggling in a wicked
— And vain — defensive battle. As a ring of hunters
Growing tighter and tighter around some wild beast flushed

From its thickets by beaters will strike and strike with spear
Until the ferocious animal exhales its last,
Wrathful breath, thus the manly Tatrans pressed the remnants
Of the Chudes, herding black legions of hapless suitors
Into the arms of Morena, into endless night.
   Now only King Bondor remained. With him Sláv engaged
On foot, as Milobrat had brought down the Chude's stallion —
The last blow that Sláv suffered others to deliver —
He wanted the king to himself, man to man, a duel
He bade the others draw back and watch. At first, ash spears
Were exchanged, whistling through the winds like fell thunderheads.
The blow our great forefather intended did not land —
Nimbly, Bondor batted the missile aside, his shield
Glancing askew the iron tip, yet he had no luck
Either in piercing his foe's heroic frame, for Sláv
Feinted low at the spear's approach and it flew past, wide.
Both were enraged at having missed, and now, they unsheathed
Their flashing swords. As two boars disputing an oak-grove
Fat with the acorns of fall will rush at each other
With sharp, curving tusks, slashing at muzzle and temple
Until a tearing blow slits the soft underbelly,
And all the while the forest crouches, low, shivering
In fright at the roars of the tuskers enraged, the shrieks
Of their ivory sabres clashing, so these two struck
And struck again, at crown and ear, at temple
And jaw and nose, neither granting the other quarter
Nor begging it, neither intending to rest until
He'd lain his foe upon the soil, never to rise again.
And as the lightning spurts from two black clouds, the bellies
Of which rest upon high peaks when the storm winds slumber
In their empty caverns, and the leafless woods are still,
So from their brightly flashing blades did swarms of bright sparks
Spill. No other sound was heard through the hushed woods except
For the clanging and clashing of their arms echoing.
However many times Sláv pierced the flesh of Bondor,
Soever many times Bondor slashed the flesh of Sláv.
Both of the battlers were bathed in black blood, yet neither
Could land a mortal blow. They fought on, with victory
Ever elusive. High up, a tall granite cliff-face
Will so often brave angry storms, and the lightning bolts

That batter its forehead will dislodge so many rockfalls
That heaps of rubble pulverised will gather at its foot
Thickly, and its base will seem awash in shoals of granite.
So did the constant pounding of swords chip loose the strength
Of Bondor and Sláv, that their legs moved but sluggishly,
As if pushing through piles of debris that impeded
The stride, like heaps of sea and shingle through which they slogged.
The ebbing of his powers served but to enrage Sláv.
At last, at the limit of his strength, he raised his sword
And with a bellow brought it down on Bondor's right arm,
Knocking, at last, the weapon from his grip. Exulting,
Sláv first lifted a prayer to his war-god Svatovít,
And, tensing one last time his sinews fairly unspooled,
Swung at Bondor with his broadsword, catching him squarely
In the face. That evil font of so many curses
For the Slovak people gushed only the blackest gore
Now, as the blade smashed his teeth, severing arteries
And tendons. Heavily, Bondor fell backwards, crashing
To earth like a mighty ash-tree felled to the forest floor.
And nether earth rumbled with the burden falling, while
The skies erupted with the victorious cheering
Sent up by the Slovaks, their joy rebounding from high
Mountain summit. 'Sláv!' they exclaimed, 'Sláva! Sláv! Glory
To Sláv! Sláva Slávovi!' The Slovaks rejoiced;
The gods Stribog and Svatovít danced on their hilltop
Beholding the triumph of the Slovak voivode;
Perún himself smiled, the ruler of the universe.
Bestriding the body of his enemy, Sláv cried:
  'Bondor! Since you refused the hand of friendship, the truce
Offered you, spurning the honest life of field labour
In rhythm with Nature, who feeds those who tend to her,
Preferring to prey upon the wealth of others, wretch!
Flouting the fire of the gods which flashed you in warning,
Which soon — had I not cut off your brigandage myself! —
Would have swept you from this life in righteous punishment —
Well? Where is your boasting now? Murder us if you can!
Ravage our Slovak motherland, strip us of our goods,
Carry it all off and us as well — born slaves, as you said —
To your Chude women yearning for your bandits' return!
Now you shall seek your spoils where none may be found,

In the black wastes of Hell's abyss, with gibbering sprites!
There, Chude, seek out the fame your kind so richly deserve,
O terror of your neighbours! O warrior since youth!'

Thus Sláv. At last, Bondor vomited forth his black soul
Which flitted away harmless into eternal night.

BIBLIOGRAPHY

PRIMARY SOURCES:

HOLLÝ, Ján. *Jána Hollého Spisy Básnické. So životopisom a zprávou o pomníku i spisoch jeho.* Sporiadal a vidal Josef Viktorin. Pešt: Sklad kníhkupectva Lauffera & Stolf, 1863.

HOLLÝ, Ján. *Cirillo-Metodiada. Wíťazská báseň w šesti spewoch s pripogením žiwotopisem swatích Cirilla a Metóda, gako též bágoslowím pohanskích Slowákow, a wistwetleňím ňekterích slow.* Buďin: Kráľowská Uniwerzita, 1835.

HOLLÝ, Ján. *Virgiliova Eneida preložená od Jána Hollého.* Trnava: J.K.J., 1828.

HOLLÝ, Ján. *Na slovenský národ (Selanky, Rozličné básne, Žalospevy a Pesne).* Bratislava: Slovenské vydavateľstvo krásnej literatúry, 1957.

SECONDARY SOURCES:

AUGUSTINUS AURELIUS (St Augustine of Hippo), *The City of God.* Tr. Marcus Dods. Edinburgh: T & T Clark, 1884.

BRÜCKNER, Aleksander. *Mitologia Słowiańska i Polska.* Warszawa: PWN, 1985.

CHOVAN, Juraj, ed. *Pamätnica z osláv dvojstého výročia narodenia Jána Hollého.* Martin: Matica slovenská, 1985.

DELL'AGATA, Giuseppe. 'S. Toscano, Ján Hollý (1785-1849) cantore di Cirillo e Metodio', *Studi Slavistici,* xvii, 2020, 2: 271–272.

DIAMOND, Jared. *Guns, Germs and Steel. The Fates of Human Societies.* New York: W.W. Norton, 1999.

GÁFRIK, Róbert. 'The Image of India in 19th-Century Slovak Literature', *Porównania* 2 (21), 2017: 163–170.

HALÁSZ, Ivan. 'Slovenská literatúra v literárnohistorických prácach napísaných po maďarsky', *Slovenská literatúra,* vol. 68, 2021, nr 4: 408–431.

HANÁK, J. 'Slovaks and Czechs in the Early 19th Century', *The Slavonic and East European Review,* Apr., 1932, Vol. 10, No. 30 (Apr., 1932): 588–601.

HORECKÝ, Ján. 'Ján Hollý — básnik a zakladateľ', *Kultúra slova,* XIII/9 (1979): 289–293.

JECHOVÁ, Lucia. 'Mytológia a mystika v epose J.Hollého – Svatopluk', *XLinguae.eu A Trimestrial European Scientific Language Review* 4/2011: 40–44.

JUNGMANN, Josef. *Sebrané spisy veršem i prosou* Vol. III. Praha: I.L. Koreb, 1873.

KIMBALL, Stanley B. 'The Austro-Slav Revival: A Study of Nineteenth-Century Literary Foundations', *Transactions of the American Philosophical Society*, 1973, Vol. 63, No. 4 (1973): 1–83.

KOLLÁR, Jan. *Sláva Bohyně a původ jména Slavů čili Slavjanů v listech k velectěnému přiteli Panu P.J. Šafaňkovi, s přídavky srovnalost indického a slavského života, řeči a bajesloví ukazujícími.* Pest: Trattner-Károlyi, 1839.

ŁOWMIAŃSKI, Henryk. *Religia Słowian i jej upadek.* Warszawa: PWN, 1979.

MICKIEWICZ, Adam. *Literatura słowiańska. Kurs pierwszy (1840–1841).* Warszawa: „Czytelnik", 1997. (*Dziela*, vol. VIII).

MILTON, John. *Poetical Works edited after the Original Texts*, ed. H.C. Beeching. London: Humphrey Milford / Oxford University Press, 1913.

MILTON, John *Ztracený ráj*, tr. Josef Jungmann, from Josef Jungmann, *Sebrané spisy veršem i prosou* Vol. III. Praha: I.L. Koreb, 1873.

MINÁRIK, Jozef. *Z klenotnice staršieho slovenského písomníctva.* Bratislava: Tatran, 1984.

PIŠÚT, M., ed. *Dejiny slovenskej literatúry*, ed. M. Pišút. Bratislava: Vydavateľstvo Osveta 1962.

PODOLAN, Peter. 'Veľká Morava a veľkomoravská tradícia u generácie Kollára a Šafárika', *Český časopis historický* 117/2019, nr. 1:59–91.

RIŠKOVÁ, Lenka. 'Z korešpondencie Jána Hollého. Niečo o vzťahu Jána Hollého k protestantským autorom', *Slovenská literatúra*, 62, 2015, nr. 6: 495–511.

ROSENBAUM, Karol. 'Poznámky' to Ján Hollý, *Výber yž básní.* Turčiansky Sv. Martin: Matica slovenská, 1947.

RŮŽIČKA, Josef. *Slovanská mythologie. Pro lid Českoslovanský.* Praha: Alois Wiesner, 1924.

SELVER, Paul. 'The Literature of the Slovaks', *The Slavonic and East European Review*, Apr., 1934, Vol. 12, No. 36 (Apr., 1934): 691–703.

ŠAFÁRIK, Pavol Josef. *Slovanské starožitnosti.* Vol I: 'Starožitnosti slovanské okresu prvního'. Praha: Bedřich Tempský, 1862.

ŠMATLÁK, Stanislav, 'Ján Hollý — Klasik slovenskej poézie', in *Pamätnica z osláv dvojstého výročia narodenia Jána Hollého*, ed. Juraj Chovan (Martin: Matica slovenská, 1985), 123–133.

ŠTÚR, Ľudovit. *A Selection of his Writings in Prose and Verse,* translated and introduced by Charles S. Kraszewski. London: Glagoslav, 2021.

TANESKI, Martina. 'Epos *Cirillo-Metodiada* v peripetiách literárnohistorickej recepce', *Konštantínovia listy* 11/2 (2018): 143–150.
VIRGIL, *The Aeneid*. Tr. Robert Fitzgerald, New York: Vintage, 1983.
VLČEK, Jaroslav. *Dejiny literatúry slovenskej.* Turčiansky sv. Martin: Nákladom vlastným, 1890.
WILKINSON, Isambard. 'Catalonia waves goodbye to "imperialist" Spanish art', *Times* 2 May 2023: 29.
WILLIAMS, R.D. ed. *The Aeneid of Virgil.* Walton-on-Thames: Nelson, St Martin's Press, 1992.

ABOUT THE AUTHOR

Ján Hollý (1785–1849) is one of the greatest writers of the Slovak *národné obrodenie* [national revival] of the nineteenth century. As a poet and translator, he is the most renowned author of the early period of *Bernolákovčina* — that codification of the modern literary language of the Slovaks, based on the western dialects of the nation worked up by Anton Bernolák. Although the language would shortly gravitate toward the central dialects, as established by those grouped around Ľudovít Štúr, Hollý continued to be revered by all Slovaks, a process which began during his lifetime. Hollý's first great work was a complete translation of Virgil's *Aeneid* (1828), which he composed following his first venture into translating the classics (*Various Heroic, Elegiac, and Lyrical Poems*, 1824), which groups together his Slovak versions of Ovid, Theocritus, Homer, Horace, and other Greek and Latin poets. The great Slovak epics — arguably his most important contribution to Slovak literature — are *Svatopluk* (1833), *The Cyrillo-Methodiad* (1835), and *Sláv* (1839). Both of the first are based on episodes from the early mediaeval period of his nation, while the last is a foray into the mythical regions of ancient Slavdom. His later lyric poetry includes idylls and hymns (Hollý was a Catholic priest). While much of his work was composed along neoclassical lines, his importance for the ideological development of Slovakia as an ethnically-based nationality, and his forays into the then-popular currents of Pan-Slavism, place him eminently amongst the great European Romantics.

ABOUT THE TRANSLATOR

Charles S. Kraszewski (born 1962) is a poet and translator, creative in both English and Polish. He is the author of three volumes of original verse in English (*Diet of Nails; Beast; Chanameed*), and two in Polish (*Hallo, Sztokholm; Skowycik*). He has also authored two satirical novels *Accomplices, You Ask?* and *At the Tone* (both San Francisco: Montag, 2021, 2024). He translates from Polish, Czech and Slovak. He is a member of the Union of Polish Writers Abroad (London) and the Association of Polish Writers (SPP, Kraków). In 2022, he was awarded the Gloria Artis medal (III Class) by the Ministry of Culture of the Republic of Poland, and in 2023 the ZAiKS award for Translation into a Foreign Tongue, presented by the Polish Society of Authors (ZAiKS).

Glagoslav Publications Catalogue

- *The Time of Women* by Elena Chizhova
- *Andrei Tarkovsky: A Life on the Cross* by Lyudmila Boyadzhieva
- *Sin* by Zakhar Prilepin
- *Hardly Ever Otherwise* by Maria Matios
- *Khatyn* by Ales Adamovich
- *The Lost Button* by Irene Rozdobudko
- *Christened with Crosses* by Eduard Kochergin
- *The Vital Needs of the Dead* by Igor Sakhnovsky
- *The Sarabande of Sara's Band* by Larysa Denysenko
- *A Poet and Bin Laden* by Hamid Ismailov
- *Zo Gaat Dat in Rusland* (Dutch Edition) by Maria Konjoekova
- *Kobzar* by Taras Shevchenko
- *The Stone Bridge* by Alexander Terekhov
- *Moryak* by Lee Mandel
- *King Stakh's Wild Hunt* by Uladzimir Karatkevich
- *The Hawks of Peace* by Dmitry Rogozin
- *Harlequin's Costume* by Leonid Yuzefovich
- *Depeche Mode* by Serhii Zhadan
- *Groot Slem en Andere Verhalen* (Dutch Edition) by Leonid Andrejev
- *METRO 2033* (Dutch Edition) by Dmitry Glukhovsky
- *METRO 2034* (Dutch Edition) by Dmitry Glukhovsky
- *A Russian Story* by Eugenia Kononenko
- *Herstories, An Anthology of New Ukrainian Women Prose Writers*
- *The Battle of the Sexes Russian Style* by Nadezhda Ptushkina
- *A Book Without Photographs* by Sergey Shargunov
- *Down Among The Fishes* by Natalka Babina
- *disUNITY* by Anatoly Kudryavitsky
- *Sankya* by Zakhar Prilepin
- *Wolf Messing* by Tatiana Lungin
- *Good Stalin* by Victor Erofeyev
- *Solar Plexus* by Rustam Ibragimbekov
- *Don't Call me a Victim!* by Dina Yafasova
- *Poetin* (Dutch Edition) by Chris Hutchins and Alexander Korobko

- *A History of Belarus* by Lubov Bazan
- *Children's Fashion of the Russian Empire* by Alexander Vasiliev
- *Empire of Corruption: The Russian National Pastime* by Vladimir Soloviev
- *Heroes of the 90s: People and Money. The Modern History of Russian Capitalism* by Alexander Solovev, Vladislav Dorofeev and Valeria Bashkirova
- *Fifty Highlights from the Russian Literature* (Dutch Edition) by Maarten Tengbergen
- *Bajesvolk* (Dutch Edition) by Michail Chodorkovsky
- *Dagboek van Keizerin Alexandra* (Dutch Edition)
- *Myths about Russia* by Vladimir Medinskiy
- *Boris Yeltsin: The Decade that Shook the World* by Boris Minaev
- *A Man Of Change: A study of the political life of Boris Yeltsin*
- *Sberbank: The Rebirth of Russia's Financial Giant* by Evgeny Karasyuk
- *To Get Ukraine* by Oleksandr Shyshko
- *Asystole* by Oleg Pavlov
- *Gnedich* by Maria Rybakova
- *Marina Tsvetaeva: The Essential Poetry*
- *Multiple Personalities* by Tatyana Shcherbina
- *The Investigator* by Margarita Khemlin
- *The Exile* by Zinaida Tulub
- *Leo Tolstoy: Flight from Paradise* by Pavel Basinsky
- *Moscow in the 1930* by Natalia Gromova
- *Laurus* (Dutch edition) by Evgenij Vodolazkin
- *Prisoner* by Anna Nemzer
- *The Crime of Chernobyl: The Nuclear Goulag* by Wladimir Tchertkoff
- *Alpine Ballad* by Vasil Bykau
- *The Complete Correspondence of Hryhory Skovoroda*
- *The Tale of Aypi* by Ak Welsapar
- *Selected Poems* by Lydia Grigorieva
- *The Fantastic Worlds of Yuri Vynnychuk*
- *The Garden of Divine Songs and Collected Poetry of Hryhory Skovoroda*
- *Adventures in the Slavic Kitchen: A Book of Essays with Recipes* by Igor Klekh
- *Seven Signs of the Lion* by Michael M. Naydan

- *Forefathers' Eve* by Adam Mickiewicz
- *One-Two* by Igor Eliseev
- *Girls, be Good* by Bojan Babić
- *Time of the Octopus* by Anatoly Kucherena
- *The Grand Harmony* by Bohdan Ihor Antonych
- *The Selected Lyric Poetry Of Maksym Rylsky*
- *The Shining Light* by Galymkair Mutanov
- *The Frontier: 28 Contemporary Ukrainian Poets - An Anthology*
- *Acropolis: The Wawel Plays* by Stanisław Wyspiański
- *Contours of the City* by Attyla Mohylny
- *Conversations Before Silence: The Selected Poetry of Oles Ilchenko*
- *The Secret History of my Sojourn in Russia* by Jaroslav Hašek
- *Mirror Sand: An Anthology of Russian Short Poems*
- *Maybe We're Leaving* by Jan Balaban
- *Death of the Snake Catcher* by Ak Welsapar
- *A Brown Man in Russia* by Vijay Menon
- *Hard Times* by Ostap Vyshnia
- *The Flying Dutchman* by Anatoly Kudryavitsky
- *Nikolai Gumilev's Africa* by Nikolai Gumilev
- *Combustions* by Srđan Srdić
- *The Sonnets* by Adam Mickiewicz
- *Dramatic Works* by Zygmunt Krasiński
- *Four Plays* by Juliusz Słowacki
- *Little Zinnobers* by Elena Chizhova
- *We Are Building Capitalism! Moscow in Transition 1992-1997* by Robert Stephenson
- *The Nuremberg Trials* by Alexander Zvyagintsev
- *The Hemingway Game* by Evgeni Grishkovets
- *A Flame Out at Sea* by Dmitry Novikov
- *Jesus' Cat* by Grig
- *Want a Baby and Other Plays* by Sergei Tretyakov
- *Mikhail Bulgakov: The Life and Times* by Marietta Chudakova
- *Leonardo's Handwriting* by Dina Rubina
- *A Burglar of the Better Sort* by Tytus Czyżewski
- *The Mouseiad and other Mock Epics* by Ignacy Krasicki

- *Ravens before Noah* by Susanna Harutyunyan
- *An English Queen and Stalingrad* by Natalia Kulishenko
- *Point Zero* by Narek Malian
- *Absolute Zero* by Artem Chekh
- *Olanda* by Rafał Wojasiński
- *Robinsons* by Aram Pachyan
- *The Monastery* by Zakhar Prilepin
- *The Selected Poetry of Bohdan Rubchak: Songs of Love, Songs of Death, Songs of the Moon*
- *Mebet* by Alexander Grigorenko
- *The Orchestra* by Vladimir Gonik
- *Everyday Stories* by Mima Mihajlović
- *Slavdom* by Ľudovít Štúr
- *The Code of Civilization* by Vyacheslav Nikonov
- *Where Was the Angel Going?* by Jan Balaban
- *De Zwarte Kip* (Dutch Edition) by Antoni Pogorelski
- *Głosy / Voices* by Jan Polkowski
- *Sergei Tretyakov: A Revolutionary Writer in Stalin's Russia* by Robert Leach
- *Opstand* (Dutch Edition) by Władysław Reymont
- *Dramatic Works* by Cyprian Kamil Norwid
- *Children's First Book of Chess* by Natalie Shevando and Matthew McMillion
- *Precursor* by Vasyl Shevchuk
- *The Vow: A Requiem for the Fifties* by Jiří Kratochvil
- *De Bibliothecaris* (Dutch edition) by Mikhail Jelizarov
- *Subterranean Fire* by Natalka Bilotserkivets
- *Vladimir Vysotsky: Selected Works*
- *Behind the Silk Curtain* by Gulistan Khamzayeva
- *The Village Teacher and Other Stories* by Theodore Odrach
- *Duel* by Borys Antonenko-Davydovych
- *War Poems* by Alexander Korotko
- *Ballads and Romances* by Adam Mickiewicz
- *The Revolt of the Animals* by Wladyslaw Reymont
- *Poems about my Psychiatrist* by Andrzej Kotański
- *Someone Else's Life* by Elena Dolgopyat
- *Selected Works: Poetry, Drama, Prose* by Jan Kochanowski

- *The Riven Heart of Moscow (Sivtsev Vrazhek)* by Mikhail Osorgin
- *Bera and Cucumber* by Alexander Korotko
- *The Big Fellow* by Anastasiia Marsiz
- *Boryslav in Flames* by Ivan Franko
- *The Witch of Konotop* by Hryhoriy Kvitka-Osnovyanenko
- *De afdeling* (Dutch edition) by Aleksej Salnikov
- *The Food Block* by Alexey Ivanov
- *Ilget* by Alexander Grigorenko
- *Tefil* by Rafał Wojasiński
- *A Dream of Annapurna* by Igor Zavilinsky
- *Down and Out in Drohobych* by Ivan Franko
- *The World of Koliada*
- *Evenings on a Farm Near Dikanka* by Nikolai Gogol
- *Georgian Folk Tales* by Marjory Scott Wardrop
- *R.U.R. (Rossum's Universal Robots)* by Karel Čapek
- *The Hermit* by Ilia Chavchavadze
- *Spark in the Dark* by Astrid Lovell
- *The Slovak Epics* by Ján Hollý
- *Masquerade* by Mikhail Lermontov
- *Letter Z* by Oleksandr Sambrus
- *The Vampire* by Władysław Reymont
- *Fu(*n*)k Bomb* by Karel Veselý
- *Liza's Waterfall: The Hidden Story of a Russian Feminist* by Pavel Basinsky
- *Biography of Sergei Prokofiev* by Igor Vishnevetsky
- *A City Drawn from Memory* by Elena Chizhova
- *Guide to M. Bulgakov's The Master and Margarita* by Ksenia Atarova and Georgy Lesskis

And more forthcoming...

Glagoslav Publications
www.glagoslav.com

www.ingramcontent.com/pod-product-compliance
Lightning Source LLC
Chambersburg PA
CBHW020514080526
44583CB00013B/594